UNDERSTANDING STREET-LEVEL BUREAUCRACY

Edited by Peter Hupe, Michael Hill and Aurélien Buffat

First published in Great Britain in 2016 by

Policy Press

University of Bristol

1-9 Old Park Hill

Bristol

BS2 8BB

UK

t: +44 (0)117 954 5940

pp-info@bristol.ac.uk

www.policypress.co.uk

North America office:

Policy Press

c/o The University of Chicago Press

1427 East 60th Street

Chicago, IL 60637, USA

t: +1 773 702 7700

f: +1 773-702-9756

sales@press.uchicago.edu

www.press.uchicago.edu

British Library Cataloguing in Publication Data
A catalogue record for this book is available from the British Library

Library of Congress Cataloging-in-Publication Data
A catalog record for this book has been requested

ISBN 978-1-4473-1327-4 paperback
ISBN 978-1-4473-2141-5 ePub
ISBN 978-1-4473-2140-8 Mobi

Cover design by Qube Design Associates, Bristol
Front cover image: istock

Contents

Biographical notes

Duco Bannink is Associate Professor at the Department of Political Science and Public Administration at VU University Amsterdam, The Netherlands. His research concerns the governance of (social) policy implementation and particularly the ways in which public managers deal with a 'double governance challenge' of combined conflict and complexity.

Evelyn Z. Brodkin is Associate Professor at the University of Chicago, USA, School of Social Service Administration (SSA), where she directs the graduate Program on Poverty and Inequality. She is an active scholar in the field of street-level organisations and has also written widely on social policy and management and welfare state politics.

Aurélien Buffat is Junior Lecturer at the Institute of Political and International Studies, University of Lausanne, Switzerland. He also works as a policy advisor to the President of the State Council (executive authority) of the Canton of Vaud. His main research interests are policy analysis and public administration, with a focus on policy implementation, street-level bureaucracy, front-line discretion and accountability issues.

Kathryn Ellis is attached to the Institute of Applied Social Research at the University of Bedfordshire, UK. Following an early career in the voluntary sector in the disability field, she has researched, taught and published in adult social care and social work, with a particular interest in the use of professional discretion. Her current work focuses on the managerialisation of front-line practice and discourses of service user empowerment.

Tony Evans is Professor of Social Work in the University of London and Head of the Department of Social Work in Royal Holloway College, University of London, UK. His research concerns the intersection of public policy, professional practice and ethics, and has focused on the idea of discretion as freedom and its continuation in the context of the increasingly managerialised public services. His current work is about discretion as judgement and the role of moral economies of care in professional decision-making.

Stephen Harrison was Professor of Social Policy and Director of the Health Policy, Politics and Organisation (HiPPO) research group at the University of Manchester, UK, until his retirement in 2011. He was formerly Professor of Health Policy and Politics at the University of Leeds, UK, and now holds honorary appointments at the University of Manchester and the London School of Hygiene and Tropical Medicine, UK. His research has focused particularly on the politics and sociology of the medical profession, the health policy process, the politics of health sector organisation, and the politics of patient pressure groups.

Michael Hill is Emeritus Professor of Social Policy of the University of Newcastle, UK. Since leaving Newcastle, he has held part-time visiting appointments at Queen Mary College (London), the London School of Economics and Political Science and the University of Brighton. His main research interests and areas of expertise are the public policy process, policy implementation and social policy. His interest in street-level bureaucracy originates from his own experience as an Executive Officer of the National Assistance Board in the early 1960s.

Peter Hupe teaches Public Administration at Erasmus University Rotterdam, The Netherlands. He has been a Visiting Fellow 2012–13 at All Souls College, Oxford. His research focuses on the theoretical-empirical study of public policy processes, particularly policy implementation and street-level bureaucracy. He discovered the relevance of the latter during an earlier career as a policymaker in national government.

Kim Loyens currently works at the Utrecht School of Governance, The Netherlands, as an Assistant Professor and is Senior Affiliated Researcher at the Leuven Institute of Criminology, Belgium. In her doctoral thesis, she conducted ethnographic research on ethical decision-making in the Belgian labour inspection and federal police. Her research interests include conflicting values at the front line, integrity management and whistle-blowing.

Peter J. May is the Donald R. Matthews Distinguished Professor Emeritus of American Politics at the University of Washington, Seattle, USA. His research addresses policy processes, environmental regulation and policymaking for natural hazards and disasters.

Steven Maynard-Moody is Professor, School of Public Affairs and Administration, and Director, Institute for Policy and Social Research, at the University of Kansas, USA. His current research interests and work are mainly about how everyday police–citizen encounters shape the meaning of policy, race and citizenship.

Michael Musheno is Faculty Director of the Legal Studies Program, School of Law, University of California, Berkeley, USA, and Professor of Law, the University of Oregon, USA. He is interested in legality, particularly the cultural force of law operating in and around the capillaries of the state's domestic policies. He is also interested in urban trouble and conflict.

Vibeke Lehmann Nielsen is Professor at the Department of Political Science, Aarhus University, Denmark. She researches in regulatory enforcement, compliance, implementation and street-level bureaucratic behaviour.

Christopher Osiander is currently a researcher at the Institute for Employment Research (Institut für Arbeitsmarkt- und Berufsforschung; IAB) in Nuremberg, Germany. His main research interests are evaluation of further training measures for the low-skilled unemployed, motivation for further training and job counselling, and placement in the German Federal Employment Agency.

Tino Schuppan holds a Professorship of Public Management and is working as Scientific Director of the Institute for E-Government (IfG.CC) in Potsdam, Germany. His research interests include transformation in the context of e-government, changing work organisation, competencies for e-government and information and communication technologies for development.

Frédérique Six is Assistant Professor of Governance and Organisation at the Department of Political Science and Public Administration at VU University Amsterdam, The Netherlands. Her research focuses on public governance puzzles in general and, in particular, the relation between trust and control.

Joss Steinke is currently Head of Department 'Work/Social affairs/ Europe' ('Arbeit/Soziales/Europa') at the 'AWO Bundesverband e.V.', a German social welfare association. Previously, he was a researcher at the Institute for Employment Research (Institut für Arbeitsmarkt- und Berufsforschung; IAB) in Nuremberg, Germany.

Rik van Berkel is Associate Professor at the Utrecht School of Governance, The Netherlands. His research interests include welfare state transformations, the introduction of new models for the provision of social services, the front-line delivery of welfare-to-work and activation policies, and the involvement and engagement of employers in promoting the labour-market participation of vulnerable labour-market groups.

Paul van der Aa is a researcher at the Dutch Municipality of Rotterdam and at Utrecht School of Governance, The Netherlands. He studies the front-line delivery and outcomes of local welfare-to-work policies within the context of regional labour markets.

Eva van Kooten works as a manager of business operations at the Rotterdam University of Applied Sciences, The Netherlands, where she also teaches Research Methodology. In her Master's thesis in Public Administration (2010, Erasmus University Rotterdam), she explored the ways in which front-line supervisors process rules.

Eelco van Wijk is a researcher and teacher at the Department of Political Science and Public Administration at VU University Amsterdam, The Netherlands. His research focuses on regulatory processes, the interaction between regulators as street-level bureaucrats and regulatees, and the governance of prostitution.

Carol Walker is Professor of Social Policy in the School of Social and Political Science, University of Lincoln, UK. Her key interests are poverty and inequality and the development of social security. Her recent research focuses on people with intellectual disabilities, in particular, their situation as they and their families age.

Jeffrey B. Wenger is Associate Professor of Public Policy at the University of Georgia's School of Public and International Affairs, Department of Public Administration and Policy. His research interests span a number of substantive areas, in particular, unemployment insurance, health insurance and pensions coverage. His theoretical work examines policy diffusion mechanisms and the role of deservingness in public policy analysis.

Vicky M. Wilkins is the Associate Dean in the School of Public Affairs and Professor of Public Administration and Policy at American University. Her primary research interests include representative bureaucracy, bureaucratic discretion, gender and race issues, deservingness, political institutions, and human resource management.

Søren C. Winter is Professor of Political Science and Public Administration at SFI – The Danish National Centre for Social Research in Copenhagen, Denmark. His research focuses on policy implementation, public management, street-level bureaucracy and environmental regulation.

Preface

Important insights may be gained via social interaction – as scholars like Charles Lindblom have pointed out. There is the instant learning of the baby touching the heating, or the spiritual reflection of the monk. Sooner or later, however, knowledge is achieved beyond the relative isolation of the individual.

This certainly goes on in the workplace of the social sciences. Intellectual cogitation is pertinent, whether or not practised during a sabbatical leave spent in a quiet resort of wisdom. Often, an empirical test of the formulated propositions will next be sought. Finally, at the end of the day, papers have to be submitted to the scrutiny of review by peers – after those papers have been presented to and discussed by colleagues at conferences.

This book is the result of a dynamic interplay between cogitation and interaction, to use the wording of Aaron Wildavsky. Parts of the ideas underlying this volume came up during stays – always too short – in splendid isolation. At the same time, most of the chapters would not have had their present form if they were not the products of inter-collegial interaction.

Coming from different directions, the editors and chapter authors found in each other a fundamental interest in studying the subject matter of this book. Aurélien Buffat combines the study and practice of public administration while currently balancing the demands of one job within and one outside the university. Before starting an academic career spanning almost five decades now, Michael Hill was a 'street-level bureaucrat' *avant la lettre*. Peter Hupe discovered the relevance of what happens on the ground floor of government when he was a policymaker in the national civil service.

Over the past five years, we have tried to build up an international network of researchers sharing our quest to understand street-level bureaucracy. We did so in flexible configurations and under varying institutional umbrellas. The latter particularly included workshops at the yearly conferences of the European Group of Public Administration (EGPA), co-chaired with Harald Sætren, and panels of the International Conference on Public Policy (ICPP), co-chaired with Evelyn Brodkin. The source from which several chapters of this book originate is the panel organised in April 2012 by Aurélien Buffat and Peter Hupe at the yearly conference of the International Research Symposium of Public Management (IRSPM) in Rome. The network comprises researchers from both sides of the Atlantic Ocean. As editors, we are pleased that a range of them present work in this book.

Apart from the boards of IRSPM, EGPA and ICPP, we would like to acknowledge our own institutional affiliations. In terms of providing favourable conditions, we owe a lot to Ioannis Papadopoulos (University of Lausanne) and, more generally, to the Institute of Political and International Studies of this Swiss academic institution for its financial support to Aurélien's travels around Europe, to Philip Haynes (University of Brighton), to Victor Bekkers and Kees van Paridon (Erasmus University Rotterdam), and to the Warden and Fellows of All Souls College, Oxford. The latter generously offered hospitality to Peter Hupe as a Visiting Fellow.

From the beginning on, Laura Vickers and Emily Watt of Policy Press have shown enthusiasm for this book project. They are thanked for thinking along the whole way through. In particular, concerning the crucial aspects that they asked for attention to be paid, some of the best ideas occurred from social interaction. Thanks also to those involved in the later stages of production: Dave Worth, Jo Morton and Ruth Harrison at Policy Press; and the copy editor, Alan Halfpenny.

Part One
Introduction

ONE

Introduction: defining and understanding street-level bureaucracy

Peter Hupe, Michael Hill and Aurélien Buffat

What is street-level bureaucracy?

The expression 'street-level bureaucracy' was coined, as far as we know, by Michael Lipsky. He introduced it in an article in 1971 and elaborated it in a book in 1980, which he further updated in 2010 (Lipsky, 2010). Most of the contributors to this volume make reference to the book, which is cited as the 2010 edition unless they have specifically quoted from the earlier one. In developing an identifiable view, Jeffrey Prottas (1979) and Richard Weatherly (1979) were collaborators. The introduction of the term obviously caught the imagination of many writers on public policy, including ourselves. Consequentially, here, we explore the 'state of the art' – which is the aim of this edited volume.

Two observations can be made head on. One is that the essential phenomena that Michael Lipsky asked attention to be paid to have been described in many ways other than in terms of 'street-level bureaucracy'. For example, here, we may note references to the 'point of entry' (Hall, 1974) and the 'public encounter' (Goodsell, 1981). Hence, if we were to engage in a computerised literature search with 'street-level bureaucracy' as the key term, we would certainly seriously undercount.

A second, and closely related, observation regards the fact that Michael Lipsky's contribution focuses particularly on certain aspects of street-level work and highlights particular problems associated with it. In so doing, he seems to be reluctant to apply his approach to all relevant public sector interfaces. In the new preface written for the 2010 edition of the book, he justifies the book as 'a search for the place of the individual in those services I call street-level bureaucracies' (Lipsky, 2010, p xi). Interactions with street-level bureaucracies are

3

'places where citizens experience directly the government they have implicitly constructed' (Lipsky, 2010, p xi).

Lipsky distinguishes two ways to understand the term 'street-level bureaucrat'. The first one is to equate it with 'the public services with which citizens typically interact. In this sense, all teachers, police officers, and social workers in public agencies are street-level bureaucrats without further qualification' (Lipsky, 2010, p xvii). In the second definition – the one originally intended, Lipsky adds – street-level bureaucracy stands for 'public service employment of a certain sort, performed under certain conditions.… Street-level bureaucrats interact with citizens in the course of the job and have discretion in exercising authority' (Lipsky, 2010, p xvii). Both of these alternative definitions highlight aspects of street-level bureaucracy in ways that make it difficult to tie down the 'state of the art' in the face of the diversity of work that either uses his term or may be seen as concerned with closely related issues without using it.

Insights on bureaucracy and beyond

Early conceptualisations of bureaucracy

Perhaps the best examination of the use of the concept of bureaucracy in political science is provided by Albrow (1970). He shows the term to originate in late 18th-century French writing by De Gournay and De Grimm, who used it to describe a form of government, broadly, 'rule by officials', in a context that was clearly critical of the phenomenon. Since this was written in pre-democratic France, it is appropriate to ask: who, then, did represent the public interest?

A later English comment on bureaucracy calls it 'the continental nuisance', and goes on: 'I can see no risk or possibility in England. Democracy is hot enough here' (Thomas Carlyle, 1850, quoted by Albrow, 1970, p 21). Interestingly, however, the English novelist Charles Dickens clearly implies that it was already here in chapter 10 of his novel *Little Dorrit* (Dickens, 1857). In that chapter, called 'Containing the whole science of government', he describes the 'Circumlocution Office', saying 'no public business could possibly be done at any time without [its] acquiescence'. Further appropriate quotes could be traded from a range of European 19th-century writers, including, notably, Balzac in France, without taking our understanding of the issues forward.

Indeed, we may see as separate questions issues about arrogation of power, whether from monarchs or parliaments (which is not our concern in this book), and issues about how bureaucracies treat people.

Bureaucracy as a mode of policy delivery

As far as the latter is concerned, the end of the 19th century saw the emergence of a view of bureaucracy as a 'rational' device to ensure the efficient and just delivery of public policy. That perspective is particularly embodied in Max Weber's (1974) notion of bureaucracy as embedded in a 'rational-legal' mode of authority. For Weber, this is not necessarily a democratic mode of authority; it is the acceptance of the rule of law in the public policy process that is significant.

At the same time, policy delivery at the local level was shifting from traditional forms, based on delegation of implementation to local elites (as in the UK Poor Law), to emergent democratic government. The most interesting discussion of these issues comes from the US, in Woodrow Wilson's (1887) famous article 'The study of administration'. There, his concern was to find a middle way between the democratic model for service delivery developed in the US – the Jacksonian spoils system (a form of clientelism) – and what he saw as the German model of efficient administration. Wilson (1887, p 20) argues:

> The ideal for us is a civil service cultured and self-sufficient enough to act with sense and vigour, and yet so intimately connected with popular thought, by means of elections and constant public counsel, as to find arbitrariness and class spirit quite out of the question.

In Wilson's work, we see the two issues about bureaucracy running side by side: bureaucracy as an overall mode of governance and as an approach to policy delivery. In his delineation of the characteristics of bureaucracy, Weber spells out the notion of rationality. From the early 20th century on, this notion would be seen as a dominant principle for the organisation of activities in a complex society. In this respect, then, a version of the bureaucratic ideal was carried forward by mass production industry, with a particular emphasis on a detailed and highly regulated division of labour, embodied in Frederic Taylor's (1911) recommendations for the Ford motor company. Much later, this led to consideration of the extent to which this version of bureaucracy is applicable to public policy delivery (see Pollitt, 1990). This generated the debate so central to this book about the extent to which policy delivery can or should be bureaucratised.

Aspects of the modern debate about bureaucratisation have echoed the 'Circumlocution Office' view of bureaucracy. Merton (1957) argues that bureaucrats are likely to show particular attachment to rules that protect the internal system of social relationships, enhance their status by enabling them to take on the status of the organisation and protect them from conflict with clients by emphasising impersonality. Because of their function in providing security, rules of this kind are particularly likely to be transformed into absolutes. Policy goals are then distorted as means are treated as ends. However, questions need to be posed about the inevitability of this process of distortion. In any case, other things are going on within a bureaucratic organisation. For Gouldner (1954), games are played around rules in bureaucratic organisations; it is not self-evident that subordinates will simply internalise the expectations of their superiors.

The bureaucratic model of policy delivery has been vehemently defended by Charles Goodsell (1983). Goodsell's (1983) book includes some cogent observations on formal modes of organisation and on rules, quoting Michael Hill (1976) on the importance of fair and predictable services for the public. Goodsell's (1983) book is primarily a defence of public administration in general, in which both rule-bound and discretionary behaviour will be in evidence. There is a need to recognise the importance of the formal organisation of public services in 20th- and 21st-century life. Perrow (1972, p 5) puts this in almost determinist terms: 'Without this form of social technology, the industrialized countries of the West could not have reached the heights of extravagance, wealth and pollution that they currently enjoy.'

Bureaucratisation or professionalisation

'In the literature concerned with formulation, bureaucratisation may almost be treated as a variable. Even within mass production industry, models that are less formal than Taylor's have been developed. This brings us, then, to the balance between bureaucratisation and professionalisation. Alongside analyses that stress the bureaucratisation of everyone, we find explorations of the development of professionalisation (for a critical evaluation of this trend, see Wilensky, 1964). Hence, then, one of the key issues for this volume is the extent to which formalisation of policy delivery and the elimination of discretion have actually occurred. Seeing street-level bureaucrats as in roles with both bureaucratic and professional characteristics, it is appropriate to raise some issues about the development of professional roles in public policy delivery. To do this, we need to recognise the transformation of public policy that has occurred since the term 'bureaucracy' was developed. To what extent were there street-level bureaucrats at the beginning of the 19th century? The answer is that they existed in a number of special situations in which a need for a public role to solve collective action problems had been recognised: flood control, fire prevention, some rudimentary policing and so on. The 19th century saw extensions of these roles, particularly in the face of needs to solve public health problems.

Going back to Dickens, perhaps his most famous street-level bureaucrat was the Poor Law official aghast that Oliver Twist should ask for more. The 1834 Poor Law Reform had made him a public official inasmuch as there was increased state funding and supervision of local services. Publicly provided education, health care, social care and social benefits were initially rare, but grew in importance through the late 19th and early 20th centuries. The gradual process of change did two things: it brought into the public sector kinds of workers who already expected a large extent of autonomy (as in the case of doctors); and it created tasks that seemed to need to involve a high degree of discretion (as in the case of child protection work). Many of the issues about street-level discretion have been set in a context in which there are varied and contested claims about the extent to which the actors are professionals rather than bureaucrats. Such issues belong very much to the late 20th century – the era when Lipsky coined the expression 'street-level bureaucracy'.

Lipsky chose to use the term 'bureaucrats' while writing about people often called professionals or 'semi-professionals' (Etzioni, 1969). Freidson's bureaucracy–professionalism contrast is therefore pertinent:

> In contrast to the negative word 'bureaucracy' we have the word 'profession'. This word is almost always positive in its connotation, and is frequently used to represent a superior alternative to bureaucracy. Unlike 'bureaucracy' which is disclaimed by every organisation concerned with its public relations, 'profession' is claimed by virtually every occupation seeking to improve its public image. When the two terms are brought together, the discussion is almost always at the expense of bureaucracy and to the advantage of profession. (Freidson, 1970a, pp 129–30)

Street-level bureaucracy and beyond

As far as street-level bureaucracy is concerned, this excursion into the discussion of bureaucracy and professionalism leaves us with two important issues. One is that emphasis on the street level represents one part of a long-standing concern about the location of power. Street-level bureaucrats are among various groups seen as arrogating power from where some people want to argue that it really belongs. Our stance in this book is to treat the questions about power as important for the study of street-level bureaucracy, in a context in which it is fundamental to recognise a wide spectrum of perspectives on the desirability and legitimacy of control.

The other issue is that this takes place in the context of many different kinds of tasks. To some extent, the latter may be arrayed along a continuum from routine activities to complex tasks implying high degrees of discretion (as with some professions), with a substantial range of tasks in-between. Our stance on this follows from the one we have taken on the first issue. As can be observed, some tasks are harder to control than others, while there are varying perspectives on the desirability of control. This being so, we do not think it helpful to try to draw too narrow lines around the empirical phenomena that may be addressed under the heading of *street-level bureaucracy*. In our view, what happens in the fulfilment of public tasks involving social interaction at the street level deserves research attention overall.

The essence of Lipsky's approach

In the previous section, we argued that street-level bureaucracy is something larger than simply Lipsky's original concerns. At the same time, his influence is such that a closer look at the issues he highlights is necessary.

What is entailed in Lipsky's contribution to the scholarly agenda? His book consists of four parts. After the Introduction, these regard, respectively, conditions of work, patterns of practice and the future of street-level bureaucracy. The chapter titles in the first part set the tone. Under the headings 'The critical role of street-level bureaucrats' and 'Street-level bureaucrats as policy makers', Lipsky elaborates on conflict, discretion, 'relative autonomy from organizational authority' and 'resources for resistance'. Conditions of work (in the second part) get attention under labels like 'the problem of resources', 'goals and performance measures', 'the social construction of a client' and 'advocacy and alienation in street-level work'. Also, the chapter and section headings in 'Patterns of practice' (the third part) speak for themselves: 'rationing services' (eg 'queuing', 'routines'), 'controlling clients', 'husbanding resources' and 'the client-processing mentality'. In the headings in the fourth and final part of the book, terms can be found like 'the assault on human services', 'accountability', 'directions for greater client autonomy' and 'the prospects and problems of professionalism'. In the expanded 30th anniversary edition, Lipsky added a new preface and a final (14th) chapter titled 'On managing street-level bureaucracy'.

These headings indicate the range of key concepts central in Lipsky's view. Giving them a closer look enables one to distil a few issues that Lipsky put on the research agenda. In our view, these issues regard theoretical, methodological, programmatic and political aspects of the study of government-in-action. We suggest the latter term to indicate the empirical object in a manner crossing disciplinary labels stemming from an academic labour division, institutionalised as it is.

The *theoretical* issue that Lipsky asked attention to be paid to regards how to understand multilayered policymaking. He grounded the assumption that street-level bureaucrats are policymakers in their own right, for example, teachers are 'street ministers of education' (Lipsky, 2010, p 12). With 'relatively high degrees of discretion and relative autonomy from organizational authority', street-level bureaucrats have considerable leeway in 'determining the nature, amount, and quality of benefits and sanctions provided by their agencies' (Lipsky, 2010, p 13). In fact, 'their individual actions add up to agency behaviour' (Lipsky, 2010, p 13): '[T]he decisions of street-level bureaucrats, the routines they establish, and the devices they invent to cope with uncertainties and work pressures effectively *become* the public policies they carry out' (Lipsky, 2010, p xiii, emphasis in original).

Hence, Lipsky looks at the daily practice of governing in contact with citizens – what happens on the ground, as Hupe (2014) has formulated it. The theoretical implication for the study of the policy process is that knowing policy inputs (for instance, a budget assigned to hire more police) does not allow 'reading off' policy outputs (more police officers effectively in street service), let alone outcomes (less crime). It is obvious that this theoretical view must have methodological implications.

The *methodological* issue that street-level bureaucracy analysis addresses regards the necessity to open up the *black box* of what literally happens in implementation organisations. Doing research on how public policies are implemented may mean walking with police officers in downtown areas, spending hours in the waiting rooms of social services

9

departments or joining environmental inspectors while making site visits. Official documents remain important and (large *n*) surveys keep their value, but there is no alternative to being on the spot while practising observation and having interviews with public officials at their own desks. It is there that 'the problem of street-level bureaucrats' is located: 'in the structure of their work' (Lipsky, 2010, p xv).

The *programmatic* issue of doing research on street-level bureaucracy is arguably the least elaborated of all by Lipsky. In the preface prepared for the expanded 30th anniversary edition of his book, he speaks of 'the street-level bureaucracy framework', entailing an 'essentially comparative approach':

> I identify the common elements of occupations as apparently disparate as, say, police officer and social worker. The analysis of street-level bureaucracy helps us identify which features of people-processing are common and which are unique, to the different occupational milieu in which they arise. (Lipsky, 2010, p xix)

The approach is characterised as 'essentially comparative' because it 'permits us to raise questions systematically about apparent differences in various service areas' (Lipsky, 2010, p xix). Lipsky (2010, p xx) goes on, stating that the 'utility of the street-level bureaucracy approach can be tested only in efforts to understand whether common features of the framework lead to common behavioural outcomes'. With these statements, Lipsky seems to make a case for research along comparative lines – although the foundation for empirical differences in 'behavioural outcomes' is given by the common elements in the *structure of the work* of street-level bureaucrats.

The *normative* issue that the theme of street-level bureaucracy puts on the academic agenda is the need for attention to the work circumstances in which contemporary 'lower-level' public officials are fulfilling their tasks. In fact, social engagement is at stake here, as expressed in the discourse. Terms like 'alienation' and the 'assault on' and 'support for' human services, used in the context of a fiscal crisis, reveal a critical political stance. Besides, Lipsky's reflections on the negative stereotyping of clients bring to our attention the differential and perhaps discriminatory treatment of citizens. More generally, the link between discretionary judgements and (in)equality of treatment regards fundamentally normative and political issues. This fact does not stand in the way of a clinical analysis, but the ultimate goal of research goes beyond academia: 'to identify conditions that would better support a reconstituted public sector dedicated to appropriate service and respect for clients – one that would be more likely to produce effective service providers' (Lipsky, 2010, p xix).

There was, and still is, research attention on various aspects of the empirical phenomena that the theme of street-level bureaucracy refers to, both before and around the moment that this label was coined. However, as a theoretical perspective – or, if you wish, a 'framework' or 'approach' – *street-level bureaucracy* provides a more or less coherent focus. As such, it offers a particular way of dealing with a range of issues, as indicated earlier. The 'proof' of its sustainability is the fact that the term became a label covering what would develop as a scholarly theme of its own. The next section, therefore, regards the present state of knowledge.

Street-level bureaucracy as a scholarly theme

Michael Lipsky introduced the term 'street-level bureaucracy' around two years before Pressman and Wildavsky's (1973) *Implementation* came onto the market. With its long subtitle ('How great expectations were dashed in Oakland …'), the latter book expressed the frustrations about what may happen with the good intentions laid down in a policy programme. That book came out in the days when policymakers, the public and, not least, researchers in political science and public administration were curious to see what had came out of big US policy programmes like the 'Great Society' project of President Johnson.

It is clear that Lipsky's book, published in 1980, also addressed 'later' parts of the policy cycle than the standard literature on, for instance, political decision-making tends to do. Although 'street-level bureaucracy' is often subsumed under the heading of 'implementation', there is a difference here. 'Implementation' refers to what happens 'after a bill has become a law' (Bardach, 1977). As such, it refers to a 'vertical' dimension of public administration, multilayered as the latter is (Hill and Hupe, 2003). On the other hand, with its focus on the 'dilemmas of the individual', street-level bureaucracy allows for the inclusion of a more 'horizontal' view. Among the 'vectors of different size directed inward', a public policy programme has alternative determinants of its implementation (Weatherly, 1980, p 9).

While both books would have a marked impact on the study of the policy process, they also expressed a continued attention on phenomena that were suddenly now framed differently. As Hill and Hupe (2014) have stressed, there was implementation before the label was used – otherwise, how would the pyramids have been built? Besides, there has been scholarly attention to the phenomena that the term refers to before and beyond the sub-discipline called 'implementation research'. Similar observations can be made of street-level bureaucracy. In introducing the literature on implementation, Hill and Hupe made a variety of connections, particularly with studies in the sociology of organisations and studies on the sociology of law. They also placed the topic within some of the concerns of political science, and of another discipline, public administration. These same connections can obviously be made here, in some respects, in terms of a dominant chain: political science and public administration – policy process – implementation – the study of street-level bureaucracy.

We note various valuable reviews of the state of the field giving, at a meta-level, interpretive overviews of the development of the scholarly theme. As such can be mentioned the special issue edited by Evelyn Brodkin (2011), who also wrote an overview article (Brodkin, 2012) and gives an account in the next chapter of this volume. Handbook chapters were written by Maynard-Moody and Portillo (2010), Meyers and Nielsen (2012) and Smith (2012).

In identifying different approaches, there is scope for elaborating a framework in which clusters of factors are distinguished as potentially explaining government-in-action (Hupe and Hill, 2014). This matrix is based on the Multiple Governance Framework presented earlier (Hill and Hupe, 2014). Here, the adapted version of that entails a matrix that may be helpful to identify which factors, on which scales of action, have got more and which ones less attention so far in the study of street-level bureaucracy.

Most street-level bureaucracy studies focus, first and foremost, on the action scale of the individual. This is hardly surprising, for it is exactly what the term 'street level' draws attention to. What, then, is being identified more precisely as the dependent variable (what needs explanation) or, at least, the unit of observation and analysis remains open. It may vary from 'discretion', via 'behavioural outcomes', to variation in 'policy outputs'. In the latter case, what needs to be explained lies outside the matrix in Table 1.1.

On the side of factors seen as potentially influencing the object studied, most accounts on street-level bureaucracy also seem to focus on the scale of the individual. There are studies on 'deservingness', stressing what happens in the direct interaction between public officials and individual clients (*Behaviour*). Often, these studies have a qualitative nature and a small *n*, but surveys are sometimes used to ask street-level bureaucrats about their behaviour (Maupin, 1993; Murray, 2006). Therefore, statements made in response to questionnaires function as

Table 1.1: Factor clusters explaining government-in-action

Action scale	Action dimension		
	Structure	*Content*	*Process*
System	Context	Orientation	Control
Organisation	Setting	Tasks	Management
Individual	Antecedents	Habitus	Behaviour

Source: Hupe (2012), elaboration of Hupe and Hill (2006, p 23). See also Hill and Hupe (2014, p 130).

a proxy for measuring individual action (*Habitus*). Under the heading of 'representative bureaucracy', there is extensive research attention on the structural characteristics of individuals in public service, like gender, ethnic background and age (*Antecedents*; for a review of these studies, see Riccucci and Meyers, 2004).

While the bulk of public management studies focus – by definition – on *management*, attention to the scale of organisations is less present in research on street-level bureaucracy than that on individual actors (with exceptions, eg, Riccucci, 2005b). Of course, a vast literature on networks has developed (for instance, Koppenjan and Klijn, 2004), some of them explicitly addressing the networks that street-level bureaucrats do their work in (*Setting*; see Provan and Milward, 1991). A focus on *Tasks* can be found in research on perceptions of red tape (Scott and Pandey, 2000), job design (Hill, 2006), automation (Wenger and Wilkins, 2009) and the role of routines, work groups and team learning (Foldy and Buckley, 2010).

Studies on implementation as the management of policy trajectories are abundant, even in the age of governance (see Sætren, 2014). Given their character as mainstream implementation studies (single case, comparing achievements with intentions), attention to the dynamics of the street level is often less prominent in those studies (Hupe, 2014). Mandating and delegation get attention in a specific stream of the literature (see the work of May, eg, 1993, 1994), but seldom in research designs encompassing attention on the street level (*Control*). The substance of policy programmes (policy goals and instruments) are the object of a different kind of studies than those on street-level bureaucracy (*Orientation*).

In rare studies on the street level, this 'level' – actually a sub-layer – is treated as, one way or another, fundamentally connected with the system level (*Context*). Nevertheless, it is clear that the latter sustainably exerts substantial influence on government-in-action. An exception is Jewell (2007). In a study of welfare administration in the

US, Germany and Sweden, Jewell observes 'three worlds of social welfare', making a connection here with Esping-Andersen's (1990) more macro-level comparative work. Jewell (2007, p 34) links 'macro-' and 'micro-'analysis by connecting 'national culture, institutional history, and agency organization to ground-level practice'. Addressing 'welfare caseworker behaviour' and 'activation caseworker behaviour' as dependent variables, Jewell places them in a context where it seems to be choices of institutional settings that are important. This theme is echoed in other comparative work, but without a street-level bureaucracy focus (Ungerson, 1995; Lodemel and Trickey, 2001).

So far, we have addressed studies on street-level bureaucracy by placing them in one of the three-by-three boxes. Obviously, some studies look in a multidimensional way (across action dimensions) or a 'multi-level' way (across action scales or administrative layers), while a few combine both. Among the latter category, the following theoretical lenses can be mentioned, each consisting of particular sets of explanatory variables:

- standards of proof, bureau-legal constraints and informal street-level standard operating procedures (O'Connell, 1991);
- community values and personal values (Weissert, 1994);
- policy design, bureaucratic incentives, political forces, task requirements and economic capacity (Keiser and Meier, 1996);
- organisational control, client characteristics and professional field (Scott, 1997);
- organisation-based verification and client-based verification (Stoker and Wilson, 1998);
- partisan control, funding decisions, values of state administrators and levels of demand (Keiser and Soss, 1998);
- professional accountability systems, trust building and the strategic behaviour of professionals (Bundt, 2000);
- organisation size, task complexity, the number of rules and stakeholder consensus (Langbein, 2000);
- professional, institutional and contextual clusters of variables (Cho et al, 2005);
- authority, role expectations, workload, client contact, knowledge and expertise, and incentives (Jewell and Glaser, 2006);
- administrative factors and political predispositions (Keiser, 2008);
- municipal politics and policy, managerial actions, street-level bureaucrats' perceptions and knowledge, and contextual factors (May and Winter, 2009); and

- policy design, the institutional and political economy of the local community, organisational strategic choices, workers' responses, and worker–client relations (Hasenfeld, 2010).

The literature on policy implementation shows a plethora of more or less comprehensive approaches, in some of which *what happens at the street level* has a more or less prominent place (for an overview, see Hill and Hupe, 2014). For instance, in Winter's (2012, p 258) *integrated implementation model*, between 'policy formulation' and 'implementation results', most clusters of variables concern the 'implementation process'. Within that relatively large centre of the model, boxes are headed as 'organisational and inter-organisational implementation behaviour', 'management', 'street-level bureaucratic skills and willingness' and 'target group behaviour'. It is clear that models like these – or, rather, theoretical approaches – have a substantial heuristic value. However, whether it is possible and desirable to develop a grounded and founded, all-embracing theory with both a multidimensional and multi-level character remains an open question.

Some matters of definition

As shown, writings on the scholarly theme of street-level bureaucracy come from various theoretical angles. Furthermore, within the scholarly theme, similar or even the same kinds of phenomena are also approached in substantially varying terms. In fact, horizontal, vertical and discursive diversity can be observed here.

Horizontal diversity concerns the question: what kind of work can be regarded as typical for street-level bureaucracy, and what not? Some authors plea for a narrow definition. Maynard-Moody and Portillo (2010, p 261), for instance, speak of research on street-level bureaucracy as having become 'a vital and generative scholarly confluence at the intersection of public administration, social welfare, criminal justice, socio-legal studies, and public policy'. Referring to court clerks, tax auditors, building inspectors, 911-call operators and public guardians, they make an interesting distinction: '[W]e emphasize that researchers need to be careful not to assume that all frontline workers are street-level bureaucrats' (Maynard-Moody and Portillo, 2010, p 263). While we have acknowledged the need to recognise diversity, we do not think it very helpful to try to draw lines in that way.

Vertical diversity refers to the question as to whether, 'down along the line', street-level bureaucrats are seen as the only ones exercising discretion. Evans (2010), for instance, stresses that discretion is not a unique prerogative of public officials doing their work in direct contact with citizens; their managers also have discretion and use it. We would like to add that this, in fact, goes for the whole range of actors on all subsequent layers from the 'top' ('Washington') to the 'bottom' ('Oakland') of a policy process. Certainly, street-level workers need to be seen at the end of a discretionary 'chain' in which the discretions exercised by their managers and their managers' acceptance of their discretions are important. However, it necessarily leaves us with a blurred view of the location of the *street*.

Discursive diversity is apparent when various terms are used for what is basically the same kind of phenomena. Some authors want to avoid the term 'bureaucracy' because of its often negative connotations, using 'public professionals' instead (Tummers et al, 2013). However, the fact that street-level bureaucrats may be seen as *professionals in public service* makes them identifiable as 'servants of the state' – and we are then back to the term 'bureaucracy' (Hupe, 2010). Against this background, we have something to say on the key concepts used in this volume.

Street-level bureaucrats

Given the arguments presented earlier, we propose a *working definition* with the following elements to define who street-level bureaucrats are. First, they are working in contact with individual citizens. The roles of the latter can vary: consumers, clients, pupils, parents and patients, but also car drivers and so on. Second, they are doing their work while in public service. Working in encounters with individual citizens, they may be employed by private companies in cases where public functions have been contracted out. Even then, however, it is decisive that they fulfil public tasks on behalf of the common good. Third, street-level bureaucrats have specific tasks for which they are likely to have had training (varying, as will be evidenced by several of the chapters in this book, from extensive formal professional education to very basic briefing). These joint characteristics make street-level bureaucrats identifiable as such. By implication: a) they have inherent discretion; b) function as policy co-makers; and c) show a certain craftsmanship in fulfilling their tasks. All these three characteristics will show to varying degrees in empirical reality.

Types of street-level bureaucracy

Once a common denominator has been established, comparison becomes justified. Detecting variation on all kinds of dimensions then becomes possible. Wilson (1989) uses outputs and outcomes as the dimensions for his typology of agencies. He distinguishes between a production, procedural, craft and coping organisation. This typology reminds us that Lipsky's delineation of street-level bureaucracy may lead us to a failure to recognise the very varied tasks for which discretion is granted and used. Within an agency, it is the 'operator' who performs the critical task of the organisation, the activities providing the raison d'être for the agency as a whole.

Rules and discretion

Earlier, reference has been made to the significance of variation in discretion within street-level work. Hence, the extent of its variation and the nature of its sources need to be examined. As Hill (2013, p 203) observed: 'much of the literature on implementation is about the various degrees of discretion accorded to those close to, or actually at, the delivery point for policy'. There is an intrinsic relationship between rules, 'which specify the duties and obligations of officials', and discretion, 'which allows them freedom of choice of action' (Hill, 2013, p 237). Public law sees discretionary action in the context of rules, specifically, as involving 'particular cases of legitimate departure from action prescribed by a legal rule structure' (Hill, 2013, p 237). A standard definition is given by Davis (1969, p 4): 'A public officer has discretion wherever the effective limits on his power leave him free to make a choice among possible courses of action and inaction'. The best metaphor to illustrate this standard definition of discretion is probably Dworkin's 'hole of the donut' (1977, p 31): 'an area left open by a surrounding belt of restriction'. In other words, discretion, both as granted and as used, is the effective decisional room for manoeuvre that a public official has in a context in which rules and regulations exist. This is why 'the study of discretion must involve … the study of rules, and may alternatively be defined as being concerned with the extent to which actions are determined by rules' (Hill, 2013, p 238).

In fact, discretion is a concept with multiple dimensions (Hupe, 2013). A distinction between two interpretations is pertinent here. On the one hand, discretion stands for the degree of freedom as prescriptively granted by a rule-maker to an actor supposed to apply the rules stemming from the latter. In an alternative meaning, the same term refers to the ways in which the freedom granted is actually used. The focus, then, is on behaviour in a given setting; the former forms the context for the latter. In most empirical studies on street-level bureaucracy, discretion-as-used will be what needs explanation, the dependent variable, with discretion-as-granted functioning as an independent variable. However, where what is to be explained is why discretionary freedom was granted, the latter will be the dependent variable. This is a distinction that we will come back to in the discussion of research on street-level bureaucracy in Chapter Eighteen.

Understanding street-level bureaucracy

Objective and contents

The present book aims at providing a state-of-the-art account of theory and research on street-level bureaucracy. It includes discussions of the varying roles of public officials who fulfil their tasks while interacting with the public. Such officials carry out public tasks in the delivery of benefits and services, and also in the regulation of social and economic behaviour. The book addresses these questions in depth, ending with suggestions for the further development of research in this field.

In Chapter Two, Evelyn Z. Brodkin provides her view on the research on street-level bureaucracy. After the two introductory chapters forming Part One, the book is divided into a further six parts, the first five composed of three chapters each. Part Two explores street-level work of the type that has probably received the most attention within the literature so far, that is, street-level bureaucrats who are in charge of delivering public services and benefits in the general context of the welfare state. Discretion is at the heart of the three chapters, in particular, the ways in which discretion is being used in various social services.

In Chapter Three, Carol Walker focuses on and reviews the issues about discretion in UK social assistance. This chapter's concern is with analysing discretion, what we earlier called the degree of freedom prescriptively granted by a rule-maker. Carol Walker highlights the evolution of the policy debate since the 1970s and the various attempts to limit discretion in a rule-based mainstream system, confining 'residual' decision-making to separate sections or organisations.

Chapter Four, by Stephen Harrison, puts UK health practitioners at the centre of the contribution. He describes the increasing development of the capacity to frame the power of street-level medical practitioners, but also investigates how some medical discretionary practices were able to survive even in such a context. Hence, the particular focus is on the freedom to act, as granted and used among relatively highly professionalised street-level bureaucrats.

In Chapter Five, by Aurélien Buffat, attention turns to the study of the exercise of discretionary power within a rule-structured context. While the chapter highlights the rather low level of discretion used by taxing officers in general, it shows that the amount of effective discretion depends much on the task at hand, the material economy of cases to be processed, the regulation framework and the existing control mechanisms.

Part Three of the book is called 'Agents of the state', and in this part, law enforcement and regulatory roles are explored. Here, we specifically look at some key 'servants of the state' who are also central figures in the street-level bureaucracy literature, that is, police officers, labour inspectors and agricultural inspectors. As in Part Two, the focus is on the ways in which these street-level agents achieve their tasks and develop discretionary practices to deal with the regulated target groups.

In Chapter Six, Kim Loyens investigates how Belgian street-level bureaucrats in law enforcement agencies, such as police officers and labour inspectors, experience and concretely deal with policy alienation, that is, situations in which frustrations and disappointments arise because the application of official procedures does not lead to the expected outcomes (solving crime, fighting human exploitation and illegal employment). Here, the focus on exploring how discretionary powers are exercised in contexts in which street-level bureaucrats have difficulty coping and putting their aspirations for their service into practice picks up on one of the key themes in Michael Lipsky's work.

In Chapter Seven, Vibeke Lehmann Nielsen addresses a similar topic, looking at the coping and discretionary behaviours of various Danish regulatory inspectors in different policy areas. Particular attention is given to the interaction between the inspectors and the regulatees and how and why the dynamics of the relationship between regulatory agents and regulated stakeholders affect the outcome of the interaction. Vibeke Lehmann Nielsen highlights two specific interaction-related factors explaining variation in the discretionary choices made by regulators: the degree to which regulators and regulatees have convergent or divergent interests; and the power relationship between these two groups.

Then, in Chapter Eight, Søren C. Winter and Peter J. May explore the relationship between the actions of regulatory agents in enforcing rules and the willingness of regulatees to comply. Here, the focus on a combination of a complex task and powerful regulatees illustrates the connection between the study of street-level bureaucracy and the wider implementation literature. The chapter considers the role of deterrent actions in bringing about compliance, that is, actions that give incentives to the regulatees to comply because they fear a risk of detection and sanction in case of non-compliance. Here, the context is Danish agro-environmental regulations.

In Part Four of the book, we look at street-level bureaucrats as public actors in their own right. While 'servants of the state', they reflect where they are coming from as *'embedded in society'*. An illustration may be helpful here.

As a taxing officer in a Swiss Unemployment Insurance Fund, Christine provides social services to citizens (Part Two) and is supposed to enforce the existing law (Part Three). Apart from this, Christine, like many other street-level bureaucrats, does her work in a context of social relationships that affect how she works and deals with people. First, Christine has a specific educational and social background (including, of course, gender here), and she has experienced unemployment herself in the past and worked in several companies. These experiences affect how she processes cases, in particular, when she has to sanction clients. In other words, her social *habitus* (Bourdieu, 2005) exerts some influence on the way in which she works as a street-level bureaucrat. Besides, daily, she encounters clients who are socially and culturally heterogeneous, this is why continuous adaptation to the situation is a requisite of front-line practice. In other words, Christine is embedded in society, the latter being heterogeneous and complex.

In this regard, the study of street-level bureaucracy must take into consideration the social and cultural environment. Working 'in public service' means undergoing sociocultural influences and this is why a part of the literature on street-level bureaucrats concerns their antecedents, such as education, training, socialisation, gender and age. We noted earlier that the literature on representative bureaucracy addresses these issues. Furthermore, street-level bureaucrats are influenced not only by *who* they are, but also by *where* they are in terms of social or institutional context.

Chapter Nine, by Vicky M. Wilkins and Jeffrey B. Wenger, develops ideas for research on the issue of representativeness of street-level bureaucrats and how their characteristics influence their behaviour. The chapter suggests a framework for the examination of the personal and institutional conditions under which bureaucrats' personal values influence the ways in which they interact with clients in terms of the notion of a 'belief in a just world'.

In Chapter Ten, Michael Musheno and Steven Maynard-Moody investigate the social, legal and cultural dynamics of doing work on the front lines of public service. Based on empirical material gathered in various street-level activities in the US (schools, police departments), the authors challenge what they refer to as the 'state-agent' narrative on street-level bureaucracy and highlight the alternative narratives provided by front-line workers. They relocate street-level discretionary judgements as having much more to do with the social context in which street-level bureaucrats act and their normative perceptions of clients than institutional and formal rules. This challenges the very concept of discretion and offers an alternative framing based on agency and structure.

Finally in this section, Chapter Eleven, by Kathryn Ellis, deals with how the reformist agenda of 'personalising' support has impacted on the nature and scope of discretion in UK adult social care. While personalisation may mean different things (a rhetorical device, a set of technologies or a true policy initiative), the chapter investigates how each one poses challenges to local authorities in this field and analyses their implications for front-line practice. Kathryn Ellis also develops a typology of social work discretion and seeks to identify the likely interplay of formal and informal frameworks of practice.

In Part Five, the focus is upon the management of street-level bureaucrats, exploring the attempts of policy decision-makers and public managers to control the ways in which street-level bureaucrats do their job. Attention is given to various modern modes and practices of managerial control.

In Chapter Twelve, Duco Bannink, Frédérique Six and Eelco van Wijk investigate the feasibility of managerial control at the street level in contexts in which public agents have to perform tasks that are highly complex and ambiguous. Based on empirical case studies carried out in a variety of Dutch public service organisations, the chapter shows how complexity (need for expertise) and ambiguity of tasks (risk of non-alignment of preferences) pose important control challenges for managers and public officials. The chapter concludes with the suggestion that 'self-defined' modes of control might be a way to address the double control challenge.

Then, using empirical material on Dutch school headmasters, Chapter Thirteen, by Peter Hupe and Eva van Kooten, looks at the pivotal managerial role played by first-line supervisors located in the middle of a hierarchy. While managing the daily work at their schools, head teachers react to the policy directives and other formal rules with which they are supposed to seek compliance. The chapter shows that in processing those rules, head teachers tend not to pass them automatically onto the teachers that they are supervising. 'Buffering' is observed, meaning that rules imposed by 'higher' authorities are filtered at this managerial level. It is therefore argued that management matters, particularly when practised by supervisors closest to the street level. This is therefore also a contribution to the need to see street-level bureaucrats in a context in which, as noted earlier, attention to discretion at a level above the 'street' is important.

This part of the book finishes with Chapter Fourteen by Tino Schuppan, whose focus is on the influence of information and communication technologies (ICT) on the work of street-level bureaucrats. The practice of control of front-line workers through electronic means and the issue of street-level discretion in a context of e-government are central here: do front-line workers have less latitude of choice due to their new 'electronic leashes'? The contribution addresses the question through a comparative case study of two German cities where centralised call centres have recently implemented a one-stop government reform. The main conclusion of the study is that ICT have only a limited power to standardise the work level and to increase the controlling capacity of management.

Part Six of the book is titled 'The promise of professionalism'. Early in this chapter, attention was drawn to the place of the study of street-level bureaucracy in relation to arguments about both bureaucracy and professionalism. Accordingly, the notions of profession, professionalism and professionalisation are at the heart of this final part of the book. In particular, the idea is to contrast the (too) simple top-down hierarchical model of control with Lipsky's bottom-up perspective on accountability to colleagues, but also clients, and thus to develop the argument about multiple accountabilities. Mechanisms of professional and participatory accountability as forms of 'horizontal accountability' may compensate for the limits to 'vertical' forms of accountability embodied in political-administrative, including managerial, modes of control. Another goal of this part of the book is to question the effects of professionalising attempts on front-line workers themselves: how do they react? What do professionalisation reforms produce at the street level?

In Chapter Fifteen, Paul van der Aa and Rik van Berkel explore the role of workers in shaping the promise of professionalism. Based on empirical data on workers in the new profession of job activation in the Netherlands, the authors argue that assessing whether professionalism is occurring requires understanding how individuals concretely deal with the various policy standards being developed to steer implementation. Their results suggest the 'promise' of professionalism, but also that this varies across policy fields and depends upon localised policy and managerial choices. More fundamentally, the way that workers deal with standards in terms of adaptation (shielding or resistance) is influential here.

Then, Chapter Sixteen, by Tony Evans, provides a critical examination of Lipsky's analysis of discretion. While the value of the latter resides in its critique of the ability of modern management to fully control front-line discretion, Evans argues that Lipsky and others have paid insufficient attention both to the role of professionalism in understanding the construction and deployment of front-line discretion, and to the discretion of managers as the new elite professionals within welfare organisations. The chapter concludes that consideration of front-line discretion should be complemented by the examination of the extensive discretion of professional managers.

Finally, in Chapter Seventeen, Christopher Osiander and Joss Steinke look at the impact of recent professionalisation reforms on German job counsellors. In particular, the concern is with the amount of discretionary choice that caseworkers in Public Employment Services have in their daily work. Using data from three different empirical studies looking at three aspects of discretion in this policy field (room for manoeuvre regarding activation measures, integration agreements and conflicts between individual needs and procedural justice), Osiander and Steinke show that formal discretion and actually used discretion do not always coincide, especially when it comes to legally complex aspects or harsh financial sanctions for younger clients.

Framework

In the third section of this introductory chapter, we identified a range of issues put forward by the introduction of street-level bureaucracy as a theoretical perspective. These regarded theoretical, methodological, programmatic and political aspects of the study of government-in-action. Leaving the last category aside here, we have asked all authors in this volume to address the following set of (meta-)questions in order to increase comparability across chapters:

1. *Central question.* What needs explanation and what has, by the end of the chapter, been explained?
2. *Theory.* What factors (variables, concepts) may, and to what extent, contribute to this explanation and what are their relations with the conceptualisation in the introductory chapter?
3. *Method.* What research design and methods have been used?
4. *Programme.* What insights have been gained in the chapter and what would be needed to be addressed in further research?

In the concluding chapter of the book (Part Seven), as editors, we, first, explore the findings from each chapter and make comparative statements answering these four questions. Next, we reflect on the agenda for future research on street-level bureaucracy by addressing the issue of generalisation. If the latter implies contextualised comparison, the question is what would be needed to make the study of street-level bureaucracy truly comparative. After all, Lipsky's argument, quoted earlier, for an 'essentially comparative approach' can be adopted, but it poses extensive methodological problems, which will be discussed in the final chapter. Therefore, we end with a rallying call for work that can solve some of these problems.

TWO

The inside story: street-level research in the US and beyond[1]

Evelyn Z. Brodkin

Introduction

Over more than three decades, street-level theory and research has captured the imagination and empirical attention of scholars, generating important insights into the links between the practical and the political. Since Michael Lipsky (1980) first offered his theoretical template for understanding street-level bureaucracies (street-level bureaucrats), the field has grown considerably, with diverse lines of research taking up issues that are central to street-level theory and also extending it in significant ways.

At the outset, it is worth noting that the term 'street-level bureaucracy' has become something of a term of art, a generic label for the public agencies that are so deceptively familiar. The term often conjures up images of prototypical Weberian bureaucracies, those relentlessly routinised people-processing agencies that represent the authority of the state and invite caricatures of 'le guichet' (the individual behind the counter) or the officious clerk with the green eyeshades. However, the term also encompasses the more ambivalent protagonists of the modern state, the social workers, police, educators, counsellors and case managers, whose interventions into people's personal lives may be appreciated or reviled. They may be celebrated as first responders to those needing help or protection, or they may find themselves the first targets of citizen dissatisfaction. The personal and, at times, invasive interactions between private individuals and street-level bureaucrats make their work deeply fraught, at once potentially helpful and potentially alienating.

A distinctive contribution of street-level research is its commitment to investigating what I refer to as the 'inside story', that is, what goes on in the often-hidden recesses of organisations that deliver public policy, what factors systematically shape those practices and the consequences of street-level practices for policy and, more broadly, for politics.

This field initially developed in the US in the context of emerging interest in the problematics of policy implementation, concerns that continue to animate contemporary policy-focused research. Over time, street-level studies expanded to take up more fundamental and also more far-reaching theoretical and empirical questions, among them, questions regarding the dynamics between organisational structures and discretionary behaviour, the influence of new managerial and governance arrangements on organisational practices, and the role of street-level organisations in the broader politics of the welfare state.

In addition, the field has advanced beyond its initial focus on street-level bureaucrats, the large public agencies that once dominated policy delivery. The role of these bureaucracies has been eclipsed by other types of organisation. More recent lines of research increasingly take account of the many new varieties of street-level organisations that now engage in policy work and play a crucial role in fulfilling public tasks. Street-level organisations may be public, private (non-profit and for-profit) or mixed (eg public–private partnerships). They operate under diverse structural arrangements, among them, contracting, fee-for-service, vouchers and philanthropic or government grants (Brodkin, 2013). As I will discuss, research on these new organisational arrangements is part of a growing scholarly project to reveal the 'inside story' of transformations taking place in governance, management and welfare state politics, not only in the US, but worldwide.

This chapter begins by discussing the origins of this field and then takes a closer look at the state of street-level research in three key areas. The first is policy-focused research, which emerged out of practical concerns over policy implementation that were much at issue at this field's inception. Policy-focused studies offer theoretically grounded strategies for examining how policies actually work, in effect, taking analysis from the formalities of policy-on-the-page to the realities of policy-in-practice. A second line of research investigates the street-level consequences of managerial and governance reforms ostensibly designed to 'make things work better'. It looks beyond conventional managerial paradigms of control to conceptualise street-level organisations as adaptive, probing the interaction between street-level discretion and changes in the managerial environment in which discretion is exercised. A third emergent line of scholarship extends beyond the particular and the pragmatic to investigate the political functions of street-level organisations as mediators of socio-legal status and welfare state politics. I will discuss these research areas separately, although they overlap and inform one another in important ways.

On the origins of street-level research and theory

In the US, interest in street-level theory and research was closely linked to the development of the field of public policy studies and, particularly, studies of policy implementation. The 1960s had witnessed a virtual transformation of the US government as it adopted far-ranging initiatives through which the federal government sought to address poverty and urban unrest. Policies launched under the banner of the 'War on Poverty' and the 'Great Society' greatly extended the federal government's reach into areas previously regarded as the domain of state and local government. However, for the most part, the federal government lacked direct authority to put its new policies in place, and, instead, depended on other units of government for implementation. The mismatch between policies-as-conceived and policies-as-executed (or *not* executed) became the central problematic of implementation research.

In their classic book, *Implementation*, Jeffrey Pressman and Aaron Wildavsky (1973) stoked the imagination of scholars, encouraging them to open up the so-called 'black box' within which policy implementation occurred. They, and other implementation scholars of the period, recognised that federal authority alone could not assure that the steps necessary for implementation would take place. Shoulder to shoulder in that 'black box' were numerous independent (or at least quasi-independent) actors at various levels of government, each of whose interests, capacities and incentives had a direct bearing on what, if anything, would happen after policies were enacted. The early implementation literature was highly innovative, yet it adopted conventional views of hierarchy, framing questions in terms of how to assert federal government control over a far-flung and decentralised intergovernmental system.

On a parallel, but largely separate, track, other theorists were concerned with the problematics of bureaucratic discretion. Although their concerns were policy-relevant, much of this research was less concerned with specific policy initiatives than with the sociology of bureaucratic behaviour (Kaufman, 1960; Wilson, 1967). Its primary purpose was to build organisational theory rather than to explain policy developments, making political context of only secondary interest.

With the introduction of Lipsky's street-level bureaucracy theory, the growing organisational literature on bureaucratic discretion (Kaufman, 1960; Wilson, 1967; Handler and Hollingsworth, 1971) came into direct conversation with the emerging policy literature on implementation (Derthick, 1972; Pressman and Wildavsky,

1973; Ingram, 1977). Lipsky's theory challenged both conventional views of bureaucracy, those that reiterated Weberian stereotypes, and conventional paradigms of the policy process that assumed the analytic relevance of hierarchy. Challenges to these common analytic conventions are central to the street-level approach and continue to animate it, underscoring its distinctiveness from other approaches to policy and organisational analysis.

The street-level view of bureaucracy, to some extent, was paradoxical, simultaneously critical and sympathetic. This becomes apparent when examining its central critiques. Drawing on Murray Edelman's (1964) profound understanding of the symbolic uses of administration, Lipsky contested the well-worn symbolism of bureaucracy. He argued that common depictions of public bureaucracies were faulty in at least two important respects: analytically, they failed to take account of the daily struggle that so many public service workers engaged in to perform their jobs well and, in the process, do good for their communities and society; politically, distorted portrayals emphasising bureaucratic malfeasance fed an anti-government narrative that threatened to undo the social policy achievements of the New Deal, Civil Rights Movement, War on Poverty, Great Society and so on.

To some extent, Lipsky's theoretical model appeared to redeem public bureaucracies, unburdening them of negative stereotyping. Its analytic framework contextualised and made more transparent the struggles of lower-level bureaucrats to do good work. This perspective allowed for the possibility that the fault for problematic practices lay not entirely with the bureaucrats themselves, but with the structural conditions that they faced.

Potentially, street-level research could redeem government bureaucracies in a more practical sense if it could inform managerial strategies that would enable agencies doing the public's business to do a better job. If realised, this could yield both practical and political benefits. Stated simply: if applied street-level analysis improved the performance of public agencies, better performance would bolster political support for the government's social welfare functions and, subsequently, lead to greater investment that could build the government's capacity to perform those functions. In this sense, street-level research might contribute to a project of improvement, creating a positive feedback loop that could contribute to building a more just and capable state.

Street-level theory also directly challenged implementation analysts, who were deeply accustomed to thinking hierarchically about bureaucracy and focused on 'gaps' and 'compliance'. Lipsky's theoretical approach moved beyond these conventional modes of thinking, setting out an innovative alternative that approached street-level bureaucrats from the inside out. It began by asking not what street-level bureaucrats *should* do, but what they *did* and why. Lipsky's novel approach launched a still ongoing debate about so-called 'bottom-up' and 'top-down' views of policy implementation. In my view, this debate is less relevant to scholarship than the more fundamental question of how to understand complex organisational behaviour, namely, what makes street-level bureaucrats tick.

Lipsky's theory built on several core propositions. First, under certain conditions, policy should be understood not as a fixed construct, but as an indeterminate one. Those conditions are present when formal policy is ambiguous or contains multiple (even conflicting) objectives and when street-level practitioners are able to exercise discretion in the course of their work. Second, under these conditions, the discretionary actions of street-level practitioners, in effect, become policy. Third, discretion is of interest not when it is random, but when it is structured by factors that influence informal behaviours to develop in systematic ways. It is these systematic, informal behaviours that impart specific practical meaning to policy-as-produced. Fourth, street-level bureaucrats occupy a position of political significance not only because they operate as de facto interpreters of public policy, but also because they operate as the interface between the government and the individual. Although what they do matters most directly for policy delivery, it also has importance for the relationship between citizens and the state.

This approach fundamentally rejected the deeply embedded notions of hierarchy and authority common to much organisational analysis. It built on implementation studies, which, as noted, had begun to demonstrate all the things that could go wrong in the process of producing policy on the ground. However, these studies were situated in a normative logic which assumed that the analyst could impute clear policy goals and the operational steps needed to achieve them. Based on these imputations, the analyst could then identify departures from the 'prescribed' implementation path.

What if one abandoned the normatively appealing idea that formal policies necessarily had clear, knowable and operationalisable goals? This idea had become increasingly indefensible in the face of both theoretical and empirical evidence demonstrating that US policymaking required compromise, making clarity and coherence unlikely, especially in politically contested areas of social policy. If one could not (or should not) impose a veneer of clarity on policies that actually had multiple and often conflicting goals (or somehow require that policymakers offer more policy clarity), then how could implementation analysis proceed? What exactly were those organisations implementing policy *supposed* to do? In addition, bureaucracy research made evident the futility of assuming that discretion could be controlled or simply stamped out by more clever management strategies. Yet, 'control' had remained central to hierarchical approaches to policy implementation.

Street-level theory offered a different perspective. It recognised that discretion is necessary to policy work that involves judgement and responsiveness to individual circumstances (as in teaching, policing and counselling). One might call these *authorised* uses of discretion. However, the theory also allowed that discretion could be used in *unauthorised* ways. Although formal policy terms and managerial strategies surely mattered, they could not fully determine what happened at the front lines of policy delivery.

Lipsky's innovative approach effectively liberated analysis from reifying formal policy as coherent and consistent and from treating discretion as potentially controllable. Rather than sticking to unsustainable assumptions about policy clarity and managerial control, Lipsky abandoned them. It would be a mischaracterisation to take the street-level model to indicate that formal policy is irrelevant, that discretion cannot be influenced or that discretion is necessarily at odds with effective policy implementation. Lipsky's theory was never that simplistic. Quite the contrary, it complicated policy analysis by treating complex organisational behaviours as part and parcel of the policymaking process, not separate from it.

The street-level perspective virtually flipped the script of conventional policy research, focusing not on what formal policy seemed to require, but on what organisations actually did in the name of policy. One central concern was to interrogate discretion in order to understand the factors that shaped its exercise *in patterned ways*. Informal patterns of practices assumed greater interest than random acts of discretion because patterns of practice structured bureaucratic interactions in systematic ways, creating systematic consequences for the distribution and content of policy-as-produced.

As I have suggested, a major, and perhaps underappreciated, innovation of the street-level project is that it sought to understand street-level work from the *inside out*. It began not with what others (eg managers or policymakers) wanted from front-line practitioners, but with an effort to investigate the realities of work for those directly engaged in policy delivery at the front lines. It recognised that these realities influenced discretion, often in unexpected (and unseen) ways.

If one could understand the logic of street-level work *as practitioners experienced it*, it would be possible to understand, and potentially predict, how changes in the work environment could alter their practices and, thus, affect what they produced as policy through their informal routines.

Street-level theory has provided fertile ground for scholarly studies that extend across several fields and disciplines. The remainder of this chapter highlights three major areas of research in which the street-level approach has introduced new questions, insights and understanding.

Policy-focused studies

The street-level approach to policy research has proved remarkably generative. There is now a corpus of studies that investigate how public policies are shaped by street-level practices in areas as diverse as child welfare, education, prison reform, health care, workplace safety, workforce development, welfare, juvenile justice, corrections and so on. Individually, these studies show that what you see (in terms of formal policy) may not be what you get (in terms of policy-as-produced). More importantly, these studies analyse *what* you actually get as policy and *how* you get it. By documenting the complex matrix of street-level practices, these studies are able to fill in the blanks between nominal policy activities (eg assessments, counselling sessions, family interventions) and outcomes, illuminating what occurs under these programmatic labels – often not what one might imagine.

Beyond their individual, policy-specific contributions, collectively, these studies have tested, refined and expanded on the theoretical template that Lipsky first elaborated. There is now a fairly substantial base of empirical evidence on factors that shape street-level practice and the types of adaptations that develop under certain conditions. As the body of policy studies has grown and the field has matured, it has begun to reveal recurrent themes that cross-cut individual policy areas and concerns. I identify a few of them here, but note that these themes have yet to be fully identified and explored, suggesting a possible research agenda for the future.

As a matter of theory-testing, street-level studies have provided empirical confirmation that the types of coping strategies that Lipsky identified are both prevalent and plentiful. They document varieties of off-the-books strategies that street-level practitioners deploy to manage their work lives in a context in which resources are rarely adequate to the demands of the job. This literature shows not only that resources matter, but, more importantly, *how* they matter. Studies examining the everyday practices of caseworkers in a variety of policy areas demonstrate that resource limitations may virtually overdetermine the development of informal practices, with the effect of virtually robbing services of their substantive value and skewing the distribution of benefits.

In addition, just as the street-level model would predict, when caseworkers lack sufficient resources to be fully responsive to individual needs or to address complex (and time-consuming) dimensions of their work, they develop varieties of 'coping mechanisms' that indirectly, but significantly, shape policy on the ground. The literature is replete with examples. To name only a few, there are the domestic violence caseworkers who avoid learning about service needs they find difficult to address (Lindhorst and Padgett, 2005), the disability assessors who reduce complex individual situations to nominal box-ticking (Gulland, 2011) and the child welfare workers responsible for family reunification who circumvent essential, but time-consuming, engagement with parents (Smith and Donovan, 2003).

Studies also show how street-level practitioners rationalise problematic practices, for example, blaming parents for not pursuing unresponsive child welfare caseworkers, or faulting domestic violence victims for reticence in revealing intimate life experiences (Smith and Donovan, 2003; Lindhorst and Padgett, 2005). This bureaucratic-style victim blaming, like other informal practices documented in policy studies, reveals a logic of street-level work that is simultaneously rational (enabling practitioners to manage their jobs with what limited resources they have got) and, at times, even functional for the organisation. It is functional, if not desirable, to the extent that these practices help to limit and delegitimate the expression of individual service needs and demands. However, there is a flip side to patterns of practice that may be individually or organisationally functional: they may be dysfunctional in terms of policy responsiveness and efficacy. To offer a single, simple example: protection against domestic violence cannot be secured if street-level practices discourage individuals from revealing it.

Cumulatively, policy-focused studies have deepened understanding of what happens to policy ideas when practitioners are confronted by the dilemmas of street-level work, most notably, by conditions in which resources are unequal to the demands of 'good' work. These studies reveal that 'doing more with less' in the name of efficiency may have hidden, deleterious effects for other important dimensions of policy delivery.

One of the striking things about the growing body of policy-focused studies is that they rarely, with only some exceptions, indicate opposition or resistance to policy aims, at least as street-level practitioners understand them. Even when practitioners favour policy ideas – or at least do not object to them – they may simply find policies that envision deeply engaged and responsive modes of practice incompatible with the realities of their work lives (Meyers et al, 1998; Smith and Donovan, 2003; Lindhorst and Padgett, 2005). As one domestic violence caseworker explained, she was concerned that her clients might suffer abuse, but 'you just don't have time to pull [domestic violence] out of somebody, unless they come here with visible observations [bruises], which doesn't happen often' (Lindhorst and Padgett, 2005, p 423). Variants on these themes are prevalent throughout the street-level literature.

Such findings are of interest beyond the specific policies under study. As an analytical matter, they suggest that practices that appear 'deviant' or 'subversive' from a principle-agent perspective may have little to do with practitioners' personal policy preferences or fealty to organisational hierarchy, but are better understood as adaptations to conditions of work. These studies also point to the limitations of seeking to explain street-level behaviour as a consequence of individual-level phenomena (eg preferences, training, etc) without accounting for organisational conditions that affect what individuals *can* do and *are likely* to do under certain conditions.

The ways in which conditions press down on front-line practitioners are central to the street-level project. At times, their influence may be revealed indirectly, for example, when practitioners recount the heroic efforts they occasionally make to 'bend the rules' in responding to the needs of selected individuals (Maynard-Moody and Musheno, 2003). If responsiveness is the exception, what are the organisational conditions that make heroic efforts necessary? In these instances, the proverbial exception may, indeed, prove the rule. Questions concerning the organisational conditions that shape policy work have clearly been a key concern of policy studies. More recently, they have been taken up in emerging areas of management and governance research.

Management and governance studies

As previously discussed, in recent decades, the world that gave rise to street-level bureaucrats has been transformed. The public sector no longer dominates policy delivery as it once did, especially in the US. Contracting and privatisation have reshaped the organisational landscape, creating new, mixed forms of provision and complex delivery arrangements. Today, policy delivery occurs not only through public bureaucracies, but also through non-profit organisations, for-profit firms and mixed public–private arrangements.

To some extent, these changes have taken place under the rubric of New Public Management (NPM), which is premised on advancing market-like approaches to policy delivery. In this new environment, the 'old' public sector bureaucracies are not only managed, but also the managers, contracting out and overseeing policy delivery in its many complex forms. In this new managerial world, direct provision – and street-level discretion – are subject to different influences, shaped by changing organisational forms and evolving managerial strategies. In light of this transformation, it is not only street-level bureaucrats that are of interest, but also the broader array of street-level organisations that are now engaged in policy delivery.

The street-level perspective has contributed to understanding changes in governance and management, exploring the mechanisms through which they alter organisational practices, particularly how they change conditions of work and to what effect. Street-level studies have taken management research well beyond questions of efficiency or control and have brought a critical perspective to bear on consideration of issues such as performance and accountability.

One line of management research has explored contracting as a method of policy delivery. Studies revealing the street-level repercussions of contracting cast doubt on the notion that private forms of provision are necessarily better than public ones. They show that whether in public agencies or private ones, street-level practitioners retain discretion to adapt to their environment. The challenge is to determine precisely *how* contract arrangements affect the conditions under which discretion takes place.

One study of contracting in Australian workforce programmes, for example, found that contract agencies appeared to perform well according to measured administrative criteria. However, it also found informal patterns of practice, influenced, in part, by contract terms, which introduced inequality and left the most disadvantaged populations as the least well-served (Considine, 2000). Discussing how contract structures influence informal practice, Considine (2000, p 292) observed that 'The reliance upon short-term financial incentives leads agencies to find innovative ways to maximize a very low-cost form of intervention and to ignore other policy values ... which do not carry a direct monetary benefit'. This finding is hardly unique to this single case, as other empirical studies in diverse policy domains have produced similar conclusions.

In a second line of management research, studies have closely examined street-level responses to management-by-performance measurement. As the search for ways to manage street-level organisations has advanced over the past few decades, arguably, few strategies have expanded as dramatically as the use of performance measurement. Today, the practice of managing-by-performance measurement seems nearly ubiquitous. In the US, it is deployed in policies ranging from education, health and welfare, to child protection and policing.

Street-level research has made a distinctive contribution to a growing literature on this phenomenon by investigating the mechanisms through which performance measurement penetrates street-level practice. Studies in this field indicate that performance measurement creates powerful inducements to focus on measured dimensions of work. However, when time and resources are limited, attention to unmeasured aspects of performance, even critical ones, are likely to be displaced. Studies adopting a street-level perspective have begun to reveal the variety of ways in which practitioners use their discretion to adapt to performance incentives. These complex adaptations lead to informal patterns of practice that can reshape policy delivery, albeit in ways that are not readily visible and, certainly, not made transparent through the performance metrics themselves.

A developing theme in these studies is that managerial demands for efficiency, coupled with perpetual surveillance of performance metrics, are bearing down hard on street-level practitioners. Studies have shown how the discretion essential to responsiveness may be squeezed out, reducing opportunities for staff to respond to client needs as they understand them (Lindhorst and Padgett, 2005; Jewell, 2007; Brodkin, 2011, 2013; Soss et al, 2011a). In short, they suggest that the dilemmas that Lipsky first identified three decades ago have intensified.

The power of performance measurement is, perhaps, most readily illuminated in those rare moments of resistance to their strictures. One case study of a contracted welfare-to-work agency (Dias and Maynard-Moody, 2007) presents a fascinating account of resistance and, ultimately, defeat as caseworkers tried to fight back against management's reductionist approach to 'services'. In this battle, there are signs of opposition to management strictures that border on what Dodson (2009) refers to as the 'moral underground'. However, in this and other studies, it is striking how little power lower-level practitioners appear to have to shape practices to fit their own, personal conceptions of policy, at least to the extent that those conceptions prioritise responsiveness to need. Yes, discretion provides possibilities for resistance to the rules and managerial pressures; however, resource constraints, coupled with unrelenting demands to meet performance measures, limit how staff can use their discretion to exploit these possibilities.

These and other studies suggest that if there is an 'implementation game' (Bardach, 1977), managers may be gaining the upper hand. This is not because they can *control* lower-level discretion, but because they have new and more powerful tools through which they can *influence* its exercise. Conceivably, these tools could be used in constructive ways. However, the empirical literature suggests that the ways in which they are used may be badly out of balance, too often favouring efficiency at the cost of responsiveness, quality and even efficacy.

As an analytical matter, street-level studies virtually upend the classic management *control* versus street-level *autonomy* dichotomy. They show that management's advantages stem less from authority than from opportunities to alter the conditions of street-level work. As Lipsky explains, there is neither control nor autonomy, but a complex dialectic. For those who might misunderstand his theory to indicate street-level autonomy, a growing body of management studies clarifies that discretion operates within limited degrees of freedom, embedded in an organisational context that shapes the possibilities for its use.

This is not to say that other factors do not matter. Studies that focus on the individual preferences or the moral reasoning of street-level bureaucrats usefully illuminate variations in the choice set among different types of practitioners, for example, professionals versus non-professionals (Sandfort, 2000; Hasenfeld and Garrow, 2012; Gofen, 2013; Tummers et al, forthcoming). However, a major contribution of street-level management research is that it also reveals how organisational conditions – and management strategies – affect the probabilities for individuals to act on those preferences or values. They do this indirectly, in effect, by altering the costs and benefits of different modes of action and, thereby, changing what I have called the implicit logic of street-level work. To paraphrase an argument made elsewhere: street-level bureaucrats do not necessarily do what they want, they do what they can (Brodkin, 1997).

Socio-political and welfare state studies

The importance of street-level bureaucrats to the 'making' of public policy is now widely recognised. They form the operational core of the state; yet, they are more than mere functionaries. Located at the intersection of individuals and the state, these organisations mediate not only the formation of policy, but also broader social and political dynamics (Brodkin, 2013). Emerging socio-political and welfare state studies are expanding the range of analytic vision to explore 'what else' these organisations do beyond their instrumental function in policy delivery.

One line of research has examined the distributive functions of informal street-level practices, exploring how they influence the possibilities for accessing services and benefits. These studies show that street-level bureaucrats produce disparities in provision, even to the point of excluding access for some populations, especially those least well-equipped to navigate the barriers of bureaucratic 'red tape' and confusing or complex agency processes (Riccucci, 2005a; Wenger and Wilkins, 2009; Brodkin and Majmundar, 2010; Moynihan and Herd, 2010; Monnat, 2011). Other research on administrative disparities is stretching the boundaries of the street-level model to examine whether political control of the government's administrative apparatus may be linked to hidden distributive effects (Keiser, 1999, 2001; May and Winter, 2009). To the extent that these findings indicate a relationship, they raise questions about precisely how this relationship is forged, pointing to the potential for new lines of inquiry investigating the mechanisms through which politics may penetrate aspects of street-level practice.

Another emerging field of study that is stretching the boundaries of street-level research explores how organisations mediate social status and identities. Studies in this area have demonstrated a turn towards organisational ethnographic research in street-level studies. The ethnographic turn takes its inspiration, in part, from the street-level project's implicit encouragement of researchers to get out from behind their desks in order to investigate and even *experience* the realities of everyday organisational life.

Researchers have used these methods to illuminate how racial and gender identities shape street-level interactions and how social status is negotiated in street-level interactions (Morgen, 2001; Korteweg, 2003; Rosenthal and Pecci, 2006; Watkins-Hayes, 2011). These studies demonstrate that street-level exchanges may be understood as part of a broader political dynamic of status construction (and reconstruction). Korteweg, for example, examines the dialogues that occur in welfare-to-work programmes in order to illuminate how the status of motherhood is constructed through street-level interactions. She probes exchanges in which women raise concerns about trade-offs between parenting and work responsibility and caseworkers dismiss them or (more incredibly) advise single mothers that 'work will make your lives easier' (Korteweg, 2003, p 325).

Patterns of street-level exchange have also been used to shed light on how class status is constructed and contested. For example, studies have illuminated how the efforts of poor and marginalised individuals to assert rights to assistance from the state are mediated by the organisations that structure claims-making and expressions of social justice (Morgen, 2001; Herd et al, 2005; Dubois, 2010; Lens, 2013). These developing lines of socio-political research offer a deeply grounded way to examine how larger social and political structures operate – and the dynamic role that street-level organisations play in maintaining and contesting them. They build on the critical case method (Burawoy, 1999) in the sense that they link micro-level experiences occurring within street-level organisations to macro-level phenomena.

Another developing line of inquiry introduces a street-level perspective to welfare state research. It recognises that street-level organisations comprise the operational core of the welfare state. This places them at the cusp of political projects of welfare state transformation and retrenchment, though rarely explicitly. As Brodkin (2013, pp 17–18) has argued, beyond their more obvious functions as mediators of policy, street-level organisations also function as:

> de facto mediators of the politics and processes of welfare state transformation. As mediators, SLOs are not overtly political, but advance political change indirectly, whether as a by-product of governance and management initiatives or through patterns of informal practices that develop in specific contexts.... [In this sense, they] function as institutional locations in which political projects of change and welfare state transformation are advanced, contested, and, at times, realized, although rarely in overtly political terms.

Studies examining changing structures of policy delivery and NPM strategies are beginning to reveal how governance reforms really work (Hupe and Hill, 2007) and how they may be used to smuggle contested policy shifts in through the administrative back door. They show, for example, that contracting arrangements can be used in ways that undermine the political power of unions and labour parties, in part, by reorganising (or, at times, eliminating) the public agencies through which they influence employment policies and their implementation (Larsen, 2013; Van Berkel, 2013).

Other studies, as previously mentioned, demonstrate that performance measurement can become a *sub rosa* instrument for advancing retrenchment. This occurs when monitoring and measurement bear down on street-level practitioners in ways that systematically bias the exercise of discretion, limiting responsiveness to claims for help from the state and increasing the difficulty of claims-making, especially for the disadvantaged, disabled and unemployed (Lindhorst and Padgett, 2005; Moynihan and Herd, 2010; Adler, 2013; Brodkin, 2011, 2013; Gulland, 2011; Soss et al, 2011a; Watkins-Hayes, 2011; Lens, 2013). Of course, these are not the manifest purposes of performance measurement, and these consequences may or may not be intentional. Nonetheless, these studies have brought a unique perspective to inquiry into managerial strategies that, essentially, target the discretionary behaviour of those street-level practitioners who effectively function as gatekeepers to the welfare state. This emerging area of research holds promise for developing a new generation of scholarship that can deepen our socio-political understanding of street-level organisations and build a broader, comparative research agenda.

Street-level research and beyond: some practical implications

In this chapter, I have emphasised the theoretical and empirical contributions of street-level research to policy, organisational and political scholarship. It would be remiss to conclude without commenting on the distinctive contribution of this field to informing the practices of policy delivery and the provision of human services.

As this literature makes apparent, glib 'solutions' or promises of simple 'reform' should be treated with great scepticism. However, even a cursory examination of this literature underscores that policymaking could benefit from giving more attention to matters of policy delivery upfront. Applied street-level analysis could be used prospectively to better assess what organisations require in order to create conditions of work that are less likely to generate the kinds of problematic coping strategies that are all too abundant. While 'throwing money at problems' is not the answer to policy delivery, neither is starving agencies of the resources they need to do their work well.

This suggests that rather than crafting policy ideas and requiring that they be realised with available resources, policymakers and managers might benefit from adopting what I call an *enabling* approach focused on creating conditions that facilitate quality and responsiveness in policy delivery. This idea recalls the 'backward-mapping' strategy advanced some three decades ago by Richard Elmore (1979), but not, to my knowledge, put to much use. In order for this kind of analysis to be fully developed, it requires a deep and complex understanding of organisational behaviour, which may be a fairly high hurdle. Still, a strategy of *enabling* rather than *controlling* street-level organisations, I believe, holds promise for capacity-building and the kinds of investments in government that Lipsky and others envision.

Street-level studies also advise caution (if not a reversal) of the rush to advance NPM reforms that substitute incentives for control. Certainly, performance measurement can be a valuable tool for monitoring aspects of practice. However, its selectivity is both a strength and a weakness. If one cannot measure and prioritise everything, then choices of what to measure assume overarching importance. As a growing street-level literature has begun to demonstrate, one may get what one measures, but this may come with unmeasured consequences of equal or even greater importance.

The US education law No Child Left Behind (NCLB) has arguably become the virtual poster-child of the anti-performance measurement movement. News accounts and sophisticated studies have revealed the hazards of the push for performance, for example, showing how schools achieved higher test scores by cooking the books or influencing educators to use their discretion to 'teach to the test'. Critics have persuasively argued that better performance scores do not necessarily indicate improvements in education or learning. As Lipsky (2010, p 233) points out, 'the law is distressingly simplistic on what constitutes a good education and it is also more or less silent on how to achieve better results'.

In a cogent critique of NCLB, Helen Ladd (2011, p 13) has observed that while some measures of performance improved:

> NCLB has generated a range of undesirable side-effects – including ... a narrowing of the curriculum, low morale among teachers who are facing pressure to achieve goals that they cannot meet, and, as has become abundantly clear ... significant amounts of cheating by teachers under extreme pressure to raise student test scores.

Among other things, Ladd suggests what amounts to the beginnings of an enabling strategy. She pointedly advises policymakers to stop assuming that teachers are shirkers, and, instead, to recognise that teachers need the resources to do a tough job, among them 'support and constructive counselling' (Ladd, 2011, p 16). To return to an earlier theme, policymakers conveniently blame street-level bureaucrats for policies that do not deliver, even when the policymakers themselves have failed to provide the conditions that would enable street-level bureaucrats to do their jobs well.

These brief lessons drawn from street-level research are only suggestive and barely scratch the surface of possibilities. A lingering concern, however, is that they do not address what is arguably an even more vexing problem than how to improve policy delivery at the street level. After all, choices about policymaking and policy delivery are more than mere technical matters; they are fundamentally political choices. To the extent that the rational legislator has incentives to produce policies with high symbolic value and low visible costs (Price, 1978; Arnold, 1990), what is the incentive to adopt enabling strategies that require upfront investment and, essentially, place greater responsibility for the fate of policy delivery on policymakers' shoulders? What is the incentive to temper the movement for performance measurement when it visibly affords the imagery of managerial control and efficiency while only invisibly undermines unmeasured aspects of performance?

In this era of divided, partisan government and extended economic crises, prospects in the US for responsible political action may seem remote. Perhaps it is precisely because these political limitations seem so daunting that it is all the more critical to pursue street-level research that reveals how policy delivery works in practice and makes visible the consequences of managerial strategies that would otherwise be unseen.

One might also consider how street-level practitioners can, themselves, benefit from scholarship in this field. Although it seems fair to say that practitioners are more the subjects than the architects of the political and organisational environment within which they work, street-level research can benefit reflective practitioners (and students as prospective practitioners) by providing a window onto this hidden world, one that is especially compelling to those who recognise their own experiences in it. By engaging with this literature, they can come to better understand how organisational conditions affect what they do and, as importantly, what the broader consequences of their practices may be. Practitioners may find that they have limited influence at 'the top'; however, they can learn how to use what degrees of freedom they have more constructively. This knowledge may encourage some practitioners to actively and self-consciously participate as part of the 'moral underground' that Lisa Dodson (2009) describes. Or, it may motivate them to take action 'above ground', using their professional and other networks to advance ideas about reforming the conditions of work in ways that would enable them to do a better job.

For better or worse, street-level organisations are a central feature of the modern, democratic state. Street-level research has both illuminated and complicated our understanding of these organisations, taking analysis beyond conventional views of street-level organisations as 'instruments' or 'agents' of the state to recognise the various ways in which they mediate the state, its policies and its politics. In this ever-changing terrain, street-level scholars will be challenged to refine their understanding of what makes these organisations tick, investigate how they respond to new efforts to reform them and continue to illuminate the opaque recesses at the operational heart of the welfare state.

Note

[1.] This chapter expands on and refines arguments initially set out in Brodkin (2012).

Part Two
Delivering services and benefits: street-level bureaucracy and the welfare state

THREE

Discretionary payments in social assistance

Carol Walker

The history of British social assistance

Social assistance, the means-tested safety net of the British social security system, has played a growing and significant role in British income maintenance provision. For most of that history, there has been a very significant discretionary element, which though a minor part of total expenditure, assumed a disproportionate amount of effort in and influence on the administration of the system, and was a major (some would argue, disproportionate) driver in the various reforms and reincarnations to which social assistance has been subjected. The British social assistance scheme demonstrates the impact of discretion on the front-line worker and on his/her relationship with management and with the public:

> At best, street level bureaucrats invent benign modes of mass processing that more or less permit them to deal with the public fairly, appropriately, and successfully. At worst, they give in to favoritism, stereotyping, and routining – all of which serve private or agency purposes. (Lipsky, 1980, p xii)

The role that discretion should play in the system and how to effectively manage its use has been a focus of debate and criticism throughout the history of British national social assistance schemes. Discretion has mainly applied to the payment of supplementary weekly additions to benefits or occasional lump-sum payments. From the outset, these were regarded as integral to the system in order to keep the main rates of benefit at the minimum level while allowing officials on the ground to respond flexibly to the additional needs of some people. As the chapter shows, despite numerous attempts to contain the growth of discretionary payments, demand increased – largely as evidence emerged that benefit rates were too low to meet all basic needs and as dependence on means-tested benefits grew far beyond that originally envisaged – with the inevitable strain that this put on the administration of the system. Increasingly, those managing the system sought to reduce the 'creative' individual discretion ('discretion as used') of front-line staff and replace it with administrative discretion ('discretion as granted') in the form of guidance (or rules) provided by the centre, though not enshrined in law. These rules both offered officials protection 'from conflict with clients by emphasising impersonality' (see Chapter One) and enabled the central bureaucracy to regain control of expenditure. The history of British social assistance shows how the way in which the scheme was operated and delivered at the local level did not reflect the stated aims of policymakers and politicians. Local custom and practice was sometimes more influential than organisational rules. Thus, the lively debate on discretion, which peaked in the 1980s, tended to focus on the widespread use of discretionary payments. The many other aspects of work where discretion (or 'judgement', as it was referred to by David Donnison, when Chair of the Supplementary Benefits Commission (SBC) came into play received very little attention. Examples included deciding whether there was a case to answer relating to 'living together as husband and wife' (the cohabitation rule) and in determining the level or impact of disability.

Over time, views on the use of discretionary payments in the state safety net varied widely, from those who saw it as a benign tool that could be used to flex the system in favour of the needs of the individual and even drive improvements in policy, to critics who argued that it rewarded those who shouted loudest rather than those in greatest need, which led to arbitrary and inconsistent decision-making based on the individual predilections and prejudices of those exercising discretionary power that could thus be used against the best interests of beneficiaries (as per Lipsky's reflections on the negative stereotyping of clients and the differential and discriminatory treatments of citizens discussed in Chapter One). The huge pressure that the rapidly increasing and widespread use of discretionary payments of the various social assistance schemes created proved to be central to the demand for development and reform of British social assistance, which came from government and the central bureaucracy.

This chapter looks at how the use of discretionary payments gradually evolved under the various social assistance schemes, beginning with Unemployment Assistance. First introduced in 1934, this scheme was extended and replaced by National Assistance in 1948, which was then replaced by Supplementary Benefits (SB) in 1966. SB itself was radically reformed in 1980, and was replaced by Income Support in

1986. By 2017, Income Support and five other means-tested benefits will be replaced by Universal Credit.

Unemployment assistance is taken as the starting point for this discussion as this was the first attempt to apply 'national rules to the relief of poverty, in a scheme designed to meet the needs of its beneficiaries in full while taking account of their individual circumstances' (Lynes, 1977, p 201). As part of the major welfare state innovations following the end of the Second World War, which included the creation of the National Health Service and followed on from the introduction of universal education in 1942, the post-war Labour government radically reformed income maintenance provision by largely, though not exactly, following the recommendations of Sir William Beveridge, who had been commissioned during the war to make proposals for the introduction of a comprehensive, national system of social security. His report (Beveridge, 1942) proposed a three-pronged approach: first, a system of universal children's allowances; second, a national insurance scheme, 'adequate in amount and duration', to cover periods of unemployment, sickness and widowhood and retirement; and, third, means-tested social assistance. Beveridge envisaged that most people's needs would be covered by the first two and that social assistance would merely provide for the small and diminishing number who would not be covered by national insurance benefits. Consequently, the discretionary elements of preceding schemes were retained. However, far from declining, dependence on social assistance increased after 1948, for two reasons: first, national insurance benefits were never 'adequate in amount or duration'; and, second, from the outset, the Labour government allowed social assistance to be paid in supplementation to national insurance – that is, when national insurance entitlement was lower than national assistance entitlement – so that the number of people claiming was higher than a scheme geared towards flexibly responding to individual need was designed to cope with. Over the next half-century, successive governments oversaw a significant increase in dependence on social assistance as the scope and generosity of the national insurance system diminished. It is this single factor which meant that the various social assistance schemes were confronted with the problem of how to reconcile the need to exercise discretion with the operation of a scheme on a mass scale. This was a dilemma also facing front-line workers who, while they might want to treat people as individuals, '[i]n practice must deal with clients on a mass basis, since work requirements prohibit individualized service' (Lipsky, 1980, p xii).

The growth of discretionary payments

The Unemployment Assistance scheme transferred responsibility for administering support to the unemployed from individual local authorities to the Unemployment Assistance Board (UAB) on behalf of the government (Briggs and Deacon, 1973). However, within this uniform national scheme, with predetermined levels of benefit, 'there was acceptance at the outset that the inclusion of an element of discretion was essential to "(modify) the standard scale rates to fit the circumstances of the individual case" (UAB 1936, p 8)' (Walker, 1983, p 12). This dual approach was retained, to a lesser or greater extent, up until the reforms of the Conservative–Liberal Democrat Coalition government in 2013, when the last vestige of discretionary payments (the Social Fund) was taken out of means-tested Income Support and transferred to local authorities, which set up local discretionary schemes of last-resort support.

The UAB's discretionary powers were broad, covering the determination of the eligibility of applicants for assistance, the definition of the household unit, the extent to which resources should be taken into account and the level of needs to be met. In addition, the final assessment of the payment could be altered in three ways. First, benefit could be reduced so that no applicant would achieve 'a sum which is equal to or greater than the amount which would obviously be available by way of earnings' (UAB, 1936, p 294), This rule was later known as the wage stop, which having been abolished over 40 years later, was effectively reintroduced in 2013 when a benefits cap was introduced. Second, weekly benefit could be increased or decreased 'in any case where special circumstances exist', a facility that was used most commonly to increase the weekly payment to claimants with special dietary, laundry or other continuing needs (UAB, 1936, p 294). Third, claimants could be paid a lump sum where there were 'needs of an exceptional character' (UAB, 1936, p 294).

Within weeks of Unemployment Assistance taking effect in 1934, it had to be suspended for two years following national 'uproar' (Davison, 1938, pp 66–7). This was because despite lower benefit rates and a harsher application of the household means test, the UAB had not, as promised, been sufficiently generous in the use of its *discretionary* powers, meaning that many were excluded from benefit or were worse off. On its reintroduction, the scale rates were more generous. The UAB also sent out guidelines to its local offices to try to establish a uniform application of discretionary powers but stressed that such instructions were 'expressly or tacitly subject to discretionary variation in individual cases' (UAB, 1936, p 39). This is perhaps the first clear example of those responsible for social assistance at the centre attempting to exercise control over the way its street-level bureaucrats exercised their discretionary power on the ground.

The cautious and more generous strategy adopted by the UAB after the standstill was reflected in its first annual reports. Considerable attention was paid to the UAB's welfare role and officers were urged 'to be vigilant in discovering cases where assistance can be offered that otherwise would be unsought' (UAB, 1936, p 40). The UAB presented domiciliary visits as a very important tool in uncovering unmet need (UAB, 1936, p 12). However, the very benign official presentation of this aspect of its work was in sharp contrast to the many contemporary criticisms of the harshness of the scheme and the hardship that its beneficiaries experienced (see, eg, Greenwood, 1933). Nonetheless, the perceived success of the UAB in paying assistance to 'the most dangerous group among the poor [the unemployed]' (Gilbert, 1970, p 191) led to it being given responsibility during the war for the victims of bomb damage, including 'many normally prosperous citizens suddenly reduced to unexpected destitution' (Clarke, 1943, quoted in Lynes, 1977, p 203). In 1940, the UAB's responsibilities were extended to older people, over 1 million of whom claimed, and, in 1943, to widows with dependent children.

With the increase in the number of beneficiaries came a commensurate increase in the number of discretionary payments made and an increased burden on the administration. Successive attempts were made to reduce them. In contrast to a later attempt to simplify the use of discretionary powers, the minister responsible told the House of Commons that:

> in this field simplification costs money. One is inclined to think of simplification and pruning ... as being something which is economical, but, of course, in this field simplification is bound to mean in a substantial number of cases a levelling up. (House of Commons, 1943, vol 395, col 1189)

In 1943, the scale rates were increased beyond the rise in the cost of living to replace the discretionary winter allowances, which, by then, were being received by 60% of all supplementary pensioners.

The National Assistance Act 1948 and accompanying regulations drew together the responsibilities of the UAB with the provisions and practices of the Public Assistance Authorities. This change was not accompanied by any rational assessment of the structure and operation of Unemployment Assistance or any consideration of this scheme's ability or suitability to administer means-tested benefits to an enlarged and disparate clientele. The government failed to anticipate that an enlarged scheme in which the 'deserving' had to mix with the 'disreputable' would be regarded in a different, unfavourable light to the UAB, which had been regarded as superior to the Poor Law. Some of the future problems of social assistance stemmed from this lack of foresight.

The new social assistance scheme was to be administered separately from the Ministry of National Insurance, by a National Assistance Board (NAB), which employed its own staff. The application of wide discretionary powers, and especially discretionary payments, inherited from its predecessors ensured that the new scheme would be extremely resource-intensive to administer. Home visits continued to be a mainstay. By the end of 1948, all the quarter-of-a-million claimants taken over from the local authorities had been visited. In 1949, 5 million home visits were made. Like the UAB, the NAB stressed in its annual reports the importance of officers making full use of these visits to establish need, in the light of which the officer was instructed either to award a special addition or grant or, where appropriate, to refer the applicant to another, more relevant organisation. The NAB officer was expected to act as a mediator between the applicant and other local voluntary and statutory services.

While the NAB presented favourable overviews of the new assistance scheme and the work of its officers, experience at the ground level could be very different. The National Assistance scheme relied on a large number of officials to make personal assessments and decide when a discretionary payment should be made. As forewarned by Lipsky, such an individualised system can be applied differently at the local level from that promoted centrally, and decisions varied between regions, between offices and between officers.

The early popularity of the NAB with many of its beneficiaries was a result of the more sympathetic attitude held by officers and the public towards older people, who were the majority of beneficiaries. However, once National Assistance became responsible for both 'deserving' and 'undeserving' groups, such as the unemployed and lone mothers, difficulties arose. Although it was acknowledged that some central training was desirable to encourage a consistent approach to the use of discretion, which was 'as much a matter of conveying an attitude of mind as of giving precise instructions' (Stowe, 1961, p 336), little was done. The main training was given on the job. Speaking of his own experience working in a local National Assistance office, Hill (1969, p 83) reported that the 'collective values of the Executive Officers, rather than the views of one's superiors', were the greatest influence on the way in which the scheme was administered, and their behaviour was more repressive than management. In contrast to the very benign picture of the use of discretionary powers and home visits painted in the UAB Annual reports discussed earlier, Hill drew a very gloomy picture of the way NAB officers exercised their discretionary powers. The result was inconsistent treatment, stemming, at one extreme, from different interpretations of need, to, at the other, deliberate 'mucking around' to make it 'more difficult for an applicant to get assistance than to get help elsewhere' (Hill, 1969, p 83).

The numbers of people claiming National Assistance in the post-war period grew exponentially from 1.75 million in 1948 to 2.8 million in 1965. This was inevitably accompanied by a significant growth in discretionary payments. Over the same period, the proportion of claimants receiving a discretionary weekly addition to benefits doubled from 26.2% (265,000 claimants) to 57.9% (1,157,000 claimants). The number of weekly additions (claimants often received more than one) to benefits grew from 319,000 to over 2.2 million. Weekly additions were paid for a wide variety of expenses, including window cleaning, but four types of expenditure predominated: laundry, domestic assistance, special diets and fuel. The emergence of fuel as an item of expenditure with which claimants needed extra help occurred despite the fall in the number of discretionary winter allowances made in 1943 following an above-inflation rise in scale rates. Nevertheless, the NAB gradually resumed such payments and in the winter of 1964/65, a fuel addition was made to all households with a person aged over 65 or a young child. This was the first time that the NAB used a rule change, as permitted within the overall statutory framework, to respond to the emerging need demonstrated by the many thousands of individual discretionary decisions made each day by front-line staff, which increased payments to a level designed to be sufficient to meet the higher heating costs of some vulnerable groups.

The second type of discretionary payment was a lump sum for occasional exceptional expenses. Following the introduction of National Assistance, claims trebled. The number of such payments, which the NAB described as 'more numerous and more troublesome' than weekly additions, continued to grow from over 100,000 in 1948 to 345,000 in 1965 (NAB, 1949, p 14).

This increasing prevalence of discretionary payments between 1948 and 1965 led the NAB, in what was to be its final annual report, to conclude that:

> there is now a strong case for compounding, in appropriate categories, the smaller and commoner special needs with the basic scale rates and providing a scale rate which they will all receive and which is sufficient for all normal needs, including small expenses for which special discretionary additions have up to now been made. (NAB, 1966, p xii)

Discretion, 'Against discretion' (Donnison, 1977) and Supplementary Benefits

In opposition, the Labour Party had put forward radical proposals to reduce dependence on means-tested social assistance in line with Beveridge's original recommendation. However, on coming to power in 1964, the new government jettisoned these plans (Hall et al, 1975) and instead took the much more modest step of replacing National Assistance with Supplementary Benefits. As in 1948, this change did not represent any detailed consideration of the role of assistance or how well it was working; it was more the 'negative outcome of the failure of the income guarantee' (Hall et al, 1975, p 453). There was an immediate increase in the number of recipients; however, this was almost entirely due to more generous scale rates rather than to any greater public acceptability of the new scheme (Atkinson, 1970). From 1966 to 1980 the Supplementary Benefits scheme was administered by the Supplementary Benefits Commission, (SBC) and from 1980 to 1986, directly by the Department of Health and Social Security (DHSS).

The aims of the reforms were, first, to make it more acceptable to potential beneficiaries and improve take-up, especially among pensioners, thus addressing the recently revealed problem of continuing pensioner poverty (Cole, 1962; Abel-Smith and Townsend, 1965). In order to achieve the second aim of diminishing the overreliance on discretionary payments, a higher long-term addition (LTA) was introduced for everyone over retirement age and others – excluding the unemployed – who had been on benefit for over two years. This higher scale rate was intended to obviate the need for the majority of weekly additions for 'special needs'. It was stressed that the LTA was not 'a preferential rate of benefit for long-term cases ... [but intended to] avoid the need for detailed enquiries into special expenses of the kind which have to be made by the Board in cases under National Assistance' (Lynes, 1977, p 211). However, and crucially, where there were exceptional circumstances, the SBC retained discretionary powers to make an exceptional circumstances addition (ECA) to meet that need if it exceeded the level of the LTA. The system of discretionary lump-sum exceptional needs payments (ENPs) was also retained.

Again, the initial decline in the number of discretionary additions soon reversed. By 1975, and despite the LTA, 39% of all claimants were again in receipt of a weekly addition. In the year to November 1980, when additional requirement payments replaced ECAs, 61% of claimants were getting such payments. A similar pattern developed with regard to lump-sum payments. Berthoud (1984, p F16) refers to an 'explosion' as the number of ENPs doubled between 1968 and 1976. The first reason for the growth was the rise in the number of claimants, especially of families. For the first time, claimants below retirement age outnumbered those over retirement age. Second, the rise of the welfare rights movement in the 1970s, including numerous very successful take-up campaigns, dramatically increased the demand for discretionary payments and the number of appeals they generated. Third, in an attempt to simplify administration and standardise practice and outcomes, there was a 'real change in [SBC] policy and practice' (Berthoud, 1984, p F16). The SBC increasingly tried to exercise administrative (agency) discretion ('discretion as granted') and minimise the use of individual (officer) discretion ('discretion as used'). Guidelines were laid down for staff, according to which some payments became almost automatic for groups of individuals or in a prescribed set of circumstances. Certain customs and practices arose in the case of lump-sum payments. For example, payments for clothing were routinely made if the claimant had been on benefits for two years' time, if there were dependent children, if there was a serious illness or if hardship would result if a payment was not made (Lister, 1976, p 23). Similar guidelines were laid down for household necessities (DHSS and SBC, 1977, para 88). This top-down approach made individual decision-making simpler but the system more complex. For example, in 1975, the SBC issued about 10,000 pages of new or revised instructions to local offices (Expenditure Committee (General Sub-Committee), 1977, vol II, p 399).

From the beginning, the administration of this rising demand for discretionary payments was to be the major headache facing the SBC. In the early years, as Deputy Chair, Richard Titmuss put up a stout defence of both administrative and individual discretion as a way of ensuring that the system retained the ability to respond to individual need. When he became Chair in 1976, David Donnison argued that the system was in danger of breaking down completely and launched a debate on the widespread use of discretionary payments and the problems this posed (SBC, 1977, ch 6). The shortcomings highlighted by Donnison included: the differential practice between regions and offices; the conflict that the system generated between claimants and between claimants and staff; and the tendency of the system to favour those with most knowledge (including the welfare rights lobby) rather than those in greatest need. Perhaps most importantly, he argued that the system of extra payments 'is ultimately a destructive process because it distracts attention from the adequacy of the basic scale rates and provides justification for keeping them lower than they should be' (SBC, 1977, para 7.50). This view was supported by claimants and many pressure groups as ENPs were made primarily for wholly unexceptional needs, such as clothing and footwear, and ECAs were given most frequently to help with the quite predictable cost of heating.

Not stated so explicitly in the SBC's critique were the expenditure implications of a discretionary decision-making process set within an Act that placed few limits on the circumstances in which an extra payment could be made (Donnison, 1982). The problem was that, like the social security system generally, and unlike almost any other area of public expenditure, these payments were demand-led; neither ministers nor the SBC had any means of controlling the costs of these extra payments. The SBC's own attempts to control them through administrative discretion were often futile as any refusals could be overturned on appeal by independent tribunals, which were not constrained by SBC guidance.

Pressure from the SBC was central to the Labour government setting up a review of the Supplementary Benefits scheme in 1976 (Walker, 1983). This team of civil servants was charged with the task of putting forward proposals for adapting social assistance to its 'mass role' by simplifying it and containing costs within a no-cost remit (see Walker, 1983). This inevitably had implications for discretionary payments. The Supplementary Benefits Review was set up in such a way as to ensure that any findings could be taken forward even if there was a change of government. In this, it was successful, and within six months of coming to office, the first administration of Margaret Thatcher introduced the Social Security Act 1980, which radically reformed Supplementary Benefits. Its goals were, first, to simplify the scheme and, second, to move from a highly discretionary system to one based on legal entitlement. The conflict between these two goals (as foreseen by Titmuss, 1971) was realised only after, but very shortly after, the reforms had taken effect. The conflict arose from the fact that means tests are, by nature, complex, and in order to reflect the diverse circumstances of the myriad of social assistance claimants, the regulations had to be complex if they were to be comprehensive. As one of the members of the Supplementary Benefits Review team ruefully told a conference shortly after the new scheme came into effect: 'Whoever thought that the law was simple?' Another more immediate problem for claimants was that 'simplification' could only be achieved by concentrating on average need rather than individual need. Without putting more money into the system, 'rough justice', with losers as well as winners, is inevitable. While this may be a familiar approach 30 years on, it was extremely radical in 1980, so much so that a recommendation by the Supplementary Benefits Review team to reduce supplementary pensioners' entitlement by 25p was dropped.

Under the provisions of the Social Security Act 1980, all decisions relating to additional payments were governed by regulations approved by Parliament, as opposed to guidance from the SBC. This did not curb the demand for extra help. The new legal framework inevitably led to a loss of flexibility in the scheme; instead of being geared to individual needs, provision was geared to the needs of broad groups of people, leading to improvements for some and losses for others. The regulations set out the conditions of eligibility and, in many cases, the actual level of payment. Weekly payments were paid automatically to certain groups of people: for example, all claimants with a child under five received a heating addition. The changes had a significantly greater impact on the system of lump-sum payments. The new legislation led to the number of single payments initially falling by one quarter; however, this owed more to the 'substance of the rules than ... their legal status' (Berthoud, 1984, p F16). The most common expenses for which payments had been made, for example, clothes and shoes, were largely excluded from the scheme. Thus, '[T]he regulations were more significant for the help they did not give than the help they did give. The 1980 Act extended claimants' rights, but it offered them less help' (Walker, 1993, p 106). The new system was also frustrating for staff, who were unable to give a payment for a claimant's most pressing need, say, for children's shoes, but could give one for sheets (Beltram, 1984). However, Beltram found that, overall, staff welcomed the shift from discretion to regulations as it shifted personal responsibility for a decision to the regulations.

The new system also had some clear benefits for claimants. For the first time, the DHSS published a leaflet setting out the availability of single payments. Consequently, despite the cuts in provision that were made, the number of single payments soon began to rise after the initial sharp fall in the first year, from 1.1 million in 1980 to 4.1 million in 1985; this was equal to an increase in the rate per 1,000 claimants of nearly two-and-a-half times (Walker, 1993, p 107). The initial fall was almost entirely due to the limited availability of clothing grants; however, grants for furniture, other household items and gardening equipment rose. The new regulation-based scheme did not overcome the disparity in treatment between different groups of claimants or eliminate regional and office inconsistencies: 'It would appear that custom and practice still had a role to play even in a regulation based system. After all, officers still had to exercise judgement and this too can lead to different treatment' (Walker, 1993, p 108).

Towards the end of discretionary additions

The reformed Supplementary Benefits scheme had been in operation for less than three years when, in 1983, the Conservative government announced a second review of the system, the main purpose of which was to bring the costs of the system under control. This second review of Supplementary Benefits had three major objectives, none of which were new: to tackle the complexity of the scheme; to reduce the number of extra additions that 'swamped' the scheme; and to target help more effectively 'to those who need help most' (HM Government, 1985, p 2). The subsequent Social Security Act 1986 replaced Supplementary Benefits with Income Support, a much less flexible system. Additional weekly payments were entirely abolished and replaced, in part, by a system of premiums. It was the rise in the overall number of lump-sum payments that was of greatest concern to the Conservative government. Far from welcoming the rise as a victory for the claim set out in the 1979 White Paper, which preceded the Social Security Act 1980, that 'all claimants will reap the benefits of the emphasis on legal entitlement and published rules, and on simplification' (HM Government, 1979, para 8), the increase was attributed to 'misuse and abuse' of the system (SSAC, 1987, p 23). It was argued that grants were being claimed because they were there, not because they were needed. Echoing the sentiments of the UAB 50 years earlier, the Social Security Advisory Committee (SSAC, 1987, p 23) begged to differ: 'One possibility [for the higher rates in some areas is] the suggestion that the regulated scheme had uncovered a reservoir of need which had not been met under the old discretionary scheme'. Nevertheless, new regulations were introduced to tighten the conditions for the receipt of a single payment and to limit the items for which a payment could be made. The 1986 changes led to a sharp reduction in the range of grants available, and to whom they could be paid. Expenditure on single payments had virtually halved by the time they were abolished in 1988.

The year 1988 marked a radical and permanent shift in social assistance provision and policy. For the first time, responsibility for meeting occasional exceptional need was removed from the social assistance scheme – Income Support – and rested with a separately administered Social Fund. The Social Fund was the most controversial aspect of the 1986 legislation. It was quite different from any previous type of British social security provision in that: it was cash-limited, not demand-led; most payments were made in the form of loans; claimants became applicants to the Social Fund as they had no rights to a payment and all decisions were discretionary (though officers worked to unpublished guidelines and the local office budget); and, finally, there was no independent right of appeal, usually seen as an essential safeguard in any discretionary system (Titmuss, 1971). In contrast to the shift to legal rights elsewhere in the social assistance scheme, especially in relation to previously discretionary weekly additions, the new regulatory framework was deemed unsuitable for 'lumpy' expenditures:

> [The Social Fund] will be better able to respond to individual needs as they arise. This does not mean there will be no guidelines or that decisions will be capricious. But it does mean that decisions will not be constrained by a very detailed framework of rules and precedents ... decisions will be made locally by specialist officers with the minimum of formality. (HM Government, 1985, p 29, para 2.120)

A study of the operation of the Social Fund funded by the DHSS concluded that it had given rise to the same kind of iniquities that were a feature of the discretionary systems previously operated by the SBC and NAB (Huby and Dix, 1992). The problems of the Social Fund, however, were compounded by the fact that applicants did not have the protection of a right of appeal. The Social Fund was widely criticised, not least by the SSAC (1990). At one stage, ministers agreed that officers were interpreting the guidance in the Social Fund Manual too strictly and a circular was sent to encourage them to use their discretionary powers more generously. Throughout, demand for help from the Social Fund exceeded the budget. In the early years, the government topped up the budget mid-year but such generosity was not to last. The Social Fund was finally excluded from the British social assistance scheme as part of the Coalition government's welfare reform agenda. From April 2013, the Social Fund will be operated by local authorities according to their own priorities and criteria. The system will be discretionary and many have no right of appeal. Policy has come full circle. This will be the first time that there has been such a local discretionary scheme since the introduction of Unemployment Assistance in 1934.

Income Support was the final capitulation to the idea that the means-tested safety net would be anything but a mass scheme: '[It] owed more to the government's desire to restrict spending, and to devise a means-tested benefit which could be computerised than to a commitment to providing better or more adequate benefits for claimants' (Walker, 1993, p 14). Given that discretionary payments could not systematised in this way, they were abolished. Those with the greatest needs were the greatest losers in the new premiums and most lost out with the introduction of the Social Fund. Never again would the main (national) means-tested social assistance scheme be overwhelmed by having to respond to a seemingly insatiable demand for extra weekly or occasional lump-sum payments from claimants. However, the resurrection of discretionary schemes at the local level lends itself to unpredictable and potentially challenging levels of demand, as happened with the various schemes of British social assistance discussed earlier. However, evidence in the first year of assuming responsibility for last-resort discretionary help to the poor indicates that many local authorities are holding a very tight rein and many have underspent even the very limited budgets that they have set aside.

Conclusion

Up until the introduction of Income Support and the Social Fund in the 1980s, the ability to increase weekly benefits through discretionary weekly additions or occasional lump-sum payments was always regarded as essential to any scheme of last-resort means-tested social assistance in the UK. Because the main levels of benefit have consistently fallen below the level needed to meet basic needs, discretionary payments have been used to meet 'normal' not, as intended, 'exceptional' needs and, as such, were much more widely applied than proved practicable to those administering the system. This was compounded by the fact that Beveridge's ideal of social assistance playing a 'minor but integral part' (Beveridge, 1942, para 369) in income maintenance policy was never realised and dependence on the means-tested system has grown, first, as the national insurance system suffered benign neglect and then as a deliberate strategy of targeting. The exercise of discretionary powers to make additional payments in response to individual need, whether governed by rules from the centre or by the decisions of front-line staff, proved to be incompatible with a system of means-tested social assistance operating on a mass scale. Ultimately, the desire to design a simply administered system proved much more influential than meeting the individual needs of claimants.

The reforms enacted in the Social Security Act 1980 brought in by a Conservative government, but based on proposals drawn up under a Labour government, were the first public acknowledgement that social assistance was, and would remain, a mass scheme. The Beveridge ideal was dead. The introduction of Income Support in the 1986 legislation abandoned all flexibility to individual need enabled by discretionary powers in favour of a relatively simple structure and rules of entitlement. The rigid structure left little scope for pressure to build up. However, as the growing demand on Income Support's minor companion scheme, the Social Fund, demonstrated, simplification could only be achieved by ignoring the financial hardship of claimants.

Titmuss (1971, p 127), and, indeed, the UAB, NAB and even SBC, argued that some discretionary payments needed to be retained in social assistance because they allow 'flexible responses to human needs and to an immense variety of complex individual circumstances'. Increasingly, recent governments have shown that this is not their concern. First, meeting individual need has been sacrificed to administrative convenience. The flexibility offered by discretionary decision-making has been replaced by a rigid rule-based system. Second, under many of the 'welfare' reforms of the Conservative–Liberal Democrat Coalition government, the concept of a safety net designed to meet need (as this chapter has shown, always the rationale for including discretionary additions in the social assistance scheme) has largely disappeared. As well as there being no discretionary additions in the current or forthcoming national social assistance scheme, levels of benefit are now explicitly determined by external factors, not the needs of claimants. The most significant demonstration of this is the benefits cap, which limits the total amount of benefit entitlement to median earnings, regardless of the circumstances of the claimant. Discretionary additions, for all their many failings, allowed for the exercise of 'compassion for special circumstances and flexibility in dealing with them' (Lipsky, 1980, p 15) and thus ensured that the needs of the individual remained central to Britain's last-resort, financial safety net. The reforms currently under way in the UK make no pretence of wanting to do so.

An analysis of the changing role of discretionary payments in the British social assistance policy illustrates key aspects of Lipsky's argument on discretion and its exercise by street-level bureaucrats. The history of this key element of last-resort help for the poor illustrates persistent tension between the centre and those working on the ground and the difficulties that arise. For example, in its early years, the NAB ran into trouble because its officers were not being generous enough; however, under the Supplementary Benefits scheme decades later, some officers, in some areas, were seen to be creating difficulties by acting too generously. All the reforms of social assistance have been triggered primarily by pressures on the system created by the widespread use of discretionary payments. This challenged effective administration as it could not cope with the workload implications of individualised decision-making in what had become a mass scheme. It also emphasised the inconsistencies in treatment between claimants, officers and offices, and regions.

The policy response was to reduce and eventually remove discretionary powers from the officials working on the ground and instead to constrain their room for manoeuvre through 'discretion as granted' from the top. These attempts were eventually successful in returning control to the centre but, at the same time, exposed the inadequacies of benefit levels and the many anomalies that arise when individualised justice is replaced by broad-brush rules under administrative justice.

As the primary concern of British social security policy has shifted from meeting the needs of the poor and vulnerable to cutting total spending, regardless of the consequences for claimants, so the role of the street-level bureaucrat has been transformed. Their scope for discretion has been virtually eliminated as computerised assessments have replaced the exercising of individual skill and judgement. The scope for officials on the ground to exercise 'inherent discretion ... function as policy co-makers, and ... show a certain craftsmanship' (Chapter One, p 17) in fulfilling their tasks no longer exists.

FOUR

Street-level bureaucracy and professionalism in health services

Stephen Harrison

Introduction

At the heart of Lipsky's analysis is the observation that the workers whom he terms 'street-level bureaucrats' exercise considerable discretion over core aspects of their work. Thus, for instance, it is police officers that 'decide who to arrest and whose behaviour to overlook.... Teachers decide who will be suspended and who will remain in school, and they make subtle determinations of who is teachable' (Lipsky, 1980, p 13).

From one perspective, this is just as it should be; Lipsky comments that, ideally, street-level bureaucrats respond to the needs of individual clients, and, indeed, may espouse this approach as a personal and professional value (Lipsky, 1980, p xii). However, this ideal is not achieved in practice; inadequacy of agency resources leads street-level bureaucrats to develop techniques for mass processing clients, the results of which may be benign but may sometimes result in 'favouritism, stereotyping and routinizing' (Lipsky, 1980, p xii). Lipsky (1980, pp 9, xii, 8) observes that this behaviour is 'far from the bureaucratic ideal' of hierarchical control since it effectively *becomes* agency policy, and concludes that 'street-level bureaucrats must be dealt with if policy is to change'. In this context, 'dealt with' refers to the transformation of agencies that employ street-level bureaucrats into organisations that:

Know what they want workers to do;

Know how to measure workers' performance;

Are able to compare workers to one another; and

Are able to deploy incentives and sanctions that are capable
of disciplining workers. (Lipsky, 1980, p 161)

At this point, we may note an apparent paradox in Lipsky's normative
position, though this is not explicitly discussed in his book. On the one
hand, his interest is in the means by which ideal-typical bureaucracy
can be substituted for street-level bureaucracy; yet, on the other hand,
he apparently approves of the ideal of street-level bureaucrats focusing
on the needs of individual clients. The central question posed by this
chapter addresses both sides of this paradox. Based on the author's 35
years of research and policy analysis in the field, it aims to assess how
far a specific group of street-level bureaucrats – medical professionals
in the English NHS – have actually been 'dealt with' by policymakers.
It also considers the relationship between bureaucracy and the needs
of individual clients (in this case, patients).

The remainder of this chapter is divided into four sections. First,
it summarises in greater detail the main elements of street-level
bureaucracy and examines the ways in which these relate to core
concepts in relation to the practice of medicine, in particular, to the
potential bureaucratisation of that profession. Second, it describes
two continuing broad areas of policy development – the NHS quasi-
market and evidence-based medicine (EBM) – which have somewhat
undermined the situation described in the preceding section over the
last two or three decades. Third, it examines the impact of selected
elements of these policies on the two main areas of English clinical
medicine – primary care and hospital care, respectively – drawing on
published research. Finally, it returns to the central question of how
far physicians can still be seen as street-level bureaucrats, and goes
on to examine the wider implications of the policies for the medical
profession, for patients and for government.

Core concepts: medicine as street-level bureaucracy

Lipsky argues that the discretion that characterises street-level
bureaucracy derives largely from work that is 'too complex to reduce to
programmatic formats' (Lipsky, 1980, p 13). In addition, it is necessary
for street-level bureaucrats to 'respond to the human dimensions of
situations', that is, to treat clients as individuals (Lipsky, 1980, p 13). On
the face of it, such work cannot be reduced to standardised bureaucratic
rules, a characteristic reinforced by clients' perception that the street-
level bureaucrat handling their case holds the key to their well-being
(Lipsky, 1980, p 13). Taken together, these characteristics provide street-

level bureaucrats with relative autonomy from organisational authority in a context where agency goals tend to be vague or ambiguous, so that performance is difficult or impossible to measure (Lipsky, 1980, pp 16, 27–8). In addition, street-level bureaucrats usually work in a context where available resources are chronically inadequate for the tasks that the agency should perform, partly because the demand for non-marketed services tends to increase so as to match any given level of supply (Lipsky, 1980, pp 27, 87). As a consequence, street-level bureaucrats develop patterns of practice that limit demand, including narrowing their operational objectives to those that can be delivered within available resources and by 'modify[ing] clients' (Lipsky, 1980, p 83). Thus, for example, information for clients may be withheld, waiting times may be allowed to lengthen and clients may be labelled or stereotyped so as to simplify decisions about appropriate courses of action (Lipsky, 1980, pp 90, 89, 142).

Although Lipsky's study does not deal with the health field to any great extent, it is clear that he does not exempt health workers from his definition of street-level bureaucrats (Lipsky, 1980, pp 3, 73–4, 138). The aforementioned central elements in Lipsky's analysis can fairly straightforwardly be associated with two aspects of the professional practice of medicine: professional discretion and health-care rationing.

Discretion in the practice of medicine may extend to a wide range of matters, from the narrowly clinical through to much broader matters of practice ownership, organisation, workload and so on (Schulz and Harrison, 1986). However, in the context of a discussion of street-level bureaucracy, it is the exercise of discretion by appropriately qualified physicians over diagnostic and treatment decisions related to the patients whose cases they constitute, along with the evaluation of such care, that is of interest. This area of discretion, variously termed 'clinical freedom', 'clinical autonomy' or 'professional autonomy' (Harrison and McDonald, 2008, pp 28–35), can never be absolute since it is bounded by, for instance, regulations about pharmaceuticals and the requirements of professional licensing bodies to avoid malpractice. The essential point is that such professional discretion is not normally subject to bureaucratic oversight, though this does not mean that other aspects of professional employment are not bureaucratised; Mintzberg (1979) coined the term 'professional bureaucracy' to denote a mainly bureaucratic organisation, such as a hospital, employing professional workers, such as physicians, whose clinical work is not subject to bureaucratic rules.

Professional autonomy for physicians was officially endorsed by the UK government for many decades after the foundation of the NHS, and was underpinned by a variety of institutional characteristics, such as professional registration with an independent self-regulatory institution (the General Medical Council), vaguely worded employment contracts, freedom of patient referral to other physicians and to hospitals, and a separate hierarchy of medically qualified policymakers within the relevant government department (Harrison, 1988). Such discretion can be seen as permitting decisions to be made about the treatment of clients in circumstances where the relevant professional knowledge is perceived to be uncertain, complex or esoteric, 'tacit' (Polanyi, 1967) and therefore 'indeterminate' (in the sense employed by Jamous and Peloille, 1970), and thus incapable of reduction to bureaucratic or algorithmic rules. In such circumstances, it may be possible for a wide range of considerations, not all of which may be fully articulated, to be integrated into a decision that can be represented as being in the client's best interests. Of course, the actual fulfilment of such a function assumes that the discretion-holder is motivated to such an end. In addition, even where this is the case, it is self-evident that professional discretion is not solely a function of the (real or supposed) indeterminacy of clinical medicine, but also functions in the profession's interests by insulating its members from supervision and management (see Friedson, 1970a, 1970b; Lipsky, 1980, pp 16–17; for a contrary view, see Navarro, 1988). Empirical studies of the NHS between the 1960s and 2000 have generally confirmed the reality of medical discretion and its insulation from managerial control, while acknowledging a slow growth over time in managerial influence (for reviews, see Harrison, 1988; Harrison and Ahmad, 2000; Harrison and Lim, 2003).

As noted earlier, Lipsky (1980, pp 29–32) argues that street-level bureaucrats are customarily faced with greater demand for their services than they are able adequately to meet. Although Lipsky does not explain matters in quite the following terms, one might say that this increasing demand for services arises from the fact that the services provided by street-level bureaucrats are non-marketed, so that there is no price to function as a disincentive to demand, either (as the case may be) on the part of clients or on the part of those who refer them to professionals (Harrison and McDonald, 2008, pp 4–7). The UK's tax-funded NHS is non-marketed (Harrison and McDonald, 2008, pp 2–3), so a parallel with the organisational context studied by Lipsky is evident. In such circumstances, some form of rationing of services is inevitable. Historically, and as several UK commentators on health-care rationing have noted (Harrison and Hunter, 1994; Klein et al, 1996), such rationing has taken the form of delays to service provision or dilution of the quality or quantity of service, rather than an outright denial of service. To the extent that the appropriate application of clinical medicine to individual patients is held to be esoteric or indeterminate, it follows that any approach to rationing that purports to employ criteria such as the expected effectiveness of treatment must itself be indeterminate and therefore left to professional discretion. Furthermore, the criteria for such decisions will also be opaque to the patient and to third parties, such as bureaucrats. Such opacity reinforces the unsupervised nature of professional work, both generally and specifically, by fostering the perhaps illusory impression that everything necessary has been provided for the patient, a process often denoted as 'implicit' rationing (Harrison and Hunter, 1994), which, crucially, is effected at the micro- (or street) level of the physician–patient relationship. Again, the parallel is with the situation described by Lipsky (eg 1980, p 89).

Professional discretion and micro-level implicit rationing are related in the sense that the former allows the latter to occur. However, both are also overlaid with an ethical dimension, at its simplest, the principle that patients ought to have their individual needs met and that the relevant professional should be best placed and well-motivated to identify and meet such needs. Of course, as noted earlier, Lipsky argues that street-level bureaucrats are usually unable to meet this ideal (even if they convince themselves that they are so doing) and must resort to patterns of practice that are feasible within the available resources (Lipsky, 1980, pp xii, 89–90).

In summary, the ostensible indeterminacy and uncertainty of medicine, along with the excess of demand over supply in the context of a non-marketed system, have historically prevented the bureaucratisation of medicine and have established physicians as street-level bureaucrats. Indeed, empirical studies prior to about 1985 have shown both the way in which the overall pattern of NHS services has effectively been the aggregate of individual clinical decisions (Haywood and Alaszewski, 1980), and that NHS managers have functioned as 'diplomats' in relation to physicians, smoothing out conflicts and helping to secure resources, rather than seeking to control or influence them (Harrison, 1988).

However, the last two decades have seen radical developments in English health policy that, although adopted for wider purposes, have combined to disrupt this long-standing situation. The next section summarises these developments.

Policy changes

The two areas of policy development outlined in this section are, respectively, EBM and the NHS quasi-market. Both are of lengthy gestation and exhibit a considerable degree of continuity across governments of different political persuasions over the period from about 1991 to the present date. The accounts given here are necessarily brief summaries; fuller accounts may be found in, respectively, Harrison and Checkland (2009) and Harrison and McDonald (2008).

Evidence-based medicine

EBM comprises a cluster of ideas originally developed within the medical profession, particularly in the work of such epidemiologists as Cochrane (1972), Wennberg (1984) and Sackett (eg Sackett et al, 1991), but was subsequently seized upon as a policy tool by UK governments. (For a brief history of EBM, see Harrison and McDonald, 2008, pp 60–4.) While there was nothing new about the use of medical research to produce evidence about the effectiveness of treatments, the novel features of EBM were its focus both on the characteristics of the research methods employed and on the findings obtained as applicable to defined classes of patient. Thus, the validity of research evidence has come to be seen in terms of the elimination of bias through a 'hierarchy of evidence', within which randomised controlled trials and aggregations of such trials through meta-analyses are regarded as the 'gold standard'. It is evident that the concept of EBM thus defined presents a considerable challenge to the notion of medical practice as esoteric, indeterminate, tacit or radically uncertain. First, the research methods required for EBM require a great deal of precise definition, including: the diagnostic, severity and perhaps demographic characteristics of the patients studied; details of the treatment(s) to be researched and to be used in control arms of studies, including timing and dose; and a great deal of statistical detail in order to ensure the adequacy of trial size and duration. Second, once findings are produced, they are seen as valid in respect of definable populations of patients with the specified diagnostic and other characteristics, and therefore as appropriate for the treatment of such groups. Consequently, research findings can be conveyed to practising clinicians through the medium of evidence-based 'clinical guidelines' or 'protocols' (Berg, 1997), essentially, algorithmic rules that guide their user to courses of clinical action, dependent upon stated prior conditions: an 'if … then …' logic.

Such findings and prescriptions are probabilistic, that is, they yield valid statements of the probable outcomes of specific treatments when applied to classes of patient rather than necessarily for every individual patient, a fact that has led to some differences of emphasis within the medical profession as to the degree of discretion required over the applicability of research findings to individuals. While some leading figures have cautioned against the development of 'cookbook medicine' (eg Sackett et al, 1996; McDonald and Harrison, 2004), on the basis of EBM as characterised earlier, clinical medicine is potentially determinate and explicit (albeit within stated probabilities) rather than indeterminate, esoteric or tacit. It would further follow that physician adherence to such guidelines can be audited, supervised and made the subject of incentives and/or sanctions: 'performance-managed' in contemporary jargon. Indeed, it might be said that clinical guidelines or protocols are simply a particular form of bureaucratic rule, an observation that led Harrison (2002) to characterise the incorporation of research derived from the 'hierarchy of evidence' into clinical guidelines as 'scientific-bureaucratic medicine'.

In principle, therefore, EBM represents a constraint on professional discretion and offers the potential to transform street-level bureaucracy into classical bureaucracy. English health policy over the last two decades or so has invested considerable effort in the construction of institutions designed to implement EBM. Perhaps the earliest relevant institution was the national research and development strategy for the NHS created in 1991, involving the appointment of national and regional research directors, the establishment of national and local research budgets to be the object of competitive bidding, and the reorganisation of the flow of research funds through NHS hospitals (Baker and Kirk, 1996). The central objective of this programme quickly became the assessment of the effectiveness of both new and previously unevaluated health-care interventions. A range of specialist institutions was publicly funded as the means of reviewing, collating and disseminating the findings of effectiveness research to the NHS. Throughout the period 1991–97, it steadily became the conventional academic and policy wisdom that valid evidence of the effectiveness of clinical interventions should be defined by the 'hierarchy of evidence'. Over the same period, the value of clinical guidelines became official received wisdom (NHS Executive, 1996a), and it became officially recognised that research should guide NHS resource allocation decisions (NHS Executive, 1996b, p 6).

The high point of institutional innovation for EBM is perhaps represented by the creation in 1999 of the National Institute for Clinical Excellence (NICE – later the National Institute for Health and Clinical Excellence and currently the National Institute for Health and Care Excellence). This organisation makes recommendations about what interventions should be made available to patients by the NHS, based largely of the results of cost–utility analysis, employing costs per quality-adjusted life year as a lowest common denominator of expected patient outcome; at the time of writing, it had undertaken some 680 appraisals of medical technology (see: http://www.nice.org. uk/guidance/). (For detailed accounts of NICE's operations, see Syrett, 2003; Rawlins and Culyer, 2004.) Since 2003, the NHS has been legally required to implement most positive NICE recommendations. NICE's second major responsibility is to commission the production of evidence-based guidelines on specific topics by groups of experts (see: www.nice.org.uk/aboutnice/about_nice.jsp), and it is expected that such approved guidelines will normally be followed. At the time of writing, some 174 such guidelines have been issued (see: http:// www.nice.org.uk/guidance/). It can be seen that the operations of NICE constitute a major (though by no means total) shift in the *locus* and focus of rationing in the NHS: from micro/street-level rationing focused on the individual patient to a more macro-level focus and explicit focus on classes of patient.

The National Health Service quasi-market

A quasi-market may be defined as a market in which an agent purchases a good or service on behalf of the user. Prior to the late 1980s, the NHS did not operate as a market in any sense. Hospitals and community services were managed by local health authorities, which received central government funds roughly related to local population size and aggregate patient flow. The apparent absence of incentives for providers to treat more patients led to a number of proposals from policy commentators to separate responsibility for the funding and for the provision of secondary and tertiary care (Enthoven, 1985; Maynard, 1986). Arrangements along these lines were officially adopted in 1989, so that the aforementioned developments in EBM coincided with the development from 1990 onwards of a quasi-market within the NHS, under which its institutions were divided into 'providers' of care (such as hospitals and community services) and government-funded 'commissioners', whose role was to purchase services from providers and pay for the care for defined geographical populations (Robinson and Le Grand, 1993). Hospitals and other providers were not guaranteed central funding, but had to rely on winning contracts from commissioners to provide services and thereby to maintain themselves in existence through payments for each patient treated. Privately owned providers were permitted to participate in these arrangements, which were competitive in principle (since providers had an interest in obtaining contracts from a wider range of commissioners), though, in practice, historical patterns of provision tended to be maintained (Flynn et al, 1996; Flynn and Williams, 1997) and the pricing of each type of case was often determined by a national 'tariff'. Nevertheless, a consequence of the adoption of such an arrangement is the necessity to specify the services that are being purchased and the standard to which they are to be provided. The first of these requires a conceptual 'currency' in which the care to be purchased and supplied can be defined, priced and exchanged. Hence, there has been increasing recourse to the 'casemix' measure, originally developed in the US as the Diagnosis Related Group (DRG) and subsequently in the UK as the Healthcare Resource Group (HRG) (Bardsley et al, 1987). In brief, such casemix measures aim to categorise health-care interventions into groups, each of which is both clinically similar (eg relating to the same organ system) and uses the same unit amount of resource. They thus aim to provide a common currency with which to describe the outputs of health services. The English NHS is currently working with a set of some 1,400 HRGs grouped into a number of 'chapters', each of which encompasses an organ system, type of intervention or type of disease (see: http://www.hscic.gov.uk/hrg), but does not distinguish between the settings (eg hospital or community) in which the care is given.

Commissioners in a quasi-market have finite funding and must therefore also develop criteria upon which to base such priorities. Coupled with the need to evaluate the care provided, this requirement has led to increasing interest in health economics, specifically, the microeconomic analysis of the cost-effectiveness of clinical interventions. Such analyses require research data about the effectiveness of interventions and generally adopt the 'hierarchy of evidence' as their criterion of validity of such research, thereby incorporating the concept of EBM into the operation of the quasi-market. The next section examines the extent to which these institutions of EBM have allowed policy to 'deal with' street-level bureaucracy by substituting a degree of classical bureaucracy for medical professional discretion.

Replacing street-level medical bureaucracy in the English National Health Service

In order to illustrate the manner in which EBM and the NHS quasi-market have contributed to the attenuation of medical street-level bureaucracy, two substantial examples can be given, one drawn from each of the major branches of English medical practice – primary care and secondary care, respectively. Only summary accounts can be given here; for more detailed accounts, see Harrison and Checkland (2009), Roland (2004) and Harrison (2009).

Incentives for primary care physicians

Most UK general medical practices are owned and run by groups of general medical practitioners (GPs) in a legal partnership, which then employs other staff, such as salaried GPs, practice nurses and receptionists. Partners share the practice's profits as personal income. Although partners are self-employed contractors to the NHS, there are limits to their independence in that they must work to national contractual terms, usually negotiated but occasionally unilaterally imposed. The 2004 national contract was negotiated and proved popular among GPs since it provided an opportunity for GPs to give up their responsibility for out-of-hours cover. The new General Medical Services contract provides a lump sum for each practice calculated to take into account factors affecting workload (such as size of practice and local population deprivation), with additional income from payments for providing additional ('enhanced') services and for meeting a series of performance targets known as the Quality and Outcomes Framework (QOF). Although the principle of partly remunerating GPs for the achievement of quantifiable targets was not new, QOF took the principle far beyond its previous incarnations in relation to the number of targets to be pursued, the proportion of practice income dependent on such performance and the extent to which the targets were evidence-based, that is, derived from research evidence about the effectiveness of diagnostic tests and treatment interventions. QOF was described by one commentator as 'the boldest such proposal on this scale ever attempted anywhere in the world' (Shekelle, 2003, p 457), while another has suggested that it is 'an unprecedented system of central control and external surveillance' (Jeffries, 2003, p 888).

From the outset of the new contract, these performance targets included 146 indicators covering both clinical and managerial areas of the practice. Roughly half of the indicators were clinical, covering

10 domains of practice, from coronary heart disease to mental health. (Further domains were subsequently added and the scheme has been periodically reviewed since then, with new indicators introduced and others 'retired'.) Within each clinical domain, points are awarded (up to specified maxima) for the attainment of specific targets. Some points are awarded simply for collecting data (eg having a record of the number of patients with epilepsy), while others relate to the care provided to these patients. Thus, for example, practices are paid according to the percentage of their patients with heart disease treated with aspirin, gaining no points until over 25% are treated, increasing linearly to seven points if 90% of patients receive the drug. The threshold at which maximum points are attained varies from disease to disease, and the number of points available for each clinical area also varies, with more points available in those categories that involve providing care than in those that simply involve collecting data. Other clinical examples include offering smoking cessation advice to diabetic patients, ensuring good control of diabetes (as measured by haemoglobin) and maintaining total cholesterol within specified target levels.

The 2004 contract was officially presented as giving practices much greater flexibility and autonomy with regard to service delivery, allowing them to choose how to organise care and to decide which QOF targets were most important and relevant for their own patients, though ignoring targets would result in a loss of income to the practice since overall point scores subsequently translate into financial awards for the practice. In practice, however, most practices responded positively to the financially incentivised bureaucratisation of substantial elements of their clinical practice, which was in sharp contrast to their previous attitude to clinical guidelines and other officially published care frameworks (Harrison and Dowswell, 2002; Checkland, 2004; see also Pope, 2003). In the first year of operation, practices achieved a mean score of 91% of available points (Cole, 2005), accounting for a substantial element (around 20%) of practice remuneration. At the end of each financial year, point scores are collected automatically by specialised software (for a fuller description, see Checkland et al, 2007). However, many general practices have used additional software that effectively generates a running progress report throughout the year, identifying by name patients in respect of whom targets remain unmet and generating 'pop-up boxes' that appear when a patient's records are accessed, highlighting any missing pieces of data. Such boxes must be actively dismissed by the clinician, though they will both reappear and also record the omission. In order to ensure that data collection is uniform and accurate, practices have developed standardised data entry tools called 'templates' for each disease domain. Templates comprise of a series of questions that must be answered with a yes/no or number (eg blood pressure or weight).

While it might seem that there is an incentive to make the points easier to obtain by reducing the number of people registered with each disease, for example, by failing to code those patients whose blood pressure is difficult to control, in practice, this is unlikely to occur for two reasons. First, the prevalence of each disease is fairly constant across an area, and a practice with an artificially low number of patients on a particular disease register would stand out. Second, in addition to providing information for QOF, records are needed to ensure that patients are correctly managed; omitting a diagnosis from the record would be potentially dangerous. Taking the evidence of high QOF scores alongside the details of software systems and the difficulty of evading or falsifying records, it is evident that, with the support of GPs, substantial areas of clinical medicine in primary care have been bureaucratised, a conclusion also reflected in the findings of organisational studies of QOF (McDonald et al, 2007; Cheraghi-Sohi et al, 2012).

Commodification of the hospital medical product

Attempts to allocate budgetary responsibility to specialist physicians (consultants), or at least those who head hospital departments, date back to the 1970s and have resurfaced at intervals since then (Bardsley et al, 1987). In the context of the quasi-market, casemix measures such as HRGs permit large-scale competitive exchange by allowing standardised product descriptions and prices. Despite some initial technical difficulties, since 2004, such HRGs have increasingly been employed as the basis of 'payment-by-results' relationships between NHS commissioning organisations and hospital care providers (both NHS and privately owned), with each HRG classification serving as the price of the individual patient intervention. Within a hospital, HRGs provide the potential for *predefining* the content of care for each category of patient (Harrison, 2004), thereby ensuring that the mean cost of each category of patient matches the tariff that the institution will receive for treating such a patient and that budget-holding clinical departments in hospitals have a powerful incentive to ensure that care is actually delivered within a cost envelope implied by any given patient caseload multiplied by the relevant HRG prices.

Moreover, casemix measures can be combined, for instance, with clinical guidelines and perhaps microeconomic analyses in order to form the basis of more complex, but, at the same time, more routinised, systems of 'managed care', 'disease management' and 'patient pathways' (Robinson and Steiner, 1998), essentially, the application to health care of industrial process management and quality management techniques. A very large number of officially recognised patient pathways exist (see: https://www.evidence.nhs.uk/search?q=patient+pathway). However, (unlike in relation to primary care) little academic research seems to have been undertaken into the extent and day-to-day consequences of this development, though one study has shown that physicians can use guidelines and pathways to override patients' wishes (Sanders et al, 2008). Nevertheless, a perusal of the websites of secondary care provider organisations in England suggests that considerable prominence is given to pathways within the descriptions of services offered. Since 2009, further incentives for the development and use of patient pathways have been provided by the Commissioning for Quality and Innovation (CQUIN) scheme, which withholds a proportion of secondary and community care providers' income until agreed quality targets have been met. Although such targets are not necessarily related to patient pathways, a perusal of the websites of such providers suggests that such pathways are commonly seen as the means of securing the required improvements.

The process of what has been termed the 'conceptual commodification' of medical care (Harrison, 2009) further undermines the view that medical practice is indeterminate, tacit or esoteric. A patient pathway typically defines the class of patient to which it applies, defines the elements of care to be delivered within the pathway, specifies the usual sequence and timing of interventions and which members of the clinical team should undertake them, and specifies expected patient outcomes. As with clinical guidelines, the underlying logic is algorithmic, and patient pathways can be seen as yet another specific manifestation of bureaucratic rules, albeit covering the work of a wider team than does a clinical guideline. The aim of pathway utilisation is to standardise care, a characteristic that makes it more susceptible to external supervision, managerial control and performance management.

The current state of street-level medical bureaucracy

The analysis so far may be briefly summarised as follows. First, the two broad policy developments (EBM and the quasi-market) that have been implemented in the English NHS over the last two decades share an underlying logic that treats medicine and health care more generally as capable of explicit specification, rather than as esoteric, indeterminate or dependent on tacit knowledge. This is not to suggest that the political/governmental motivation for these broad policies is to be found in a crude desire to bureaucratise medicine. In fact, both EBM and the quasi-market probably owe their adoption largely to a search for, respectively, legitimate criteria for rationing health care and mechanisms for controlling expenditure (Harrison and McDonald, 2008, pp 74–6, 100–1).

Second, the pursuit of these broad policies has permitted the introduction of organisational arrangements in primary care (QOF) and secondary care (casemix measures and clinical/patient pathways) that offer the possibility of attenuating professional discretion and of governing clinical medicine through media such as clinical guidelines/ protocols, casemix measures and patient pathways, which are particular forms of bureaucratic rule. It is, of course, invalid to simply 'read off' the social or behavioural changes that may be assumed to result from organisational or institutional changes. In the present case, empirical evidence of the real bureaucratisation of medical practice is much stronger in the case of primary care than in secondary care.

Third, the fact of increased bureaucratisation within elements of medicine does not imply that the NHS has become the kind of organisation characterised by Mintzberg (1979) as 'machine bureaucracy' or that physicians have become analogous to call-centre operatives. An important element in the philosophy of patient pathways is the analysis of variance of actual treatment from pathway specifications as a means for reviewing pathway content for future use (Beazley and Brady, 2006). Nevertheless, physicians in the English NHS have come to exhibit less of the characteristics of street-level bureaucrats. It seems clear that QOF (in primary care) and patient pathways (in secondary care) are, indeed, capable of meeting Lipsky's specification of the kind of organisation that would be able to 'deal with' street-level bureaucracy, even though evidence for their actually being used in this way is much stronger in respect of primary care than in secondary care. In summary, the potential for the bureaucratisation of clinical medical practice is somewhat greater than long-established theories about the esoteric and tacit nature of medical practice would suggest.

A final analytic point flows from all this. British health service managers are rarely medically qualified (unlike in many countries), but it might be observed that there is a good deal of unremarked-upon commonality between the underlying assumptions of medicine and those of management. These have been explored more fully elsewhere (Harrison, 2009) but may be summarised as follows. Notwithstanding its supposed indeterminacy of treatment and outcome, in practice, since the late 19th century, clinical medicine has proceeded from a perspective of illness usually termed the 'biomedical' (or sometimes simply 'medical') model. This model takes illnesses to have specific knowable causes (such as micro-organisms, trauma or biochemical imbalances), causing physical lesions that alter the patient's anatomy and/or physiology and their consequent symptoms. Although scarcely credible as a complete view of disease in the contemporary age (eg since it ignores social factors), the model evinces a reductionism and a mind–body dualism that is clearly discernible in medical practice: disease resides in individual bodies and is best treated by specific appropriate interventions. It follows that individual patients can be grouped into classes, in medical terminology, 'cases': a particular patient is a case of a specified disease. The biomedical model has traditionally been treated by sociologists as conferring authority on physicians (since they are the experts on particular types of cases). However, its basis in diagnostic classes of patient for whom specific interventions are indicated allows it to be co-opted for managerial purposes; as has been seen, interventions can be bureaucratised and classes of patient can be conceptually commodified into health-care 'products' that can be costed, priced, counted and traded in a health-care market or quasi-market. The implication is that the claims of medical indeterminacy and the appearance of physicians as street-level bureaucrats may have always been illusory.

The developments examined in this chapter may have consequences for the structure of the medical profession. As Hupe and Hill (2007) have observed, Lipsky has little to say about the role of management in street-level bureaucracies; however, the aforementioned developments raise questions about new forms of stratification within the medical profession since it is clear that some doctors are firmly implicated in the spread of commodification as a managerial tool in both hospitals and primary care settings (McDonald et al, 2007; Timmins, 2007). The most recent organisational developments in the English NHS have reallocated the commissioning of a substantial proportion of health care to local groups of GPs, termed 'clinical commissioning groups' (see: http://www.england.nhs.uk/wp-content/uploads/2013/03/a-functions-ccgs.pdf). This may represent the development within English medicine of what Freidson (1994) described in a US context as a medically qualified 'administrative elite', which seems likely to further entrench the commodification of medical practice and undermine professional discretion and any remaining resistance to its bureaucratisation.

The bureaucratisation of medicine may also have consequences for patients. It is certainly possible that some primary care patients will be better cared for as a result of QOF. At the same time, there is a risk that GP attention will focus disproportionately on the diseases covered by QOF at the expense of non-incentivised conditions. A patient with asthma and marginally raised blood pressure may receive regular and duplicated invitations to attend for blood pressure checks, while a cancer patient will receive no reminder to attend for a potentially life-preserving hormone implant. More generally, the reduction of information about patients to the yes/no and quantitative measures risks ignoring complicated issues such as lifestyle modification, health beliefs, stress and attitudes to food (Checkland et al, 2007, 2008). As already noted, the empirical literature about the impact of patient pathways is not extensive, but such literature as does exist does not demonstrate unequivocal benefits for patients (eg Kwan, 2007; Hunter and Segrott, 2008).

Finally, the bureaucratisation of medicine may have consequences for governments. As noted earlier, one feature of street-level bureaucracy is its ability to perform an implicit micro-level rationing function in circumstances where demand for services exceeds available resources. A consequence of classical bureaucratisation is to undermine the feasibility of implicit rationing by medical street-level bureaucrats and to partially substitute macro-level explicit rationing, most obviously by NICE. If physicians are required to follow rules, then (to the extent that those rules prescribe what service each patient of a given class should receive) rationing becomes explicit and the responsibility for it logically transfers to the rule-makers, thereby rendering such rationing potentially more difficult to justify politically.

The policy and organisational detail set out in this chapter has been narrowly focused on the medical profession in England. However, it is important to note that the broader picture of developments in EBM, bureaucratisation and commodification can be discerned across several other countries in Northern Europe and North America. The international origins of EBM and international interest in its institutions have been noted earlier. Casemix measures analogous to HRGs are now common in the health systems of developed countries. Similarly, there is widespread international interest in medical 'pay-for-performance' systems, such as QOF (Mannion and Davies, 2008), and in patient pathways (Beazley and Brady, 2006). The 'naturalisation' of management ideas as relevant to medicine has also occurred elsewhere. For instance, Potter and McKinlay (2005) have suggested that the increasing corporatisation of medical care supply in the US has led to the transformation of the doctor–patient relationship into a series of isolated encounters, while, in Finland, Kurunmaki (2004) has shown that concern with hospital costs co-opted physicians into managerial perspectives. In summary, there may be an international 'epistemic community' (Haas, 1992) that is challenging street-level medical bureaucracy.

FIVE

When and why discretion is weak or strong: the case of taxing officers in a Public Unemployment Fund

Aurélien Buffat

Introduction

This chapter is about discretion exerted by public agents at the front line. Davis (1969, p 4) defines discretion as follows: a public officer has discretion wherever the *effective limits* on his power leave him *free* to make a choice among possible courses of action and inaction. For Vinzant and Crothers (1998, p 37), discretion means the power of *free* decisions or the latitude of choice *within certain legal bounds*. For Hupe (2013, p 435), discretion consists in *granted freedom to act within prescribed limits*. In addition, the distinction that Hupe (2013, pp 434–5) makes between *discretion-as-granted* and *discretion-as-used* will be of particular relevance in this chapter, where the analytical focus is mainly on the level of discretion used by front-line workers, while also considering granted discretion as one factor – among others – influencing it.

Discretion is, hence, both about the existing capacity for agents to take decisions in a free way and about deciding in a context where rules and legal bounds exist and influence the effective latitude that people use. This is why the image of the hole in the donut – an area left open by a surrounding belt of restriction (Dworkin, 1977, p 31) – is a suitable metaphor for what discretion is fundamentally about.

Hence, the literature indicates that the effective degree of front-line discretion varies according to individual factors (age, gender, work socialisation, job experience), organisational factors (work organisation, type of front-line agency, available resources) and institutional factors (political systems, policy designs and sectors, administrative cultures, types of welfare state regimes, etc) (for an overview, see Maynard-Moody and Portillo, 2010; Brodkin, 2012; Meyers and Nielsen, 2012). Any study of discretion, therefore, needs to take context seriously into account and has to consider the factors influencing the degree of discretion used at the front line.

In this chapter, the main goal is to study discretion in context and to look at the main factors influencing it. To do this, I use data from my PhD research, which investigated discretion exerted by Swiss taxing officers in a Public Unemployment Fund (Buffat, 2011). Two results will be highlighted. On the one hand, the analysis provides a case characterised by a generally low level of discretion. This constitutes an interesting result for the literature on street-level bureaucracy since the latter has been dealing so far with officials that tend to have much higher levels of discretion than the front-line workers studied here. On the other hand, the research shows that discretion is a highly task-dependent phenomenon and that many factors account for explaining why some tasks involve high or weak discretion.

The chapter is divided in the following way. In the next section, information is provided regarding the Swiss unemployment insurance policy at the front-line level. After a section presenting the research design of the study, I comparatively analyse two contrasting tasks in terms of degree of discretion being used, that is, one characterised by a rather weak amount of discretion (determining clients' eligibility for unemployment benefits) and one characterised by a rather important amount of discretion (sanctioning clients). The latter forms the basis for a concluding discussion about the factors influencing discretion and the theoretical lessons that can be more generally derived.

Swiss unemployment insurance policy at the street level

The Swiss national unemployment insurance policy was born after a popular vote in 1976 that rendered unemployment insurance compulsory for all workers. It is mainly contained in the Federal Law on Unemployment Insurance and Insolvency, enacted by Parliament in the early 1980s (Federal Assembly, 1982). Official policy goals are to guarantee insured people with financial compensation for losses due to unemployment, but also in case of a significant reduction in the amount of working hours or employers' insolvency. The unemployment insurance is equally funded by contributions from workers and employers.

The Swiss unemployment insurance policy is a typical case of executive federalism (Kissling-Näf and Wälti, 2007, p 503). The content of the legislation is decided at the federal level while the implementation is a responsibility delegated to the local level, that is, to the 26 cantons and semi-cantons. At the federal level, the State Secretariat for Economic

Affairs (SSEA) is in charge of the unemployment insurance. At the cantonal level, two types of implementing agencies exist. On the one hand, regional job centres deal with unemployment and seek the reintegration of people into the labour market. On the other hand, unemployment benefits are managed by Unemployment Insurance Funds (UIFs). Each canton has one Public Unemployment Fund and there are also several private organisations, mainly from trade unions (Pasquier and Larpin, 2008).

Any UIF has two missions to achieve. The first one is to determine clients' eligibility for unemployment compensation; formal eligibility criteria are contained in the federal law and enforcement orders. Their second task is to pay beneficiaries on a monthly basis. More generally, UIF employees follow up claimants and beneficiaries for all matters linked to unemployment compensation. In addition, taxing officers[1] may sanction beneficiaries who do not comply with formal rules. Sanctioned clients will have their benefits temporarily suspended for one to 60 days, depending upon the gravity of their transgression.

The UIF that was investigated in my research is the public UIF of a French-speaking canton in Switzerland. The organisation is divided into several units: an administrative department, a legal department and a benefits department. In 2009, the UIF had 36 full-time workers, almost half of them being taxing officers. Taxing officers are in charge of determining clients' eligibility, paying beneficiaries, following up clients and sanctioning clients if necessary. They are active in field units that cover the socio-economic regions of the canton. The most important field unit (six taxing officers) is located at the central branch office. Workers are aged 40 on average and women represent a majority in the group (62.5%). All taxing officers have an education as clerical clerks. Two thirds of them come from private companies active in the insurance or the accounting sectors, and one third from local public sector organisations (tax offices or labour courts).

Research design

The cantonal UIF has been investigated through an ethnographic approach. Data were gathered through extensive fieldwork at the UIF, in which I was integrated for a period of six months (September 2008–March 2009). Two methods were central: first, direct observations of taxing officers' work were conducted for approximately 40 days; and, second, 19 semi-structured interviews took place with UIF staff on their daily activities, room for manoeuvre regarding federal regulations, control mechanisms, and so on.

When used discretion is low: assessing clients' eligibility

Taxing officers decide whether a person is eligible for unemployment benefits or not. To do this, they have to assess if the claimant's situation complies with seven criteria contained in the federal law (Article 8: right to compensation):

a. to be (fully or partially) jobless;
b. to have one's home in Switzerland;
c. to have lost a job;
d. to be finished with school, not to be at the age entitling one for a pension or not to be receiving one;
e. to have financially contributed for a minimum of 12 months to unemployment insurance funds within the past two years, or to be released from this obligation for specific reasons (training, illness, disability, divorce, imprisonment);
f. to be fit for employment; and
g. to comply with control requirements.

These criteria are further specified in other articles of the law and in enforcement orders. At the UIF, the eligibility assessment process starts with a meeting between the claimant and the taxing officer. Claimants have to fill in a registration template asking them about personal information, their current work situation and capacity, and whether they receive benefits from other welfare institutions (a pension or illness or disability insurances). The central part of the template is about the claimant's last work contract(s) and employer(s), about the reasons for its termination, and about the professional and financial situation of the person over the previous two years. Registering a new claimant may last between 15 to 45 minutes, depending on the cases and whether additional information is needed.

My data collection had the purpose of assessing the extent to which taxing officers use discretion in the process of assessing clients' eligibility. Based on field observations and interviews, the research shows that UIF workers enjoy a relatively limited degree of discretion in this task. All taxing officers perceive their general room for manoeuvre as being weak, sanctioning clients being the only exception:

> "Regarding processing registrations, I think we come to know very well whether a claimant has a right to unemployment benefits or not or to determine the insured income. However, it is always a bit blurred as far as sanctions

are concerned, in particular in case of guilty unemployment, which is more or less left to our own interpretation." (TAXO1, L603–6)[2]

"In general, we don't have a great deal of room for manoeuvre.... For assessing eligibility, we have enforcement orders, the law, you don't have much autonomy here. Then it is obvious you can decide 31 or 40 days of sanctions in a given case, lowering sanctions is possible. However, regarding room for manoeuvre, we don't have a lot in general." (TAXO3, L230–4)

"It is only when sanctioning clients that room for manoeuvre exists, this is all. For the rest, there is not, it is yes or no, all the rest is about calculating." (TAXO10, L1440–1)

UIF workers perceive a varying amount of used discretion according to the task at hand: very low room for manoeuvre in assessing claimants' eligibility and much more in sanctioning clients. Therefore, discretion seems highly task-dependent. These subjective assessments were generally confirmed in the observations made at the front and back offices. In the next sections, I will present three elements that restrain the use of room for manoeuvre in the realm of eligibility assessments.

The material economy of cases: 90% of simple cases versus 10% of complex cases

A first element diminishing the amount of used discretion in eligibility assessments is linked to the general distribution of cases between simple or complex ones. Observations at the registration desk indicate that an overwhelming majority of new cases are easily processed because they rapidly match the formal criteria of the law. As the service manager of the taxing unit states, these are situations that directly fall within the scope of the law (SEMA, L1178–9), that is, situations that do not require particular interpretation efforts and can therefore be processed almost automatically. These simple cases are clearly in the majority:

"Regarding law enforcement, there is 80% to 90% of cases for which it is easy to assess eligibility and then 10% of more complex ones.... Generally speaking, eligibility assessment is just about article 8, it's rapidly processed you know." (TAXO5, L838, L1140)

"For me, in 99% of cases things are very clear, law and enforcement orders are enough. Then you have extreme cases for which the law seems clear but is actually not. But those cases do really represent a low percentage." (TAXO6, L040–50)

Therefore, as far as eligibility assessments are concerned, it is only in a very limited number of situations that taxing officers need to personally appreciate or interpret cases, that is, to make discretionary judgements. This means that discretion exists but only for a minority of specific and complex cases. Furthermore, even for the (relatively few) situations requiring interpretation efforts, UIF workers tend to avoid using their discretion. Indeed, in case of serious doubts as to whether entitlement to benefits should be accepted or not, taxing officers prefer to let their service managers decide instead of acting in their own individual ways. In other words, they auto-limit themselves and the room for manoeuvre that they can use.

A very clear and highly specified regulatory framework

A second element limiting taxing officers used discretion is the existence of very clear and highly specified attribution criteria. Due to their factual and rather binary nature, criteria leave very little room for interpretation in practice: one is jobless or not, one lives in Switzerland or not, one has contributed to unemployment insurance for a minimum of 12 months or not, and so on. With the noticeable exception of control requirements, UIF workers can hardly interpret these narrow regulations:

"There are some aspects for which rule interpretation is necessary, but there are many aspects for which no interpretation is possible. For example, either the claimant has contributed during 12 months to the unemployment insurance or he has not." (SEMA, L1518–20)

"There is no grey zone here, or very few, it is either black or white." (TAXO5, L480)

Furthermore, eligibility criteria are narrowly specified in the other articles of the law, in several articles of the governmental enforcement ordinance (Federal Council, 1983) and in directives provided by the SSEA (2002) and the UIF. Taxing officers are literally surrounded by formal rules and specific regulations, that is, by a strongly delimited belt of restriction. This is why taxing officers perceive their institutional role as being mainly about *enforcing* state rules, rather than *interpreting* them. Significantly enough, caseworkers talk about the bible when they refer to the book containing all the articles of the federal law and the enforcement ordinance. Therefore, rules do matter and have a restraining effect on discretion used at the front line.

Tight controls, harsh consequences

Formal rules matter even more because of the existence of strict controls with potentially harmful consequences in case of incorrect eligibility assessments. Taxing officers are controlled at different levels and from different actors. The internal control system (ICS) requires service managers to check a minimum of 5% of registrations processed by taxing officers annually, in particular, whether eligibility decisions comply with regulations, whether financial benefits were correctly calculated, and so on. The main goal of the ICS is to detect and correct mistakes before the SSEA does through its team of federal inspectors. The latter inspect the UIF annually through an in-depth investigation of selected cases. Taxing officers are well aware of these external and internal controls. These controls make them act very carefully when they assess eligibility:

> "We are very much controlled, the system wants it so. Each operation we make leaves a trace in the electronic system. I think such an important control is normal because we pay so much money. Everywhere a lot of public money goes out, there must be a lot of controls. I think it cannot be different." (TAXO1, L980–9)

> "It is clear you must not make mistakes; our responsibility is mainly in case assessment because if you make mistakes, then it has financial consequences.... Enforcing the law, calculating the insured income and payments are the three aspects one need to be particularly careful to." (TAXO6, L621–5)

Financial sanctions referred to in the interviews might, indeed, be imposed by the SSEA on the UIF in case of mistakenly paid benefits. Regulations do, indeed, provide that when entitlements to benefits or payments based on incorrect assessments are decided by the UIF personnel, the primary and, hence, financial responsibility for covering undue but nevertheless paid benefits goes to the canton and not to the federal insurance funds, particularly in case of serious mistakes. The risk responsibility and its financial burden will mainly be placed on the implementing agency and not on the federal insurance budget. Given the severity of SSEA policy on that issue, UIF managers and personnel are particularly careful to strictly comply with federal regulations regarding eligibility assessments:

SEMA: "At the SSEA, inspectors are very nitpicking, they let nothing pass, they don't make you gifts …"

Buffat: "Why is this the case?"

SEMA: "Well, if they are able to detect mistakenly paid benefits…. Their mission is really to monitor the spending of the unemployment insurance. We do often disagree regarding the risk-responsibility system because for the SSEA, all mistakes we make are considered as serious mistakes. And it is the only social insurance in Switzerland where this is the case. Think about the disability insurance: there, if you have mistakenly paid, you have mistakenly paid, period. If you try to get the money back and you can't at the end, never mind. But here, in the unemployment insurance system, you always get serious mistakes. They consider if you do something wrong, for example, mistakenly calculating an insured income, it is a serious mistake. And this amount of money, they will not take responsibility for it." (SEMA, L2081–100)

These potentially harsh financial consequences for the UIF, coupled with the existence of several control mechanisms, render taxing officers very careful and risk-averse when eligibility is assessed. They stick to the rules as much as they can and avoid any unconsidered risk likely to happen when one would interpret regulations. Therefore, a strong administrative culture of caution exists in eligibility assessments, a culture that clearly inhibits discretionary behaviours in that task.

When used discretion is high: sanctioning clients

In some situations, taxing officers also have to sanction clients. In Article 30 (suspension of the right to compensation), the law states that the UIF must sanction when a beneficiary:

a. is unemployed due to his or her own fault (guilty unemployment);

b. has renounced a claim for salaries or compensation from his former employer, and this being to the detriment of the unemployment insurance;

c. has given wrong or incomplete indications or has contravened the duty of providing information to the unemployment insurance agencies; and

d. has obtained or has attempted to unduly obtain unemployment benefits.

According to the governmental enforcement ordinance, the appropriate level of sanctions depends upon the gravity of the fault at hand. A light fault requires from one to 15 days of benefits suspension (up to three weeks without unemployment benefits), a medium fault requires from 16 to 30 days (up to one-and-a-half months without compensation) and a serious fault between 31 to 60 days of sanction (three months being the legal maximum). Guilty unemployment is typically considered by the law as a serious fault.

A specific directive (SSEA, 2002) further states that the duration of the sanction has to be established according to all circumstances that are case-specific, such as: the motive/cause of unemployment; personal circumstances, such as age, civil status and state of health; whether the person has an addiction; their social environment, level of education, linguistic skills and so on; specific circumstances, such as the behaviour of the employer or work colleagues and work atmosphere (eg pressures at work) (Article D60). The directive does not include a specific grading scale regarding the number of sanctioned days to be inflicted.

Data collection had the purpose of assessing the extent to which taxing officers use discretion in the sanctioning activity. Data show that UIF workers both formally enjoy a certain freedom of action in this task (discretion-as-granted) and do use this freedom in practice (discretion-as-used). First, taxing officers have leeway in determining the gravity of the fault to be considered – variation exists. Second, when taxing officers sanction similar cases, they tend to inflict different amounts of days without benefits:

> "For a similar case, processed by one or the other taxing officer, one will decide 40 days, another one 31 and another one 15. It is quite awful." (TAXO1, L21–2)

> "I can decide 35 days while my colleague, for the same case, might estimate 25 days. And it might be the case that

colleagues in other branch offices would say 'no, it is 40 days'." (TAX08, L1185–8)

In the following sections, I will present three aspects that favour the use of an important room for manoeuvre in the realm of sanctions.

Decisions of sanction as de facto complex cases

The fact that discretion is used is linked to the intrinsic complexity of the sanctioning decisions. At the opposite of the material economy of cases in eligibility decisions, sanction decisions are intrinsically complex for taxing officers for many reasons.

First, sanctioning is a humanly complicated task because it implies cutting financial resources for (generally) needy people. This is why all taxing officers negatively perceive that task. It constitutes an official duty that they would prefer not to have to achieve but nevertheless have to deal with: "This is the dark side of the job" (TAX01, L506). Facing human and complex situations, taxing officers need to interpret rules in the light of cases and cases in the light of rules.

Second, the complexity of sanctioning can be observed in the reflexive relationship that taxing officers have with their power to sanction. Some workers highlight the severity of the sanctions regime through a comparison drawn with traffic fines:

> "In terms of money, when you compare with someone acting badly when driving, you really need to screw up a lot on the road to get a fine of 3,000 to 5,000 Swiss Francs! I do not think financial sanctions in the unemployment policy are appropriate." (TAXO2, L525–8)

Other workers reflect on the risk of power abuses:

> "One needs to be very careful because it's a job in which you have a power, I mean you need to put yourself at the people's place because you clearly have the power to say I'm going to pay you, I'm not going to pay you, I'm going to sanction you. One needs to avoid playing with that power because it could be dangerous otherwise.... Sometimes, I would like to take from some people to give to others but we can't do that. Fair, the word fair, being fair, a difficult thing to be fair!" (TAX02, L545–50)

Third, sanctions are complex because deciding whether a claimant is responsible for being unemployed or whether a claimant has left a job that was suitable render interpretation necessary for taxing officers. Assessing whether a client is responsible for being unemployed is, in itself, less immediately obvious than assessing compliance with clear-cut criteria, such as 12 months of contributions to unemployment funds. In sanctions, things are grey instead of being black or white:

> "When you sanction a client, you need to reason, you need to look at the current situation and think about it: have they children? Are there travels for going to work? We have to take into consideration a whole range of aspects, you cannot say I am systematically tough, I am nasty or I am not because you have to consider the whole situation of the client, its circumstances.... Each situation is specific and you never have twice the same situation." (TAXO5, L1417–31)

Hence, all sanctioning cases are complex cases, that is to say, cases that require taxing officers to think, to interpret and to make their own judgements about the situations at hand. In this activity, the material economy of cases is just the opposite as the one prevailing for eligibility assessments: 90% of complex versus 10% of simple cases. This is why they need to use the discretion that they have been formally granted, an element that is presented in the next subsection.

A discretionary space created by the regulatory framework

Another factor enhancing the use of discretion in sanctioning is the regulatory framework itself. Two distinctive features matter. On the one hand, directives state that in order to establish the duration of any sanction, UIF personnel have to consider a whole range of circumstances that are specific to the case at hand, such as personal characteristics or work-related aspects. However, the directive does not further specify exactly *how* those specific circumstances have to be considered. On the other hand, the directive does not provide any specific grading scale.

At the front line, these two features have the combined effect that taxing officers assess each case requiring sanctions as a case per se. More importantly, every case-specific circumstance might be considered either as an aggravating or as a mitigating one. According to the personality and social background of taxing officers, similar circumstances can lead to different or even opposite assessments. This is the case for the circumstance regarding having children or not. For some agents, having children is perceived as a mitigating circumstance for establishing the amount of sanctioned days, while for others, it represents a rather aggravating one:

> "I am likely to have more empathy for a client who is a family man with children and who has given his resignation letter than for a young guy who is single and lives at his parents' house, I do consider that circumstance all the same. Well, we have to take specific circumstances into consideration, directives require that from us. It must be a sanction, this is obvious, but we have to consider the person's situation. But then you have colleagues who remain unmoved and would rather say, 'Well, it is precisely when you have children that you should not resign from your job!', so they judge the case as being grave. They will justify it saying: 'I decide that amount of sanctioned days because I think the person should have thought about that before!'" (TAXO6, L1358–79)

> "Important circumstances are does the person have children? But this is a circumstance I do not like because, for me, if you have children, precisely, you need to take your own responsibility by not leaving your job like this! Therefore, I do not always agree to say 'There are children in the household, I shall not sanction too much' because if you precisely have children, you should ... I think we tend to judge cases in the same way as we would judge ourselves. I am quite tough with me, if I am sick, I go to work." (TAXO2, L528–37)

In this example, it is important to understand the underlying mechanism: the way the directive is formulated de facto grants taxing officers with a discretionary space within which they might freely move when assessing specific circumstances. Both taxing officers acted in conformity with existing regulations (they respect the formal requirement to consider circumstances) but they came to opposite conclusions. In other words, the directive makes it possible for taxing officers to interpret the same circumstance in opposite ways, and they do. Instead of limiting the use of discretion, as is is the case for eligibility assessments, the rules have an enhancing effect on it. It is precisely because taxing officers are formally required to interpret specific circumstances (discretion-as-granted) that they effectively exert their discretionary judgements here (discretion-as-used).

Soft controls, few consequences

The nature of the existing control mechanisms constitutes a last contextual factor enhancing the use of discretion in sanctions. For federal inspectors, controlling sanctions is mainly a matter of verifying whether UIF personnel have administered sanctions when this action is formally required. Federal inspectors only check that faulty behaviours have been sanctioned and do not enter into more detail. As long as a sanction has been inflicted, they will not verify whether the sanctions are too harsh or too soft:

> "Regarding SSEA controls of sanctions, I think they do not really control. It means they check the concept of fault but they don't care whether we have decided 1 or 60 days of sanctions. For sanctions, we don't have real problems with federal inspectors because they're fully aware they did not have any direct contact with the client. For example, sometimes, we write in the file decision issued in accordance with oral 'discussion so federal inspectors cannot really assess whether this was a right or wrong decision'. What the federal inspector does really want to see is ok, the guy didn't respect that, UIF has sanctioned, it's all right but they don't mind whether we have sanctioned for 10 or 40 days." (TAXO7, L1039–49)

This leniency of control and the relative absence of consequences have a positive influence on the latitude of choice that taxing officers effectively use in sanctioning clients, especially for deciding the number of days to be inflicted. Nobody really checks the number of days that UIF personnel decide and no official grading scale exists for that matter.

In fact, the latter is quite logical because sanctioning is a task that has been formally delegated twice. First, federal authorities have delegated the operational responsibility of sanctions to all public and private UIFs acting at the local level, only providing them with broad guidelines contained in the enforcement directives. A second delegation happens within the UIF itself: managers have given full decisional autonomy to the taxing officers, in particular, in the realm of sanctions. This organisational choice has consequences for the way in which internal control is conceived and achieved. As the head of the UIF legal office explains, managers do not want to infringe too much upon the decisional autonomy that they have granted to employees:

LEGO: "For sanctioning clients, they have a great deal of autonomy. As head of the legal office, I try to respect their autonomy.... Normally, I always try to leave untouched the amount of days they have decided. For example, I would consider inappropriate from me to rule out a 35 days decision and bring it back to 31 days."

Buffat: "Why not?"

LEGO: "We grant them with a discretionary power, so I would find it intellectually dishonest from me to leave the decision in the same category of fault but at the same time to suppress four days, because it would therefore mean I do not recognise their decisional autonomy and their discretionary power regarding cases any longer." (LEGO, L1267–87)

In such a context, taxing officers do effectively enjoy an important amount of discretion in determining the appropriate level of sanctions.

Conclusion: the various sources of discretion

In this chapter, the goal was to investigate the factors influencing the degree of used discretion in a given street-level context. From the empirical analysis previously presented, some theoretical lessons can be more generally derived. To start with, the research shows that four types of factors matter for explaining variation in the use of discretion at the front line.

A first important factor to consider is the *type of task at hand*. As the data show, taxing officers have a lower degree of discretion in determining eligibility and a comparatively stronger discretionary power in sanctioning clients.

A second explanatory factor, closely linked to the first one, is the *material economy of cases*, that is, the relative proportion of simple and complex cases within the total amount of cases that front-line workers have to process. The more important is the number of complex cases, the more necessary are discretionary assessments. In assessing eligibility, discretion could be considered as low because, in practice, it was only used for a tiny percentage of all processed cases. At the opposite extreme, the degree of discretion is higher in sanctioning clients because this specific activity transforms each case into a complex one.

Third, the *regulation framework and rules* do influence the degree of used discretion. In assessing eligibility, attribution rules are very specific and of a very clear-cut nature, and therefore drastically limit taxing officers' possibilities to freely interpret them in practice. For sanctions, specific rules exist as well, but they have the opposite effect due to the nature of enforcement directives: since taxing officers must assess all case-specific circumstances for establishing the duration of sanctions, this de facto leads to providing front-line agents with substantial room for interpretation. In one case, rules inhibit used discretion, while in the other one, they favour it. In both cases, rules matter.

Finally, control mechanisms influence the amount of front-line discretion. UIF eligibility assessments are very strictly controlled, both through internal (ICS enforced by managers) and external procedures (in-depth check by federal inspectors). Implementing agents (and the agency itself) are very careful and stick to the rules because they fear the (financial) consequences that they will have to undergo in case of mistakenly paid benefits. Contrastingly, such a fear does not exist for sanctions because federal and organisational controls are much softer in terms of procedures and consequences. In both cases, therefore, it is important to understand how accountability regimes function and what effects they have at the street level (Hupe and Hill, 2007).

From this analysis of contextual factors, three additional lessons can be drawn regarding the phenomenon of discretion as used at the street level. First, the research highlights the importance of an *empirical and analytical disaggregation of discretion* as a concept into the specific *tasks* that street-level workers achieve. Indeed, the degree of discretion varies from one task to another; it is a highly task-dependent phenomenon. The effective room for manoeuvre is more or less pronounced depending on the task at hand. Such conceptual disaggregation represents an innovative point for the research on street-level bureaucracy. Instead of considering discretion, it is more relevant to talk about *discretions*. Instead of analysing *the* discretionary *power* of some given front-line workers, one should rather study discretionary *powers*. As the analysis shows, front-line workers do indeed have differentiated *rooms* for manoeuvre according to the task at hand instead of an undifferentiated *room* for manoeuvre. Acknowledging the latter means that progress is being made on two fronts, at the theoretical and methodological levels.

From a theoretical point of view, it suggests that the concept of discretion can be approached through a new unit of analysis, which is the type of task at hand. Such a conceptual and analytical disaggregation of discretion suggests a further specification of what happens at the micro-level of street-level practice: street-level behaviours *in specified tasks*.

From a methodological perspective, such disaggregation requires researchers to use approaches characterised by a strong sense of contextualisation because the ways in which tasks are concretely carried out at the street level are closely linked to their immediate institutional and organisational environment. In that sense, organisational ethnographies (Brodkin, 2008; Ybema et al, 2009) or comparative strategies of in-depth case studies like Qualitative Comparative Analysis (Rihoux and Ragin, 2009) represent particularly promising approaches.

A second aspect regards the distinction between *discretion-as-granted* and *discretion-as-used*. Actually, the empirical analysis has shown how much legal regulations regarding the benefits attribution process, accountability and control rules systematically influence the amount of discretion that is effectively used by taxing officers. Rules aiming at granting little discretion, coupled with harsh accountability mechanisms in case of non-compliance, lead to very limited use of discretion at the front line (eligibility assessments). At the opposite extreme, rules granting the possibility of discretionary interpretations to workers, coupled with soft control procedures, favour a more important use of discretion (sanctioning clients). In other words, the investigated case highlights the necessity for street-level bureaucracy theory and research to reflect much more upon the causal linkage between the level of formally granted discretion and the amount of practically used discretion.

Third, the research more generally shows how much street-level discretion is a complex *multi-causal phenomenon*, as some authors argue (eg Evans and Harris, 2004; Maynard-Moody and Portillo, 2010). At the UIF, the degree of used discretion is *jointly* influenced by macro-institutional-related factors (such as policy design, the nature of the regulatory framework and federal control mechanisms), organisational-related factors (such as managerial decisions regarding taxing officers' spheres of decisional autonomy or the administrative culture of cautiousness) and person-bound factors (such as taxing officers' preferences and attitudes towards the formal autonomy that they are granted). This multi-causality strengthens the need for contextualised approaches when investigating front-line discretion. It also indicates that discretion-as-used is influenced by the way in which discretion is institutionally and organisationally granted, but that this factor alone is far from sufficient in explaining what is observed at the street level.

Finally, the research provides the literature with a case characterised by a rather *weak* amount of used discretion in general. A provocative but logical question could then be: are Swiss taxing officers true street-level bureaucrats? I would definitely answer 'yes' to the question, going back to the working definition given in the introductory chapter of this book: street-level bureaucrats are public officials (or fulfilling public tasks) working in contact with individual citizens, having inherent discretion and functioning as policymakers. The important thing is that all these definitional traits have always shown varying degrees in the empirical reality documented by research achieved so far.

This is why the generally weak amount of used discretion discovered in my research appears as an interesting result for the literature on street-level bureaucracy as the latter has rather dealt with officials who have higher levels of discretion. Such a result reinforces the argument that street-level discretion has to be analysed in terms of a continuum between high and low discretion (Evans and Harris, 2004). While the literature on street-level roles has covered a wide range of functions with varying amounts of discretion, Swiss taxing officers constitute a group of people located near the bottom end of that continuum. Therefore, the interesting question becomes: why is it the case? How do we explain that these taxing officers generally use a weak amount of discretion?

Hence, this result represents an opportunity for thinking about potential explanations of such a negative case. Interestingly enough for the literature, it appears that a specific combination of conditions is particularly conducive to a limited use of discretion at the front line: a strongly specified and condensed regulatory framework; strict and potentially severe external accountability mechanisms; central tasks to be achieved (eligibility assessments, payments) being closely connected to a professional culture of cautiously enforcing regulations; coupled with a structural weakness of taxing officers as a professional group compared to other semi-professional public bureaucracies (at the opposite extreme of teachers or doctors, taxing officers have not organised into unions or professional associations to defend their interests and autonomy). Therefore, such a combination of factors could be of particular interest for analysing other front-line agencies achieving similar tasks (eligibility assessments for social benefits with administrative competence of financial sanctions), whether they are characterised by a relatively low or high degree of discretion used by its agents.

Notes

[1.] English does not provide a fully accurate word for translating the French *taxateurs de l'indemnité de chômage*. Even though the front-line work described in this chapter is not about imposing a tax, but about deciding on the amount of unemployment benefits that will be paid to the beneficiaries, I will use the shorthand expression 'taxing officers' in my subsequent references to this role. In French, a *taxateur* literally means someone who decides on a tax or a sum of money. In the context of the unemployment insurance system, a *taxateur* decides on the sum of money that the insurance funds will pay to beneficiaries.

[2] All interview with front-line workers are coded with the acronym TAXO (taxing officers) followed by a number between 1 to 10 (since 10 people were interviewed). Other codes used are SEMA (service manager of the taxing unit) and LEGO (manager of the legal office). L603-6 means that the interview extract comes from lines 603 to 606 in the original interview transcript.

Part Three
Agents of the state: street-level bureaucracy and law enforcement

---

Law enforcement and policy alienation: coping by labour inspectors and federal police officers

Kim Loyens

From work alienation to policy alienation

Front-line officers in law enforcement agencies inspect whether or not laws are complied with. They operate in various fields of law, such as criminal, environmental, social and labour law. As typical street-level bureaucrats, law enforcement officers perform their tasks with limited resources within a restricted amount of time, while having 'substantial discretion in the execution of their work' (Lipsky, 2010, p 3). These front-line officers might, however, experience frustration when their regulatory activities do not lead to lawbreaking being stopped. This could result from perpetrators finding creative ways to circumvent the rules, while officers' legal powers are limited. Furthermore, when enforcement activities do not actually address societal problems, frustration might arise among these officers. Laws that are created to stop human misery could, in fact, aggravate victims' distress or increase injustice.

Such forms of frustration relate to the concept of 'policy alienation' in the implementation literature. This concept is partly connected to, but clearly distinct from, 'job alienation' (Blauner, 1964) and 'work alienation' (Lipsky, 2010). Blauner's (1964) work on job alienation particularly focuses on how various aspect of the job (eg the impersonal control system) lead to workers feeling powerless. When workers have a lot of discretion, they might feel more powerful, which could reduce job alienation. Lipsky's (2010) research on work alienation confirms that street-level work is alienating when front-line officers experience a lack of discretion to assert influence over the type of sanctions and rewards they issue in dealing with clients. However, he adds that alienation could also result from work that requires officers 'to deny the basic humanity of others' (Lipsky, 2010, p 75) or from feeling unable

– as a result of restraints in time and resources – to fully respond to clients' needs. In other words, work alienation is, in Lipsky's research, intrinsically bound with the relationship between the front-line worker and their clients. Policy alienation, however, deals between front-line workers and their clients. Tummers, Bekkers and Steijn (2009, p 686) define policy alienation as the 'general cognitive state of psychological disconnection from the policy programme being implemented'. The concept is multidimensional and consists of policy powerlessness and policy meaninglessness. The powerlessness dimension refers to 'the expectancy or probability held by the individual that his own behaviour cannot determine the occurrence of the outcomes, or reinforcements, he seeks' (Seeman, 1959, p 784), while the meaninglessness dimension is linked to 'a professional's perception of the contribution the policy makes to a greater purpose' (Tummers et al, 2009, p 689). Street-level bureaucrats experience policy meaninglessness when they consider the contribution of the policy they (need to) implement to the general interest to be rather limited. Previous studies aimed at identifying organisational factors that influence policy alienation (Tummers et al, 2009) and at explaining how policy alienation impacts change willingness (Tummers, 2012). However, more research is needed on how street-level bureaucrats cope with the tensions and frustrations that result from policy alienation and how such coping styles impact the alienation experience.

From classifications of coping styles to systems theory

Coping can be defined in various ways. Folkman and Lazarus (1980, p 223) define coping as 'the cognitive and behavioural efforts made to master, tolerate, or reduce external and internal demands and conflicts among them'. In the street-level bureaucracy literature, coping routines have been referred to as 'defenses against discretion' (Lipsky, 2010, p 149) and even 'strategies of survival' (Satyamurti, 1981, p 82). Different scholars in the street-level bureaucracy tradition have identified various ways of coping that front-line officers develop to deal with tensions and pressures in their job, such as creaming, reutilising and controlling clients (Lipsky, 1980; Moore, 1987; Fineman, 1998; Nielsen, 2006a). These ways of coping are, however, particularly aimed at trying to achieve a fair and manageable workload. In other words, they are a way of dealing with work alienation, and thus not explicitly linked to dealing with policy alienation. To broaden the perspective, inspiration can be drawn from the general coping literature. Skinner and colleagues (2003) have developed a model of 12 core families of coping, which each consist of several ways of coping (see also Skinner and Zimmer-Gembeck, 2007; Zimmer-Gembeck and Skinner, 2011). Tummers, Bekkers, Vink and Musheno (2015) have enriched this literature by conducting a systematic review with the central aim to integrate scholarly work on coping in the domain of policy implementation and clinical psychology, on the basis of which they constructed a classification of ways of coping in policy implementation.

Previous scholarly work on coping – both within and beyond the street-level bureaucracy literature – can provide useful inspiration for the identification of coping styles in this study. However, this study aims at bringing this literature further by also addressing the issue of how these coping styles impact street-level bureaucrats' alienation experience. In other words, the question is asked as to whether the coping styles that street-level bureaucrats use either reduce or increase feelings of policy meaninglessness. Systems theory is proposed as a useful perspective to shed some light on this issue. In this theory, a system (eg an organization) is defined as 'a set of components interacting with each other' (Berrien, 1968, p 32) that has 'boundaries which delineate them from some broader suprasystem' (Kast and Rosenzweig, 1973, p 11), such as the economy, the legal and political systems, or social institutions (Harrison et al, 1999, p 45). Systems theory further suggests that organisational systems are dynamic and change through positive and negative feedback mechanisms, which are considered to be the two basic forces that explain how a system is maintained (Jervis, 1997).

This chapter focuses on how enforcement officers in a specific organisational system (ie the Belgian labour inspection and federal police) deal with a particular policy (ie the federal immigration and asylum policy in Belgium), which is one element of the broader suprasystem. The central research question that will be addressed in this chapter is: 'How do labour inspectors and police officers cope with the policy meaninglessness that they experience in implementing the federal immigration and asylum policy in Belgium and how do these coping styles impact street-level bureaucrats' alienation experience?' In this study, coping will be understood as positive and negative feedback mechanisms, in which 'positive' and 'negative' are not used in a normative way, but in the tradition of systems theory. The former refers to a process in which, more or less like a vicious circle, a phenomenon's characteristics are constantly being reinforced (6, 2003, p 399). Applied to the topic of this chapter, positive feedback occurs when enforcement officers deal with the frustrations of policy alienation in a rather fatalistic (or alienated) way by, for example, resigning themselves to their fate or burying their heads in the sand. Typical for positive feedback is that a phenomenon ultimately radicalises itself. Then, feelings of alienation encourage alienated behaviour that, in its turn, reinforces the feelings of alienation. Negative feedback, on the other hand, is 'transformational', leading to the system 'deviating from a prescribed course and ... readjust[ing] to a new steady state' (Kast and Rosenzweig, 1972, p 450). Applied to the topic of this chapter, this means that other coping styles are used to break the vicious circle created by positive feedback. Enforcement officers then attempt to reduce feelings of alienation. This study aims to identify the coping styles that street-level bureaucrats apply that either reinforce (positive feedback) or reduce (negative feedback) policy alienation.

Methodology

The central research is addressed by means of a comparative case study. The following section will further elaborate on the methodological choices that have been made, focusing, respectively, on the general research design, the ethnographic data collection methods and the approach of sophisticated inductivism.

Comparative case study design

A comparative case study has been conducted in two field organisations of a Belgian labour inspectorate department (INSP1 and INSP2) and two investigative units of the Belgian federal police (POL1 and POL2) in a medium-sized and a large judicial district. The units that are included in the study consist of eight to 16 street-level bureaucrats and one to three supervisors. To ensure comparability of both groups of street-level bureaucrats, the choice was made to focus on how the respondents deal with investigations in the overlapping domain of illegal employment and economic exploitation, which is only one part of their job description. Policy meaninglessness is particularly high in such issues as a result of the ambiguous and ineffective immigration and asylum policy in Belgium (as will be illustrated later), making this an interesting case.

The labour inspectors in this study perform inspections on illegal employment, unregistered work violations and labour conditions. Labour inspectors' legal discretion in Belgium is founded on the Labour Inspection Law (16 November 1972) and has remained largely unchanged with the introduction of the new Social Penal Code (6 June 2010). They have the authority to respond to the aforementioned types of violations in a threefold way: (1) giving a warning (implying no immediate consequences for the employer); (2) offering employers the chance to rectify the violation (eg retrospective payment of deprived wages or social security taxes, improvement of labour conditions); and (3) making a formal report, after which the public prosecutor could dismiss the case or prosecute the employer. When labour inspectors encounter illegal workers during inspections, they should call the local police, who will put those workers in custody to await the decision of the Public Service of Immigration Affairs.

The federal police officers in this study conduct investigations on human exploitation and trafficking in human beings. They cooperate with a public prosecutor specialised in these matters, who formally leads the investigation, or with an examining magistrate if special coercive measures are needed (eg telephone tap, infiltration, systematic observation, arrest). In practice, these police officers first discuss the general strategy with the public prosecutor, after which they take the necessary investigative steps. Unlike labour inspectors, Belgian police officers do not have the discretion to give a warning or offer perpetrators the chance to rectify the violation (see Article 40 of the Belgian Law of the Police Function and Article 53 of the Belgian Code of Criminal Proceedings). When they encounter illegal workers during inspections, they should arrest them to await the decision of the Public Service of Immigration Affairs.

Ethnographic research methods

Data collection was carried out by using several ethnographic research methods (Hammersley and Atkinson, 1995). In particular, data were collected during 21 months (between September 2009 and May 2011) through approximately 555 hours of observation and informal conversation, and approximately 118 hours of in-depth interviewing with 59 respondents (ie 42 street-level bureaucrats, nine supervisors, five regional directors and three magistrates).[1] The observations and informal conversations aimed at gaining insight into the work context of labour inspectors and police officers. Particular attention went to analysing how these street-level bureaucrats perceive their job, which factors contribute to policy meaninglessness, which coping styles they apply to deal with it and how this impacts their experience of alienation. For this purpose, the researcher accompanied the respondents in as many different situations as possible (eg inspections, house searches, interrogations, meetings and informal meals), during both day and night, on weekdays and on the weekend. In addition, the researcher attended several classes that newly recruited inspectors need to take as part of their one-year internship in the organisation before they can be officially appointed. The observations and informal conversations were summarised in detailed reports. In addition, in-depth interviews were conducted in which both groups of street-level bureaucrats were asked to think about recent investigations in which they had experienced policy meaninglessness. They were asked to give a detailed narrative of the situation and how they dealt with it. The interviews were recorded and transcribed literally. The combination of these qualitative data collection methods – which can be considered a type of within-methods triangulation (Denzin, 1978) – resulted in rich data and 'thick description' (Geertz, 1973). The data were analysed with the software Nvivo using topic coding and analytic coding (Richards and Morse, 2007).

Analytic generalisation and sophisticated inductivism

The empirical findings discussed in this chapter result from a qualitative, exploratory case study in a relatively small number of research settings. The decisions that are analysed are thus not necessarily representative for labour inspectors' and police officers' coping behaviours in general. However, the goal of this qualitative study is not generalisation to a wider population, as in quantitative research, but theory-building by developing hypotheses that can be tested in future research, which can be perceived as analytic generalisation (Smaling, 2003; Yin, 2003). In this process of theory-building, an iterative-inductive approach is used, which starts from the premises that 'all data are theory driven' and that the 'researcher should enter into an ongoing simultaneous process of deduction and induction, of theory building, testing and rebuilding' (Ezzy, 2002, p 10). This approach has been referred to as 'sophisticated inductivism', in which theory is considered the 'precursor, medium and outcome' of the study (O'Reilly, 2005, p 27). Insights from previous research (as presented in the previous parts) will thus provide an important source of inspiration for this study, without them strictly guiding data collection and analysis. In other words, the iterative-inductive approach is merely used to organise the rich and 'messy' data of this ethnographic study in a well-considered, focused and consistent manner.

Various sources of policy meaninglessness

As explained earlier, this study has been conducted in units that investigate human exploitation. Such crimes bring about tragedy and distress for victims, who are often trafficked by criminal organisations from less prosperous countries to more wealthy areas in which they are either employed in illegal sectors (such as the prostitution industry) or in legal sectors under degrading conditions. Victims' illegal status, lack of foreign-language skills and outstanding debt to their traffickers add to their precarious situation. Investigating such crimes is not an easy task because they are often hidden and covert, and therefore extremely difficult to detect. Moreover, enforcement officers who conduct such investigations regularly doubt whether their actions adequately address victims' needs or general societal problems. The latter can be considered a manifestation of policy meaninglessness. It mainly results from the conflict between the policy goal to support the victims and those victims' unwillingness to be saved from their exploiters. According to Article 61 of the Belgian Immigration Law of 15 September 2006 and the ministerial circular on the multidisciplinary approach in human exploitation affairs of 26 September 2008, an illegal person who is exploited can be officially recognised as a victim of human exploitation under three conditions: (1) they have to file a complaint with the police against the perpetrators; (2) they have to accept support from a recognised refugee centre; and (3) they have to abandon the network in which they are exploited. Illegal workers or prostitutes who reside in Belgium and comply with these conditions can obtain a Belgian residence permit if the information they provide leads to a successful investigation. However, several respondents in this study explain that many victims of human exploitation do not want to comply with these obligations because they do not feel victimised. Although their living and working conditions are below Belgian legal standards, they prefer being exploited in Belgium over returning to their home country, where living and working conditions are even worse. For example, they earn more money in Belgium (although is it below the minimum wage) and they have a roof over their head, which they perceive to be better than being homeless. Moreover, some illegal workers and prostitutes prefer staying in Belgium because it allows them to regularly send money to their families who stayed abroad. This attitude is encouraged by exploitative employers, who do not use as much aggression as they did in the past, who give the victims more individual freedom and who pay them more than they would earn in their home country. Although this improved treatment is obviously a good evolution, it might discourage victims from filing a complaint against their exploiters, leading to government officials being unable to stop exploitation.

When exploited illegal workers do not cooperate with the police, the only legal option that police officers have is detaining them and contacting the Public Service of Immigration Affairs, which will most likely order the forced repatriation of the 'victims' to their home country or give them an order to voluntarily leave the country within five days, which is scarcely possible to enforce. By not complying with the procedural provisions of the exploitation victim recognition policy, the 'victims' thus risk being victimised again. Police officers in this study express disgust with their share in this 'dirty' work. This can be illustrated by referring to the arrest of three Romanian prostitutes during an inspection of a brothel. Because these victims did not want to file a complaint against the manager of the brothel or their traffickers, the police officers had no other option than to arrest them and await the decision of the Public Service of Immigration Affairs. One of the involved police officers stated afterwards:

> "And I think it's so pathetic because, you know, we do an inspection and the only result is that those girls are put on a plane tomorrow. Tonight, they have to sleep in a stinking cell in police department X.... Those cells stink like hell. And we have to put the victims in there!... Then, you pick them up in a van, almost like the Nazis transported the Jews by train. You drop them off at the transit centre and there they have to stay behind barbed wire in order to be deported."

The police officers in this study experience policy meaningless not only because they cannot save victims from the criminal underworld if they do not cooperate, but also because they are aware that many victims who are repatriated later return to Belgium, which creates a vicious circle that they are unable to stop.

Labour inspectors experience similar kinds of policy alienation because they perceive a conflict of interest between the official policy goal to stop labour exploitation and workers' need to earn money (if necessary, even through illegal work). The labour inspectors in this study stated that many 'victims' do not inform the labour inspectors of being exploited because they perceive the exploitation to be a win–win situation, in which employers are able to employ cheap workers and they are themselves grateful to be employed because their illegal or low socio-economic status does not give them any alternative. In addition, many labour inspectors perceived some of their actions to be useless, in a similar way as the aforementioned police officers. A particular labour inspector stated: "If you let an illegal person be arrested, then tomorrow he will be back on the streets. So it's useless." This is confirmed by many other inspectors, who added that most illegal persons only receive an order to leave the country within five days but nevertheless stay in Belgium.

This section has illustrated that various sources of policy meaninglessness can be identified in the fight against human exploitation. The next section will focus on how the labour inspectors and police officers in this study dealt with this type of policy alienation and how these coping styles influenced their alienation experience.

Police officers and labour inspectors coping with fatalism

In this study, five ways of coping to deal with policy meaninglessness were manifested, two of which are a form of positive feedback that reinforces feelings of alienation and three of which are a form of negative feedback that attempt to reduce them. An overview of these ways of coping, as well as an illustration of how they are applied by the street-level bureaucrats, is shown in Table 6.1.

Coping as a form of positive feedback

The positive feedback type of coping is not aimed at mitigating or decreasing policy meaninglessness, but at reconciling oneself to the situation. Two such coping styles were observed: acquiescence and emotional habituation. While the former can be understood as a conscious coping style, the latter seems to occur at a rather unconscious level.

Acquiescence

As explained earlier, police officers and labour inspectors often consider their actions towards illegal workers to be ineffective because most of them immediately return to Belgium when repatriated or are released shortly after being arrested. Several police officers in POL1 explained that the importance of such arrests lies merely in drawing the workers' attention to their illegal residential status. To cope with such policy meaninglessness, they reconcile themselves to the fact that their efforts have only little impact, which, in this study, is conceptualised

Table 6.1: Five ways of coping with policy meaninglessness

WAYS OF COPING	ILLUSTRATION
Positive feedback	
Acquiescence	"Realise that what you do is just a drop in the ocean." (Instructor in INSP) "Well, it's what they say, all we do is move paper around." (Inspector in INSP2)
Emotional habituation	"Yes, indeed, the first time it really gets to you. The second time it is still rather difficult, but ... you get used to it." (Inspector in INSP1) "It is hard, but you get tougher." (Inspector in INSP1)
Negative feedback	
Do your job from a sense of duty	"I think it is your duty to just do your job, just do what is expected of you." (Inspector in INSP1) "I am not convinced that victims should be put in a police cell like criminals, but the procedure prescribes it, so I comply." (Police officer in POL2)
Get your share	"We didn't solve organised crime or round up a gang, but here they say: 'Yes! We are rid of the zero in the administrative arrest list'." (Police officer in POL1)
Bond with the victim	"What I prefer to do is keep them here, try to bond with them, hope that when they see something go wrong in the criminal underworld or themselves experience something they don't like, that they will say: 'I will call X'." (Police officer in POL1)

as 'acquiescence'. A similar attitude can be found among labour inspectors. A labour inspector in INSP2 explained how she sees her job: "Well, it's what they say, all we do is move paper around." She explained that a lot of the reports she makes and sends to the public prosecutor only lead to the perpetrator being condemned to pay a fine, after which the latter can continue committing fraud. By trying to accept that her role is only to 'move paper' from her desk to the public prosecutor's desk, she tried to resign herself to the idea that she can only barely affect societal problems. This was also emphasised by an instructor in the inspection department under study who teaches newly recruited inspectors. During one of the classes that was observed, he emphasised that, as an inspector, you should always look at things in perspective and "realise that what you do is just a drop in the ocean". This coping strategy can be considered an example of what has been called 'the skill of powerlessness' (Loyens, 2012). It also relates to 'acceptance', which Skinner and colleagues (2003) consider an example of 'accommodation'.

Emotional habituation

The second type of positive feedback coping – emotional habituation – results from continuous exposure to manifestations of policy meaninglessness. Several labour inspectors explained that the first time they encountered illegal workers was quite shocking because they then had to call the police, who treated these victims almost as if they were criminals because they did not want to cooperate. A respondent in INSP1 stated: "Yes, indeed, the first time it really gets to you. The second time it is still rather difficult, but ... you get used to it." One of his colleagues confirmed this by saying: "I have often had the remark that you cannot be a social worker in this job.... It is hard, but you get tougher." A young labour inspector in INSP2 explained that while he still feels sorry for illegal workers being arrested by the police, more experienced inspectors have habituated themselves to the idea that illegal workers who do not comply with the stipulations of the exploitation victim recognition legislation are to be put in custody. This way of coping strongly relates to the cognitive phenomenon of normalisation that Cohen (2001 pp 188–9) explains in his seminal book *States of denial*: 'What was once seen as disturbing and anomalous – a sense that things are not as they should be – now becomes normal, even tolerable.' As acquiescence, emotional habituation does not reduce feelings of policy meaninglessness, but it does help labour inspectors to deal with it by making them emotionally numb and disengaging them from the misery of exploitation victims that only seems to increase when being arrested.

Coping as a form of negative feedback

Street-level bureaucrats also use strategies in an attempt to reduce the fatalism of policy meaninglessness. From the perspective of systems theory, this can be conceptualised as a form of negative feedback. In this study, three such types of coping have been identified: the style of 'Do your job from a sense of duty'; the opportunistic style of 'Get your share'; and the emphatic style of 'Bond with the victim'.

Do your job from a sense of duty

Several respondents in all four settings explained that every agency has its role and responsibilities. Even though the actions of individual enforcement officers might not always lead to the aspired results, they are convinced that they should dutifully do their job. A police officer in POL2 stated: "I am not convinced that victims should be put in a police cell like criminals, but the procedure prescribes it, so I comply". By referring to the procedure, which is part of a legitimate system of rules and laws, individual police officers do not feel personally responsible for being unable to really help victims. They consider themselves to be just one link in the chain. Rather than becoming emotionally numb (as in emotional habituation, which increases the alienation experience), they emphasised the legitimacy of the criminal justice system that they are a part of when implementing this policy, thereby actively justifying for their acts. Moreover, they also refered to victims' responsibility: if they cooperate they receive help, but if they do not cooperate, they have to bear the consequences themselves. A police officer in POL1 stated: "If illegal prostitutes refuse to give a statement, then you cannot save them; all you can do is let them be repatriated." This is linked to a sense of duty or an inner obligation to having to perform one's role. This way of coping is also observed in the studied labour inspections, which is illustrated in the following quote of an inspector in INSP1:

> "Look, I truly sympathise with the illegal person for whom I called the police, but that does not stop me from having him arrested, and running after him if he flees. And if the police will take him away and he will be repatriated, then I will have compassion for him … but that does not keep me from doing my job, like some other colleagues. Because then I think you are doing the wrong thing. I think it is your duty to just do your job, just do what is expected of you."

Also in INSP2, some respondents stated that doing one's job is the only correct way of coping with policy meaninglessness. While they mostly dislike calling the police, they are convinced that they have no other legal options. One inspector explained that when he encounters illegal persons who do not want to return to their home country, he tries to "act like a robot, because if you would act like a human being then you would not call the police". He adds that sometimes you need "a heart of stone", but you can only just do your job.

Get your share

Some street-level bureaucrats in this study responded to policy meaninglessness in an entirely different, and rather opportunistic, way. They explained that in situations in which you cannot address victims' need by performing your official role, you should at least try to personally gain something from the situation. Hence, you should aim at getting your share and thereby trying to compensate for the frustration that those situations bring about. In POL1, this coping style is expressed by perceiving the 'meaningless' situation from a performance-oriented perspective. This police unit had been criticised over the past few years by the general director and the public prosecutor for not having delivered the aspired results, in terms of the number of arrests, number of investigations and number of coercive measures used. When illegal persons who refuse cooperation are arrested, some police officers in this unit applaud the arrest because it is beneficial for the performance indicators, particularly the number of arrests. Not all police officers in this unit appreciate this performance management attitude, as illustrated in the following quote:

> "What I am averse to is that a colleague here then states: 'Oh wow you have got three administrative arrests!' No, we have nothing, Kim. There are two options. One, they come back and continue working in the Belgian prostitution business. Two, they don't come back, but start working in the prostitution business in X (Eastern European country), for a lot less money with nastier men. We didn't solve organised crime or round up a gang, but here they say: 'Yes! We are rid of the zero in the administrative arrest list'."

Some labour inspectors in this study also used this coping style, albeit with a different motive. During a particular inspection, a labour inspector decided not to call the police when she encountered an illegal worker. On the contrary, she decided to let him continue working. However, her main motive was not to show compassion to the illegal worker. She explained that having this illegal worker arrested does not add anything to her investigation because the employer can be convicted without the illegal worker having to be repatriated. Contacting the police would only cost her time and administrative burden, without it being beneficial for society or for her specific investigation. Therefore, she only made a report against the employer for the detected crime. By allowing this illegal worker to continue working, she bent the rules (which are, in her opinion, useless), but simultaneously 'gets her share' by making a report on the basis of which the employer will most likely be convicted. Moreover, she avoids losing time. This way of coping is related to the problem-solving kind of rule bending that benefits various actors (Tummers et al, 2013, p 26).

Bond with the victim

The third and final way in which the street-level bureaucrats in this study (particularly police officers) tried to reduce feelings of policy meaninglessness is a rather empathic way of coping. As explained earlier, police officers who encounter illegal persons who do not want to file a complaint have to arrest them and await the decision of the Public Service of Immigration Affairs. However, by doing so, victims are often condemned to return to worse living conditions than in Belgium and police officers are still not able to start an investigation against their exploiters. Therefore, police officers in this study sometimes tried a different approach, as explained by a respondent in POL1:

> "If I enter a brothel and I see three girls who like working there, whose freedom is not restricted, who have come to Belgium of their own free will … and they don't want to leave, they feel okay, they feel fine, they do not feel exploited, they work in a good atmosphere … then arresting them and letting them be repatriated is not useful for me. I don't gain anything from it. If I arrest them, the manager of the brothel will probably not be prosecuted, neither will the pimp, but, in the end, those girls will be screwed the most. What I prefer to do is keep them here, try to bond with them, hope that when they see something go wrong in the criminal underworld or themselves experience something they don't like, that they will say: 'I will call X [respondent]'."

By bonding with the victim, this police officer tried to avoid the negative effects of applying the official procedure. This would, in his opinion, only bring misery to the victims without offering any options to help them. This way of coping relates to the political reaction of professionals to work pressure, which is aimed at creating coalitions to tackle its sources (Hupe and Van der Krogt, 2013). In this case, a coalition is formed with the street-level bureaucrats' clients (ie exploitation victims), who are considered valuable assets in the joint fight against human exploitation crimes, with the central aim to subvert or bypass the policy that brings about policy meaninglessness.

Conclusion

In his seminal work, Lipsky (2010) already introduced the problem of alienation in front-line work. He focused on work alienation, which is strongly linked to the relationship that street-level bureaucrats have with their clients. This chapter focused on the type of alienation in which front-line workers become estranged from the policy they (have to) carry out, rather than from the job or the clients they deal with. It particularly addressed the question of how law enforcement officers cope with the tensions that a contested policy brings about and how these coping styles impact the alienation experience. The idea of 'coping' is not new in the street-level bureaucracy literature. Various authors (Lipsky, 2010; Moore, 1987; Fineman, 1998; Nielsen, 2006a) have identified ways in which front-line officers deal with the constraints and pressures that come with the job. Whereas these coping mechanisms explain how front-line workers try to achieve a fair and manageable workload, or deal with work alienation, this study aimed to illustrate how front-line workers cope with policy alienation and how these coping styles influence the alienation experience. By bringing together insights from various strands of literature (eg street-level bureaucracy, policy implementation and coping), this study aimed to broaden our understanding of the repertoire of front-line coping and its effects. In particular, this study has led to the identification of five coping styles that the enforcement officers in the police and inspection agencies under study apply to deal with the alienation they experience in implementing the Belgian asylum and migration policy. Inspired by systems theory, two of these coping styles can be considered positive feedback mechanisms that reinforce feelings of fatalism: acquiescence and emotional habituation. However, the street-level bureaucrats in this study also tried to reduce feelings of policy alienation by applying the coping styles 'just do your job from a sense of duty', 'get your share' and 'bond with the victim', which are conceptualised as negative feedback mechanisms.

These results could be beneficial for practitioners and researchers. As for practitioners, this study shows that front-line officers in enforcement agencies, being overwhelmed by policy alienation, can sometimes find ways to reduce the frustration and tensions that result from policy alienation. Street-level bureaucrats in similar (and possibly also in other types of) organisations could thus find support and inspiration for their own practice in the coping styles presented here.

Researchers could benefit from this exploratory study by further exploring and complementing the proposed model. Both qualitative and quantitative studies would be beneficial. As for the latter, quantitative survey research could be done to study the extent to which various groups of law enforcement officers in different organisations within different countries apply the five coping styles, and whether or not the respondents consider them constructive ways of dealing with policy alienation. In addition, more in-depth qualitative studies on coping with policy alienation are needed. On the one hand, the nature and origin of policy alienation in various policy domains could be studied, taking the political-administrative setting into account. Relevant questions are whether and, if so, how asylum and migration policies in other countries evoke similar feelings of policy alienation among law enforcement officers as have been identified in this study, and whether other policies that are less (or more) ambiguous result in similar manifestations of policy alienation. On the other hand, more ethnographic research in law enforcement agencies within various countries would deepen our understanding of how these street-level bureaucrats cope with policy alienation. Relevant questions are the following: are the coping styles identified here relevant for police officers and labour inspectors in other countries? Do enforcement officers in other types of enforcement agencies apply similar ways of coping? Can other coping styles be identified that reinforce or reduce the policy alienation experienced by enforcement officers? In conclusion, this study has provided inspiring tools to support front-line workers in law enforcement (or other public) agencies and valuable building blocks for future research on street-level bureaucrats' coping with policy alienation.

Note

[1.] To protect the respondents' identity, neither the judicial district where the organisations are located nor the individual characteristics (such as age or years of experience) of the respondents will be mentioned. Male and female pronouns will be used randomly. The respondents' quotes were freely translated from Dutch by the researcher.

SEVEN

Law enforcement behaviour of regulatory inspectors

Vibeke Lehmann Nielsen

Introduction

Every year, almost every day, and in almost every country in the world, regulatory inspectors working in different policy areas get into their cars and go on inspection visits. Before the visits, they have spent some time at the office answering emails, returning phone calls and going through the case files of the businesses that they are going to. The businesses are often quite various; some are large, some small; some are public businesses, others are private; some are on the verge of bankruptcy, others are booming. Some businesses have everything under control and may even have trained employees responsible for observing the regulations. Other businesses have no idea about the regulations and what the inspectors are telling them. During a year, it adds up to several thousand kilometres on the road, hundreds of handshakes, countless instructions, injunctions, recommendations and agreements, and a huge number of meetings, telephone conversations and follow-ups.

According to Lipsky's seminal definition, regulatory inspectors are street-level bureaucrats (SLBs) since they 'interact directly with citizens in the course of their jobs, and have substantial discretion in the execution of their work' (Lipsky, 2010 (1980, p 3)). Regulatory inspection includes health and safety, environment, fire precaution, veterinary inspection, nursing homes, and so on. As all SLBs, regulatory inspectors work at the interface between citizens and the state and they act as state agents, but because direct citizen interaction is difficult to assess and monitor, regulatory inspectors exercise considerable discretion, and, as such, they have significant opportunities to influence the implementation of public policies (Meyers and Nielsen, 2012). This presents two important questions: how and why do the dynamics of the interaction between inspector and regulatee affect the behaviour and discretionary choices of regulatory inspectors? And how does the behavioural outcome of the interaction fit with the normative requirements and expectations about those who work as 'law enforcers at the frontier of the state'?

Based primarily on Danish empirical studies in various policy areas, this chapter focuses on the behaviour and discretionary choices of regulatory inspectors. Focus is on the interaction between inspectors and regulatees, and on how and why the dynamics of the interaction between regulatory agents and regulated stakeholders affect the outcome of the interaction. Hence, within this chapter, the central question is the behaviours of the individual SLB (equivalent to 'behaviours' in Hupe, Hill and Buffat's Table 1.1 in Chapter One). However, I argue that the concept of behaviour should be split into two, namely, *enforcement behaviours of the individual SLB* and *interaction behaviours* arising within the interaction between the client and SLB. These two understandings of behaviours should be split because variation in interaction behaviour explains variation in enforcement behaviour. In other words, 'interaction, and hence client, matters' in explaining SLBs' discretionary authority enforcement behaviour.

First, regulation is defined and its central characteristics are discussed. Concepts to measure and understand the behaviour of the regulatory inspector are presented. Here, there is a particular focus on enforcement styles. This concept was developed by May and Winter (1999, 2000; Winter and May, 2001) using Danish data concerning the environmental inspection of farmers. It leads to a discussion of the need to conceptually differentiate between the characteristics of the actions of the regulatory inspector and those of the interactions between the inspector and regulated business. The third and last section discusses how and why the dynamics of the interaction between regulatory inspectors and regulated stakeholders affect the discretionary choices of the inspector and the outcome of the interaction by drawing on my own studies of Danish inspectors' enforcement of occupational health and safety, environmental, and fire regulations. Hence, the empirical material behind the chapter is two separate – Danish – studies. May and Winter's study was conducted through surveys among famers and environmental inspectors of farms in Denmark, while my own study likewise was conducted through a survey among inspectors and regulated businesses in Denmark, but covered both occupational health and safety, environmental, and fire regulations. Furthermore, my study covered data registered through case-file reading. While agency level was explicitly studied in the first study, it was controlled for in the second.

Regulation and law enforcement: the command, control and sanctioning task of the modern state

Regulation is a popular subject of study in disciplines across and beyond the social sciences and from different theoretical and methodological perspectives. As a consequence, regulation has many different definitions (Jordana and Levi-Faur, 2004). In its broadest sense, regulation encompasses all mechanisms of social control, including unintentional and non-state processes, while in its narrowest sense, it is defined as 'a specific form of governance: a set of authoritative rules, often accompanied by some administrative agency, for monitoring and enforcing compliance' (Baldwin et al, 1998, p 3). If we focus on public regulatory inspectors, this last definition is the relevant one. This does not mean that law enforcement tools such as command, control and sanctioning are the only tools available to regulatory inspectors in changing people's behaviour. They may offer guidance, or the enforcement may be supplemented with economic incentives. Nevertheless, command, control and sanctioning remain the core elements of the regulatory inspector's job, and they define the interaction between inspector and regulated business as an interaction that always takes place in the shadow of the state's legitimate power. Hence, regulatory inspectors 'deliver obligations, rather than services' (Sparrow, 2000, p 2), and they have the power to sanction. Another feature of regulation is that it seeks not to maintain the status quo, but to address the externalities that a system without regulation would otherwise create (Kagan, 1984, p 2). Hence, regulation is a law-based, politically defined restriction of people's freedom to act, and is mostly reasoned by reference to the common good.

These fundamental features lead to certain characteristics of regulatory inspection in general. First and foremost, the regulated businesses do not represent an infinite demand on the regulatory inspector. Most businesses would prefer to run their business without the interference of regulatory inspectors. This characteristic is contrary to most SLBs within public services and it fits badly with Lipsky's argument which claims that incessant client demands are a precondition for coping. Since there is no stressful never-ending demand for more and better services, there should not – according to Lipsky – be any reason for coping (Nielsen, 2006a). Second, regulatory inspection of businesses is often perceived – especially by the regulatee – as potentially criminalising of law-abiding citizens who create value to society in terms of workplaces and revenue. Third, the regulatory rules are often complex and not common knowledge. Therefore, the inspectors meet lawbreakers among the regulatees who unintentionally broke the law. Fourth, regulatory work is characterised by the fact that many breaches are of controversial nature. Standards, measurements and boundaries are often debatable and only presumed correlates of the desired outcome. What level of emissions harms the environment and/or the public health? How dangerous is a two-decibel breach of the noise standards to employees?

Fifth, since leaving the country is not an option to most businesses, another characteristic of regulation is that – to most – it is hypothetical to exit the interaction. To file a complaint or an appeal is, in most countries and within most regulator policy areas, a formal, legal opportunity, but it requires knowledge and resources. Furthermore, sixth, most regulatory inspections are an ongoing interaction, and the inspector and the regulatee will meet over and over again as long as the firm stays in business. However, the frequency of interaction is commonly fairly low – perhaps only once a year or every second year.

In addition, the task of a regulatory inspector has the classic features of an SLB. It involves a direct citizen/client interaction that is difficult to regulate, assess and monitor, and it gives the inspector great latitude as far as how to act before, during and after inspection, and in case of problems, but, at the same time, inspectors depend upon the cooperation of the regulated business. Additionally, regulatory inspectors are public employees and, as such, they are not employed with a free mandate, but act on behalf of their political and administrative principals (Meyers and Nielsen, 2012). Finally, we must not forget that the behaviour and specific decisions of SLBs have consequences (sometimes very serious ones) for others. First, they have overall economic consequences for society and taxpayers in general since the SLBs' working efficiency, decision-making, choice of action, and so on influence government spending. Moreover, their behaviour and authoritative decisions have substantial consequences for the individual regulatees in terms of instructions, injunctions and recommendations that interfere in some way or other with their way of running their businesses.

Since inspectors act on behalf of others, and since these acts may have substantial consequences, they must demonstrate accountability towards several parties: the principals, the regulated businesses and external stakeholders, for example, non-governmental organisations (NGOs), the neighbours of the regulated business and its employees and consumers. Hence, regulatory inspectors have to exercise discretionary judgement in a situation with many, often conflicting, interests and a great deal of uncertainty in interaction with the regulatees on whom they impose restrictions, duties and indirect moral statements.

Finally, it should be noted that by focusing on public regulation and regulatory inspectors instead of, say, social services, we focus on a group of SLBs that often interact with a highly heterogeneous and quite powerful group of 'clients' (Nielsen, 2005, 2007). By way of example, there is a world of difference between the knowledge and the economic and political resources of the local motor mechanic compared with a large international enterprise in relation to environmental regulation. Contrary to many studies of SLBs, which focus on the interaction with the unemployed, social clients, criminals, the early retired and so on, regulatory inspectors interact with a group of clients where – at least a good part of them – may be comparatively resourceful regarding knowledge and economic and political power. In addition, society's social support for the businesses is mostly positive (Schneider and Ingram, 1993, 1997; Winter et al, forthcoming), but it may vary within the group of regulated businesses.

Discretion, interaction, interdependence and a heterogeneous but comparatively powerful group of clients increase the likelihood of clients' success in affecting the regulatory inspectors' behaviour, but with different weight. Therefore, a worry might be that variation in administrative practice and, hence, differential treatment occurs (Wood, 1981; Jacobsen et al, 1982; Smith, 1988; Nielsen, 2002). However, differential treatment is not the only potential effect of regulatory inspectors trying to cope with the special features of their work task. Within the literature on regulation and business compliance, the following three worries in particular have been identified (Bardach and Kagan, 1982; Baldwin et al, 1998):

- too lenient law enforcement and, hence, ineffectiveness;
- too harsh law enforcement and, therefore, over-regulation and illegitimate use of power; and
- differential treatment.

The normative requirements imply that the regulatory inspector's law enforcement behaviour should be effective, reasonable and just. How the regulatory inspectors act and navigate the troubled and conflicting waters of their job is discussed later. This discussion is, as mentioned, based on findings of Danish studies of different regulatory inspectors. The findings tell us how to conceptualise the inspectors' enforcement behaviour during different aspects of the regulatory enforcement process, how to understand the behaviour and, in particular, how the dynamics of the interaction between regulatory inspectors and regulated stakeholders affect the inspectors' discretionary choices.

As mentioned, we hereby highlight the importance of splitting our conceptual understanding of SLB behaviour into two, and hence differentiate between *enforcement behaviours* and *interaction behaviours* arising within the interaction between the client and SLB.

The inspectors' enforcement behaviour: the tale of a concept

The literature on regulation and regulatory inspectors has traditionally used the word 'regulatory style' to desribe the ways of implementing and enforcing regulation (Bardach and Kagan, 1982; Kagan and Scholz, 1984; Braithwaite et al, 1987; Scholz et al, 1991; Kagan, 1994; Gormley, 1998; May and Burby, 1998). However, like all theoretical concepts, 'regulatory style' constantly develops. It has had a number of 'teething problems' (Kagan, 1994; May and Burby, 1998). First, the different styles have had a variety of names. Harsh enforcement is termed 'legalistic', 'deterrent', 'going-by-book' or 'coercive' enforcement, while a more collaborative style is called 'cooperating', 'flexible', 'accommodating', 'conciliating', 'reasonable' or 'advisory'. Meanwhile, a very soft regulatory style has been termed as either 'soft', 'ritual', 'symbolic', 'easygoing', 'permissive' or 'reluctant' (May and Winter, 2000). Such linguistic variation is confusing, but could be acceptable if it did not cover another problem: that the authors operationalise the concepts in different ways and, hence, attach slightly different meanings to them. For example, in 1984, Kagan derived the regulatory styles 'legalistic', 'accommodating', 'retreatistic' and 'flexible' from both the willingness to punish and the regulatory inspectors' opinion of the regulated businesses: are the businesses on the whole trustworthy? Are most breaches thought to be caused by a lack of knowledge or by calculated greed (Kagan, 1984)? Soon, the question of the regulatory inspector's attitude towards the regulatees was regarded as an explanatory factor instead of a dimension of the behavioural-style concept (Hedge et al, 1988). Some years later, Kagan still named the different styles as 'retreatistic', 'accommodative', 'flexible' and 'legalistic', but another dimension was added, namely, the matter of effort (Kagan, 1994). In other words, effort – often measured by frequency of inspection and/or whether the inspection was reactive (provoked by complaints) or proactive – became part of the operational definition of the style concept. Other studies, however, regarded effort as separate from the matter of style since both a legalistic and a cooperative regulatory style can be performed with high or low levels of activity (Scholz, 1991; May and Burby, 1998). However, to leave out the matter of effort makes it very difficult to identify a more or less symbolic regulatory behaviour since studies show a strong correlation between low effort and a very accommodative regulatory style (Scholz, 1991; May and Burby, 1996; Winter, 1996, p 5).

The differences in defining regulatory styles can primarily be seen as an evolutionary process towards a stricter concept. However, the evolution and debate about the concept uncovered two more fundamental issues concerning how to define and measure regulatory behaviour. First, it highlighted whether or not regulatory style is to be understood as one- or multidimensional (Bardach and Kagan, 1982; Gormley, 1998; May and Burby, 1998). Second, the debate uncovered variation in levels of analysis. Some studies consider style as a micro-phenomenon (Winter, 1994), in the form of the individual supervisor's behaviour towards the regulated firms, while other studies focus on the level of the organisation – that is, the level of the regulatory agency (Braithwaite et al, 1987; May and Burby, 1996).

The confusing multiplicity of names and definitions led to a study of environmental regulation of Danish farmers where May and Winter examined the empirical relationships between the different variables traditionally used to measure regulatory style. Their research (May and Winter, 1999, 2000; Winter and May, 2001; May and Wood, 2003) adds empirical evidence on two aspects. First, they showed that a useful distinction can be made between *agency enforcement strategies* and *inspectors' (agent) enforcement styles*. The label 'enforcement strategy' is best used when referring to the enforcement choices of regulatory agencies, while 'enforcement style' is best used when referring to the behavioural choices of the individual inspector. The crafting of an enforcement strategy entails decisions at the regulatory agency level about what to enforce (targeting and the priority of regulatees), how to allocate resources for inspections and, hence, the frequency of inspection, and which enforcement tools to emphasise (rule enforcement, persuasion, education or management advice) (May and Winter, 2011, p 225). Hence, agency enforcement strategies might be understood as actions at the organisation level made by administrative and political managers concerning task content in respect of the definition of tasks and task priority (see Chapter One). An important point in the work of May and Winter is that choices by agency officials – both administrative and political managers – affect the actions of their inspectors. Agency choices about enforcement strategies set the boundaries for inspectors by establishing priorities and inspection targets. Additionally, the choice of which enforcement tools to emphasise and how much effort to spend provides the toolkit for enforcement actions and limits the scope of the actions of inspectors. Finally, the choice of enforcement strategies serves as a means of 'signalling' to inspectors the desired tone to emphasise as they carry out inspections: in other words, 'management matters'.

Moreover, May and Winter's empirical studies showed that the inspectors' enforcement styles are best depicted by two dimensions, rather than one. They labelled these two dimensions 'formalism' and 'coercion'. The dimensions were measured by the inspectors rating on a five-point scale their typical approach towards regulated entities when considering a set of polar opposite approaches: 1) written versus verbal communication; 2) enforcement through strict rules versus negotiation; 3) compliance through formal rules versus influencing attitudes; 4) rule- versus result-oriented; 5) consistent versus flexible; 6) sceptical versus trusting; and 7) the use of versus the non-use of threats of sanctions (May and Winter, 2011, p 227). Their further research on the two underlying dimensions of enforcement styles suggests that the degree of formalism and coercion employed by inspectors need not go hand in hand (May and Winter, 2000). In practice, they identified three clusters of inspection patterns in the two underlying dimensions of enforcement style. The largest category of Danish inspectors (40%) was identified as having an 'insistent' enforcement style, made up by a moderate score on formalism and a relatively high score on coercion. The second-largest group (37%) scored low on formalism and moderately on the use of coercion, constituting a 'token' enforcement pattern. The remaining 23% scored high on formalism but varied in coercion, constituting a 'rule-bound' enforcement pattern.

However, in studies of differential treatment of regulated businesses based on data from the three Danish regulatory areas of environment, fire precaution and occupational health and safety, I found it fruitful to measure the regulatory style slightly differently, and to further fragment the dimensions of the inspectors' regulatory behaviour (Nielsen, 2002, 2006a, 2006b, 2007). Since the focus of my studies was differential treatment at the street level – that is, if and why business A is treated more harshly than business B by inspector C, even when we control for the history of the overall regulatory performance of A and B – it did not make much sense to measure the inspectors' regulatory behaviour as a *typical approach* towards the regulated entities. Instead, data was a mix of information registered through the reading of actual case files, and through questionnaires that the regulatory inspectors were asked to fill in related to named businesses (equal to the ones registered through the case files). Therefore, instead of the typical approach, the inspector rated the behaviour towards different individual businesses. Furthermore, by focusing on variation and the reasons for variation within each individual inspector's enforcement behaviour across businesses, the character of the *interaction* between inspector and regulatee was hypothesised to play an important role in creating enforcement variation. Consequently, to avoid the risk of mixing causes with consequences, I chose – contrary to May and Winter (1999, 2000, 2011; Winter and May, 2001) – to separate the measures of interaction (eg questions about written versus verbal communication, enforcement through strict rules versus negotiation) from variables measuring the enforcement action/attitude of the inspector (eg questions about sceptical versus trusting, the use versus the non-use of threat of sanctions). To measure the action and attitude of the inspectors towards the regulated businesses, I included direct behaviours that measure the harshness of the authoritative decision (length of respite to mend problems, average sanction – coded on a nine-point scale going from 'doing nothing/acceptance/wait and see' to 'going to the police/legal charge' – and gap between the level of sanctions and gravity of violation) and more indirect attitudes (the use of threats of formal sanctions, personal versus impersonal attitude, sceptical or trusting attitude – in other words, formalism and coercion as uncovered through the studies of May and Winter). Direct behaviour – both length of respite and legal sanction – and, hence, the harshness of authoritative decisions are registered through a review of case files and thus mirrors objective measures of actual behaviour.[1] On the other hand, formalism and coercion are measured through several questionnaire items regarding inspectors' regulatory behaviour and attitudes towards specific named businesses (the same as those studied through the case files). Thus, coercion and formalism were measured more subjectively. Ideally, to ensure source triangulation and, hence, a more valid measure, the regulated businesses could have been asked to answer the same items measuring formalism and coercion. However, positive correlation between harshness in direct behaviour and formalism and coercion enhance the trustworthiness of the inspectors' subjective assessments of their own attitudes. Therefore, all in all, in regard to *enforcement behaviours*, lenient regulatory enforcement was characterised by comparatively long respites and comparatively gentle sanctions; the firm is met with a more personal and trusting attitude and is rarely threatened with formal sanctions. In contrast, harsh enforcement was characterised by comparatively short respites and harsh sanctions compared with the gravity of the violation; the inspector is impersonal and sceptical, and frequently threatens with formal sanctions.

I defined the character of *interaction behaviours* as communicative interaction and operationalised it as 'regularities in the actors' social behaviour that reflect the level of communicative interaction between the inspector and the regulated firm'. Communicative interaction has two dimensions, however: frequency of interaction and quality of interaction. Communicative interactions may never take place or may take place very often, and communication may have no depth at all or it may be very deep, reflecting total reciprocity in sharing information and total recognition of the other actor's interests. Hence, the level of communicative interaction may be viewed on a continuum, from legal control with no communicative interactions at all, other than formal ones, at one extreme, to interactions characterised by a high level of reciprocity and attention at the other extreme; symbolic communicative interactions and different degrees of attention and reciprocity fall in-between these extremes. To enable deeper and more sophisticated analyses, I distinguished between negotiation and cooperation: 'negotiation' is measured on the part of the continuum going from 'no communicative interactions at all' to the point where the regulator and regulatee interact to present their interests and arguments. However, at this point, there is no guarantee that they actually pay attention to each other, or that they regard regulation as a mutual problem. On the other hand, 'cooperation' is measured by the last part of the continuum, going from the end of the measure of 'negotiation' to the point where the regulatee and inspector share responsibility for keeping in touch and for finding mutually acceptable solutions. 'Negotiation' and 'cooperation' were measured through the indicators outlined in Table 7.1. It is important to point out that the character of interaction is not solely defined by the inspector. The regulated business can independently contribute to a relatively high level of interaction. The regulatory inspector cannot just decide on a certain level of interaction.

Controlling for the seriousness of violations, the study showed that public-owned companies are subject to a more lenient inspection than private-owned ones, and that large private companies are subject to a more lenient inspection than small private companies (Nielsen, 2002, 2005). Furthermore, it showed that regulatory behaviour is partly explained by differences in levels of negotiation and cooperation between the business and inspector. Hence, part of the differential treatment in enforcement behaviour may be explained by reference to differences in the character of the interaction between the inspector and regulated firm. To explain variation in the behaviour of the inspector, it therefore seems important to separate interaction behaviour from

Table 7.1: Items measuring negotiation and cooperation within regulatory inspection

Variable	Indicator
Negotiation	Meetings regarding formulation of approvals and other forms of planning (yes/no)
	Meetings regarding problems (yes/no)
	Average number of meetings regarding formulation of approvals and other forms of planning
	Average number of meetings regarding problems
	The political level is involved in inspection issues at the firm
	The head of office is involved in inspection issues at the firm
	The firm's technical arguments are recorded in minutes
	The firm's economic arguments are recorded in minutes
	The inspector communicates by phone with the firm
Cooperation	The firm feels that it has influence on the regulation
	The firm feels that the inspector listens
	The firm reports complaints and accidents
	The firm communicates by phone
	The firm and inspector are equally responsible for keeping in touch

the inspectors' enforcement behaviour and instead include variation in the interaction between the inspector and regulatee as an explanatory factor.

Put together, the reported Danish findings of May and Winter and of Nielsen suggest several points. One is that to separate causes from consequences, it is important to differentiate between behaviours at the levels of, respectively, the agency and the individual regulatory inspectors (agent level) – in other words, to differentiate between the action scale at the agency and individual SLB level. Likewise, to separate causes from consequences, a second point is that our studies of behaviour at the individual SLB level need to differentiate between enforcement behaviours and interaction behaviours. A third point is that the enforcement behaviour of the regulatory inspector may fruitfully be defined as a mix of three dimensions: the two dimensions of regulatory style – formalism and coercion – and a dimension measuring the harshness of the authoritative regulatory decisions. A fourth point is that the style of inspectors varies, not only across individual inspectors, but also across regulated businesses regulated by the same inspector. The lessons from the Danish studies are put together and illustrated in Figure 7.1.

In sum, the enforcement behaviour of regulatory inspectors may fruitfully be conceptualised as mixed patterns of behaviour on three dimensions: formalism, coercion and harshness of authoritative decisions – going from too lenient and, hence, ineffective law enforcement to a

Figure 7.1: Conceptual and causal lessons from the Danish studies of regulatory inspectors

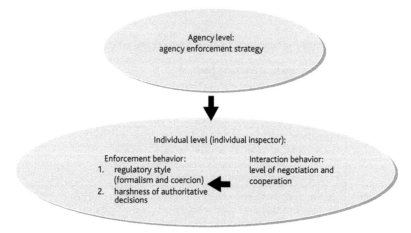

too harsh and therefore perhaps illegitimate use of power. Furthermore, the studies suggest that it may not be a question of either/or. On the contrary, differential treatment with a systematic biased mix of leniency and harshness may be the inspectors' discretionary choice in navigating the waters of multiple expectations of accountability characterised by interdependence and interaction with a heterogeneous – but comparatively powerful – group of clients. Figure 7.1 only illustrates the Danish evidence concerning the conceptualisation and measurement of regulatory inspectors' behaviour, which splits causes from consequences, and does not give a comprehensive model to explain regulatory inspectors' behaviour. The next section focuses on the Danish studies' contribution to explaining the inspectors' discretionary choices. While May and Winter's studies pinpointed the importance of explanatory factors at the agency level (agency enforcement strategy), the next section explores in depth the clusters of factors related to the client (regulatee) and SLB (regulatory inspector) and how the characteristics of these two affect the characteristics of the enforcement and interaction behaviour of the SLB.

Discretionary choices and the dynamics of the interaction

How do we explain the discretionary choices of the regulatory inspectors? Scholars have attempted to explain the variation by pointing to various policy design, organisational, political, situational and personal considerations that shape inspectors' behaviours (Lundqvist, 1980; Hedge et al, 1988; May, 1993, Kagan, 1994; Winter, 2002; see also Chapter One). As the studies of May and Winter show, there is a clear connection between decisions made by agency officials about enforcement strategies and the styles and decisions that the inspectors adopt (May and Winter, 2011). However, inspectors are not public employees who simply follow dictates from above when carrying out their inspections or when taking action once violations are observed. Among scholars of regulation and scholars of SLBs in general – and as mentioned in Chapter One – broad discretion has been pinpointed as the precondition for behavioural variation at the street level (Meyers and Nielsen, 2012).

When explaining variation in street-level bureaucratic behaviour, much focus has been on professional norms, policy preferences, personal beliefs about policy instruments and the target population, their own moral judgements, workload preferences, economic incentives, and so on (Sandfort, 2000; Winter, 2001; Maynard-Moody and Musheno 2003). Less focus has been on the dynamics of the interaction between the client and bureaucrat and how this interaction affects the SLB's behaviour.

However, when explaining differential treatment of regulatees, the Danish studies of environmental, occupational health and safety, and fire precaution inspectors presented in the previous section showed that power resources, such as organisational match and knowledge, directly enable the regulated companies to entice the inspector to a more lenient inspection, or indirectly through a higher degree of negotiation and cooperation between the company and inspector. By possessing local economic strength, the regulatee is able to compel the inspector to negotiate and cooperate more and, hence, to achieve a more lenient inspection (Nielsen, 2002, 2006a). To fully understand the discretionary choices of the SLB, we need to widen the examination of the range of interests that motivate the bureaucrat and the assumptions about the characteristics of the relationship between the SLB and client than mostly considered.

Looking at scholarly work on motivation, it becomes clear that the field of study is complex. Basically, theories of motivation may be divided into three main categories, each focusing on specific structures of interest (Scheuer, 2000). Based on *scientific management*, one might argue that the important interests of the individual are economic (least possible work for most possible money). However, a second category, based on the theories in the school of *Neo-human Relations*, is Maslow's hierarchy of needs. Using this hierarchy as point of departure, it is argued that people seek self-realisation through work (Argyris, 1957, 1964; McGregor, 1960). Hence, the motivational factor is not economic benefits, but rather the actual purpose of the job according to professional norms and policy preferences, and, through that, pride and self-respect. The third school category is the *Human Relations perspective*, which argues that social interests are the basic motivational factor (Roethlisberger and Dickson, 1947; Homans, 1950). According to this view, the individual is, first and foremost, a social creature whose main interest with regard to work is to be part of a social context. However, none of the theories have been able to explain empirical observations satisfactorily. Empirical observations frequently contain more differentiated motives than provided for by the theories (Scheuer, 2000, p 18). Therefore, reducing human beings – and, hence, regulatory SLBs – to 'economic man', 'self-realisation man' or 'social man' may hinder the formulation of sufficiently advanced and nuanced hypotheses about SLB motivation, and, hence, theories that are meaningful as well as capable of explaining actual SLB behaviour. In fact, classic empirical studies show that the 'joy in work' is a complex, almost relative, phenomenon, depending on the job itself, social relations at work, the wage, management and the employee's expectations (Roethlisberger and Dickson, 1947; Goldthorpe et al, 1968a, 1968b, 1969; Burawoy, 1979). To a large degree, contemporary scholars of motivation build upon the insight of the classics mentioned, but instead of viewing the three different 'men' as distinctive categories, most scholars of today regard them as dimensions inherent, to various degrees, in each individual. Claiming that the prime motivator for street-level bureaucratic behaviour is a fair and manageable workload may thus very well be wrong. However, saying that the workload has no effect at all would be equally wrong. The point is that to make a meaningful analysis, we must admit that a plurality of interests motivates people at work. Therefore, a 'complex people' approach may very well be the most fruitful in terms of what motivates the behaviour of SLBs (Scheuer, 2000).

Furthermore, it is well known that people react not only to negative pressure – the stick – but also to positive pressure – the carrot (McGregor, 1960; Barnard, 1968; Herzberg, 1990). In addition, there seems to be no evidence that the different interests have a specific point of saturation; we will always strive to be even more satisfied by minimising frustrations and maximising pleasure. Thus, as Nielsen (2006a) suggests, it may be very useful to regard each possible interest as part of an overall barometer of satisfaction/frustration, where pressure, either positive or negative, on each interest increases the overall satisfaction or frustration and, in continuation of that, causes action. We react to negative pressure because we want to minimise frustration, but we also react to positive pressure because we want to maximise satisfaction. When regarding the motivation of SLBs in this way, it becomes clear that they may be compelled as well as enticed to act, and that the interaction with the clients plays an important role in their everyday challenge of minimising frustration and maximising satisfaction. If, in accordance with theories of Human Relations, we assume that SLBs are interested in, among other things, good social relations with their clients, they may react positively to obliging and understanding clients and negatively to hostile and complaining clients. However, at the same time, in line with Neo-human Relations, we may also assume that SLBs are interested in autonomy in their work tasks. Consequently, we may expect them to react if the client is able, either negatively or positively, to affect the political and/or administrative leaders. However, whether the behavioural discretionary choice of the SLB is caused by a wish to minimise frustration, that is, by negative pressure, or by a wish to maximise satisfaction, that is, by positive pressure, depends on the behaviour of the other person in the interaction, namely, the client. Does it converge with or diverge from the interests of the SLB? This cannot be determined a priori, but, as Haas (1964, p 39, emphasis added) points out, 'the interests and behaviour of others *may* converge – that is to say being unlike, but still possible to be satisfied by the same means'. However, interests and behaviour *may* also diverge. They may be so unlike that neither can be satisfied. Nevertheless, there is no reason to assume that the behaviour of the clients always diverges from the interests of the SLB.

However, as shown in Nielsen (2005, 2006a), determining whether the interests and behaviour of the SLB and the client are converging or diverging is not enough to determine whether the SLB is being enticed or compelled to behave in a certain way. The balance of power is equally important. In case of converging interests between the SLB and client, it is relevant to know whether or not the two actors are strong enough to resist pressure from diverging external factors, for example, scarce resources. If this is the case, the interaction between the inspector and regulated entity may be characterised as a win–win situation, and, if not, a lose–lose situation. On the other hand, in case of diverging interests between the client and bureaucrat, we need to know who, perhaps in alliance with other actors, is the more powerful of the two. If the bureaucrat is the most powerful, it is a win–lose situation to the bureaucrat, who will then act in accordance with their own preferences simply because it provides an opportunity to enhance their own motivation. If the client is the most powerful, it is a lose–win situation to the bureaucrat, who will then be compelled to behave in the way that the client does. Thus, to determine whether the bureaucrat is compelled or enticed to certain behaviour, we must clarify the character of the interaction between the bureaucrat and the client on the following two conditions:

1. Does the client's behaviour diverge from or converge with the interests of the bureaucrat?
2. What are the power balances between the SLB and client, respectively, and between the bureaucrat and client jointly, when compared to other external actors?

Each answer leads to different interaction scenarios between the client and bureaucrat and, therefore, to different conclusions about the reason for the behaviour of the SLB. Making variation in the characteristics of the very interaction leads, at least theoretically, to four different reasons for the SLB's behaviour (Nielsen, 2006a, p 871):

- unconstrained behaviour, the discretionary choice of the SLB is determined by preferences;
- enticement by the client;
- compelled by the client; and
- compelled by external actors.

The outcome depends upon the constellation of interests (broadly defined based on a 'complex man' approach, as discussed earlier) between the actors involved, and on the balance of power characterising the interaction. The argument is illustrated in Figure 7.2.

Therefore, by studying the behaviour of regulatory inspectors and the dynamics of their interactions with the regulated businesses and, hence, focusing on a group of SLBs dealing with a heterogeneous but relatively powerful group of clients, the research reported here contributes to the work on SLBs by clarifying the relation between the SLB and client as a power relation in which the SLB is not necessarily the most powerful actor, and in which the clients by no means have equal preconditions to handle the interaction. Moreover, it pinpoints the need for widening our explanations of coping mechanisms and discretionary choices. The classic studies of SLBs understand street-level bureaucratic behaviour as a kind of self-defence: a way to minimise negative aspects of the job and thereby minimise job frustration (Lipsky, 2010 (1980)). However, as shown, it is also relevant to consider at least part of some SLBs' behaviour as positively motivated, that is, as a way of maximising job satisfaction. Several of the resources used effectively

Figure 7.2: Model of behavioural outcomes concerning reasons to cope

Condition 1: Does the behaviour of the client diverge from or converge with the motivations of the SLB?	Condition 2: How are the power balances between the SLB and client, respectively, and between the bureaucrat and client jointly, when compared to actors external to the interaction?	Conclusion about the behavior of the SLB

```
                                                                        ┌──────────────────┐
                                        ┌──────────────┐                │ Enticed by client │
                                        │ There is no  │         Win–Win └──────────────────┘
                        Converging      │  conflict of │
                                        │ interests, but the            (C – B)
┌──────────────────┐                    │  client and SLB │
│ The 'complex man' │                   │  may be strong or             Lose–lose
│ motivations of the│                   │  weak compared │
│        SLB        │                   │  to pressure from             (C – B)       ┌──────────────────┐
└──────────────────┘                    │  external actors │                          │ Compelled by     │
                                        └──────────────┘                              │ external actors  │
                        Diverging       ┌──────────────┐                              └──────────────────┘
                                        │ There is a conflict│                        ┌──────────────────┐
                                        │ of interest and   │                         │ Compelled by client │
                                        │ therefore a       │           Win–Lose      └──────────────────┘
                                        │ power battle      │
                                        │ between the       │           (C – B)
                                        │ client and        │
                                        │ bureaucrat. Is the │          Lose–Win
                                        │ client or the     │
                                        │ bureaucrat the    │           (C – B)       ┌──────────────────┐
                                        │ strongest         │                         │ Unconstrained SLB │
                                        └──────────────┘                              │ behaviour         │
                                                                                      └──────────────────┘
```

Source: Based on Nielsen (2006a, p 872).

by regulated stakeholders to affect the behaviour of the SLB are seen as attractive to the inspector and therefore create a kind of mutual win–win situation between the company and the inspector. In the last section, we noticed that the interaction behaviours of the SLB matters to his or her enforcement behaviour. However, it takes two to tango and, therefore, in explaining variation in interaction, the characteristics not only of the SLB, but also of the client, matter. Hence, to understand SLB behaviour, we should add an 'interaction matters' hypothesis (and, behind that, a 'client matter' hypothesis) to the existing clusters of explanatory factors – not as a competitive, but as a supplementary, hypothesis as SLB behaviour is a complex phenomenon with no single cause. However, future research might look deeper into the dynamics and causes of the interaction between the SLB and client in order to further understand SLB behaviour and its consequences, in particular, if we want to untangle one of the main worries of scholars of SLBs, namely, the differential treatment of clients and citizens.

Note

[1.] The harshness of the legal sanction was seen in relation to the gravity of the violation. The gravity of each violation was evaluated by independent regulatory experts.

EIGHT

Street-level bureaucrats and regulatory deterrence

Søren C. Winter and Peter J. May

Introduction

One important strand of scholarship about street-level bureaucrats concerns those who serve as enforcement agents at the front lines of regulatory activity. These include, to name but a few, building inspectors, environmental enforcement agents, fish and game officers, health and safety inspectors, immigration and customs agents, licensing and fraud inspectors, police on the beat, and revenue agents. Given the increased role of employment and social workers in assessing compliance with work and welfare rules, social service front-line employees have also taken on important regulatory enforcement roles. As with any street-level bureaucrat, regulatory agents typically have a good deal of autonomy and discretion in how they go about enforcing regulations within broad parameters established by agency guidelines and routines. They have discretion over the thoroughness with which they conduct inspections or reviews, and latitude in the manner with which they interact with those they regulate.

Much of the literature about regulatory agents (see May and Winter, 2011) focuses on their behaviours in enforcing regulations, as typified by studies of inspectors charged with assessing compliance with rules and taking actions when non-compliance is found. Consideration of the enforcement behaviours of regulatory agents draws attention to different ways of bringing about compliance. The literature concerning this suggests that individuals and firms comply with rules because they either fear detection of violations and punishment for them, feel a civic duty to comply, or feel social pressure to comply (see Burby and Paterson, 1993; Winter and May, 2001; Nielsen and Parker, 2012). These constitute calculated, normative and social motivations for compliance. While such motivations are important for compliance, the willingness to comply is hardly enough if those who are regulated do not have the ability to do so in terms of their awareness of rules and capability to comply.

These considerations about compliance raise a basic question that is the focus of this chapter: how do the actions and behaviours of regulatory agents affect regulatees' perceptions that non-compliance with rules will be detected? Answering this gets at the perceptions and consequences of the use of discretion by regulatory agents in choosing what to inspect, the thoroughness of inspection and the style of interactions with regulated entities. While much of the literature about discretion and street-level bureaucrats addresses factors that affect the use of discretion (see Keiser and Soss, 1998; Maynard-Mooney and Musheno, 2000), the more relevant issues for this research are the implications of the use of discretion in action within regulatory settings.

Our research approach entails an empirical study of the enforcement of and compliance with Danish agro-environmental regulations. Compliance with these rules is enforced primarily by local governments and municipal inspectors, who have wide discretion as to how they enforce the rules. We address perceptions of enforcement activities and relationships through surveys of municipal inspectors and of farmers who are subject to the agro-environmental regulations. We develop a set of hypotheses drawing from the regulatory literature concerning decisions made by regulatory agencies in establishing priorities for enforcement and by inspectors concerning their day-to-day actions and interactions. These are examined using the survey data and multivariate methods to provide a multifaceted understanding of deterrence in practice.

Conceptual foundations

The degree to which those who are regulated perceive that non-compliance will be detected – 'detection risk' – is of particular importance in the calculated compliance calculus. It serves as the primary focus in this chapter for the development of hypotheses about deterrence and calculated compliance. Hypotheses about these are developed with respect to the role of inspections, the interactions of regulators and those who are regulated, the heuristics with which the latter gauge detection risk, and a set of conditioning factors. While the interactions of regulators and those who are regulated directly relate to the interactions that characterise studies of street-level bureaucracy in action, as described in Chapter One, our consideration of additional factors and hypotheses underscores the multidimensional nature of both regulatory enforcement and compliance with rules by regulated entities.

Deterrence and regulatory compliance

Regulatory agencies mainly rely on a deterrent approach to compelling compliance. The pioneering research of Becker (1968; also see Stigler, 1970; Ehrlich, 1972) predicts that regulated entities comply with a given regulation when they conclude that the benefits of compliance, including averting fines or other sanctions, exceed the costs of compliance. While this calculus can be framed in a variety of ways, depending on how one calculates the benefits and costs of compliance, the calculation is based on expected utility, which involves choosing the option – compliance or not – that has the higher net return.

As discussed by Scholz (1994), deterrent-based regulatory enforcement takes two forms. General deterrence is aimed at putting classes of regulated entities or individuals (industry groups and individuals subject to the same rules) on notice that violations will be aggressively addressed. Through publicising 'showcase' actions in sanctioning violators, regulators seek to draw attention to the costs of non-compliance (see Thornton et al, 2005). Specific deterrence is directed towards all who are subject to a given set of regulations and entails regular inspections and the sanctioning of violators. This is the routine basis with which regulatory agencies and inspectors seek to bring about compliance.

Regulatory agencies and, by extension, inspectors make three sets of decisions as to how to implement a deterrent enforcement strategy. The first is the frequency with which inspections are undertaken. Requirements concerning the frequency of inspections are sometimes prescribed in regulatory provisions, but discretion about this is more often granted to the regulatory authorities that enforce the regulations. Deciding how often to inspect entails a balancing of inspection resources, the number and heterogeneity of entities to inspect, and the complexity involved and time required to undertake inspections.

A variety of empirical studies of compliance have shown that the perceptions of those who are regulated that violations will be detected is the most important aspect of the deterrent calculus and much more important than their perceived risk of sanctions. These studies have also shown that the perceived detection risk is greatly influenced by the frequency of inspections. These findings have been reported by, among others: Burby and Patterson (1993) in studying compliance with erosion control standards; Feinstein (1989) in considering safety violations among nuclear power plant operators; Gray and Scholz (1991; also see Scholz and Pinney, 1995) in studying taxpayer compliance; and Helland (1998) in studying firm compliance with water quality regulations.

A second decision, which is typically left to inspectors, concerns the particular items to inspect. As a practical matter, it is often impossible to inspect all elements of a given set of regulations. Doing so would take too much time and effort and would not be necessary unless the regulatory situation entailed very high-risk situations, as with a nuclear power plant. Bardach and Kagan (1982, pp 123–51) provide a compelling argument that emphasis on the inspection of major categories of violations is an important aspect of effective regulation (see also Sparrow, 2000, pp 109–22). May and Winter (1999) provide empirical support for this in studying Danish farmers' compliance with agro-environmental regulations. Particularistic enforcement of minor rules is both petty and a time-consuming waste of agency and inspector resources.

A third choice regarding inspections concerns the particular categories of regulated entities to target for inspection. The enforcement literature is consistent in arguing that effectiveness is increased by going after categories of cases that have historically higher rates of violations, or by other ways of identifying higher-risk entities (Scholz, 1994; Sparrow, 2000, pp 255–78; Black and Baldwin, 2010).

The preceding discussion provides a basis for a set of hypotheses about the influence of inspection efforts and the targeting of inspections on detection risk. In particular, this perceived risk is expected to increase if inspections are more frequent (H1a), inspectors perform more thorough inspections (H1b) and regulatory agencies and inspectors target those for inspection who have a higher chance of being out of compliance (H1c).

Regulatory interactions and deterrence

Inspectors are not functionaries who simply follow dictates from above in carrying out their inspections or in taking action once violations are found. As regulatory situations differ, inspectors necessarily have discretion in how to perform these functions. How they exercise this discretion affects the thoroughness of inspections and the way with which they interact with those who are regulated. A variety of empirical studies suggest that there is a good deal of variation in inspectors' interactions, even in the same regulatory setting (Hawkins, 1984; Hutter, 1989; Gormley, 1998; May and Winter, 1999, 2011; Nielsen, 2006a; Pautz, 2010).

Enforcement style concerns the interactions of inspectors and regulated entities: are they friendly and helpful, sceptical and questioning, or threatening and picky? While originally conceived as varying along a single dimension concerning the rigidity with which rules are applied (see Kagan, 1994), a variety of empirical research suggests that enforcement style is best depicted by two dimensions, rather than one. May and Winter (1999; see also Winter and May, 2001; May and Wood, 2003) have labelled these two dimensions 'formalism' and 'coercion'. These dimensions are verified as part of this research. It is logical to hypothesise that increased use of coercion by inspectors will cause those who are regulated to perceive a greater likelihood of detection of violations (H2).

Regulatory heuristics and deterrence

Given that those who are regulated are motivated to comply by more than calculations about the costs and benefits of compliance, it is useful to consider how normative and social motivations also relate to perceptions of detection risk. Scholz and Pinney (1995) point to the difficulty that individuals have in obtaining accurate information about the risk of being caught for cheating on taxes. Given this, Scholz and Pinney (1995) theorise about and show empirically that taxpayers unconsciously rely on their sense of duty to derive their best guess about these risks. In this manner, the sense of duty functions as a heuristic. Heuristics are decision aids or cognitive short cuts that are used to minimise cognitive efforts for routine decision-making. In a different study of taxpayer compliance, Scholz and Lubell (1998) extended the research about the duty heuristic to show that taxpayers' trust in government and trust in other citizens also increased compliance, even after controlling for risk of punishment and perceived duty to obey tax laws.

In addition, various studies have shown that citizens and firms are more likely to comply, and, in turn, accept the need for enforcement, if they believe that regulatory provisions are legitimate and that the regulatory enforcement process is fairly implemented (see Tyler, 1990, pp 57–68). They gauge legitimacy and fairness in several ways that relate to the behaviours of regulatory inspectors. One consideration is the degree to which they believe that inspectors are competent. A second consideration is the degree to which they perceive inspectors to treat them fairly. A third consideration is the degree to which they believe that others are doing their part to comply (Levi, 1988).

The preceding discussion of these factors leads to a set of hypotheses about the interplay of regulatory heuristics and detection risk. Detection risk is increased if there is a strong duty to comply (H3a), perceptions of competent (H3b) and fair inspectors (H3c), and a belief that others are doing their part to comply (H3d).

Conditioning factors for deterrence

Not all regulatory situations are the same. Individuals and firms differ not only in their willingness to comply, but also with respect to their knowledge of rules and their ability to comply. In earlier analyses of compliance with agro-environmental regulations by Danish farmers, Winter and May (2001) found that farmers' awareness of rules was the most important factor in explaining compliance. It not only directly influenced compliance, but also conditioned the impact of other factors. For this reason, awareness of rules is considered here as a conditioning factor for which there are no a priori expectations regarding effects.

The ability to comply is also potentially important in influencing perceptions of risk detection. Those with larger-scale production and practices present more challenging situations for compliance and are arguably more likely to be targeted for inspection. Given this, it is useful to consider the degree of potential environmental problems as an additional conditioning variable that should be taken into account in controlling for differences in compliance situations.

Research setting, data and measures

Agro-environmental regulations in Denmark provide a fruitful case for studying regulatory deterrence given the way in which the rules are enforced and the unique standing of farmers in Danish society. The latitude granted to municipalities and inspectors in enforcing the agro-environmental regulations fits the classic street-level bureaucratic criterion of discretion in everyday actions. The role and standing of farmers give them the qualities of firms, as well as highlight their civic roles. Farmers are businesspeople who can be expected to act like profit-making firms in their compliance decision-making. In addition, many farmers in Denmark are important citizens in their communities, for which they have strong stakes in being viewed as good citizens. This duality provides an excellent basis for considering the interplay of calculated, normative and social motivations for compliance.

Agro-environmental regulations

The main agro-environmental regulations that are the foci of this study entail: (1) requirements that farmers have sufficient capacity to store manure; (2) prohibitions on the spreading of liquid manure during winter months; (3) 'harmonisation' rules limiting the maximum number of livestock allowed per area unit; (4) cultivation-free zones along creeks and lakes; and (5) the required degree of nitrate utilisation from manure to reduce use of other fertilisers. Each of these rules entails a number of technical specifications (e.g. concerning nitrate levels) and alternative means of compliance. Given that the regulations are highly intrusive and require major changes for most farmers in farming practices and substantial investments, compliance with the regulations is not automatic.

Regulatory enforcement of the agro-environmental rules is shared among several national-level agencies. At the time of the data collection, the 14 counties issued permits to environmental risk farms, and 258 municipalities that had farms with animal husbandry have to inspect farmers' compliance with most regulations (see May and Winter, 1999). Municipal inspectors provide advice to farmers about the regulations and have authority to issue warnings and to recommend stronger penalties for non-compliance by notifying the police. The Danish Environmental Protection Agency oversees regulatory enforcement by municipalities. The Plant Directorate of the Ministry of Food, Agriculture and Fisheries checks all farmers' annual reports on fertilisation plans and accounts, and performs some on-site inspections (fewer than 5% of farms in 1999). Farmers also have contact with other farmers in their locality on a bilateral basis or through meetings in local branches of farmer organisations or smaller experience exchange groups. Some also rely on agricultural consultants for advice about requirements and ways to comply (see Winter and May, 2002).

Data for this study

The data for this study are based on two mail-out surveys, which are discussed in more detail in May and Winter (1999) and Winter and May (2001). One is a survey of 1,562 Danish farmers with cattle or pigs administered in 1999. Questions addressed farmers' experience with the enforcement of the rules, their motivations for compliance with the rules and measures of their efforts to comply with the rules. The 1,562 valid responses provide an unweighted response rate of 69%.

The second source of data is a survey of 216 municipal inspectors administered in 1997. Questions addressed the frequency of their enforcement actions and their behaviours when interacting with famers to bring about compliance with the rules. This was a mail-out survey administered to each of the 258 Danish municipalities containing farms with animal husbandry. Responses were obtained from 216 municipalities, providing a response rate of 84%.

Measures employed in the study

The measures used in the study operationalise the key concepts discussed in the earlier section about the conceptual foundations for the study. The key dependent variable is a measure of farmers' perceived detection risk, defined as their perception of the likelihood that violation of rules will be detected. The explanatory variables relate to the deterrent actions of regulatory authorities and inspectors, the enforcement style with which inspectors interact with farmers, the regulatory heuristics that shape farmers' perceptions of detection risk, and conditioning factors. The measures for each of these categories of factors are summarised in Table 8.1.

A few comments about these measures are relevant. The focus on the perceived risk of detection of violations follows from the findings noted in the earlier discussion about the importance of this factor in shaping the calculations of those who are regulated about compliance. The index is the most direct measure of regulatory deterrent effects that could be devised from these data. The measures of regulatory actions and heuristics are straightforward, as summarised in Table 8.1. The derivation of measures of two dimensions of enforcement style – 'formalism' and 'coercion' – are based on a Principal Component Analysis (PCA) of a set of ratings by farmers of the way that inspectors interact with them according to the scales shown in Table 8.1. The results of these ratings were subjected to the PCA statistical analysis in order to reduce the six items into a more manageable and meaningful set of underlying dimensions (see Winter and May, 2001). The formalism dimension varies from an informal, flexible style to a formal, inflexible style. The coercion dimension varies from trusting inspectors, who avoid threats of sanctions, to sceptical inspectors, who use threats of sanctions to induce compliance. The scores that are calculated by the PCA statistical analysis for each dimension are used in the analyses that follow.

Table 8.1: Measures used in this study

Deterrent effects: Perceived likelihood of detection of violations: Index based on a scale of 1 (very small) to 5 (very large) measuring farmers' expectation that each of six possible violations would be detected: Capacity to store manure is one month too short; The farmer is spreading liquid manure during winter months; The farm has 20% too much livestock per hectare and has no agreements with others for delivery of surplus manure; 20% of the agreed manure delivery to other farms has not been implemented; The farmland is cultivated to the very brink of creeks or lakes; and The farm spreads 10% more nitrate than allowed.
Deterrent actions: **Inspection frequency** – Farmers' responses to question of how many times they have received inspection visits over the last 10 years.
Inspection thoroughness – two indicators: Duration in minutes of last inspection visit according to farmer responses. Percentage of items inspected constructed as an index from farmers' responses to how often eight key requirements have been examined by inspectors during the last five years.
Inspection targeting – An index on a 0–8 scale of inspectors' responses as to the importance of different situations in considering enforcement targeting (2 = important; 1 = one of several factors; 0 = not considered) given that: Environmental problems were observed on the last visit; The farm is close to environmentally sensitive areas; The farm is a large, factory-like farm; and The farm is a pig farm.
Enforcement style: Identification of underlying dimensions of farmers' ratings on a five-point scale of the degree to which they perceive inspectors as having the following characteristics: rules- versus results-oriented; Compliance through formal rules versus influencing attitudes; Enforce through strict rules versus negotiation; Consistent versus flexible; Use versus avoid threat of sanctions; and Sceptical versus trusting.
Regulatory heuristics: **Duty to comply** – An index of farmers' evaluation of the extent of agreement, on a scale of 1 (completely disagree) to 5 (completely agree), with statements that: Farmers have a moral obligation to comply with environmental regulations for farming. Rules about manure are so unreasonable that one needs not comply (reversed for the index). Environmental authorities should take stronger action with the few environmental sinners who are spoiling the name and reputation of farming.

Competence of inspectors – Index measured by farmers' responses to a question as to how they would rate the expertise on a five-point scale of each of four listed regulatory authorities, including the person who made the last municipal inspection on the farm.
Fairness of inspection – Index of the mean of each farmer's agreement on a five-point scale with items reporting that the municipal inspection has given them fair treatment and that the municipal inspection treats individual farmers unreasonably different (latter reversed in calculating the index).
Trust in others – This is measured by farmers' ratings on an 11-point scale (from 0 to 10) of how they assess the mean compliance with the environmental regulations for the storing and application of manure by livestock farmers in the farmers' municipality.
Conditioning factors: **Awareness of rules** – The extent of farmers' agreement, on a scale of 1 (completely disagree) to 5 (completely agree), with the statement: 'I believe I am well informed about environmental rules that apply to farming'.
Potential environmental problems – The livestock density on each farm.

The livestock density on each farm is employed as a measure of potential environmental problems, with the logic that complying with the agro-environmental regulations becomes harder as animal density increases. Density is measured by the number of livestock units per hectare. A livestock unit is a standard measure across all species and ages (a proxy for size) of livestock to assess the amount of nitrate in manure that each animal produces. The livestock density was calculated by first calculating the total number of livestock units based on each farmer's report of the number of livestock of each species and age interval. This value was then divided by the amount of cultivated land in hectares reported by each farmer.

Examining variation in detection risk

Multivariate analyses are employed to explain variation in farmers' perceptions of detection risk, with attention to the hypotheses concerning the role of deterrent actions, enforcement style, regulatory heuristics and conditioning factors. Given the prior findings of the importance of awareness of rules as a conditioning factor in influencing farmers' overall compliance (May and Winter, 1999), separate multivariate models are examined for high and low levels of farmers' awareness of rules.

Variation in regulatory situations and practices

It is useful to discuss the descriptive statistics that depict the variation in regulatory situations and practices. These are provided in Table 8.2.

One of the more interesting points is the high degree of variation in the perceived likelihood of detection of violations, which serves as the key detection risk-dependent variable. More than 40% of farmers report scores of 3 or less, indicating perceptions of lower likelihoods. Only 19% report scores of 4 or more, indicating perceptions of higher likelihoods.

Table 8.2: Regulatory deterrence descriptive statistics

Item	Minimum	Maximum	Mean	Standard Deviation
Perceived likelihood of detection	1	5	3.3	0.9
Deterrent actions				
Inspection frequency (last 10 yrs)	0	15	3.5	4.2
Inspection thoroughness:				
Inspection duration (minutes)	0	180	36.9	30.8
Inspection scope (% inspected)	0	100	62.0	30.4
Inspection targeting	0	8	3.4	2.2
Enforcement style				
Formalism index	−2.5	3.1	0	1.0
Coercion index	−2.0	3.1	0	1.0
Regulatory heuristics				
Duty to comply	1	5	3.9	0.7
Competence of inspectors	1	5	3.4	1.1
Fairness of inspectors	1	5	3.7	0.8
Trust others to comply	2	10	7.9	1.3
Awareness of rules	1	5	3.8	0.9

The data about deterrent actions provide a mixed picture concerning the extent of deterrence. Farmers report being inspected on average 3.5 times over the past 10 years. This is generally consistent with the agreements in place at the time of the study, which specify that all municipalities must inspect within a given three-year period all pig farms and 50% of other farms. Yet, some 64% of farmers report being inspected two or fewer times over the past 10 years. The average duration of inspection of 37 minutes would suggest relatively cursory inspections, but the reported average 62% of items inspected suggests attention to a range of considerations. There appears to be limited targeting of inspections given that only 10% of farms have a score of 6 or greater on the eight-point scale for targeting.

Many farmers report a relatively strong sense of duty to comply, with 42% reporting scores of 4 or greater on the five-point scale. On average, farmers view inspectors to have greater fairness than competence (*t*-test of paired differences, $p < .01$). Nonetheless, inspectors are rated fairly highly by farmers for each measure. In addition, there is a fairly high degree of trust in others to do their part in complying with the rules: 76% of farmers report a score of 7 on the 10-point scale.

For the key conditioning variable, farmers' awareness of rules, 72% responded that they mostly or completely agree with the statement 'I believe I am well informed about environmental rules that apply to farming'. This indicates a high level of awareness of the regulations. Nonetheless, 28% had lower levels of awareness. These are the two groups that are the basis for separate analyses of the conditional effects of levels of awareness.

Explaining variation in detection risk

The detailed regression models are presented in the methodological appendix to this chapter. These statistical findings are summarised with summary statements in Table 8.3. The first two columns of the table show the various hypotheses and expectations about the implications for detection risk. The entries for the last column provide a text summary of the statistical findings.

Three things stand out from these findings. One is that farmers' awareness of rules plays a critical role in conditioning the effects of other enforcement factors, including the role of street-level bureaucrats. Six of the positive effects of factors that affect detection risk were conditioned on the level of awareness of rules. A second notable set of findings is that deterrent actions and inspectors' coercive enforcement styles have positive effects on detection risk, but these generally only hold when awareness of rules is strong. A third set of findings is that various heuristics regarding the competence of inspectors, fairness of inspection and trust in others positively affect detection risk, regardless of the level of awareness of rules. The exception is the failure to find an effect for farmers' sense of duty to comply. Key aspects of these findings are discussed in the remainder of this section.

Effects of deterrent actions and inspection style

The finding that deterrent actions and a coercive enforcement style have a positive influence on detection risk only when awareness of rules is strong is a notable refinement on past findings. As noted in the

Table 8.3: Summary of findings

	Effects on perceived risk of detection	
	Hypothesis	Finding
Deterrent actions:		
Inspection frequency (H1a)	Positive	Only when awareness high
Inspection thoroughness (H1b):		
Duration	Positive	Only when awareness high
Scope	Positive	Holds regardless of rule awareness
Inspection targeting (H1c)	Positive	Only when awareness high
Enforcement style:		
Coercion (H2)	Positive	Only when awareness high
Regulatory heuristics:		
Duty to comply (H3a)	Positive	No effect detected
Competence of inspectors (H3b)	Positive	Holds regardless of rule awareness, stronger when awareness high
Fairness of inspection (H3c)	Positive	Holds regardless of rule awareness, stronger when awareness low
Trust in others to do their part (H3d)	Positive	Holds regardless of rule awareness
Conditioning factors:		
Awareness of rules	No expectation	No direct effect detected, only interactions
Potential environmental problems	No expectation	No effect detected

conceptual discussion, prior studies (Feinstein, 1989; Gray and Scholz, 1991; Burby and Paterson, 1993; Helland, 1998) generally show that increased inspections lead to greater compliance. However, the prior studies did not take into account the awareness of rules. In addition, inspectors' use of coercion in dealing with farmers only had a detectable effect on detection risk for those who had a high awareness of the rules.

However, why is it that a high awareness of rules makes a difference in the seeming effectiveness of deterrent actions and behaviours in influencing detection risk? Simply put, those who are regulated need to know enough about what they are not doing to comply with regulations to worry about non-compliance. Ignorance may be bliss, at least as it relates to fear of detection of non-compliance. The positive impacts of inspectors' use of coercion on detection risk for well-informed farmers may also result from their needing to know enough in order to see the potential consequences of inspectors' threats. In addition, inspections may be so infrequent and of so limited duration as to not serve as credible deterrent threats. As noted earlier, the evidence about farm inspections is somewhat mixed in suggesting relatively infrequent inspections of limited duration on average, but with attention to a range of relevant items.

The one exception to the conditional relationships is the finding that inspections with greater scope, that is, inspecting more things in any visit, lead to increased perceptions of detection risk, regardless of the level of awareness of rules. Scope may be a better measure of inspection thoroughness than duration. More important is that farmers are likely to be more sensitive to what is inspected than how long inspections take. Almost by definition, having more items inspected is a good guide to the risk that they incur of being found out of compliance, regardless of the awareness of the reasons for being non-compliant.

Effects of regulatory heuristics

With the exception of no detectable influence of duty to comply upon perceived detection risk, the findings concerning regulatory heuristics are notable for several reasons. One is that these findings hold regardless of the level of awareness of rules. This underscores the basic notion of a heuristic in acting as a short cut to decision-making in order to overcome information problems, whether limited information or overloads. A second notable aspect of these findings is the strength of the effects, which are stronger than the effects of deterrent actions or behaviours, as shown by comparing the magnitude of the standardised coefficients for the regression results in the appendix. This underscores the fact that detection risk is far from an objective, probability-based calculation. Rather, as the label suggests, it is a subjective impression based on limited information and short cuts to calculations.

A final aspect of the findings about regulatory heuristics concerns the differential impacts of the perceived competence and fairness of inspectors. The effects of perceived competence on detection risk are stronger when awareness of rules is high, while the effects of perceived fairness in inspection are stronger when awareness of rules is low. This duality reflects different aspects of the relevant heuristics. If one knows more about the rules, it is possible to better gauge the difference between competent and less competent inspectors. That assessment, in turn, influences perceptions of risk detection. In contrast, fairness in inspection is perhaps the most important concern of those who do not know much about the rules.

The effect that farmers' perception of the compliance of other farmers has on perceived detection risk can be interpreted in two ways. One is as a heuristic in that one turns to peers for cues as to how to behave, regardless of the level of awareness of the rules. This may be a simple judgement as to what one can get away with, or a more complex judgement as to whether one will stick out like a sore thumb. A second interpretation is that the overall compliance of peers with rules serves as a signal of the general deterrence effect of inspections. Put simply, one might reason that if others cannot get away with non-compliance, then he or she will not be able to either.

The failure to find statistical support for an effect of farmers' sense of moral duty to comply with the agro-environmental regulations on detection risk is unexpected. This finding contrasts with Scholz and Pinney's (1995) finding of an effect in their study of taxpayers' subjective probability of being caught cheating. Yet, in other analyses of the data for this study, Winter and May (2001) found that duty to comply is an important consideration in farmers' overall compliance with agro-environmental regulations. It may well be, as suggested by these earlier findings, that the normative aspects of duty to comply as a basis for compliance far outweigh their heuristic functions.

Conclusions

This chapter has considered the role of street-level bureaucrats in regulatory deterrence. This is an important aspect of many of the day-to-day activities of those inspectors and regulatory agents who are charged with enforcing compliance by citizens, firms and other entities with laws, regulations and other provisions. The decisions that regulatory agencies make as to how to allocate enforcement resources set the broad parameters for regulatory agents. Inspectors' choices about the regulatory provisions to inspect and how to interact with those who are regulated establish the realities of regulatory enforcement.

This chapter has addressed the role of deterrent actions on the part of regulatory agencies and the deterrent behaviours and actions of those on the front lines of regulatory enforcement. The specific focus has been a fundamental aspect of deterrence: how these actions and behaviours affect the degree to which those who are regulated perceive that non-compliance will be detected. The literature reviewed here led to a set of hypotheses concerning the role of inspections, the interactions of regulators and regulated entities, the heuristics with which the latter gauge detection risk, and a set of conditioning factors. These hypotheses have been examined in this chapter for data concerning the enforcement of agro-environmental regulations in Denmark and for the compliance behaviours of farmers who are subject to these regulations. Although the data for this study were collected over a decade ago, the basic enforcement and compliance situations differ little today from that of the time of the data collection.

Implications for effective deterrence

The findings highlight the important role of the awareness of rules in conditioning the effects of other enforcement factors. Deterrent actions and inspectors' coercive enforcement styles have notable effects on farmers' perceptions that violations will be detected, but these generally only hold when farmers' awareness of rules is strong. Simply put, those who are regulated need to know enough about what they are not doing to comply with regulations to worry about non-compliance. A key implication for strengthening regulatory enforcement is the need for greater emphasis on clearly communicating regulatory requirements. This often entails more than simply producing documents and publicising them in the media and on websites. The involvement of third parties, such as industry associations, relevant consultants and other intermediaries that regulated entities trust, can be invaluable in this regard (see Winter and May, 2002).

Inspectors' threats appear to have a positive effect on increasing the perceived likelihood of the detection of violations for those who are more aware of the rules, which, in turn, can be presumed to increase overall compliance. When those who are regulated are not aware of the rules and do not understand why inspectors use what they perceive to be unnecessary threats, they are much more likely to regard the use of threats as bullying. Taken together, the findings reported in this chapter and those of the May and Winter (1999, 2001) study suggest that the use of coercion in enforcement strategies is risky business. A key implication is that getting tough is not, in itself, a blanket strategy for improving compliance.

Traditional enforcement strategies of frequent and thorough inspections can be made more effective by targeting inspections towards regulated entities and items that present a higher risk of violations and harm. Inspectors' use of coercive styles can be effective, but only if they are targeted towards those who are well informed about the rules. Otherwise, such threats are likely to backfire. This underscores the importance of educating those who are regulated about rules as a precondition for the emphasis on deterrent enforcement practices.

Stated differently, deterrent strategies become more effective if they are backed up by an information strategy.

Also notable are findings that various heuristics regarding the competence of inspectors, fairness of inspection and trust in others positively affect farmers' perceptions of the likelihood of violations being detected, regardless of their level of awareness of rules. Indeed, these effects were stronger than those of deterrent actions and behaviours on the part of inspectors. These findings underscore the basic notion of a heuristic in acting as a short cut to decision-making when adequate information is missing. Danish farmers seem to be relying more on cues from their interpretation of regulatory interactions and the broader regulatory environment than from the concrete steps that are taken to enforce regulatory provisions. This may be because the latter are too infrequent and too episodic to interpret as signals about the likelihood of detection of violations.

Applicability to other regulatory contexts

The results reported here about regulatory enforcement are likely to apply in other regulatory settings involving inspectors and other street-level regulatory agents. The most applicable situations are those for which inspections are relatively rare, as is often the case for regulatory environments that entail many regulated entities and few inspectors; consider the low ratio of police on the street to citizens, revenue agents to taxpayers, food and safety inspectors to food establishments, and the like. When inspections are relatively infrequent, averaging each third year in the Danish case, and there is large variation in the circumstances of regulated entities, it is harder for those who are regulated to calculate the risk of violations being detected. In these situations, various cues that we document, such as trust in inspectors, assessments of inspectors' competence and perceptions that others are complying, are more likely to be used as aids for calculating the odds of being found out of compliance.

These findings also have important theoretical implications for thinking about regulatory deterrence. Several studies reviewed here have questioned the crucial role that classic deterrence theory assigns to the risk of punishment as opposed to the risk of detection of non-compliance. Our research shows that this risk can be affected by the actions of regulators but more typically only for those who are more informed about rules. Put differently, further development of deterrence theory needs to consider the awareness of rules more fully and how that, in turn, affects calculated bases for compliance.

In addition, the research in this chapter underscores the role of normative and social motivations for obtaining compliance. These are notable alternative bases for compliance than deterrence, which have been discussed in the regulatory literature (see Winter and May, 2001). Yet, as also shown here, they are important factors in the subjective calculations of those who are regulated as to the likelihood of detection of non-compliance. In particular, this research shows that social considerations – perceptions of fair and competent inspectors and trust in the compliance of others – are important heuristics for calculating this risk.

Street-level bureaucrats and regulatory interactions

This chapter also demonstrates the important roles that street-level bureaucrats fulfil on the front lines of regulatory enforcement. They are more than functionaries who act like parking meter enforcement personnel in issuing tickets for failure to pay parking fees. Rather, they often deal with very complex regulatory environments comprised of extensive requirements that present challenges in assessing the degree of compliance of regulated entities. More than faceless bureaucrats, inspectors need to be a combination of consultant and critic, applying the right combination of these to the situation at hand. In addition, they need to establish trust with regulated entities in order to have a credible basis for acceptance of their advice and appreciation of the basis for applying sanctions.

These findings underscore the importance of fair and competent inspectors for improving compliance. This may seem like a truism, as any regulatory organisation seeks to hire and deploy capable and fair-minded regulatory agents. However, herein lies one of the key dilemmas of street-level bureaucracy. Given the variation in the situations of regulated entities and the discretion granted to inspectors, it is inevitable that what seems fair to some may not seem so to others. Furthermore, inspectors who do their best to judiciously enforce rules may come across as picky and inflexible, leading those who are regulated to question their competence.

One of the unique aspects of regulatory enforcement is that it is not typically a one-shot undertaking. Regulated entities are subject to re-inspections to assess whether deficiencies have been corrected, and to repeat inspections over time. Often, these interactions involve the same inspectors. Much of the street-level bureaucracy literature concerns one-shot or limited duration interactions that may involve different street-level bureaucrats. All of this suggests that an important avenue for future research concerns repeated interactions over longer time periods. Both the repeat situations and duration need to be considered as variables that shape perceptions of both the street-level bureaucrats and of those who are subject to the interactions.

One illustration of this line of research is scholarship that views regulatory enforcement as a set of 'regulatory conversations' that play out over time (Black, 2002). What regulated entities come to expect rests heavily on the nature of the interactions with inspectors over time in setting both expectations about what constitutes compliance and in establishing a credible basis for following up with sanctions or other enforcement actions. The clear implication is that deterrent enforcement is not simply a one-shot set of actions in detecting violations and issuing sanctions. Rather, it is an ongoing activity that is often played out over years and involves multiple inspectors. The consistency of their behaviours and actions is critical in establishing an implicit regulatory contract (see May, 2005) that serves as a basis for compliance with regulations.

Acknowledgements

The authors are especially grateful to the following: the Danish farmers and municipal environmental inspectors who participated in the study; the survey firm, GfK, and Finn Villemoes for collecting the farmer survey data; the Danish agencies and organisations that provided statistical information for the farmer sample frame; and Vibeke Lehmann Nielsen, who provided research assistance in designing and collecting data for the inspector survey. The research was supported by the Danish Strategic Environmental Research Program for a project directed by Søren Winter. The findings are not necessarily endorsed by the sponsoring organisation.

Methodological appendix

This appendix presents the regression models that were employed in this study. The models were estimated using ordinary least squares (OLS) regression with appropriate transformations of relevant variables to meet assumptions of linear relationships. Visual inspections and statistical tests were conducted to verify that OLS regression assumptions were met for these models. Because the coefficients for the models are standardised values, they can be used as a gauge of the relative importance of different factors. Table 8.A1 presents regression models for all farmers, as well as for those with high and low awareness of the agro-environmental rules.

Table 8.A1: Explaining variation in detection risk

Explanatory factors	Standardised coefficients[a]		
	Combined model	Awareness of rules low[b]	Awareness of rules high[c]
Deterrent actions			
Inspection frequency (ln)[d]	.04 (1.23)	.01 (0.10)	.05* (1.36)
Duration of last inspection (ln)[d]	−.04 (0.78)	−.03 (0.51)	.05* (1.33)
Interaction of duration and awareness of rules	.10* (1.46)	−[e]	−[e]
Scope	.12*** (3.88)	.12** (1.99)	.12*** (3.31)
Targeting	.05** (1.66)	−.03 (0.52)	.07** (2.14)
Enforcement style			
Coercion in style	−.03 (0.48)	−.03 (0.47)	0.14*** (3.89)
Interaction of coercion and awareness of rules	.15*** (2.51)	−[d]	−[d]
Regulatory heuristics			
Duty to comply (sq)[f]	.03 (0.91)	.02 (0.26)	.03 (0.87)
Competence of inspectors (sq)[f]	.15*** (4.73)	.09* (1.41)	.17*** (4.51)
Fairness of inspection (sq)[f]	.08*** (2.45)	.12** (1.77)	.07** (1.77)
Trust others to do their part	.20*** (6.52)	.19*** (2.96)	.20*** (5.75)
Conditioning factors			
Awareness of rules	−.02 (0.45)	−[d]	−[d]
Potential environmental problems (ln)	−.01 (.18)	−.04 (.66)	.01 (.19)
Model statistics			
Number of observations	966	233	726
Adjusted R^2	.11	.11	.12
F-value for overall model	10.76***	2.85**	10.72***

Notes: [a] Dependent variable is farmers' mean perceived likelihood of detection of violations of six types of environmental regulations, scored on a scale of 1 to 5. Cell entries are standardised regression coefficients from OLS modelling with the absolute value of t-statistics in parentheses. [b] Farmers that report not being well-informed about environmental rules. [c] Farmers that report being well-informed about environmental rules. [d] natural log transformation. [e] Variable not relevant for this model. [f] square transformation. *** $p < 0.01$; ** $p < 0.05$; * $p < 0.10$ (one-tailed). Transformations for meeting linearity assumptions are shown in parentheses.

Part Four
Embedded in society: street-level bureaucrats as public actors

NINE

Street-level bureaucrats and client interaction in a just world

Vicky M. Wilkins and Jeffrey B. Wenger

Introduction

The bureaucrats working in public agencies are often the first, and sometimes the only, contact that the public has with the government. As this contact is most often with street-level bureaucrats who exercise discretion, understanding how the characteristics of street-level bureaucrats influence their behaviour is important in understanding policy implementation (Lipsky, 2010). There is a long literature examining bureaucratic representation that focuses on the identity of the street-level bureaucrat, primarily, race, ethnicity and gender. Instead, we theorise about how an individual street-level bureaucrat's values alter the use of discretion. This is an important question as discretion provides street-level bureaucrats with the opportunity to shape outputs and reward or disadvantage clients (Meier, 1993).

Researchers have long been concerned with understanding how street-level bureaucrats use discretion to provide public services. The concern stems from questions about the impact of discretion on democratic governance and the knowledge that as street-level bureaucrats exercise discretion, they may alter policy outcomes for clients. Bureaucrats on the front lines of service provision work in an environment governed by rules and procedures, and although their work is 'rule-saturated', it is not 'rule-bound' (Maynard-Moody and Musheno, 2003, p 10). In addition, monitoring bureaucratic behaviour is costly and often not possible. This environment results in street-level bureaucrats making decisions about which rules to apply, and, in doing so, they make choices that have an impact on the lives of their clients. Given this, it is important to develop theoretical models to identify the factors that affect the interactions between street-level bureaucrats and the clients of their agencies, particularly how the personal values of the bureaucrat influence her or his behaviour.

Work in the area of representative bureaucracy concerns how the identity of a bureaucrat affects the distribution of outputs to clients when the bureaucrat and client share demographic characteristics. The extant research on representative bureaucracy almost exclusively focuses on three identities – race, ethnicity and gender (notable exceptions are Thielemann and Stewart, 1996; Van Gool, 2008; Pitts and Lewis, 2009). However, recent work has expanded to consider a broader range of identities, including mutable identities (ie veteran status, profession and language). Implicit in much of the representative bureaucracy literature is the conflation of identity and other personal characteristics, including values. This research assumes that women and African-Americans hold certain values as part of their gender or racial identity. We argue that conflating identity and values is problematic because it leads to an inaccurate understanding of the role of identity in bureaucrat behaviour. Our goal is to offer a framework and an example to disentangle values from identity. To our knowledge, no work examines the role of personal values. We contend that personal values (not captured in any one identity) influence the relationship between street-level bureaucrats and the clients they serve, and ultimately alter the provision of public programmes.

Using the research on representative bureaucracy, our theoretical framework identifies the conditions under which a street-level bureaucrat's personal values will influence their interaction with clients. The framework identifies a necessary, but not sufficient, condition for the link between values and behaviour to occur in the workplace. We also hypothesise about how several institutional arrangements will influence whether a bureaucrat's values will alter their interactions with clients. In this chapter, we examine a well-known value in the psychological literature, namely, the 'belief in a just world' (Lerner, 1980).

We argue that when the world is believed to be a just place, where people get what they deserve, individuals, including street-level bureaucrats, will see differential outcomes as part of a fair process that is socially just. Street-level bureaucrats who believe that the world is just are more likely to believe that individuals deserve their observed outcomes as a result of their choices, abilities and attitudes. Street-level bureaucrats with particularly strong beliefs about people getting what they deserve may believe that if one works hard enough, then he or she can get ahead and avoid requiring assistance from the state. Under this condition, people who fail to succeed are viewed as less deserving of government help.

The theory of representative bureaucracy

The literature on representative bureaucracy focuses on how shared demographics and experiences, constructed as identities, influence the interaction between the bureaucrat and client. The literature distinguishes between two forms of representation: passive and active. Passive representation is concerned with the bureaucracy having the same demographic origins as the population it serves (Mosher, 1968). Active representation, in contrast, is concerned with how representation influences policymaking and implementation. Active representation assumes that bureaucrats will advocate on behalf of clients because of common experiences that result from a shared identity (Pitkin, 1967; Mosher, 1968).

The assumption underlying research on active representation is that identity shapes and differentiates an individual's attitudes and behaviour (Meier and Nigro, 1976). Theoretically, active representation occurs because bureaucrats share core attitudes and beliefs with the groups they identify with (Meier, 1975; Meier and Nigro, 1976; Salzstein, 1979). Given this, bureaucrats will advocate for the interests of individuals who share their group identities when setting or implementing policy.

Early scholars assumed that passive representation would naturally translate into active representation; however, researchers identified a couple of necessary, but not sufficient, conditions for this link to occur (Meier, 1993; Keiser et al, 2002). First, the policy area must be salient to the identity of the bureaucrat (Meier, 1993; Selden, 1997; Keiser et al, 2002). The second necessary condition is that the policy area must be one in which bureaucrats exercise discretion (Meier and Stewart, 1992). Discretion is a necessary condition because it provides bureaucrats with the opportunity to shape outputs. Several institutional factors also influence the link between passive representation and active representation. These factors include the mission of the organisation, the role that hierarchy plays within the organisation, stratification and the professionalisation and socialisation of the individual (Keiser et al, 2002).

Adapting the model offered in Keiser et al (2002), we theorise about the relationship between a bureaucrat's personal values and his or her response to clients. It is important to note that the theory of representative bureaucracy examines how the identity of the bureaucrat alters outcomes for a client *when* the bureaucrat and client share an identity. Our model of the link between personal values and behaviour does not require such a match. In other words, we expect that the influence of personal values will not vary according to the identity of the client, but will instead differ according to the context. Like the linkage between identity and behaviour, we contend that the personal values of a street-level bureaucrat will not always change his or her interaction with clients. Given this, we theorise about the conditions under which we expect this association to occur.

First, we posit that bureaucratic discretion is a necessary, but not sufficient, condition. Street-level bureaucrats who do not exercise broad discretion will not be able to change outcomes for their clients, regardless of their values. In addition to discretion, it is also important to theorise about how certain institutional arrangements can promote or suppress personal values from influencing the interaction between the client and bureaucrat.

Following the Keiser et al (2002) model, we argue that several institutional arrangements can deter (or encourage) street-level bureaucrats from letting their personal values influence their behaviour and change policy outcomes. First, the mission of the agency will be an important determinant of whether values influence client outcomes. The mission and function of the organisation in which the street-level bureaucrat works must be related to the personal value in question. In other words, we expect that a value like the belief in the just world may only be significant in certain policy arenas, particularly redistributive policies. However, other personal values (ie equality, fairness, honesty or trust) may be relevant in other policy contexts.

Second, we consider the structure of the organisation. In less hierarchical organisations, the street-level bureaucrat may have more opportunities to inject their values into the administration of the public programme. In addition, the bureaucrat's place within the hierarchy of the organisation is also likely to influence their behaviour and consequently to what degree his or her personal values enter into his or her decision-making. In the same vein, the values of the leadership of the organisation will also be translated into the behaviour of the street-level bureaucrats working in that agency.

Third, a street-level bureaucrat may belong to a profession that will also influence their behaviour. Professions are defined by shared specialised training, terminology, codes of conduct or ethics, testing, and often professional associations (Beckman, 1990; Torstendahl, 1990). Professions can shape or even override an individual's values because professionals receive some of their material rewards from groups outside of the organisation. Given this, street-level bureaucrats working in professions may adopt the values of the profession and be less likely to rely exclusively on their own values in their interactions with clients. Organisational norms and expectations are introduced and solidified through the socialisation process, where actors adopt behaviours and preferences that are consistent with organisational goals, thereby minimising the influence of their own personal values on bureaucratic behaviour. Therefore, we cannot understand bureaucratic behaviour without taking into account the institutions in which the behaviour takes place and how the institutional arrangements may influence whether or not the personal values of the bureaucrat alter the provision of public programmes (Keiser et al, 2002).

The belief in a just world

The framework we propose could apply to any personal value (eg equality, fairness, honesty, trust, etc) across a variety of policy areas and institutional arrangements. However, in this chapter, we use the value of the belief in a just world to explicate a model of bureaucratic behaviour and derive specific hypotheses. In the 1960s, Melvin Lerner began a series of experiments to determine how people would react when faced with an innocent victim who they could not help. The motivation for these studies was to investigate a troubling discovery that Lerner had made while working at a mental hospital. Observing and participating in hospital staff interactions with mentally ill patients, Lerner came to observe disconcerting behaviour by the hospital staff. Lerner describes sessions where the therapist would aggressively question patients about their efforts to find employment in the local community. Many patients were frightened at the prospect of leaving the hospital, and did not actively search for work and regularly missed interviews. However, they were aware that the staff wanted them to become employed. In the sessions, the therapist would push and prod the patients with questions about their search and interviews until, cornered, they admitted their lie – they had not searched or interviewed. The patients subjected to this treatment ended the sessions dejected and degraded as a result of the confrontation. At weekly staff meetings, Lerner and his colleagues planned how to get rid of the 'manipulators' who would not seek work. Lerner was plagued by this question and wondered why trained professionals would treat vulnerable patients cruelly (Lerner, 1980, p 2).

Lerner's hypothesis was that this dysfunctional and cruel behaviour was a defence mechanism that was 'needed for anyone to be able to function for so long with so many people who were suffering, hurt, and would stay that way for a long time' (Lerner, 1980, p 2). Lerner argued that people had a fundamental need to believe that the world was a just place, and that these mentally ill patients were a constant threat to that belief. In general, it is easy to see that some belief in a just world is necessary. In the absence of a just world, routine activities such as planning, saving and investing would be constantly called into question.

Furthermore, Lerner theorised that people would go out of their way to avoid threats to the just world belief. He argued that there are certain compensatory strategies for dealing with injustice. First, people will seek to prevent injustice from happening. In the event that prevention is impossible or impractical, then people seek restitution for the harm done and to restore some semblance of justice. Second, people deal with injustices by accepting the limits of what they can do. Lerner also identified a set of non-compensatory responses that individuals use when their belief in a just world is threatened. First, and most obviously, we have denial and withdrawal. In this case, people are selective about the information that they expose themselves to. With the passage of time and some distractions, the unjust event will leave your mind. Perhaps the most interesting of the set of non-compensatory responses is *reinterpreting the event*. This non-compensatory response consists of reinterpreting the outcome, reinterpreting the cause and reinterpreting the character of the victim. In a set of classic experiments, Lerner demonstrated that all three of these effects took place when people witnessed injustice happening to an innocent victim who they were unable to aid.

Classic experiments

In a series of experiments, Lerner demonstrated that the inability to help an innocent victim led to significant increases in victim derogation. In the most famous experiment, Lerner had students (the experimental subjects) come and observe a 'learning experiment' – ostensibly to provide observational aid with the faculty member's research. Unbeknownst to the students, the subject in the 'learning experiment' was an actor. The actor entered the room and was informed that the negative treatment for the 'learning experiment' was going to be conducted on that day. The negative treatment was to be an electric shock, which would be painful but not create lasting damage. The actor protests, indicating that she was unaware that the experiment was to include electric shocks. Ultimately, she is 'pressured' to submit to the experiment (recall that she is acting – although the students are unaware of this). Eventually, the actor fails the learning experiment and is administered a shock. All of the interactions are observed by the students. The experiment randomly assigned to one set of students the option of giving the actor an alternate treatment after she is shocked (reward treatment); the other set of students was not allowed to alter the actor's treatment.

The results of the experiment are startling. Groups that were not able to alter the actor's outcome were much more likely to hold negative attitudes about the actor. There was a statistically significant difference in students' willingness to derogate the victim *if they were not afforded the option to alter the outcome of the treatment (shock)*. People were very angry about the experiment; however, none of the people who watched the actor suffer demonstrated their disapproval in any overt way. Not one of literally a thousand or so students in medicine, dentistry, nursing, psychology, the arts and sciences – people with experience in the helping professions – complained. Not even a mild protest. The reasons given included: that the participant did not act to end her own suffering; denial of the event – the shocks were mild and she overreacted; and reshaping the event – she knew what she was signing up for. The facts are that the shocks are described as strong and painful, but will not cause any lasting damage.

The experimental evidence validates the 'belief in a just world' (BJW) phenomenon and demonstrates the ubiquity of its effect and strength. Threats to a person's belief in a just world are met with increases in victim derogation. This occurs in the complete absence of any evidence that could be used to justify the derogation.

Measurements of the degree of belief in a just world

Beyond validating the belief in a just world experimentally, researchers have developed instruments that rely on self-reporting to assess the content of this value. The resulting questionnaires seek to measure the degree to which individuals perceive others as deserving of their fates in a wide range of situations. There are now several scales used to measure the belief in a just world or features of it (Dalbert et al, 1987; Furnham and Proctor, 1989; Lipkus et al, 1996). Using these scales, several studies confirmed the value and validity in differentiating between people who believe that their experiences are generally just or whether the world is generally just (Lipkus et al, 1996; Bègue and Bastounis, 2003; Bègue and Muller, 2006).

Relationships between the belief in a just world and other social outcomes

Using measures derived from scales like the one discussed earlier, researchers are working to identify correlates associated with varying levels of belief in a just world. High levels of belief in a just world are positively correlated with measures of authoritarianism (Rubin and Peplau, 1973), trust (Fink and Wilkins, 1976), attendance at religious services (Rubin and Peplau, 1973; Furnham and Gunter, 1984; Lerner, 1991) and a strong Protestant work ethic (Lerner, 1974; Smith and Green, 1984).

The research examining the relationship between demographic characteristics and belief in a just world produces limited and mixed finding. Smith and Green (1984) and Calhoun and Cann (1994) found that white people score marginally higher on belief in a just world than African-Americans. However, other studies found either no relationship (Lempert, 2007) or that African-Americans had higher belief in a just world (Umberson, 1993). The findings are similarly mixed for sex and age. Several studies (O'Connor et al, 1996; Stowers and Durm, 1998) found no significant difference based on sex. Conversely, Whatley (1993) and Furnham et al (2009) found that males score higher on belief in a just world than females. Findings for age are also inconsistent. In a few studies, age is also positively correlated with belief in a just world; studies find that older individuals report higher just world beliefs (Furnham and Proctor, 1989; Furnham et al, 2009). However, Rubin and Peplau (1973) found that scores for belief in a just world were negatively correlated with age for men, but not related to scores for women. Overall, these findings are weak and inconsistent, suggesting that identities primarily used in the representative bureaucracy literature may not capture the variation in beliefs about the justness of the world and are insufficient proxies for this value.

Researchers have also demonstrated that scores for belief in a just world are significantly correlated with certain beliefs and behaviours. One of the most studied relationships is between belief in a just world and victim blaming. Using self-report scales, researchers have analysed the association between belief in a just world and victim blaming across numerous categories of victims: poor people in third world countries (Montada, 1998), disabled people, AIDS patients (Connors and Heaven, 1990; Furnham and Procter, 1992), accident cases, rape victims (Kleinke and Meyer, 1990) and cancer patients (Montada, 1998; Braman and Lambert, 2001). These studies offered support for the expectation that higher levels of belief in a just world lead to increased victim blaming. These findings are unsurprising since blaming the victim is one of the fundamental ways to mitigate threats to just world beliefs. In a study focused on how individuals preserve their belief in a just world, Reichle, Schneider and Montada (1998) demonstrate how belief in a just world and the responsibility to help the needy and willingness to act pro-socially are related. They found that just world beliefs motivate individuals to blame the needy for their affliction (finding that it is self-inflicted), minimise need levels and justify their own advantage. Additionally, they found that people with high levels of belief in a just world were not disposed to assist the disadvantaged (Reichle et al, 1998). Similarly, Rubin and Peplau (1973) found that high levels of belief in a just world were correlated with a tendency to prefer 'winners' and to justify the victimisation of certain groups.

Belief in a just world and bureaucratic behaviour

Thus far in the chapter, we have theorised broadly about how values can alter the interactions between street-level bureaucrats and clients. We also introduced the concept of the belief in a just world and demonstrated how it is distinct from other characteristics, such as race and sex. In addition, we provided evidence of how this belief can alter perceptions of clients requesting benefits. Now we offer a set of predictions (see Figure 9.1) regarding the bureaucratic response given a bureaucrat's belief in a just world and his or her capacity to address the needs of the client. As discussed earlier, a determinant of how a bureaucrat's belief in a just world will influence their behaviour is the ability of the street-level bureaucrat to alter the outcomes for the client and minimise the threat to their own belief in a just world. Capacity to assist can stem from several sources, including the institutional arrangements noted earlier. In Figure 9.1, the rows represent the bureaucrat's level of belief in a just world (high or low), while the columns of the table represent the bureaucrat's capacity to assist the client in a given situation. Examining the convergence between belief in a just world and this capacity allows us to hypothesise about the type of response (compensatory or non-compensatory) that we expect from the bureaucrat and the type of bureaucrat that the client will likely encounter.

Research on bureaucratic discretion produced several different views of how bureaucrats use their discretion and how this ultimately impacts the outcomes for clients. One view of how bureaucrats use their discretion argues that they 'stretch the law' to respond to the needs of their clients (Keiser, 1999; Maynard-Moody and Musheno, 2003). Maynard-Moody and Musheno (2003) examine the stories of 150 street-level bureaucrats and offer evidence that street-level workers act as agents of the clients (or citizens). According to Maynard-Moody and Musheno, these street-level bureaucrats assess the needs

Figure 9.1: Bureaucratic response typology

Capacity to assist

		Low	High
Belief in a just world	**Low**	Response type: COMPENSATORY Behaviour: APPLY RULES	Response type: COMPENSATORY Behaviour: ASSIST
	High	Response type: NON-COMPENSATORY Behaviour: PUNISH	Response type: COMPENSATORY / NON-COMPENSATORY Behaviour: ASSIST/PUNISH

Note: Response types include compensatory and non-compensatory: when bureaucratic responses are 'compensatory', they include providing remuneration and aid, and preventing further harm; in cases where responses are 'non-compensatory', they include reinterpreting the events, outcomes or client in an effort to maintain the belief in a just world.

and worthiness of individual clients in determining eligibility, and do not rely exclusively on the rules and hierarchies of the organisation.

Some scholars posit an alternative view of the use of discretion by street-level bureaucrats. In contrast with the street-level bureaucrats previously discussed, these street-level bureaucrats are guided by rules and hierarchy, use their discretion to enforce the policies and procedures of the agency, and are less concerned with serving the needs of the clients. Maynard-Moody and Musheno (2003, p 12) argue that 'the workers process rather than engage clients'. From this perspective, bureaucrats become symbols of authority and use their discretion to act as gatekeepers for the services they provide.

A third view of street-level bureaucrats posits that bureaucrats may use their discretion to 'disentitle' clients that they deem unworthy (Lipsky, 2010). These street-level bureaucrats use procedures and rules to punish and, at times, abuse citizens (Maynard-Moody and Musheno, 2003, p 151; Wenger and Wilkins, 2009). They give in to favouritism, stereotyping and routinising and use the rules to discourage and harass citizens (Lipsky, 2010, p xii; Maynard-Moody and Musheno, 2003, p 151). The clients who face the harshest treatment are those who the street-level bureaucrat has constructed as unworthy or undeserving (Lipsky, 2010). A client deemed undeserving receives 'the least possible service and the greatest possible punishment' (Maynard-Moody and

Musheno, 2003, p 151). At the extreme are the cases of police officers who use excessive force to punish 'bad guys'. Clearly, these types are not mutually exclusive and most street-level bureaucrats probably vacillate between type based largely on the context; however, we contend that most street-level bureaucrats will have a predisposition when dealing with clients seeking their assistance and it is likely that the bureaucrat's belief in a just world will influence their client interactions.

In Figure 9.1, we predict how a street-level bureaucrat may respond (compensatory – provides restitution or prevention; non-compensatory – reinterpretation of outcome, cause or victim) for each of the four cells in the two-by-two diagram. We first consider a street-level bureaucrat with low belief in a just world and limited ability to address the needs of the client (upper-left cell); our theoretical model predicts that the street-level bureaucrat would have a compensatory response to the injustices they observe. However, the lack of capacity to help will raise the likelihood that the street-level bureaucrat will simply apply the rules of the agency when interacting with the client. In contrast, we hypothesise that a street-level bureaucrat with high belief in a just world and low capacity to help the client (lower-left cell) will have non-compensatory responses when interacting with clients seeking assistance. These non-compensatory responses are a function of the inability to assist the client through restitution or prevention. Instead, this lack of capacity leads the street-level bureaucrat to reinterpret the cause of the injustice, the injustice itself or the client. Ultimately, we posit that these street-level bureaucrats will use their discretion to disentitle the client, providing the client with the minimum benefit at the maximum cost.

Next, we consider street-level bureaucrats with low belief in a just world and greater capacity to assist clients (upper-right cell). These bureaucrats see and accept the injustices in the world but have the ability to help. We posit that these street-level bureaucrats will have compensatory responses and use their discretion to improve outcomes for the clients of the agency. Finally, we expect that street-level bureaucrats with high belief in a just world and capacity to assist (lower-right cell) will likely behave similarly, using their discretion to improve the client's situation, while also minimising threats to his or her belief in a just world. However, it is important to note that the street-level bureaucrat with high belief in a just world could, under certain circumstances, also opt for a non-compensatory response even when he or she has the ability to assist the client.

To illustrate our hypothesis more fully, we provide the specific case of an AmeriCorps member applying for food stamps. AmeriCorps members are paid a poverty-level wage, making them eligible for food stamp benefits. Consider an AmeriCorps member applying for benefits and encountering a street-level bureaucrat with low belief in a just world and limited capacity to help. In this case, the street-level bureaucrat is likely to merely apply the rules and provide benefits. Consider the same client applying for benefits with a street-level bureaucrat with high belief in a just world who has a limited capacity to help. In this case, the street-level bureaucrat is frustrated by his or her inability to help but still needs to defend his or her belief that the world is a just place where people get what they deserve; consequently, he or she will have a non-compensatory response to the client's situation and will reinterpret the need or cause, or blame the client for his own misfortune. This leads the street-level bureaucrat to seek to disentitle the client, making it more difficult for the client to receive food stamps. In the case when the street-level bureaucrat has low belief in a just world and high capacity to help, the client will encounter a street-level bureaucrat who is willing to stretch the law to provide the greatest benefit. In our final scenario, the client applies for benefits from a street-level bureaucrat who has high belief in a just world and the capacity to help. In this situation, there are two possible outcomes: the street-level bureaucrat may opt for a compensatory response, providing restitution or prevention of further harm; or the street-level bureaucrat could opt for a non-compensatory response. In the case of the AmeriCorps member, the street-level bureaucrat knows that the member will also receive a one-time stipend/award at the end of their service that is not considered when determining eligibility or food stamp benefit amount. This knowledge may provoke a non-compensatory response and may lead the street-level bureaucrat to increase the cost of applying for benefits (eg lose paperwork, treat the client poorly during the interaction, wrongly accuse the claimant of fraud, contact other agencies to curtail other benefits, etc).

Conclusion

The previous research on representative bureaucracy focuses almost exclusively on the role of shared demographic characteristics between the client and bureaucrat. In this chapter, we extend the standard representative bureaucracy model to incorporate the role of street-level bureaucrats' personal belief systems to generate hypotheses about how this will influence the client–street-level bureaucrat interaction. This extension helps to explain previous mixed findings in the active representation literature, where identity and values were conflated.

We theorise about how personal values (not captured in any one identity) influence the relationship between street-level bureaucrats and the clients they serve, and ultimately alter the provision of public programmes. Lipsky (2010) argues that bureaucrats adopt certain behaviours when using their discretion; however, no one has theorised about the underlying factors that may lead a street-level bureaucrat to respond differently to client needs. Using the value of a 'belief in a just world' and street-level bureaucrats' capacity to assist the client, we provide a set of hypotheses to predict the response type and behaviours that a client is likely to encounter. In particular, the street-level bureaucrat may act in a compensatory or non-compensatory way given the resources at her disposal. Interestingly, non-compensatory responses are a function of the inability of the bureaucrat to assist the client. This leads to the street-level bureaucrat's reinterpretation of the client's need or deservingness. Under these circumstances, street-level bureaucrats may use their discretion to disentitle the client.

While the theoretical framework we offer is most concerned with how the behaviour of street-level bureaucrats is influenced by personal values (in our case, belief in a just world), we also hypothesise about how values interact with the structure and processes of the organisation. In Chapter One, Hill, Hupe and Buffat argue that government actions occur across scales (system, organisation and individual) and structure (content and process dimensions). Our theoretical contribution focuses on agent behaviour and the antecedents of that behaviour. These individual effects will also have aggregate effects at the organisational level. For example, agencies with difficult-to-serve clients will alter the service delivery setting and range of tasks undertaken by the agency.

This chapter lays the groundwork for a research agenda that extends the field of representative bureaucracy and policy implementation. We argue that scholars should look for opportunities to test the relationship between a street-level bureaucrat's values and policy outcomes. Since valid scales exist for measuring an individual's belief in a just world, this would be an excellent starting point. Collecting data that measure the demographic characteristics of a street-level bureaucrat, their belief in a just world and client outcomes would allow future researchers to test the hypotheses offered earlier. Second, the belief in a just world is only one of numerous belief systems that might influence a bureaucrat's behaviour and the client's experience with the agency. Values such as fairness, equality and trust are likely to alter bureaucrat and client interaction and, ultimately, the provision of public services. Given this, researchers should test additional personal values across a variety of policy contexts and institutional arrangements.

TEN

'Playing the rules': discretion in social and policy context

Michael Musheno and Steven Maynard-Moody

Introduction

Many researchers who turn to the street-level bureaucracy literature are concerned about policy variation and how to manage the front-line workforce of the state to secure policy fidelity. In earlier work, we have depicted this prevailing grain of research as the 'state-agent' or implementation–control–discretion narrative (Maynard-Moody and Musheno, 2000; 2003, pp 4, 9–24). Our work over the last 15 years has challenged the singularity, but not the importance, of this narrative and, instead, focused on an empirical rendering of front-line work and the implications of theorising this work accurately for a democratic polity. It is important to stress, as we did in the conclusion of *Cops, teachers, counsellors* (Maynard-Moody and Musheno, 2003, p 156), that front-line workers 'cannot reject the state-agent role and the demands and tensions it brings to their work. [They] cannot shed the responsibility that comes with the state-assigned power over others'. Aware of the salience of the state-agent narrative, but pushing beyond it, our work carries forward the foundational purpose of street-level bureaucracy inquiry and theory: to understand the work of public employees who interact directly with the citizenry and 'mediate ... the constitutional relationship of citizens to the state' (Lipsky, 2010, p 4). Here, we pursue two questions: (1) 'How do our earlier empirical findings about the judgements of front-line workers square with theoretical renderings of culture, agency and structure?'; and (2) with a focus on the worker as agent and drawing upon our current fieldwork, 'How does "playing the rules" produce both local equities and inequities?

Discretion on the front lines of governing has been, and remains, a dominant frame in street-level bureaucracy and policy implementation research. Research within this frame has produced, and may continue to produce, important new insights into policy and governance (for reviews, see Hupe and Hill, 2007; Maynard-Moody and Portillo, 2010). However, like all frames, the discretion frame has drawn attention to certain issues, while others have remained largely outside the gaze of this scholarly discourse. We argue that the concept of 'discretion' inadequately and incompletely represents the central referents that shape front-line worker judgements and stands in the way of imagining a path for reconciling judgements with social justice and a democratic ethos that demands transparency and accountability. We are not arguing for rejecting 'discretion', but rather to look beyond it to build a different theoretical frame to better weld front-line work to social justice. In earlier work, we made the empirical case for viewing workers as cultural or 'citizen-agents' through story-based analysis of their judgements in three professional fields – law enforcement, social work and public education – and across two municipal jurisdictions in the US (Maynard-Moody and Musheno, 2003, pp 3–24). We revealed a schematic evident across professions, wherein workers concentrate their judgements on who people are (their perceived identities and moral character), engage their agency in pragmatic improvisation and *use* law to secure cultural abidance. The 'precedents' they deploy are derived more from the stories that circulate among themselves than policy, rules and management directives.

In this chapter, we move in two directions: first, retrospectively, in order to deepen our argument by aligning our empirically derived framing of front-line work with theorists' articulations of culture, agency and storytelling; and, second, turning to our current projects on front-line work to advance our claims about what is produced by street-level decision-making and what can be done to better align that production with social justice and a democratic ethos. These empirically grounded field projects add research features absent in our previous work, namely, an ability to see how large-scale policy interruptions rebound on front-line work. Here, we are talking about forceful pushes for change, or what Llewellyn and Hoebel (1941, pp 35–8) call 'constitutional troubles' and Swidler (1986, pp 278–80) articulates as 'unsettled cultural times' brought about by social movements, state policy institutions and media forces combining to interrupt the orientations and practices of established institutions. The constitutional troubles or institutional interruptions we study are: the policy moves to transform US public education into a punitive institution that prioritises security and discipline over education; and the social movement and policy push to stop US law enforcement engagement in racial profiling while legally permitting more aggressive racialised policing. Also, our current projects enable investigation of how both street-level workers and citizen-clients account for the same encounters, what we call interactional 'hitches' (Llewellyn and Hoebel, 1941, p 21), which arise during unsettled times of institutional interruption. Few studies to date have engaged in grounded empirical research of front-line work that investigates worker–client interactions under conditions of institutional transformation (Soss et al, 2011a; Harrits and Møller, 2013).

Beyond discretion

New insight often requires shifting the frame of reference, especially in mature areas of research such as street-level bureaucracy theory. Looking beyond 'discretion' to depict the decisional framing of front-line work may, we argue, advance scholarship on democratic accountability and the production of equities in front-line work and management. The prevailing normative theory of street-level decision-making portrays the democratic state as an edifice built on law and predictable procedures which insure that like cases are treated alike in public service delivery. In this formulation, adjustments to legal requirements are allowable only if workers concentrate on behaviour and adapt law to the circumstances of cases in a manner consistent with policy, rules, hierarchical authority and professional practice. Adapting law and policy to the circumstances of a case is the empirical referent of discretionary decision-making. The apparatus of public administration – management and performance measurement – is designed to align discretion with law and policy abidance or generate a form of legal equity wherein like cases are treated alike. For at least 35 years (Lipsky, 1978, 2010), scholars have focused empirically on explanations of adherence to and deviations from discretionary decision-making, and evaluations of management efforts to align front-line work to discretionary decision-making and legal equity. We now know that street-level work exists in complex, multidimensional webs of accountability and that 'street-level bureaucrats must constantly weigh how to act' while coping with multiple stakeholders and competing demands (Hupe and Hill, 2007, p 296). The challenge for future research is to better understand how front-line workers operate within these webs of obligations, relationships and meanings.

Clearly, discretion and its embedding referent – the state-agent narrative – are anchored in the conscience of front-line workers, such that if you ask them, as we did in our inquiry, to describe their work and decision-making in the service of 'justice', they respond with flat, one-dimensional answers: 'Treat everyone the same; follow the rules, follow the law; don't let your own views or prejudices affect your decisions; be professional' (see Maynard-Moody and Musheno, 2003, pp 33–4). With time, we came to understand that these articulations of the state-agent narrative serve as a buffering tool for legitimating public expectations and managerial scrutiny of their work. Workers know that the state-agent narrative is *the* institutional narrative of public service delivery. It is *the* narrative to convey to outsiders, including researchers, and public exposure of their acting outside the paradigm of discretionary decision-making may undermine the legitimacy of their organisations, generating disciplinary actions against them, often described as 'lone wolves' or 'bad apples', to restore the institutional narrative of public service delivery.

As we gained the trust of front-line workers, engaged in observations and collected their stories over the course of many months, we discovered that workers convey a strong orientation towards 'faces' or making judgements about who people are (their identities, character and moral worthiness), and, in doing so, use their agency to impose cultural abidance. We called this viewpoint of front-line workers a cultural or 'citizen-agent narrative' and documented the constructive and destructive elements of their localised cultural production of worthiness and badness among the citizens they encountered. Most challenging to the edifice of the state-agent narrative and the fixation on discretion to characterise front-line work is our discovery that stories shape judgements more than rules and that morality often trumps legality: cops, teachers, and counsellors first make normative judgements about offenders, kids and clients and then apply, bend or ignore rules and procedures to impose cultural abidance.

These discoveries, derived inductively from three years of fieldwork, prompt our call for looking beyond discretion as a frame for understanding and managing street-level decision-making. Here, we move retrospectively to connect our field findings to early works that theorise the centrality of culture, storytelling and agency to human judgement. Shearing and Ericson (1991) point to the attractiveness of rules to explain the regularities of social ordering, but claim that there is little evidence that rules operate as independent instructions that people look to in constructing their actions. They write: 'People simply do not walk around with rules in their heads that they apply in situations, in the midst of action, to decide what to do' (Shearing and Ericson, 1991, p 482). Shearing and Ericson note that the rule-based paradigm did not die; instead, scholars spent years searching for more implicit rules within an organisational sphere, commonly referred to as 'subcultural rules', which may guide front-line decision-making (on policing, see, eg, Reuss-Ianni, 1983; Reuss-Ianni and Ianni, 1988).

Scholars pursuing implicit rules did find that work cultures are, at best, 'sort of rule-guided' (see Manning, 1997), and, as a result, Shearing and Ericson formulated and investigated an alternative perspective of action in which the continuous telling of stories by workers forms a cultural toolkit that 'invites them to consider particular sorts of gambits and strategies to use in constructing action and show how this has been done on particular occasions in the past' (Shearing and Ericson, 1991, p 500). Stories, and the tropes they convey, are cultural precedents that guide and allow for improvisation in constituting normative ordering; stories 'materialise' who and what practices are valued and why. This perspective, consonant with our findings, recognises that front-line work is full of unexpected opportunities and ambiguities, and that front-line workers are not 'cultural dopes blindly following ... rules' (Shearing and Ericson, 1991, p 500), but, instead, possessors of agency and power intent on playing rules and putting fixes on people in the micro-processes of enforcing (or reinforcing) normative ordering.

Shifting our language from 'discretion' to 'agency' adds four essential elements to our understanding of street-level work (Maynard-Moody and Musheno, 2012). First, agency, or the ability to form judgements and take actions, is inherent. It is not delegated or legitimated by laws, rules or procedures, but is an essential aspect of being human. In William Sewell's (1992, p 20) analogy, the 'highly generalized capacity for agency' is as inherent as our 'capacity to use language'. Second, the capacity to form judgements and to act does not exist apart from social systems. Building on the work of Anthony Giddens (1979), Sewell argues that structure – rules, roles and resources – shape and give meaning to agency. Agency cannot exist absent structure, just as structure becomes lifeless without agency (Hallett, 2010). The concepts of 'structure' and 'agency' presuppose each other. Giddens (1979, p 161) insisted that 'structures must not be conceptualized as simply placing constraint on human agency, but as enabling'. Knowledge about normative ordering or the prevailing rules, customs, norms, roles, resources and practices enables what Giddens calls 'knowledgeable agents' to both recreate and modify existing practices and structures.

Third, for Giddens and Sewell, agency is not equally or evenly distributed. Position, status and socially advantaged or disadvantaged identities – all the socially defined characteristics that mark our place in society – give individuals and groups 'knowledge of different schemas and access to different kinds and amounts of resources and hence different possibilities for transformative action' (Sewell, 1992, p 21). Street-level workers occupy the bottom tier of our public and private bureaucracies. At the same time, they occupy liminal positions or interstitial space and must navigate between state policy and local community sentiments and between institutional norms, such as crime fighting or school discipline, and social welfare or educational values (on the position of liminality generally, see, Turner, 1977; on front-line workers dealing with such tensions, see Gilliom, 2001; Soss et al, 2009; Kupchik, 2010). Their position, training and work shape the nature and expression of their agency. It is essential to underscore that the agency framework goes well beyond the concept of discretion in acknowledging the inescapable presence of street-level judgement and action; we cannot conceive of structure without it.

Sewell (1992, p 21) makes an additional fourth point of relevance to understanding street-level work: the presence and expression of agency is 'profoundly social'. Individual agency is not only defined by social position and institutionalised schemas, but also expressed in interaction with and against others. Often, workers express and engage their agency as oppositional to the expectations of management and as a 'play' on or 'playing with' formal rules. These practices and schemas may become deeply ingrained and acted upon with little or no conscious thought or reconsideration. In our formulation, the schemas are the drivers of workers' citizen agency and shape their enforcement of cultural abidance (Maynard-Moody and Musheno, 2003). They tend to constrain and reproduce action; this is the meaning of structure. Nonetheless, practices and schemas are never a perfect fit for circumstances and experiences, and even the effort to reproduce structures promotes some level of change and adjustment (Sewell, 1992, p 27).

Dual narratives amid institutional interruption

Our current book projects – Morrill and Musheno (forthcoming; see also Morrill et al, 2000; Morrill and Musheno, 2009) and Epp, Maynard-Moody and Haider-Markel (2014; see also Epp and Maynard-Moody, 2010) – focus on a particular genre of front-line workers who have direct contact with citizens: Musheno on US urban high school teachers and Maynard-Moody on US municipal cops. Both projects utilise mixed methods, particularly observational and conversational interview techniques, and provide added dimensions to the study of front-line work that are absent in our earlier collaborations (Maynard-Moody and Musheno, 2000, 2003; Oberweis and Musheno, 2001). The first of these dimensions is our ability to look at how both front-line workers and their clients imagine the same incidents differently, what we call 'interactional hitches', or what Llewellyn and Hoebel (1941, p 38) refer to specifically as 'personal-experience trouble cases involving common man'. Here, the guiding question is: how do workers and clients view encounters similarly and differently through their respective narratives and why?

The second new dimension is our ability, in each project, to study interactional hitches that arise when there are large-scale, social movement-promoted and media-hyped policy interventions to transform presumed institutionalised practices where front-line workers ply their trade. Here, we are referring to more than the interruption of a new statute or judicial ruling, but state action from above and social movement activity from outside, combined with broad and deep media attention, coalescing with the intent to bring about a shift in institutional regimes. Here, the question we pursue is: how does constitutional or institutional interruption influence the decisional judgements of front-line workers and evaluative assessments of clients who bear the effects of front-line work?

School teachers in the US have faced nearly 20 years of 'safe-schools' rhetoric, social movement activity, federal and state mandates, social and physical technologies, and architectural designs to implant a new regime of discipline, security and punishment in US public schools (Lyons and Drew, 2006; Simon, 2007; Kupchik, 2010). Morrill and Musheno (forthcoming) have conducted a 12-year ethnography of youth conflict in a multi-ethnic urban high school, focusing, in part, on the interactional hitches that arose when the full bore of this new regime hit a public high school – Cotton River High School (CRHS) – in the late 1990s and subsequently.

Maynard–Moody and his colleagues examine the interactional hitches that arise when two contradictory institutional interventions take hold of law enforcement in the US. Specifically, they focus on police stops during a sustained decade of: (1) social movement activity, legislative, executive and state mandates, and law enforcement rulemaking to prohibit the police from practising racial profiling; and (2), during this same decade, broad media support, political encouragement, judicial rulings and law enforcement initiatives to encourage aggressive policing on the sidewalks, streets and highways of urban America. Racial profiling began as a much-lauded police practice to efficiently target drug couriers on US highways by basing stops on 'rigorous, evidence-based' criminal profiles, but ended as a disgraced practice employed by a few 'bad apple' racist cops (for a review, see Epp et al, 2014, ch 2). At the same time that police departments officially abandoned the practice of racial profiling, they turned to the heightened use of investigatory stops in the ever-spreading US war on crime and drugs (Provine, 2007). Promoted as good police practice and supported by court rulings, the new form of colour-blind racial profiling has remained central to modern policing in the US and elsewhere.

Convergent narratives in the mediation of punitive schooling

"It's important to know that Cotton River High has been a multicultural high school from the days of its origins." (Randy Neilson, CRHS teacher)

"I am still flying under the radar." (Mr Lopez, CRHS teacher)

CRHS is a historic school, built during the territorial years of the American West in a municipality supporting the emerging commercial needs of a fertile agricultural valley now grown into a metropolis. From its beginnings, the high school stood in close relationship with the town whose name it bore and an emerging college located only a few blocks away. Children of long-standing Hispanic families who historically worked in agriculture, white settler families that gained control of many ranches and related town commerce, and college families whose adult members occupied the ranks of administration, teaching and support services attended CRHS. Early in Morrill and Musheno's 12 years of fieldwork in the school, they met Mr Nielson, a graduate of CRHS and teacher in the ranks for over 30 years, who implored them to remember that CRHS has 'been a multicultural high school from the days of its origins', indeed, well before the construct of school multiculturalism was coined.

The mid-1990s marked the era during which safe-schools policies, with their punitive logic and practices, were imposed on the school, a period when the school was shrinking in size and increasingly populated by youth from low socio-economic families and immigrant populations. CRHS was transformed from an open school to a fortified, closed school with an administration dedicated to tightly controlling student movement, imposing strict disciplinary rules and building close ties with local law enforcement. All of these features of the safe-school movement were put into place despite little evidence that the student body had turned unruly or that street gangs had claim to the turf of the school. As part of their triangulation of mixed field methods, Morrill and Musheno (forthcoming) deployed student ethnographers in the field to document interactional hitches and collected narratives of trouble for students and teachers alike when constitutional transformations were being imposed on CRHS. During the period of institutional interruption, the hitches often involved, on one side, the school administration and a small group of teachers aligned with the central office. On the other side, activist students joined with a larger contingent of 'youth-centred' teachers, many whom attended CRHS themselves, and opposed the disruptive effects of the safe-schools punitive logic.

The triangulation of collected narratives with cases of interactional hitches assembled from participant observation reveal a sizeable portion of the teachers as youth-centred, characterised by: 'keeping their ear to the ground'; recognising that youth have a repertoire of skills to manage much of the trouble that they have with one another; taking stock of the many difficulties that youth at CRHS 'have to face'; and actively mitigating many of the draconian features of the punitive measures initiated by the school board and campus administration. One of these teachers is Carol Robinson:

> "You gotta know what's going on.... All that [rules, discipline and security], it only goes so far.... I take a different approach.... You have to know when you need to intervene, give guidance, and when to let 'em [youth] deal with it on their own."

The narratives of the youth and of this sizeable portion of the faculty are convergent. They tell stories of muting the effects of negative images of the youth, new forms of punishment and the spatial confinement of the youth, all aspects of the cultural and material markers of the 'safe-schools' regime. Here, we draw on one interactional hitch to demonstrate the convergence of judgements, teachers' and students' alike, in contestation with the school administration. Like many of the hitches related to youth–adult interactions, this account depicts the school administration, bent on imposing this new regime on the school, as against the best judgements of youth-centred teachers working in support of students engaged in local cultural expression.

Hip hop culture, particularly break-dancing, is the passion of a diverse group of boys and girls at CRHS. Whenever and wherever they performed, they would draw an enthusiastic audience, including a crowd of students 'cheering and clapping' a performance on the sidewalk visible to a main business street and school parking lot. In the story, 'flying under the radar', recalled by students, teachers and

administrators, one of the assistant principals, Mrs Tilly, checked out
the loud music and commotion outside the school one day. While she
was 'impressed' by the performances, she expressed worries about the
public display and the possibility of liability issues should anyone be
hurt because the crew was not an officially sanctioned school activity.
Rather than trying to bar the crew's activities on campus, an act she
seemed to prefer, she turned to Mr Lopez, asking him to find 'suitable
space' where they could practice and perform less visibly. Mr Lopez,
who juggles many after-school activities, agreed and first found time
for them to use the gym when no school athletic teams were practising.
This was also unsatisfactory to the administration and, consequently,
Mr Lopez moved them to his very large classroom, where the crew
practised and performed after school, but was much less visible to the
student body and to the public. He checks in on them occasionally, but
unlike the administrator, who expresses a host of worries, Mr Lopez
dismisses such concerns, saying simply that they "police themselves".

The crew members have their own view of what's on the minds of
adults, including the administration. They report that they are always
getting stereotyped as a gang because of the clothes they wear and their
tattoos. They go to great lengths to repel the gang label. Furthermore,
without 'breaking', they would be getting into trouble – maybe "doing
drugs" or "doin' crime" all the time. They deeply appreciate the efforts
of Mr Lopez to make space for them on campus. Bing, one of the
crew, says that Mr Lopez is 'playing the rules', which he characterises
as using the rules to their (the crew's) benefit in some way, but not
necessarily as intended. When they express their thanks and show
respect for Mr Lopez, he returns it by casually letting them know that
the place will be there for them, saying simply that he would see them
all again tomorrow.

By 2008, in the last phase of their ethnography, Morrill and Musheno
(forthcoming) found that youth-centred teachers and students did keep
their 'ears to the ground', continuing to sustain an evolving school
multiculturalism and engaging in what they viewed as improvisational
production of localised equities, like the reported facilitation of break-
dance crews and hip hop culture. The core of the school administration,
those that were committed to imposing the strict implementation
of the new safe-schools regime on CRHS, had moved on to other
schools and districts. Students were regaining mobility on campus.
The current administration includes faculty who Morrill and Musheno
(forthcoming) identified in the late 1990s as youth-centred and fully
committed to a local normative order of inclusiveness. In the late
1990s, they rarely heard open dialogue and expressions of difference,

and narrative reconciliation by reference to the prevailing norm; while in the final phase of fieldwork, openness, difference and reconciliation were apparent in the local school culture.

One such moment of their observing a democratic ethos in practice revolved around an institutional interruption produced by a new state policy intervention directing all schools in the state to deploy English-only teaching practices in dealing with new immigrant youth. This standard, reflective of a state legislature hostile to immigrant rights, conflicted with the long-standing local school culture of honouring cultural differences while promoting educational opportunity. In focus group meetings with a range of teachers and administrators, Morrill and Musheno (forthcoming) heard a full range of stories openly told among many of the teachers and administrators of the progress being made at CRHS with immigrant students and how media reports and state policy mandates could undermine their localised practices. At one meeting, a key administrator, explicitly addressing the new legislative edict, said that CRHS is "just not going to follow the law". In this setting, teachers less sympathetic to youth cultures, and particularly the new immigrant youth, felt comfortable telling dissenting stories which asserted that the new wave of students was 'mushrooming' and calling them a 'hard core' of youth who could disrupt the forward momentum of CRHS. These contrasting narratives or interactional hitches were woven into the prevailing discourse of inclusiveness as teachers and administrators from across the spectrum of beliefs agreed that the new edict would be harmful to the immigrant youth of the school and therefore should be resisted while acknowledging that this population was the least incorporated into the school and the most vulnerable to creating and experiencing trouble.

Enacting colour-blind racism: police–citizen encounters

Whether of cars or pedestrians, police stops are the most common encounter between police officers and citizens; they are routine moments when citizens experience the coercive power of the state. In 2005, there were 18 million traffic stops in the US (Durose et al, 2007). Half of all contacts between the police and public occur during a traffic stop (Harris, 2002), and about 12% of all drivers are stopped while driving in a given year (Lundman and Kaufman, 2003). Yet, we know that these stops are not evenly distributed. Over a wide range of studies and controlling for a wide range of alternative explanations, in the US, black people are stopped about twice as often as white people. The disparity of stops is present, but not as pronounced, for other

Americans of colour. Whether the driver is white, black or brown, each stop is an instance of a relational hitch, when police momentarily interrupt a driver's mobility and freedom; drivers describe a traffic stop as a momentary incarceration. The persistent and pervasive racial disparities in stops and stop outcomes are evidence of a policy trouble that cuts to the heart of norms of equity.

The persistent and pervasive racial disparity in police stops poses important questions for our understanding of street-level judgement. Most police districts, including those that we studied, now ban racial profiling or stops based on a driver's or pedestrian's race (Epp et al, 2014). Such actions are explicitly against law, policy and rules, and could lead to an officer being dismissed from the force. Police chiefs confidently state that racial profiling is not permitted in their jurisdictions and that it is bad policing; racial profiling is considered officially repugnant and unprofessional. This extends to the front lines. Our interviews and focus groups with police officers suggest that they consider any form of racialised policing to be ineffective and wrong. There are, of course, racist police officers, but contemporary police departments, like most US institutions, no longer exhibit an overtly racist culture and many are highly diverse (Sklansky, 2008).

Yet, black people and other minority ethnic groups are stopped at a much higher rate than white people. After controlling for a wide range of socio-economic and behavioural variables, Epp, Maynard-Moody and Haider-Markel (2014) found that black people are stopped by the police more than twice as often as white people. When the focus is narrowed to investigatory stops, or those stops that involve hunting for other crimes and not merely enforcing good driving, two-and-a-half times more black people are stopped than white people. In stops that officers describe as 'must-stop' situations, such as excessive speeding or indications of drunk driving, racial disparities disappeared. This evidence thus indicates that racial disparities occur almost exclusively in the less common investigatory stops. Such stops are evidence of the dangers of street-level judgement – or are they? Rather than evidence that street-level police officers across the US engage in collective 'sabotage' of the laws and procedures banning racial profiling, Epp, Maynard-Moody and Haider-Markel uncover evidence that state mandates both legitimate police officers enforcing aggressive investigatory stops and – and here is the 'hitch' – foster the race-based policing. These competing mandates – one that prohibits racial profiling and the other that encourages aggressive stops, as detailed later – generate divergent narratives or interactional hitches between police officers and citizens in their assessments of stops for which there has yet to be reconciliation (on the ambiguity and contradictory qualities of state legality and policy generally, see Edelman, 1992).

Police officer narratives

Police stops are a major element of modern policing, although only some of them are focused on traffic enforcement. As driving to work, for leisure and for other life necessities became embedded in our social and economic life, roads and streets have become increasingly policed public spaces. Although, on one level, no police stop is routine, most traffic-safety stops are thoroughly mundane and predictable responses to typical traffic-law violations. For traffic officers, pulling drivers over for these violations is a repetitive part of every day. One officer told Epp, Maynard-Moody and Haider-Markel (2014) that she made 15 to 20 stops a night. For some officers they interviewed, routine stops were so common that the officers blurred several together in their narratives.

Investigatory stops are fundamentally different. Here, an officer stops a driver not primarily because he or she has violated a traffic law, but because the officer wants to investigate whether the driver is engaged in crime. In investigatory stops, this suspicion appears to precede identification of a legal justification for the stop. The basis for suspicion is commonly something – perhaps something inchoate – about the driver and vehicle in its particular location and time of day. For example, an officer might try to stop a driver who "just left the hotel district after three minutes there". They also make more investigatory stops late at night, as one officer put it to us: "Midnights, you're looking for DUI's [driving under the influence] and drugs.... Midnights, you search a lot of cars".

Epp, Maynard-Moody and Haider-Markel (2014) asked officers what sorts of justifications they typically use to make a stop when they want to investigate the driver or vehicle. They learned that unless the driver seriously violates a traffic safety law, they use trivial technical violations of the law when they want to stop a driver to investigate. The laws governing traffic and vehicle conditions are remarkably detailed, and any violation of traffic laws or vehicle codes, no matter how minimal, may be used to justify an investigatory stop (Harris, 1997). Officers in focus groups observed that "people will always give you some reason to pull you over if you wait long enough". These include improper turns, littering, the licence plate light being out, the lack of a turn signal and so on.

It is important to stress at this point that these 'pretextual' stops are not primarily the result of aggressive individual police officers, but the core practice of modern proactive policing. They are the traffic equivalent of the 'broken-windows' theory of using small infractions to track, punish and discourage serious violations. Such stops are supported by police practice, training and court decisions. To soften the harsh edges of this more intrusive approach to policing, officers are trained to always remain polite and courteous to those that they are scrutinising. Most police officers consider such stops as an effective – even essential – crime-fighting tool. In their view, they are just doing their jobs. Nonetheless, when we shift our perspective from the police officer to the black driver who is the subject of these investigatory stops, a different picture emerges.

Black driver narratives

"One time that I particularly remember, I was just, I don't know how to explain it – I felt violated. I was doing the speed limit, I got pulled over and was asked for my driver's licence and registration. I went and asked why I was being pulled over. He just pretty much stated that there was a warrant check. And pretty much ran my licence and asked if I had any warrants for my arrest and I told him, 'No'. And he ran my plate and driver's licence and asked if that was my current address and all that good stuff and then released me."

This black man's experience appears inconsequential. The officer was professionally courteous, did not search the vehicle or handcuff the driver, and, in the end, issued no citation. It was all over in a few brief minutes. From one perspective, the driver suffered no more than a moment of inconvenience, yet the driver's emotional response was palpable and raw. This African-American man was not just annoyed or angry, common feelings associated with traffic stops, he felt violated.

At first glance, the racial injustice so evident in investigatory stops looks like evidence of the misuse of police discretion; evidence of the dark side of street-level judgement. Indeed, police officers themselves often refer to such stops as 'discretionary stops': they did not have to stop the driver because of their egregious behaviour, they chose to stop the driver because there was a chance – in practice, a remote chance – that they were committing a crime. Closer examination underscores that officers were acting within a well-established policy regime. The problem of racial disparities in police stops arises less from individual biases or street-level worker judgement than from a broad policy favouring investigatory stops. Investigatory stops are not the isolated choices of individual police officers, they are a key crime-fighting policy; they are deeply imbedded in the US War on Crime. This policy targets people for intrusive police stops based on their membership in a group, whether it be a racial group or a crime-prone neighbourhood. Targeting in this way generates pernicious social costs: it turns increasing numbers of the targeted groups into convicted criminals and treats others so targeted as distrusted subjects of surveillance. This policy exempts others from police scrutiny, giving them comparative freedom from such control (Harcourt, 2007). Furthermore, it stands in stark contrast to the institutional intervention to end racial profiling. Ironically, racial profiling – or 'being profiled' – provides the normative ordering that African-Americans draw upon to render their interpretation of aggressive stops, an interpretation that stands in stark contrast to the view espoused by the police officers carrying out these stops.

Cultural barriers to local equities

For researchers, stories provide detailed cognitive maps about front-line decision-making. They reveal mosaics of pragmatic improvisations and the interplay of structure and agency; they reference the salience of both rules and morality, acts and identities, and the reverberations of judging others as one judges oneself. For workers, the exchange of stories is the lifeline for learning how to ply one's trade in the mix of the particularities of people, places and events. Through the exchange of stories, workers acquire precedents for guiding improvisational decision-making. However, for too many public managers, stories are treated as subversive acts; we have observed instances when workers have brought their stories into the open only to have them slapped down by supervisors. Even as managers are fully aware of the centrality of stories to front-line work, they routinely discourage or ban their telling from the official discourse of public agencies because they undermine the state-agent narrative and the tools of supervision that legitimate *their* work. We regard the blockage of stories as the cultural barrier that ruptures front-line work from management.

In our earlier and current work, we have documented moments when managers invite stories into hierarchical spaces of public agencies. When this occurs, managers weave the street knowledge of stories into the discourse of supervision. In the law enforcement agencies we have studied, managers routinely suppress street-level stories that do not conform to the state-agent narrative in their meetings with 'the troops'. However, in two vocational rehabilitation offices and CRHS, we documented particular work sites where managers encouraged group storytelling and story analysis as a central feature of case supervision. 'Story-telling and analysis were routine parts of managing [the vocational rehabilitation] agencies, as the supervisors created a context in which stories were told, dilemmas were discussed and moral reasoning was critically examined' (Maynard-Moody and Musheno, 2003, p 162). The managers helped stitch together an organisational narrative of achieving localised equities and, in so doing, bridged the gap between front-line storytelling and case management.

Musheno, in collaboration with Morrill on their current public school ethnography (Morrill and Musheno, forthcoming), finds an active exchange of stories between students and youth-centred teachers in the mediation of interactional hitches. This exchange was prompted by an institutional policy intervention to incorporate punitive technologies and spatial confinement into the high school under investigation. Central administrative personnel of the school sometimes passed off to these teachers the power to manage trouble prompted by the new punitive regime, as exemplified earlier in the hitch over finding space for the boy and girl break-dancers. The fieldwork revealed a more recent dialogue among school teachers, administrators and students over a new state regime for forcing schools to adopt practices of English-only education for a new wave of students who immigrated with their families, often outside the law, from Mexico and Central America. Here, as documented earlier, school managers shaped or choreographed a localised discourse that incorporated the stories of pro- and anti-immigrant teachers while holding onto their school-based social technologies for teaching and socialising the new student population.

Maynard-Moody, in his collaboration with Epp and Haider-Markel in their study of police stops, reveals a disjuncture in their meanings between police officers and African-American citizens. It is a disjunction prompted substantially by the dual adoption of two conflicting institutional policy interventions related to police stops, one demanding aggressive policing and the other prohibiting racial profiling. Could the inequities revealed by police officers who feel that they are wrongly accused of racial profiling and African-Americans who bear the brunt of aggressive policing be bridged if police managers created a forum for and choreographed the storytelling of both parties (with regard to policing and democracy, see Sklansky, 2008)? We see the possibility. Management practices that incorporate and legitimate the stories of both front-line workers and their clients are acts consistent with participatory democracy, a mode of public service delivery fully in line with the normative orientation of most democratic nations. Moreover, our work suggests that interactional story exchanges between administrators and their workers, and between front-line workers and their clients, show promise to produce local equities and to locally interrupt or blunt state-mandated inequities through playing the rules (see also Cheung and Ngai, 2009; Zinner, 2011).

While story exchange among administrators, front-line workers and clients shows promise to promote local equities, there is much more to learn about the dynamics of local adaptation or locally playing the rules, particularly uncovering the factors that condition equities and inequities. Currently, scholars are pursuing the importance of cultural structures to advance the understanding of the production of local inequities (see Harrits and Møller, 2013), while others are advancing evidence that 'decentred governance' strategies are crucial to the production of local equities (see Griggs et al, 2014). Whether uncovering evidence of local inequities or equities, all of these studies converge in their focus on local adaptation over policy fidelity and worker and client agency over legal discretion to understand the realities and potentialities of front-line work (see Dubois, 2010; Zacka, 2011).

ELEVEN

Personalisation and adult social work: recasting professional discretion at the street level?

Kathryn Ellis

Introduction

The author's empirical investigations of adult social care as a site of street-level bureaucracy have been centrally concerned with the distinction drawn in Chapter One between discretion-as-granted and discretion-as-used. These studies of social workers' assessment practice within English local authority social services departments span two decades, a period marked by policy reform and major shifts in the approach to governing front-line behaviour. Under the National Health Service and Community Care Act (NHSCCA) 1990, social services departments were required to contract out directly provided services to private and third-sector organisations. This transformation of function from provider to purchaser was underpinned by a managerialised system of assessment and care management designed to curtail professional discretion and manage resources in line with strategic priorities. Criticisms of the resource- and service-led practice to emerge served to legitimate subsequent moves towards 'personalising' adult social care and a return to more traditional social work roles, values and professional authority.

Three of the author's studies centre on the impact of care management on front-line social work practice; the fourth is a study of direct payments, which represent the origins of personalisation in the allocation of cash budgets for people to purchase their own support. In a meta-analysis of the findings (Ellis, 2011), the author attempts to show that changes in discretion-as-granted attendant on shifts in the mode of governance have consequences for the nature and scope of discretion-as-used. Much of the empirical work is based on direct observation in line with a phenomenological approach to investigating the negotiated order of front-line practice (for overview, see Ellis, 2011). The descriptive detail of the findings is analysed within a broader critical framework that reflects Lipsky's (2010) concern with the multilayered nature of policymaking highlighted in Chapter One. Both policy ambiguity at the macro-level, for example, and the nature of strategic and operational management at the meso-level are shown to affect the scope and type of discretion and the way in which it is used on the front lines of contemporary adult social care. In contradistinction to Lipsky's approach, however, which generalises across a range of settings to provide a homogeneous account of street-level bureaucracy, the author identifies differing patterns of behaviour under specific organisational conditions.

A feature of the resulting taxonomy concerns the framing in both reforms of the relationship of central interest to this field of investigation, that between social worker and service user, which has been reshaped by and within discourses of user rights and empowerment since Lipsky's (2010) classic account. The NHSCCA was heralded as reconstructing an exchange relationship of professional authority and client dependency into one in which the consumer exercised greater choice in the construction of customised 'packages of care' from the newly formed marketplace. Given that purchasing power lay with the commissioner rather than the user of services, this representation was widely discredited, including by the disability activists who led campaigns for direct payments legislation. The rhetoric of personalisation is similarly of giving greater choice and control to the end user but, as will be discussed, this time by changing the process of resource allocation in such a way as to place the social worker in a position of supporting the user to achieve their aspirations rather than gatekeeping access to resources.

Adult social care: modes of governance and street-level decision-making

The author's taxonomy of discretion under care management distinguished four types – *practitioner, bureau-professional, street-level bureaucrat* and *paternalistic professional* – each representing an exercise in the power to manage encounters with service users and to control access to resources. Given the nature and content of their work, all social workers in the author's studies are street-level bureaucrats within the broad definition adopted in Chapter One. The means by which power was exercised in empirical reality, however, differed from Lipsky's classic account of street-level bureaucracy, which was the basis of the author's analysis of discretion–as–used in adult social care (for detailed discussion, see Ellis, 2011). The key variables were degree and type of formalisation.

When social services departments were established in 1970, they typified the bureau-professional regime of welfare organisation (Clarke et al, 1994). As such, they embodied normative assumptions that, within a framework of rules, social workers used professional expertise to respond flexibly to the individual when assessing need. Empirical studies of social work, however, suggested that front-line practice should be understood in terms of the characteristics of street-level bureaucracy identified by Lipsky (2010), that is, rules were open to negotiation and professional knowledge and values had low salience relative to the informal rules and understandings driving street-level decision-making (Hall, 1974; Rees, 1978; Smith, 1980; Satyamurti, 1981).

Developed in the era of bureau-professional organisation, Lipsky's approach to discretion was challenged by the full implementation of the NHSCCA in 1993, when assessment and care management systems made it possible to manage front-line practice hierarchically. Computerisation, in particular, was instrumental in routinising social work tasks and enforcing compliance with organisational rules (Lymbery, 1998, 2001; Bradley, 2005; McDonald et al, 2008; Parrott and Madoc-Jones, 2008). This generated a form of assessment practice prefigured in government guidance to local authorities on implementing the new systems, which used the term 'practitioner' in preference to professional or social worker. In the author's studies, social workers at the point of entry to care management were prone to behave as practitioners, most obviously when completing computer screens during an initial assessment. Procedures designed to allocate resources in line with eligibility criteria meant that there was little call for either professional expertise or implicit rationing strategies. As practitioners, social workers practised legitimately as gatekeepers.

Traditional forms of discretion did have some purchase among teams that were both beyond the disciplinary reach of information and budget management systems and protected from the immediate pressures of managing social care resources in encounters with service users. Hospital social workers, or social workers in specialist teams for disabled people of working age, people with sensory impairments or people with learning disabilities, had some freedom to operate as *bureau-professionals*, their decision-making being mediated by norms drawn from older bureaucratic traditions, such as equity, as well as by professional commitments, such as advocacy.

The two remaining patterns of behaviour were observed within and across teams in situations where social workers were not only required to control front-line pressures for which formally sanctioned means were ineffective, but also had sufficient latitude to manage service users in other ways. Professional identity played little part in the *street-level bureaucrat*'s assessment practice, whose covert rationing strategies strongly resembled those described by Lipsky. Whereas these methods were legitimated by popular notions of deservingness, however, the *paternalistic professional* mobilised professional authority in the face of rights or any other means by which service users threatened to assert control over the assessment encounter.

By definition, Lipsky largely discounted the direct impact of discretion-as-granted on the nature of street-level discretion. Yet, the author found that both neo-Taylorist tools of management and older bureau-professional traditions of prioritising need could affect discretion-as-used. Put simply, the former had the potential to manage those pressures that led to informal rationing, whereas the latter was influential in spaces absent of such pressures. Where informal pressure management was required, more familiar strategies were observed across the same teams. In the case of professional paternalism, however, the taxonomy distinguishes a type of discretion deployed in response to a pressure less evident at the time that Lipsky was writing, that of user empowerment and rights.

At the point at which the governance of adult social care shifts once again, personalisation affords the opportunity to review the continuing value and strength of these distinctions. Changes in the policy and operational environment are considered first as a means of considering their impact on the key variables of degree and type of formalisation.

Personalisation and the challenges of governance

The policy agenda for personalising adult social care in England, set out in *Putting people first: a shared vision and commitment to the transformation of adult social care* (HM Government, 2007), reflected increased interest across advanced welfare states over the previous two decades in moving from services in-kind to 'cash-for-care' schemes in which eligible individuals receive cash payments, vouchers or personal budgets to purchase care instead of receiving in-kind domiciliary care (Arksey and Kemp, 2008). In common with other countries, the underlying principles are of personalised, responsive and flexible delivery that affords people greater choice and control over the way their needs are met (Arksey and Baxter, 2012). Individual budgets, as they were initially called (DH, 2005; Prime Minister's Strategy Group, 2005), were designed to extend the reach of direct payments by permitting the delegation of flexible levels of control to those unwilling or unable to take charge of a cash budget.

The author has described the personalisation agenda elsewhere as 'symbolic', the term used by Matland (1995) in his model of policy implementation for interventions incorporating high levels of ambiguity and conflict (Ellis, 2013a). While the symbolism of choice and control is consistent with both neoliberal policymakers' and disability activists' agendas, these are rooted in ideologically opposed positions. Despite drawing on the language of radicalism, far from pursuing greater autonomy on the basis of collectivist goals for social justice and inclusive citizenship, the core purpose of the policy agenda was to enable the individual citizen-consumer to make lifestyle changes based primarily on participation in the social care market (Roulstone and Morgan, 2009; Houston, 2010; Ferguson, 2012). These contradictions were at least partially obscured at the policy formation stage, however, by a broader *Putting people first* agenda of early intervention and prevention, building community capacity, and improving people's access to universally available services.

Personalisation also appeared to offer a range of possibilities for an enhanced role for adult social workers in capacity building at the individual and community level through empowering, outcome-focused assessment and support planning, brokerage, risk enablement, and safeguarding (Duffy, 2010; Lymbery and Postle, 2010; Tyson et al, 2010; Leece and Leece, 2011). Issued in the wake of a report from a government task force set up to make recommendations for reforming the profession, a joint statement by key social work organisations in England (ADASS et al and DH, 2010) endorsed the potential for a wider role for adult social work, as well as an advanced practitioner and consultant social worker career structure. Evaluations of individual budget pilot schemes similarly lent credence to an expanded role for adult social work, indicating both that professional support in care planning was valued (Hatton et al, 2008; Beresford and Hasler, 2009; Rabiee et al, 2009) and that personalisation implied a level of responsibility that not everyone requiring support was either willing or able to take (Glendinning, 2008).

At the point of implementation, however, local authorities had to translate symbols and aspirations into operational reality. According to Newman et al (2008, p 547), adult social care in England is 'positioned at the interface between a highly centralising government and the rhetoric (and to some extent the practice) of local autonomy and control'. They argue that compliance with centrally determined outcomes is secured through the top-down transactional change processes of hierarchical and managerial governance, whereas bottom-up trajectories of power work through transformational processes of network-based and self-governance (Newman et al, 2008, pp 538–40). The *Putting people first* policy agenda did initially imply transformational processes of change. Local authorities would address the longer-term goals of a preventive network of support based on early intervention, information sharing and participation through community capacity building. People's potential for self-governance would be correspondingly increased by maintaining their independence, well-being and safety for longer, while recommendations for an enhanced career structure for social workers suggested a greater capacity for professional self-governance.

Yet, personalised budgets run counter to the public sector values and bureaucratic traditions upon which social services departments were founded. The evaluation studies identified principled concerns about balancing the contradictory imperatives of promoting individual choice and managing their duty as democratically elected councils to have regard for equity and fiscal integrity when allocating public funds (Henwood and Hudson, 2007; Rabiee et al, 2009; Jones and Netten, 2010; Needham, 2011; Stevens et al, 2011). More pragmatically, local authorities faced the dilemma of reconciling the move towards greater choice and control for individuals with their duty of care and adult safeguarding responsibilities (Lymbery, 2010; Warin, 2010; Leece and Leece, 2011). In adult social care, need is measured against risk with eligibility criteria governing entry based on the level of risk to independence and well-being. Consequently, only people at critical or substantial risk gain access, and tight means-testing means that they are also likely to be the most economically and socially disadvantaged. The result was widespread scepticism about the model of the reasonable and responsible consumer underlying personalisation (Ferguson, 2007; Kemshall, 2010; Lymbery, 2010; Lymbery and Postle, 2010).

By 2010, moreover, the original vision of personalisation had been undermined by significant cuts in local council budgets, imposed by the incoming Coalition government, which limited the capacity for funding preventive interventions. Despite the initial resurgence of faith in social work expertise, government guidance also made it clear that the roles of support planning and brokerage were not confined to qualified social workers (DH, 2010a, p 3). In line with Beddoe's (2010) argument that social work is less contested when it relates to statutory power or mandated action, a narrower role for qualified workers was emerging of assessing mental capacity and related support planning for people deemed most at risk (ADASS, 2009; Lymbery and Postle, 2010; Schwehr, 2010). Whatever the rhetoric of transformational change, the implementation logic was for transactional change processes. The rest of the chapter considers the question of their purchase on front-line behaviour in the light of the challenges of managing policy ambiguity combined with high demand, which drive street-level bureaucracy.

Challenges for front-line management

Evans (2013) identifies an enduring tension for statutory social work in England between fulfilling organisational roles and exercising professional autonomy. The loss of a community-facing role notwithstanding, social workers appear to have been granted a wider margin of discretion in their relations with individuals under personalisation. In terms of resource management, they not only retained their existing powers to determine eligibility and the way in which eligible needs should be met (ADASS, 2009), but indicative guidelines governing resource allocation also afforded professional judgement about specific allocations to meet individual situations within funding bands (DH, 2010b). Similarly, an intensification of focus on risk assessment and management potentially increased professional autonomy in relation to support planning given the credence attached to social workers' capacity in this regard (Kemshall et al, 1997; Schwehr, 2010; Gardner, 2011). Yet, the managerialisation of adult social care suggests that this assumption of a greater potential for self-governance on the part of social workers warrants closer examination, as does any assumption that professional discretion would be used to enhance the potential for self-governance on the part of service users. These issues are explored next by considering the interplay of discretion-as-granted and discretion-as-used within the explicit and implicit frameworks of front-line practice opened up by the personalisation agenda.

Managerial and bureau-professional governance of front-line practice

This exploration starts by examining the likely impact of personalisation on the two types of formalisation previously identified by the author as giving rise to practitioner or bureau-professional behaviour on the front line. The original proposal to identify an appropriate allocation to personal budgets on the basis of self-assessed need was declared unlawful once it was confirmed that local authorities retained responsibility under existing legislation, both for identifying and costing eligible need and for final support-planning decisions (ADASS, 2009). The early promise of greater professional autonomy and a return to traditional social work skills and methods proved as uncertain as that of user control. Observers noted a shift in emphasis over 2009 in government task-force reports on social work reform, from highlighting the impact of bureaucracy on workloads to the centring of the final recommendations on 'supply side' strategies of recruitment, education and training (Dickens, 2011; Stanford, 2011). Following implementation, the evidence is that bureaucracy has proliferated rather than reduced under personalisation, with a number of councils initiating a duplicate process of self-assessment and traditional community care assessments in order to give a lead to service users in identifying their needs while simultaneously testing eligibility and identifying potential risks in line with local authorities' duty of care to prevent foreseeable harm (Schwehr, 2010).

In terms of the consequences for the way in which discretion is used, the author previously found that front-line social workers behave as practitioners when adopting the 'managerial-technicist' approach to practice, which Harlow (2003, p 29) identifies as developing under care management. A practitioner, however, does not simply follow rules. Indeed, as Evans (2010) points out, a multiplicity of often-competing rules in adult social care can serve to widen discretion by creating uncertainty and the scope for interpretation and choice. Outside of certain prescribed circumstances, such as inputting data on computer screens, studies show that social workers retain the freedom to choose how to use standardised documentation and what to include (Ellis, 1993; Foster et al, 2006). Given the pressures to control demand, these are the enabling conditions for street-level bureaucracy. Yet, the literature on front-line practice in contemporary adult social care would suggest that managerialisation has given rise to a type of defensive practice that sits outside of Lipsky's (2010) classic account. Before considering practitioner discretion further, however, evidence for the enduring influence of bureau-professionalism on behaviour is first considered.

In making this case, Evans (2011, 2013) points to an internal fracturing of control between strategic and first-line management in adult social care, either side of which arguably lie the *practitioner* and *bureau-professional*. In a study of professional approaches to organisational rules among first-line managers and front-line social workers, Evans (2013) argues that belonging to the same professional group creates a shared commitment to professionally validated goals, which stands in contrast to strategic managers' prioritisation of expenditure control and performance targets. Whereas all his participants were committed to organisational rules in terms of ensuring procedural justice, one group prioritised their ethical commitment to individuals, even if this meant bending or breaking rules, while the other group placed greater emphasis on fair treatment for current and prospective service users, albeit with scope for responding flexibly to individual need.

Other researchers, too, have shown that social workers' justification for complying with organisational rules draws on older traditions of welfare governance, such as the significance of eligibility criteria in guaranteeing objective assessments and a fiscally responsible and equitable distribution of resources (Sullivan, 2009; Ellis, 2011). Whereas some research has found little professional judgement in participants' decision-making (McDonald et al, 2008; Sullivan, 2009), other studies have identified a form of front-line practice that still bears the hallmark of professional reflexivity in balancing the tensions inherent in the bureau-professional tradition (Ellis et al, 1999; Evans, 2011, 2013). Indeed, Evans (2011, 2013) argues that the two are mutually reinforcing: the language of need and risk in eligibility criteria assumes professional judgement, whereas service users' procedural rights are supported by the bureaucratic standards of equity and accountability underpinning resource allocation.

Evidence for the lingering influence of bureau-professionalism on personalisation practice lies in the uncertainty, even hostility, invoked by the threat that policy implementation is perceived to pose to the principles of traditional welfare bureaucracy. Personal budgets and direct payments have generated considerable uncertainty about their implications for the equitable treatment of the local population as a whole, as well as the legitimacy of expenditure on items that some might regard as 'luxuries' (Ellis, 2007; Glasby and Littlechild, 2009; Needham, 2011; Stevens et al, 2011). Even if purchases are technically legal, they nevertheless risk damaging local authorities' reputation and budget security if they are regarded as profligate or irresponsible (Henwood and Hudson, 2007). Such attitudes among first-line managers and social workers have been linked to front-line behaviour, with criticisms of personal budgets as an overly individual approach to collective social welfare (Henwood and Hudson, 2007) and concerns about a two-tier system of direct payments and direct services (Priestley et al, 2010) both translating into ideological barriers to promoting access to self-directed support.

Direct observation of practice, however, would suggest that front-line social workers tend only to act in line with bureau-professional principles in environments where managerial technology and practices have limited purchase (Ellis et al, 1999). In the case of first-line managers, McDonald et al (2008) found little appreciation for the ethical principles of social work in their supervision practice, which focused on managing workloads and monitoring front-line adherence to procedures rather than professional issues and dilemmas. At the sharp end, managerial governance offers a more secure means of dealing with the ambiguity of front-line practice than an ethical balancing of traditional bureaucratic standards and professional codes of conduct. It is not that practitioners' adherence to procedures in pressured front-line environments can simply be attributed to the 'tick box' mentality described by Crisp et al (2006). Rather, what Hudson (2009) characterises as social workers' search for organisational 'permission to act' represents a deeper-seated disposition of compliance rooted in the priorities of strategic management. Thus, Foster et al (2006, pp 129–33) found a tendency among social workers to manage the assessment process by selecting topics to raise according to assumptions based on the initial referral or on current managerial priorities, such as meeting practical, self- and home-care needs. Even social workers using documentation designed to encourage the exploration of an extensive range of user-preferred outcomes identified only a narrow range of preferred outcomes and service types, notably, equipment and daily living aids (Foster et al, 2008, p 557). This is similar to Sullivan's (2009, p 1314) observation that social workers not only valued clients who 'fit the system', but also, when required, shifted from routine to strategic behaviour in assessment encounters to effect a fit.

Such findings, as Foster et al (2006, pp 131–3) note, represent a considerable challenge to the transformational potential of personalisation for moving assessment and support planning beyond the service-led approach of care management and towards identifying new and imaginative ways of meeting people's support needs; furthermore, the vision of a participatory process is thrown into doubt by the practice of completing documentation after, rather than during, the assessment encounter. Adult safeguarding, a further strategic priority under personalisation, led first-line managers within the individual budget pilots to adopt a conservative stance on risk when discharging their duty of care by guiding or monitoring what could go into support plans before signing them off (Stevens et al, 2011, p 270). The imperatives of risk management also reinforce the transactional power immanent within managerial-technicist approaches to assessment and support planning. In pressured front-line environments, this is likely to find expression in defensive strategies to avoid blame, such as recording information in ways that minimise professional and corporate risk rather than capturing what is right for the service user (Foster et al, 2006; McDonald et al, 2008; Beddoe, 2010; Pollack, 2010).

Front-line practice: an informal order

Whatever the commitment to managerial priorities and bureau-professional standards, studies of direct payments and individual budgets suggest that access is still influenced by implicit knowledge and attitudes (Ellis, 2007; Henwood and Hudson, 2007; Glasby and Littlechild, 2009; Priestley et al, 2010). These are types of discretion that are used but not granted, or at least explicitly, and have been identified earlier as those exercised by social workers operating as *street-level bureaucrats* and *paternalistic professionals*. Their respective impact within the new environment created by personalisation is considered next.

Lipsky (2010) saw occupational stress, rooted in low morale and responsibility for unmanageable demand, as a factor in the subversion of formal frameworks of front-line practice. Constraints on professional autonomy under care management, coupled with the stress created by the gap between professional expectations and the everyday reality of high-volume, low-intensity work, were identified as leading to demoralisation and cynicism about policy intentions (Bradley, 2005; McDonald et al, 2008; Curtis et al, 2010; Foster, 2010). Commentators suggest that personalisation is also more likely to be regarded as yet another policy imposed on social workers for which, in view of its implied criticism of the approach to professional practice to develop under care management, any lack of progress in implementation will be blamed on them rather than on systemic weaknesses in adult social care (Beresford, 2009; Duffy, 2010; Lymbery, 2010). Nor are managerialist technologies likely to afford front-line professionals full protection against the pressures of demand management. Unsurprisingly given the proliferation of bureaucracy, an increased number of social workers and first-line managers participating in the 2012 Community Care/Unison survey felt that personalisation had led to a higher volume of paperwork, largely relating to longer assessment processes. Time constraints predispose towards short cuts in decision-making, and where these cannot be managed or legitimated in terms of managerial tools and priorities, street-level means of rationing demand and managing workloads are likely to come into play.

Beliefs and values drawn from personal and social worlds have been shown to exert a continuing influence on front-line decision-making in adult social care (Foster et al, 2006; Ellis, 2013b). The valorisation of self-reliance that permeates this field, from policy through to eligibility criteria, is reinforced by street-level beliefs about the legitimacy of claims on resources. To be deserving means eschewing voluntary dependency, as exemplified by social workers' beliefs that some people are too active and independent to warrant an in-depth assessment for adult social care (Foster et al, 2006) or stereotypes of older people as less motivated to engage in assessment (Sullivan, 2009; Priestley et al, 2010). Both carry implications for assessments for personalised support, predicated as these are on people's active participation in the articulation and formulation of preferred outcomes (Foster et al, 2006). Being adjudged dependent, moreover, requires evidence of genuine need, which is confounded by the suspicion surrounding individual budgets that people will seek to get as much out of the system as possible (Henwood and Hudson, 2007) or fears that public money for direct payments and individual budgets will be used to meet extravagant 'wants' rather than 'needs' (Ellis, 2007; Henwood and Hudson, 2007; Stevens et al, 2011).

Turning to the *paternalistic professional*, the challenge represented by the displacement of direct services under personalisation is a powerful driver of this type of discretion. Resource-allocation systems developed during implementation were designed to replace discretion with citizen entitlement, disrupting what Duffy (1996, 2005) identifies as 'the professional gift relationship', according to which the pre-paid services into which people were slotted were treated as a gift bestowed on the basis of an assessment of their needs. Preferential treatment given to service users showing gratitude (Ellis, 1993; Sullivan, 2009) evidences the dominance of the gift relationship in adult social care, as do terms such as 'let', 'allow' and 'give', which social workers frequently used when dispensing direct payments (Ellis, 2007). Fears about self-assessment and the loss of direct services have been shown to act as barriers to accessing direct payments (Ellis, 2007; Priestley et al, 2010). Paradoxically, in contradistinction to concerns about budgetary control, Henwood and Hudson (2007) identify a cultural challenge to self-directed support in the 'giving and doing' tradition, according to which social workers try to secure as much support for service users as possible.

The contemporary valorisation of individual responsibility – which, Kemshall (2010, p 1252) argues, has led to the replacement of the good client of adult social care, who passively accepts professional decisions, by the good citizen, who plays an active part in decision-making and risk calculations – reinforces both the legitimacy of professional discretion and the potential for professional paternalism. Social workers' expertise in risk enablement is important in making a reality of more person-centred ways of managing risk (Tyson et al, 2010). Yet, as the individual budget pilot schemes demonstrate, sanctioning risk-taking represents a particularly difficult cultural shift given that adult safeguarding responsibilities require social workers to manage the tension between positive risk-taking and their organisational duty of care (Glendinning et al, 2008; Stevens et al, 2011). In managing the risk of personalised support in the pilot schemes, Stevens et al (2011, p 269) reported that professional discretion was used in more or less directive ways to support, empower or constrain people in their decision-making. In an earlier study of paternalism, Clark (1998, p 389) found that although professional beneficence is not formally articulated as a principle of practice ethics, social workers were intuitively convinced that this is the single most important justification for their work. There is support for this finding in Stanford's (2011) study of the personalisation of risk, where social workers who sought to act in clients' best interests by advocating for and protecting them drew on personal and professional morals, ethics and values in framing their responses. Yet, Clark also identified an implicit acceptance of constraint as compatible with an ethical approach to practice, where social workers could justify this in terms of acting in a person's best interests, and, as Evans (2013) observes, acting in a person's best interests can shade into disempowering professional patronage.

Research suggests that the greater the focus of risk management strategies on protecting the organisation, the less confident and supported social workers and first-line managers are likely to feel in their practice (SCIE, 2010), and uncertainty and fear of blame or liability reinforce defensive practice. Social workers in Clark's (1998, p 392) study regarded organisational factors, such as the expense of meeting self-determined choice or the negative consequences of risk to the authority, as qualifying people's right to self-determination. In Stanford's (2011) study, too, organisational context was a significant influence on those social workers who adopted a stance of controlling and dismissing clients, and feelings of isolation and fear of sanctions reinforced their sense of being at risk from or a risk to vulnerable clients. Personalisation is likely to exacerbate risk aversion given concerns about the use of unregulated services, physical, emotional or financial abuse, and misuse of public funds (SCIE, 2010, p 19). This may, in turn, give encouragement to the *paternalistic professional*, as evidenced by Henwood and Hudson's (2007) finding that front-line social workers' mistrust of people's ability to manage self-directed support included an implicit assumption that significant professional input was required to safeguard public money.

In Clark's (1998, p 389) study, acting in a person's best interests on the basis of risk meant that a judgement about mental capacity could justify legal coercion, deception and withholding information. Given that risk stands as a proxy for need when determining type and level of support, implicit judgements about resource allocation can shade into determinations of deservingness. Studies of direct payments and self-directed support illustrate what might be termed 'street-level professionalism' in linking generalised decisions about who should access them to stereotyped assumptions about the capacity of certain groups, such as older people, people with learning disabilities and mental health service users, to manage these options (Spandler and Vick, 2005; Ellis, 2007; Henwood and Hudson, 2007; Arksey and Kemp, 2008; Carr and Robbins, 2009; Priestley et al, 2010).

Conclusion

This chapter has adopted a multilayered approach to the impact of a significant policy shift on the author's previous modelling of front-line discretion in adult social care, developed primarily under care management (Ellis, 2011). The author's taxonomy challenged Lipsky's representation of the exchange relationship between managers and street-level bureaucrats as one incorporating both mutual dependency and antagonistic interests. Rather, where managerialist technologies provided an orderly environment for front-line practice, they encouraged compliance with strategic objectives. Only where the purchase of technology on uncertainty and competing priorities was incomplete were street-level techniques used to secure orderly relations with service users. Furthermore, contrary to Lipsky's dismissal of the possibility of discretion deriving from professional values as the 'myth of altruism', the typology incorporated manifestations of discretion that derived from professional as well as bureaucratic forms of governance. Nonetheless, however deeply inscribed within English social services departments, neither social work values nor bureaucratic traditions had a direct influence on discretionary behaviour towards service users in pressured conditions but were mediated by the need to manage high demand and uncertainty.

Under personalisation, proposed changes in the scope of both professional discretion and user control during policy formation potentially reconfigured the front-line worker–manager–service user exchange relationships at the centre of this modelling of discretion-as-used. Coupled with inadequate resources relative to demand, the ambiguities of personalisation recreate many of the enabling conditions for street-level behaviour. At the point of implementation, however, local authorities continue to rely on transactional technologies of care management to manage both demand and elevated levels of risk. The nature and scope of discretion granted under such circumstances mean that social workers are likely to continue to behave as practitioners who ally themselves to strategic objectives in ways that reduce the need for street-level discretion. Nonetheless, where allegiance to managerial priorities, or adherence to managerial controls, is weakened, the evidence is that social workers use their power informally, but equally defensively, to control both resources and risk.

In granting social workers greater professional authority, personalisation could lend credence to the notion of an expanded scope for bureau-professionalism. Yet, the emphasis on individual choice has debased local authority legitimacy – stemming as this does from democratic accountability to the local population as a whole – and, by extension, the ethical underpinnings of front-line practice. The continuing circulation of counter-values and traditions rooted in earlier forms of governance is not necessarily evidence of ethical forms of practice. Decision-making has to be understood within the material conditions of practice to avoid the danger of conflating front-line actors' views with their behaviour. Eligibility criteria continually expose social workers to the tension between choice and equity, a conflict heightened by the dissonance between what personalisation ought to represent for professional aspirations and front-line realities. Reinforced by their duty of care and the risk-averse stance of local authorities, social workers feel justified in exercising their paternalistic authority as professionals to override choice and control, which, given its relationship to eligibility criteria, can shade into determinations about deservingness for support. While social workers' accounts bear testimony to the continuing impact of bureaucratic traditions and professional aspirations on practice, direct observation of practice in pressured environments suggests that they can be equally convincingly understood as a rhetorical strategy for justifying resistance to the transfer of greater control over resource allocation to end users, such as creating stereotypes of voluntary dependency in order to manage demand.

In some respects, given the familiar challenges of managing demand in an environment of policy ambiguity and inadequate resources, this analysis of the uses and abuses of front-line discretion confirms the enduring features of street-level bureaucracy. Yet, the formalisation of decision-making since 1980 has given rise to a level of conformity with bureaucratic rules unimagined in Lipsky's classic account. Personalisation represents a further shift in governance that merits closer examination – particularly through observation of practice – to empirically test the anticipated impact of shifts in professional and user control on street-level behaviour. The analysis presented here may also have wider interest and research application. Although it is rooted in certain institutional characteristics of adult social care in England, notably, the civic values and traditions within which discretion is granted, personalisation is a feature of neoliberal policy and practice across a number of policy fields, nationally and internationally, responding as it does to the common and contradictory challenges of managing risk, the struggle for professional identity and the assertion of user control.

Part Five
The management of street-level bureaucrats

Bureaucratic, market or professional control? A theory on the relation between street-level task characteristics and the feasibility of control mechanisms

Duco Bannink, Frédérique Six and Eelco van Wijk

Introduction

Street-level bureaucracy is two things: it is an effort to have policy implementation conform to general and abstract rules; and it is an effort to apply rules to specific and concrete cases. This central assumption informs our analysis of the managerial control of street-level action. The first assumes control of action through general regulation; the second assumes adjustment of action to specific case conditions. These are necessarily incongruent functions. Bridging the distance between general and abstract rules and specific and concrete cases requires action that cannot be fully defined by either. This is why, as Lipsky (2010) phrased it, street-level bureaucrats are policymakers. Street-level bureaucrats do not simply implement given rules in cases that can be fully understood on the basis of these rules, but instead translate rules into client-level decisions, building upon information (not fully defined in the rule) on clients' conditions and upon expertise (also not fully defined) on client treatment.

There is an abundant literature on managerial and bureaucratic control over street-level bureaucrats. Meyers and Vorsanger (2003, p 246) argue that 'the questions of whether, and how, policy making principals control the discretion of their implementing agents have dominated much of the empirical research'. Winter (2003) asks whether 'bureaucrats [are] servants or masters, and to what extent ... bureaucrats [can] be controlled by their political superiors' and argues that there is 'differentiated and limited control' over street-level bureaucracies that varies according to the extent of information asymmetry. Meyers, Riccucci and Lurie (2001, p 165) argue that the achievement of 'goal congruence' between political control actors and street-level bureaucrats might increase 'implementation fidelity and policy achievement'. The main thrust of the insights in this literature is that control over street-level action is limited and indirect.

These arguments conceptualise the issue of street-level control as placed on a single dimension of increased control versus increased street-level discretion. We disagree with this conceptualisation. Our central assumption is that street-level bureaucracy does not have one manifest function, but two: the control of policy implementation given existing regulations; and the translation of policy rules to clients given the street-level information on client conditions and expertise on client treatment. Brodkin (2011, p 254, emphasis in original) argued that street-level organisations 'not only *do* policy work, but are manifestly responsible for making policy *work*'. Discretion is accepted as 'an inherent – at times even necessary – feature of implementation' (Brodkin, 2011, p 254). Through control systems, managers seek 'to align employee capabilities, activities, and performance with organisational goals and aspirations' (Sitkin et al, 2010, p 3). They do not minimise the application of employee capabilities in order to achieve maximum implementation fidelity. There is an autonomous contribution that the street-level bureaucrat makes to street-level bureaucracy; this is the second function of informing the street-level bureaucratic system with client information and treatment expertise. Also, the political decision-maker makes an autonomous contribution to the street-level system: the control of street-level bureaucrats' action. These functions are *both* necessary functions of a street-level bureaucratic system. In Brodkin's phrasing, street-level bureaucrats *do* the work and make it *work*.

We transferred this insight to a discussion on control mechanisms in street-level bureaucracy. Street-level bureaucrats do their work in different contexts (Hupe and Hill, 2007). These contexts determine street-level task characteristics and pose the different control challenges that managers need to deal with. The two context variables critical for determining task characteristics and the corresponding nature of the control challenge are complexity and ambiguity. Social problem complexity is about the uncertainty of the factual estimation of social problems. Social problem ambiguity is about the uncertainty of the normative evaluation of social problems and solutions.

In this chapter, we propose a *theory* about the relationship between two variables: street-level task characteristics (the levels of task complexity and ambiguity) and the control mechanisms (enforcement, incentives and competence control) that may be applied. When both the ambiguity and complexity of tasks are low, the control challenge entails how to achieve conformity. Managers may achieve this by means of enforcement: process control or standardisation of work processes (Mintzberg, 1989). When ambiguity is high but complexity is low, the control challenge is how to achieve the alignment of preferences and interests. Managers may control street-level bureaucrats by means of incentives: output controls (Bouckaert and Halligan, 2008) or the standardisation of outputs or results. So, incentive-based government is one of the main governance arrangements suitable for the organisation of street-level action, where tasks are highly ambiguous but complex to an only limited extent. When complexity is high but ambiguity is low, the challenge is one of expertise, and managers may control street-level bureaucrats, who act more or less autonomously as experts, by competence control: autonomous task execution and mutual adjustment of action, with expertise normally being guaranteed through competence controls or the standardisation of skills (see Table 12.1).

Table 12.1: Control challenges in relation to the complexity and ambiguity of social problems

		Ambiguity: heterogeneity of preferences or interests	
		Low	High
Complexity: factual uncertainty of risks	Low	Conformity	Alignment
	High	Expertise	Double control challenge

In situations of simultaneous high ambiguity and high complexity, there is a double control challenge of simultaneously controlling the application of the necessary expertise and controlling to ensure that preferences and interests are sufficiently aligned. This interaction of complexity and ambiguity, we argue, is the normal state of affairs for broad segments of street-level bureaucracy. This poses an important problem since extant theories on governing or controlling SLBs, or public professionals for that matter, provide adequate explanations and guidance for the first three situations but not for the bottom-right-hand situation of the double control challenge (eg Terpstra and Havinga, 2001; Bannink et al, 2006).

The dimensions of our matrix are almost, but not completely, similar to the dimensions in Matland's (1995) well-known ambiguity–conflict matrix. Matland makes a distinction between the dimension of ambiguity, in which he includes complexity, and the dimension of conflict. We diverge from Matland's conceptualisation because we try to convey that conflict may concern either factual estimations or normative evaluations, or both. The interaction of factual and normative uncertainty creates the double control challenge that is of central interest to the discussion in this chapter.

The *central question* we address in this chapter is a normative or, rather, prescriptive one and concerns this double control challenge: which governance mechanisms are functional responses to the double control challenge of combined task complexity and ambiguity? In this chapter, we present an empirical study made up of 42 case studies of task characteristics and governance mechanisms. The study supports our theoretical point of departure that tasks and governance mechanisms are related and that a double control challenge – where it is difficult to choose a governance mechanism – is, indeed, important in street-level bureaucracies.

We studied cases comprised of a set of tasks and governance mechanisms applied in a human service organisation. The tasks vary widely: judge's rulings, community policing, inspecting chicken factories, providing care at home, re-employment services, caring for troubled youth in institutions, child protection services and so on. We show that instead of finding a new governance solution that integrates the requirements of ambiguity (alignment) and complexity (expertise), most of these organisations 'flee' to a partially adequate governance approach in which only one of these requirements is addressed.

Some cases, however, appear to make an effort to stay in the double control challenge box. They appear to seek a way to address the double control challenge. We study the following empirical question: what are the mechanisms that they make use of? The (not yet theoretically understood) roots of a solution to the double control challenge are empirically located in the smaller cases that we studied.

This leads us to an additional, conceptual, question that we briefly address at the end of our chapter: how may control systems be designed specifically to deal with the double control challenge? In the situations where the double control challenge is present, ambiguity needs to be overcome through interactive processes that lead to the alignment of preferences and interests, while, at the same time, managers and collaborating professionals need to trust the expertise of the street-level bureaucrats that they are in disagreement with. In a *programmatic* sense, we make one central claim: the double control challenge posed by task complexity and ambiguity is, indeed, important for the understanding of the governance of street-level bureaucracy but the relation between task and governance is as yet not fully understood. Some authors have begun to explore possible solutions to the double control challenge but, so far, without adequate theoretical explanations (eg De Bruijn, 2007; Bouckaert and Halligan, 2008, Noordegraaf, 2011; Thomas and Hewitt, 2011). We look, among others, at research that integrates trust-building and control as complementary managerial activities (Long and Sitkin, 2006) and the role of intrinsic motivation (Deci and Ryan, 2000; Ryan and Deci, 2000; Weibel and Six, 2013).

Control challenges and governance mechanisms

We discuss how existing organisations that have to perform in contexts of simultaneous high complexity and ambiguity respond to the double control challenge in terms of the governance principles they apply. We apply an explicitly normative approach, in which we define the appropriate solution to the control challenge in relation to the task at hand. This does not lead to a single statement on appropriate organisation, however. Our normative position includes both functions: alignment of street-level bureaucrat action to regulations and input of autonomous street-level bureaucrat expertise. As outlined in Table 12.1, where complexity and ambiguity are limited, appropriate control is oriented to 'conformity'. Where ambiguity is high but complexity is low, the control challenge concerns the 'alignment' of normative orientations. Where complexity is high but ambiguity is low, street-level bureaucrat 'expertise' in the task execution is sought. When complexity and ambiguity are simultaneously high, seeking expertise weakens alignment and seeking alignment weakens the input of local expertise. As such, the control challenges of alignment and expertise appear contradictory and create a double control challenge. Our normative position with respect to this double control challenge is that the 'integration' of alignment and expertise needs to be sought. Table 12.2, then, outlines through which governance mechanisms the various control challenges can be addressed.

We define three types of governance with their respective main governance mechanisms. In bureaucracy, enforcement is the main mechanism to steer the action of subordinates; this presupposes compliance by subordinates and the capacity of the controlling actor to define tasks. In managerialism, incentives function as the main mechanism to direct the action of service providers; this presupposes a conflict of interests (to be overcome by incentives) and the capacity of the controlling actor to define the required performance. In professionalism, competence control is the main mechanism in

Table 12.2: Ability of governance mechanisms to deal with complexity and ambiguity

		Ambiguity: heterogeneity of preferences and interests	
		Low	High
Complexity: factual uncertainty of risks and policy objectives	Low	Bureaucracy (enforcement)	Managerialism (incentives)
	High	Professionalism (competence control)	

professional governance to accommodate expertise and task; this presupposes a natural willingness by experts to engage in mutual adjustment and requires (but also allows) the controlling actor not to define tasks and performance.

Addressing the need for conformity: bureaucracy

When both complexity and ambiguity are low, conformity to the wishes and preferences of management may be achieved through governance based on bureaucratic rules and authority (cf Bradach and Eccles, 1989; Thompson et al, 1991; Terpstra and Havinga, 2001; Hupe and Hill, 2007). The aim here is full control of policy implementation. In such a hierarchical governance mechanism, management operates as the regulator of the actions at the street level (Kirkpatrick, 1999; Terpstra and Havinga, 2001; Keast et al, 2006; Bannink et al, 2006). Management defines the social problems that street-level bureaucrats respond to and the way in which the latter need to implement the desired response, that is, how they execute their task.

The Dutch General Pension Act is a standardised retirement arrangement in which central government defines that a pension benefit is provided when clients reach 65 years of age. The central (supra-organisational)-level regulation defines how age is determined (by checking personal records) and how the benefit is disbursed. Such a governance arrangement is only feasible under highly demanding conditions as it requires sufficient information and expertise at the control level and street-level compliance with the regulation and definition of the policy objectives, or – the other way around – a sufficiently simple task that allows the management-level definition of policy goals and implementation.

Addressing the need for expertise: professionalism

Addressing high complexity and facilitating the accompanying need for local expertise is structurally achieved by granting policymaking autonomy and implementation discretion to street-level officials, be they called street-level bureaucrats (Lipsky, 2010) or (hybrid) public professionals (Noordegraaf, 2007). The terms are not interchangeable; they differ in the extent that officials have 'ownership' of their expertise. Our central assumption of street-level bureaucracy being 'two things', however, holds that street-level bureaucracy necessarily includes aspects of both. When ambiguity is low, this may be geared towards support of the street-level official fulfilling his or her professionally defined role obligations, with management possibly enforcing competence control, but without intervening in the actual work process. When ambiguity is low, preferences and interests are aligned, so that street-level bureaucrats are assumed to naturally comply with management objectives.

The public professional literature distinguishes 'pure' forms of professionalism from 'hybrid' ones (cf Noordegraaf, 2007, p 2011). In the pure, traditional form, professionals are autonomous from organisational management and are accountable to professional peers and the professional association. This form of organisation is chosen because professionals command relevant information and expertise about important issues at the street level that management does not have (Abbott, 1988; Freidson, 2001; Bannink et al, 2006; Keast et al, 2006). Lipsky (2010, p 3) defines SLBs as 'public service workers who interact directly with citizens in the course of their jobs, and who have substantial discretion in the execution of their work'. The inevitable human aspect of public service delivery to citizens means that – although street-level bureaucrats are 'bureaucrats' and need to implement rules; they can only be 'semi-professionals' (see Chapter One) – managers *intentionally* give discretion to street-level bureaucrats so that they may tailor the service delivery to the specific needs of the citizen concerned by applying their expertise to the case.

In effect, however, such an arrangement places implementation under 'weak control' (Héritier and Eckert, 2008) and may empower street-level actors, possibly allowing them to give priority to street-level interests at the expense of management interest. However, the other way around, discretion may also be given because managers intend to shift the blame for lacking implementation effectiveness to the street level (cf Evans and Harris, 2004).

Addressing the need for alignment: managerialism

High ambiguity is addressed by measures to align preferences and interests. When complexity is low, alignment may be imposed by management onto street-level bureaucrats as little resistance may be expected. Management may choose to impose this alignment via rules, that is, bureaucracy, but when there is a natural discrepancy between the interests and preferences, elaborate control systems will be needed to enforce alignment. Hence, New Public Management (NPM)-type reforms were introduced, which aim to improve the performance of public service delivery while still controlling and prescribing which interpretation of preference and interest is to prevail. In managerialism, preference/interest alignment is, in a sense, 'bought' by the prospect of rewards when the imposed performance targets are achieved.

Such a control arrangement is aimed at influencing the choice options of street-level bureaucrats. Although the street-level bureaucrat is given implementation discretion, a specified output, or outcome, component is measured and rewarded (Brodkin, 2011). The establishment of a specified performance indicator supports increased management control over street-level performance, while 'performance' is defined in such a way as to conform to management objectives. Related to Brodkin's (2011, p 254) observations, we argue that NPM, at the same time, assumes and underestimates the extent of autonomous street-level bureaucrat input in policy implementation. It assumes street-level bureaucrat input in the sense that compliance is actively bought through incentive-based governance. It underestimates the extent of street-level bureaucrat input where unintended effects of incentive-based control mechanisms are evoked. For example, the objective that is implied in the performance indicator may evoke 'shirking' behaviour, or such arrangements may give rise to a so-called 'performance paradox' (Van Thiel and Leeuw, 2002), in which street-level bureaucrats comply with the limited output components measured and rewarded in the system, while broader objectives disappear out of sight and may not be realised.

Addressing the double control challenge

In 'double challenge' situations, both the application of local expertise on a case-by-case basis and the alignment of preferences and interests are asked for. Extant theories of governance mechanisms fail to address these situations properly. The three governance mechanisms – as ideal types – each address one of the three cells in Table 12.1, but not the bottom-right-hand one with the double control challenge (see

Table 12.2). Where social risk complexity rises, market governance faces the performance paradox (Van Thiel and Leeuw, 2002), with disconnects (Bouckaert and Halligan, 2008) and blurred (Pollitt and Bouckaert, 2004) or unexpected outcomes (Hood and Peters, 2004). Where market issues come to inform professionalism, processes of closure (Abbott, 1988; Ackroyd, 1996) and double closure (Ackroyd and Muzio, 2007) indicate the increasing orientation of professional actors to organisational or individual interests.

Some authors have begun to explore possible solutions to the double control challenge (eg De Bruijn, 2007; Bouckaert and Halligan, 2008; Noordegraaf, 2011; Thomas and Hewitt, 2011). Network governance mechanisms are proposed by Klijn and Koppenjan (1997). An implicit assumption seems to exist in the network literature that interaction supports the mutual adjustment of interests and eventually action. This implies, we argue, that conflict is *underappreciated*: a constellation of interests is postulated that allows discursive mechanisms to produce effective cooperation. Where interests enter the debate – and they necessarily do – the horizontal coordination of networks becomes hybrid coordination. The network literature, of course, acknowledges the need to combine discursive methods of coordination and hierarchical ones, but the problems that the interaction of these mechanisms engenders seem to be underestimated. Furthermore, when they are discussed, as for instance by Klijn et al (1995), no new mechanism (comparable to incentives, enforcement or competence control) is introduced. The only 'new' aspect of network governance is a different constellation of actors that are supposed to engage in inter-organisational cooperation or institutional design. The proposed methods described to manage these constellations are bureaucratic (enforcement) or managerialistic (incentives). When problems of conflicting norms and perceptions are addressed, they opt for a top-down approach called 'reframing' in network structuring (Klijn et al, 1995, p 449). In this sense, network governance is nothing new and is, in itself, not able to deal successfully with combined complexity and ambiguity at the street-level bureaucrat level.

In the performance management literature, authors have proposed ways to address situations where accurate or unambiguous performance indicators are hard to come by (eg De Bruijn, 2007; Bouckaert and Halligan, 2008). The general gist is that managers and street-level bureaucrats collectively agree on the design of the performance management system, jointly make sense of the measurements, and agree on the conclusions drawn.

From an opposite angle, in the professionalism literature, Noordegraaf (2011, p 1365) proposed the concept of organised or 'connective' (Noordegraaf, 2013) professionalism since 'various changes in and around professional services ... call for organized responses.... This means that so-called "secondary" aspects of service – efficiency, communication, cooperation, safety, reputation management and so on – become of primary importance, also for professionals.' This builds upon a distinction between primary and secondary aspects of the task by Jamous and Peloille (1970). However, Noordegraaf does not give clear guidance on how to structurally address this control challenge, that is, what controls are appropriate.

In sum, we argue that there is currently no adequate conceptualisation of how to best address the double control challenge of simultaneous input of local, case-specific expertise and the alignment of preferences and interests. In so far as research has begun to address this, answers appear to include 'discursive contestation' (Thomas and Hewitt, 2011), 'dialogue' (Noordegraaf and Abma, 2003) and 'diplomacy' (Rhodes, 1997). However, while the ideal-typical form of dialogue – conflict-free suspension of and inquiry into beliefs and subjective knowledge (Isaacs, 1999) – may be feasible for highly complex situations, it may be very difficult to achieve in highly ambiguous ones.

We argue that management needs to in some way 'integrate' the objectives of bureaucratic, managerial and professional governance arrangements. Theoretically, this is difficult to devise. What, exactly, would such activity include? We turn to the analysis of a large number of empirical cases in order to shed light on this issue. In the next section, we present the results of an empirical study that inventoried the street-level control arrangements that were devised to address the double control challenge.

Research method and findings

The model developed earlier is applied to 42 cases where street-level bureaucrats perform public tasks that combine medium to high complexity with medium to high ambiguity. The 'case' (Yin, 1994) is comprised of the set of a task and a governance mechanism applied in a human service organisation. We studied the complexity and ambiguity of tasks and the governance mechanism (enforcement, incentives, competence control) that was applied. These cases were analysed by master's students in the context of a seminar, 'Governance of public and third sector organisations', taught at VU University Amsterdam. Students were required to select a street-level organisation in which 'personal-interactive' (Mills and Margulies, 1980) 'human services' (Hasenfeld, 1983) were implemented. Within these confines, the selection of cases was a convenience sample. In Table 12.3, an overview of all cases is given. The tasks vary widely: judges' rulings, community policing, inspecting chicken factories, providing care at home, re-employment services, child protection services and so on. street-level bureaucrats are civil servants employed by public organisations (eg judges, community police officers and inspectors), employed by not-for-profit organisations (eg teachers, nurses and youth care workers) or employed by commercial organisations who won contracts to perform public tasks (eg re-employment services and providing care at home). All tasks are performed in the Netherlands.

For each case, on average, two street-level bureaucrats plus their supervisor were interviewed and relevant documents were studied. Data were collected by pairs of public administration master's students enrolled in the seminar during the academic years 2009/10 and 2010/11. We only included the studies with good grades and removed cases where the ambiguity and/or complexity were not high enough.

Data

We analysed the data in terms of relatively high or low complexity and ambiguity on SLB task level. Complexity increases where tasks are more personally interactive (Mills and Margulies, 1980) and where information gathering is linked to client interaction (Van der Veen, 1995). Ambiguity is operationalised in terms of the possibility of competing normative assumptions about ends and the degree to which clients or peers are able to influence these normative assumptions. Ambiguity also rises where there is a relative vagueness of the goals to be achieved. Where street-level bureaucrats meet civilians, there is a certain degree of negotiation about goals between the street-level bureaucrat and civilian.

In the earlier discussion, the control mechanisms were discussed as 'ideal types'. In our research, we measured the different control mechanisms in terms of their relative dominance within one organisation. Professional control is measured by looking at the level of freedom and trust that street-level bureaucrats are given by their managers in performing their task. High levels of freedom correspond with high levels of professional control. Bureaucratic control is measured in terms of the presence of a hierarchal structure and the amount of prescribed modes of working. A strong hierarchy and strictly prescribed task result in high levels of bureaucratic control. Managerial

Table 12.3: Relative dominance of control mechanisms (professional organisations)

Case number	Applied control mechanisms		
	Professional	Bureaucratic	Managerial
24	Dominant	High	Low
18	Dominant	High	Medium
67	Dominant	High	None
46	Dominant	High	None
50	Dominant	High	Low
15	Dominant	Low	Upcoming
17	Dominant	Low	High
22	Dominant	Low	Low
29	Dominant	Low	Low
68	Dominant	Low	Low
8	Dominant	Low	Low
44	Dominant	Low	Low
2	Dominant	Low	Low
41	Dominant	Low	Low
65	Dominant	Low	Low
9	Dominant	Low	Medium
11	Dominant	Low	Medium
38	Dominant	Low	None
32	Dominant	Low	Upcoming
36	Dominant	Low	None
42	Dominant	Low	Low
39	Dominant	Medium	Low
48	Dominant	Medium	Low
30	Dominant	Medium	Low
3	Dominant	Medium	Low
21	Dominant	Medium	Low
35	Dominant	Medium	Medium
37	Dominant	Medium	None
31	Dominant	Medium	None
27	Dominant	Medium	Low
40	Dominant	Medium	Low
1	Dominant	None	Low
16	Dominant	None	Low

control is operationalised in terms of output control and accountability. Where the amount of clients to be helped is prescribed and controlled for, and where other performance measures such as client satisfaction are used as a method of control, managerialism is high. The level of relative dominance of each mechanism is based on the estimations of our respondents. Thus, 'dominance' means the dominance as experienced by the street-level bureaucrats. We scored the influence of the different mechanisms that they experienced for each individual case. This means that the 'high' in one case does not have to be exactly the same 'high' in another case, but that in that specific case, there is a relatively 'high' amount of one mechanism experienced by a street-level bureaucrat compared with the other mechanisms.

To operationalise adequacy, we have limited data to work with. It is only in the report of street-level bureaucrats and, in many cases, their managers that clues about adequacy can be found. We could not measure whether organisations perform optimally (ie solve or diminish the social dilemmas that they have been set up for). However, in the interviews, street-level bureaucrats and their managers brought up conflict in some cases between different demands originating from different control systems. There are also cases in which no complaints or conflicts were reported.

Analysis

What types and constellations of mechanisms have we found? At first, it should be no surprise that ideal types have not been found. Instead, all organisations studied are a mix of several mechanisms applied simultaneously. In Table 12.3, the organisations are ordered on the basis of the dominant mechanisms at the street-level bureaucrat level. The professional mode of control is dominant within most organisations. Furthermore, almost all professionally dominated organisations also have some form of bureaucratic and managerialistic control systems. The relative dominance of control mechanisms among professionally dominated organisations in our case studies is presented in Table 12.3.

We first focus on those organisations where professional control is dominant. Only five cases (18, 24, 46, 50, 67) combine professionalism with a high level of bureaucratic control. Two of these cases (18, 46) are organisations providing elderly care. Case 50 is a criminal court. The bureaucratic control in both the elderly care cases takes the shape of detailed instructions about how to treat the clients under prescribed circumstances. The tasks performed here are mostly day-to-day routine; therefore, complexity in these cases is relatively low, while ambiguity is also relatively low but not absent in the sense that street-level bureaucrats have to make judgements about the well-being of their client and adapt their services to clients' needs where possible. If we do not take into account the question of adequacy, it is not surprising that, within our logic of suitability of control mechanisms, lower levels of complexity in practice could be suitable for more hierarchical control. The last case (a criminal court) is an exception. Complexity and ambiguity are extremely high for the street-level bureaucrats in this case: judges. However, the high level of bureaucratic control stems from the fact that in their judgements, the law itself is the cornerstone of their work and, as such, controls the way in which they come to decisions in the courtroom.

The same can be said for case 24, the Immigration and Naturalisation Service, where street-level bureaucrats judge refugees in order to grant them residential status. Again, here, law (constantly changing) prescribes a big part of decision-making, but street-level bureaucrats are left almost completely free in their judgements. Control over their decisions is mainly via peer review and sometimes through random selection by the supervisors. In case 67, the level of complexity is relatively low (day-care for the mentally ill and disabled). The task at hand is not described in detail, but is performed within a strong hierarchical structure. High bureaucratic control in this case also stems from the nature of the task.

Furthermore, there are a few cases where dominant professionalism is accompanied by a high level of another form of control. Apart from the former cases, only case 17 combines professionalism with high levels of other control mechanisms. This case is a social work organisation that aims at helping adolescents (aged 13–23) in order to prevent issues in the public domain of so-called problem neighbourhoods. The street-level bureaucrats' task here is patrolling the streets looking for adolescents who skip school, have drug-related issues and so on – a highly complex and ambiguous task. They show a high level of inter-organisational action, which derives from their street-level position as key player/case manager. It is their responsibility to redirect their clients to other organisations and to monitor their behaviour in everyday life. Therefore, a central task is to communicate with other specialised organisations (schools, addiction clinics, etc). This is combined with a high amount of managerialistic control. The combination of control mechanisms leads to tension. The interviewed street-level bureaucrats report relatively high pressure from management for accountability in terms of how many clients they have helped and in what way.

Other cases where the professional control is substantially accompanied with other forms of control are those with a medium level of bureaucratic control. Cases among these are police officers working in strong hierarchical structures, elderly care homes, inspectorates and home-care organisations.

In sum, most of the control mechanisms found seem to primarily respond to the nature of the task at hand. Where tasks are highly complex, professional control prevails. Organisations do not aim to integrate the requirements of complexity and ambiguity, but, instead, seem quite apt in designing a control strategy around the nature of the task that they have to perform at the street level. The organisations where professionalism is *not* the dominant control system, on the other hand, appear to opt for a bureaucratic control mechanism that also does not integrate the requirements of complexity and ambiguity, but is unilaterally aimed at street-level bureaucrat conformity. Table 12.4 displays the level of ambiguity and complexity among these seven cases.

Table 12.4: Relative dominance of control mechanisms (non-professional organisations)

Case number	Characteristics of SLB tasks		Applied control mechanisms		
	Complexity	Ambiguity	Professional	Bureaucratic	Managerial
14	Medium	High	Low	Some tasks high	Medium
7	Low	Low	Low	Dominant	Low
34	Low	Low	Low	Dominant	Upcoming
49	Medium	Medium	Medium	Dominant	Low
25	Medium	Medium	Medium	Dominant	Low
33	Medium	Medium	Medium	Dominant	Low/upcoming
20	Medium	Medium	High	Dominant	Low
45	High	High	High	Low	None
4	High	High	High	Low	None

In these seven cases, complexity is relatively low to medium, as is ambiguity. It may hardly be surprising that these organisations are dominated by bureaucratic control systems because the level of street-level bureaucrat expertise required in the task at hand is relatively low. Given their task, these organisations are able to emphasise the objective of conformity. The one organisation (14) where ambiguity is high shows a relatively high level of managerial control, which is the adequate response to a control challenge of ambiguity, when complexity is low. The street-level bureaucrats in this case are restaurant managers whose task it is to promote neighbourhood cohesion. The ambiguity is high because there is no clearly defined idea of when cohesion is achieved and which organisations should participate. It is by no means a complex task however. The governing organisation has described in detail what the restaurant should look like, what should be served at what price and so on. More than in the cases with high complexity and ambiguity (where a double control challenge applies for which a single response has not yet been found), in the low complexity cases, the relative dominance of different control systems can be explained using the nature of the task as a starting point.

The same can be said for the two cases that do score high on both ambiguity and complexity. These organisations show a dominant orientation to inter-organisational governance. Thestreet-level bureaucrats support multi-problem individuals. In case 4, judicial partners (police, public prosecutor), social work-oriented professionals (psychologists) and teachers develop a customised approach for every individual client. Trade-offs are negotiated (ie obligatory psychological treatment instead of judiciary punishment) between the different partners. Dialogue between professionals (with expertise guaranteed through competence control) is the dominant control mechanism, which stems from the nature of the task.

There is, however, one control mechanism that does not seem to stem from the demands of the task at hand: managerialistic influences. Cases 9, 11, 18 and 35 report medium levels of managerialistic control combined with high levels of professional control. Cases 15 and 32 report an increasing importance of managerial control systems in professional environments. In cases 17, 33 and 34, where bureaucratic control is dominant, managerialism is also a profound factor. Furthermore, more than half the cases (25) report low managerialistic control.

As we have explained, this would be logical if complexity were low. However, that is not the case. Instead, in all cases where managerial control is found, this seems a relatively new influence that has been imposed from outside the organisations. In most cases, this takes the form of output control. Street-level bureaucrats report administrative tasks demanded by managers, who themselves have to account for the output that their organisation produces. To understand why these mechanisms have been introduced (and, in some cases, are being introduced), we need to look beyond the nature of the task and consider the institutional context of these organisations. It seems that the policy trend of managerialism is at the root of the existence of these mechanisms. Theories of sedimentation (Cooper et al, 1996) and institutional layering (Thelen, 2004) point our attention to the idea that institutional change is an incremental and slow process in which new elements are attached to existing institutions. This view is particularly useful for our analysis because these managerialistic influences 'do not come alone'. With the heightened attention to accountability and output control, bureaucratic control also rises. For the measurement of output, measuring tasks in a detailed way is necessary. To measure street-level bureaucrats' performance, detailed descriptions of tasks are needed. In almost all cases where managerial control systems were implemented, street-level bureaucrats report a rising standardisation of work processes, which can be characterised as bureaucratic control. It appears that where control systems are imposed on organisations by governing actors or political policy developments, conflicts between task-related mechanisms and externally imposed mechanisms arise. This implies, in other words, that these organisations appear unable to solve the double control challenge that is imposed upon them. While the complex nature of the task requires a strong position for street-level bureaucrat expertise (professionalism), the output control imposed upon the organisation is an indication of ambiguity, requiring the alignment of street-level bureaucrat policy implementation to policy goals (managerialism). Instead of integrating these requirements, control mechanisms are simply combined, which leads to tensions in the policy implementation system.

Discussion and conclusion

In this chapter, we addressed the following central research question: which governance mechanisms are functional responses to the double control challenge of combined task complexity and ambiguity? We posed a theory on the relation between the variable of task characteristics (complexity and ambiguity) and governance mechanism (enforcement, incentives, competence control). Programmatically, we argued that the relation between street-level bureaucrat tasks and governance is, as yet, not fully understood. In order to improve our understanding of this issue, we studied governance mechanisms in a large number of cases where task complexity and ambiguity were high.

High complexity of tasks and the task environment create a high degree of discretion for individual street-level bureaucrats and blocks the effectiveness of rule-based and, to some extent, incentive-based governance mechanisms. Where control incentives are strong, however, political and organisational managers tend to apply rule-based or incentive-based control mechanisms anyway, even if task characteristics block the effectiveness of these controls. This normally leads to tension and relatively strong unintended effects with respect to case treatment and/or employee well-being. This indicates that the appropriateness of such methods is limited. In eight cases, street-level bureaucrats and their managers openly complained about the bad fit between different control mechanisms (see earlier). We observe a dilemma in which political and organisational leaders need to choose between allowing discretion in order to respond to task complexity and controlling task implementation through rule- or incentive-based governance mechanisms in order to retain control. In other words, we have observed that it is difficult to design a control mechanism that forms an appropriate response (defined here as a control mechanism that does not lead to tension) to the double control challenge of combined complexity and ambiguity. In some way, the control mechanism needs to integrate the requirements of complexity (expertise) and ambiguity (alignment).

Shielded professionalism

In one third (14) of the cases, managers have found a way to shield SLBs from the external pressures of upcoming managerialistic and bureaucratic systems. This solution does not imply the integration of control challenges, but, instead, is best described as 'decoupling' (Meyer and Rowan, 1977; see also Chapter Thirteen). Five of these cases are in (lower, higher or special) education. In these cases, managers explicitly report that their teachers should be free to teach and spend all the time they have on their primary task. The street-level bureaucrats in these cases are aware of this shielding and praise their managers for it. Problems with conflicting mechanisms, therefore, do not seep through to the street-level bureaucrat level. In case 11, the direct supervisor of the street-level bureaucrats even openly admits to manipulating output indices to create more freedom for the street-level bureaucrats.

Shielded professionalism strongly acknowledges the complexity challenge of governance arrangements, *but underappreciates high ambiguity*. This mode of control is aimed at the maximised utilisation of professional expertise through allowing professionals or street-level bureaucrats to infuse the work process with their own values and preferences. The demanded accountability and transparency, however, is not being fully provided. In these organisations, street-level bureaucrats and managers seem to view control and professional autonomy as mutually exclusive alternatives.

Integration

A number of other cases also showed a rather 'organic adaptation' (Hernes, 2005) to conflicting demands. In these cases, management appeared able to devise a control mechanism that responds to the challenges of both complexity and ambiguity, without leading to tension in the implementation system. This is what we call the 'integration' of control challenges. In a number of small or start-up consultation firms, the owner of the firm operates both as the top managerial official and a co-worker, operating as a *primus inter pares* among the workforce. While we have observed that a response was devised to the combined control challenge of complexity and ambiguity (and so, in a functional sense, have observed that integration has apparently been achieved), we do not fully understand the structure of the mechanism that is applied. This suggests two important implications. In the first place, it actually seems to be possible to devise a mechanism that integrates control functions in response to the double governance challenge of combined complexity and ambiguity without leading to tension. However, and this is the second conclusion, our understanding of the structure of such a mechanism is still underdeveloped.

Although it appears difficult to define the structural characteristics of the governance mode that these managers apply, a number of central structural characteristics of the context in which it is produced can be identified. Management and co-workers simultaneously define the governance arrangement and its application is also strongly bound to the personal interaction between the management and street-level bureaucrats. This seems an echo of an already-old idea by Maynard-Moody et al (1990, p 844), who argued: 'Moving beyond Lipsky's thesis, our exploratory research suggests that delegating authority and including the perspectives of street-level workers in programmatic decisions is one realistic alternative to managerial control when the objective is to reduce the dangers of discretion.'

Lacking knowledge, alternative approaches?

Extant theories on how street-level bureaucrats should be controlled are found to be lacking in situations of the double control challenge. The double control challenge is about achieving *both* the expertise to address high complexity *and* the alignment to overcome high ambiguity.

We argued that bureaucracy, managerialism and professionalism do not properly address the double control challenge. The empirical results support our conceptual analysis. We have found support for our argument that the double control challenge of simultaneous high complexity and high ambiguity is important in street-level bureaucracies and that it is difficult to devise a response. In most cases, one of the challenges is simply ignored. Where a response to both control challenges is devised simultaneously, tensions occur because some of the mechanisms conflict with each other. We found very few organisations that have found appropriate solutions.

How may the expertise that street-level bureaucrats possess be applied in ways that align the interests and preferences of street-level bureaucrats and their managers? The assumption that control engenders dysfunctional effects also appears to be dominant in the professionalism literature; formal controls are assumed to crowd out intrinsic street-level bureaucrat motivation. When managers impose controls on professionals, professionals see this as a sign of distrust; when managers grant professionals autonomy, no controls may be imposed. The 'Third Logic' (Freidson, 2001) of professionalism is a logic of horizontal coordination of substance, without the application of hierarchical controls. Power (1997) even argued that the insertion of controls in governance relations evokes the further insertion of even more controls in order to control the application of the controls.

Formal controls generate resistance and dysfunctional effects when street-level bureaucrats perceive them as coercive (Adler and Borys, 1996), restrictive (Elias, 2009) or constraining self-determination (Weibel, 2010). When this happens, ambiguity is not overcome in a productive way as intrinsic street-level bureaucrat motivation is likely to be crowded out (Frey, 1997; Weibel, 2010). Controls may also be perceived by street-level bureaucrats in more constructive ways, enhancing intrinsic motivation and organisational value internalisation (Weibel, 2007, 2010). This happens when controls are perceived to be enabling (Adler and Borys, 1996), promotive (Elias, 2009) or supportive of self-determination (Deci and Ryan, 2000; Ryan and Deci, 2000; Weibel, 2007, 2010). The more street-level bureaucrats are able to participate in the development of the formal controls, the self-determination theory poses, the more their self-determination is enhanced.

This might actually resemble the structural form of organisational governance that the managers of the small firms discussed earlier apply. 'Self-defined' control may, on the one hand, force street-level bureaucrats to conform to organisational demands (responding to the ambiguity problem) while, on the other, support their capacity and their preparedness to infuse the work process with their expertise (the complexity problem). This supports self-definition (related to SLBs' need for autonomy), but also control (related to external demands). Self-defined control is also related to Noordegraaf's (2013) concept of the 'connective professional'. The emphasis De Bruijn (2007) and Maynard-Moody et al (1990) placed on the need for SLBs to be involved in programmatic decisions, such as the design and evaluation of performance, supports self-determination theory. This is, indeed, what we see in a few of the smaller organisations in our sample. Further research on the applicability of governance mechanisms related to self-determination theory and related approaches might shed more light on the structural form of these mechanisms.

THIRTEEN

First-line supervisors as gate-keepers: rule processing by head teachers

Peter Hupe and Eva van Kooten

Introduction

First-line supervisors are, literally, positioned in the middle. Working in the hierarchy of 'vertical public administration', they are, on the one hand, truly managers, aiming to control the work of their subordinates. On the other, they are doing their job close to the work floor, more or less immediately receiving signals from there. It is in this pivotal position 'in-between' that first-line supervisors fulfil a crucial role. In public service, they co-determine the effectiveness of public policies while contributing to the outcomes of policy processes. In fact, they are policy co-makers in their own right.

The focus in this chapter is on the ways in which head teachers of primary schools process rules. While functioning as 'school managers', these school principals are daily receiving rules to comply with. These rules stem from a variety of sources: applicable rules are made by the Ministry of Education, local government, the school board and other institutional actors. At the same time, these head teachers are supervisors: the received rules have a particular applicability to the teachers working at their school. As *street-level bureaucrats*, the latter are supposed to 'implement' the rules. Therefore, it matters how head teachers react when confronted with new rules coming from relevant stakeholders, especially those at the top of a formal hierarchy. As managers working in the 'first line', head teachers can process those rules by just passing them downward, by formulating additional rules in order to specify the received ones or by buffering them. Therefore, if variation in the processing of rules can be observed, the question is which factors influence that rule processing.

This chapter reports on qualitative research into these matters undertaken in a city in The Netherlands. For reasons of anonymity, the city has been given the fictitious name of 'Gluton'. The empirical data were gathered as part of the work of a master's thesis of one of the authors. The objective of the study was to contribute to the knowledge about the ways in which head teachers as first-line supervisors are doing their work – the latter being a relatively under-studied subject matter in the study of public administration and public management. The level of scientific ambition concerns that of a systematic description combined with an identification of relevant factors as qualitative steps towards a causal explanation.

The central question is: how do head teachers of primary schools process rules, and what are the factors that influence this rule processing? Hence, the following questions are relevant: a) 'Which sorts of rules do head teachers have to deal with?'; b) 'What characteristics define the interviewed head teachers?'; c) 'What characteristics define the work circumstances of the head teachers involved?'; d) 'How do head teachers process rules?'; and e) 'Why do the head teachers process rules the way they do?'

In the next section, a theoretical lens is developed, ending with an operationalisation of a robust causal model. In the third section, the research design is explicated. In the central part of the chapter, the research object is first placed into its empirical context before the findings are presented in the fourth section. In the fifth section, some conclusions are drawn.

Theoretical lens

In classic sociological studies of complex organisations, insights have been gained about the expressive leadership, loyalty to subordinates and supportive role of supervisors (cf Etzioni, 1961). How middle managers in the public sector are doing their work, by contrast, seems an under-studied subject. While the literature on public management is abundant, specific studies are scarce. In that literature, 'management' most often refers either, in a general way, to a range of activities without specification of the managing actor, or to the work done by the functionaries positioned at the top of organisations. Seldom do middle managers get attention (for exceptions, see Schartau, 1993; Brewer, 2005).

Studies of the policy process show a similar picture in fact. The usual orientation in mainstream implementation research is a top–down one. In the view going from the policy as formulated and decided upon in Washington to 'dashed expectations' in Oakland – to use Pressman and Wildavsky's (1973) exemplary phrasing – there is no specific attention to the role of work supervisors. Interestingly, however, the same can be said about the so-called bottom-up view on implementation, as expressed in Lipsky's (2010) seminal book on street-level bureaucracy. Indeed, stating that policies are made at the street level, Lipsky (1978) 'stands the study of public policy implementation on its head'. He does so in a literal way; with his focus on social workers, police officers and teachers, he hardly gives attention to their managers. To the extent that Lipsky does address the latter, managers are seen as a unified category and, in terms of labour relations, as opposites of street-level bureaucrats and their dilemmas. It is this aspect of Lipsky's approach that Evans (2010) criticises, pointing out the possibility that managers have a similar occupational background as the public workers they supervise. As 'one of us', these first-line supervisors are facing constraints to a certain degree comparable to the street-level bureaucrats' dilemmas (see also Chapter Sixteen).

Our point of departure here is the observation of empirical variation in the way in which head teachers practise management. In particular, some of them seem to be more directive than others. This observation made us curious about the ways in which head teachers process rules.

Ostrom (1999, p 50, emphasis in original) describes rules as 'enforced prescriptions about what actions ... are *required, prohibited, or permitted*'. Hupe and Hill (2007) differentiate 'action prescriptions' into public-administrative rules, professional norms and expectations from society. In this study, the focus is on the first category: formal rules and regulations stemming from various political-administrative authorities. More precisely, formal rules and regulations are defined as action prescriptions stemming from official sources with a legitimate authority and the possibility of imposing sanctions on non-compliance.

As a dependent variable, the processing of these rules by actors has been operationalised as: a) formulating additional rules; b) passing on rules; or c) buffering rules. This operationalisation is derived from Meier, O'Toole and Hicklin (2010; see also O'Toole et al, 2005). They have looked at the ways in which public managers react to the 'environmental shocks' that their organisations see themselves confronted with. Organisations can buffer such shocks, or they can cope with them. Both structural and managerial aspects determine the way in which the performance of the public organisations involved is influenced by these shocks. Here, we assume that the repertoire of possible reactions to external influences with a more than incidental character, such as an increase in the number of formal rules, is not fundamentally different from the range of possible reactions to major singular events like natural disasters. Therefore, *strengthening* means that public managers add rules to be followed by their subordinates, and *passing* means that these managers just transfer received rules downward to their subordinates. *Buffering* implies that rules imposed by authorities 'downwards' in the vertical dimension of public administration are captured by tempering or blocking them. Hence, we have documented the actions that head teachers take when they receive new rules, specifically in terms of the actions that these head teachers take (or not) when they receive new formal rules from the Ministry of Education, local government or other sources.

On the side of potentially explanatory factors, a distinction was made between organisational characteristics (on the level of the organisation) and, on the level of individual actors, action characteristics, work perceptions and person-bound characteristics (see Figure 13.1).

Figure 13.1: Conceptual model

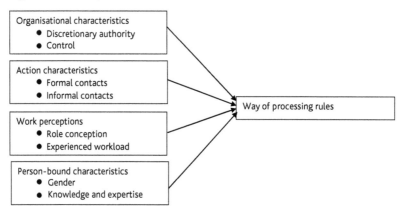

Organisational characteristics have been measured in terms of discretionary authority and control. Discretionary authority concerns the nature and degree of freedom of first-line supervisors to act. Such freedom is 'objectively' indicated in the management statutes of schools, but also subjectively experienced by the head teachers involved. The granted and experienced freedom regards both what to do and how to do it. Control concerns the degree of direct attention from political-administrative superiors to the fulfilment of tasks by first-line supervisors, including formal and informal systems of rewards and sanctions. This control was measured subjectively. The head teachers were asked about the frequency of such direct attention, and also about its possible consequences.

Additionally, it was assumed that 'networking matters'. The basis for this assumption is also found in the work of O'Toole and Meier (1999).

Since they developed their formal model of public management, they provided ample empirical evidence for this assumption (for an overview, see Meier and O'Toole, 2007). In the present research, action characteristics have been defined as formal and informal contacts. Formal contacts refer to the required interaction between first-line supervisors and their subordinates, with their peers within and beyond their own organisation, and with the functionaries by whom they are supervised themselves. Hence, indicators for such contacts are the span of control (number of teachers and non-teaching staff) and the head teachers' estimate of the frequency and duration of formal contacts with the other actors. Informal contacts refer to interaction with the same range of actors but without necessarily being formally required. The indicators are similar.

Work perceptions regard role conception and experienced workload. A role conception has been defined as the view of first-line supervisors of their role within their organisation. It is measured by asking the head teachers to describe what they see as their major task. Experienced workload concerns the way in which first-line supervisors experience the demands related to their work and its volume. The head teachers were asked to assess the workload they experienced and its perceived causes.

Concerning person-bound characteristics – next to gender (Portillo and DeHart-Davis, 2009) – the head teachers were asked to give a self-assessment of their knowledge of rules and regulations and of their skills to deal with these. The head teachers were also questioned about their education and training, number of years of experience in their present job, and years of experience in the field of education in general.

It is obvious that the theoretical lens explicated here has been developed with an eye to applying it to the research object at hand. It is not a full 'theory' in the sense that Elinor Ostrom (1999) refers to when making a distinction between 'models', 'theories' and 'frameworks'. Here, rather than testing hypotheses, applying a theoretical lens is what is involved. The lens can be called a 'conceptual model' because it expresses expectations about relationships between a limited range of elements.

Research design

In order to find how the observed empirical variation relates to the factors seen as potentially explaining this variation, data were collected via document analysis and semi-structured interviews. The document analysis included the study of research reports, policy documents and relevant documents from within the school board. These documents were used to gather understanding of the rules that the head teachers have to deal with. In addition, several documents from within the school board were used to gather data about potential respondents. This information was used in the selection of the respondents, which will be discussed later, and was an addition to the information obtained from the interviews.

In this study, semi-structured interviews were the main source of information. During the interviews, a list of topics was used. This list was compiled based on the operationalisation of the central concepts. All 16 interviews took place at the school in which the respective head teacher was working. The interviews were recorded with permission from the interviewees. Hence, the interviewer could pay more attention to the respondent and his or her non-verbal reactions. The transcripts of the interviews were sent to the respondents, enabling the respondents to check their transcript for factual correctness. After gathering the data, the recordings of the interviews were transcribed. Thereafter, the text was coded and categorised (the data collection is obtainable from the authors). By doing so, it was possible to review the data and to find similarities, differences and connections. The data were analysed using the indicators for the central concepts explicated in the previous section.

The respondents were selected from the population of head teachers employed by the central school board of public education in Gluton. Given the intention of compiling a diverse group of respondents, several school and personal characteristics were taken into account when selecting the respondents. First, schools were chosen so that attention could be given to variation between the approaches to management adopted by school district managers (the next layer up in the hierarchy). The schools in the study were located in four districts, with each one having its own manager. Second, the criterion of school size, in terms of size of the student and personnel population, was taken into account. It is expected that head teachers working at a small school maintain contact with their personnel in a different way than their peers working at a larger school. They may also have a different role conception. The third and last criterion is the gender of the head teacher. As indicated earlier, gender is expected to affect the ways in which head teachers process rules. At the start of this study, the intention was to select for age as well. This criterion was dropped because of the limited age differences within the research population. Except two (born between 1967 and 1977), all respondents were born between 1946 and 1960. Two thirds of the head teachers were born before 1955.

As not all approached head teachers were willing to participate, the final group of respondents is not ideally spread among the selection criteria of school location and gender. In one of the four districts, only three head teachers were prepared to participate. This resulted in a small group of three to five respondents per district. Only a third of the head teachers working for the school board are female and not all approached female directors wanted to take part in the study. As a result, a quarter of the interviewed respondents are female. The results of the final four interviews proved to be similar to the results of the former 12 interviews. Therefore, it was concluded that extra interviews were not likely to produce new insights. However small the number, from a substantive point of view, the 16 interviews that were held are therefore expected to provide a reasonably accurate representation of reality.

Findings

Empirical context

The head teachers in this study all work at elementary schools in Gluton, belonging to the non-confessional denomination. The head teachers, each managing one school, report to a school district manager. The latter is not directly employed by the municipality, but by a foundation, labelled here with the acronym 'SCHOOL' for reasons of anonymity. At the time of this study, there were four school district managers responsible for a total of 64 elementary schools, all in the area of the municipality of Gluton, a mid-sized city in a European context. This larger urban area includes several towns.

The school board, managed by a committee of directors, has formulated management bylaws in which tasks, powers and responsibilities of the directors, the district managers and the head teachers have been written down. In the context of those management bylaws, head teachers are responsible for the day-to-day management of education at their elementary school. They receive rules from a variety of sources, the school board being one of them. The school board developed their own strategic policy plan through which general objectives are communicated. The three main goals set forth via this policy plan are:

• increasing educational performance and strengthening talent development;

- enlarging the market share in education in Gluton; and
- further developing social entrepreneurship.

These objectives are materialised into further objectives and obligations for individual schools. In addition, the school board can also generate rules based on agreements within (new) partnerships. SCHOOL also has formulated action prescriptions regarding the schools' finances. For specific actions, the head teachers have to explicitly ask permission from the board. Finally, the school board generates rules following government policies, rules and regulations. By doing so, they determine how the head teachers should handle government rules.

Government rules targeting elementary schools stem from national and local government. Government layers in The Netherlands entail (viewed 'top-down') the European Union, the ministries, the provinces, local government and, in Gluton, also the city district administrations. In the field of Dutch primary education, the Ministry of Education, the Ministry of Social Affairs and Employment, and the municipalities (there are about 400 of them in Netherlands, but the number changes over time) are the three largest rule-makers (Ecorys-NEI, 2004). The formal rules concern compulsory schooling, the contents of lesson materials and the teaching process, personnel matters, housing, the security and integrity of pupils, financial management and accounting, audit and supervision, additional needs pupils and policy programmes on educational disadvantages, and childcare (Berdowski and Vennekens, 2008). Next to these general rules, the Gluton local government also addresses parental involvement and the conception of a *brede school* ('*brede*' means broad), implying extra attention given to pupils before, during and after school hours.

Rule processing

As discussed, it was expected that head teachers will process rules by formulating additional rules in order to specify the received ones, by passing the latter on downward or by buffering the received rules. The interviews made it clear that all three of these reactions to rules occur. There is variation both among the head teachers and per person, dependent on the type of rules involved. Two respondents indicated that they sometimes add additional rules, seven respondents pass them on now and then, while all respondents stated that they buffer rules. As far as buffering rules is concerned, the head teachers described different manners of acting. All head teachers stated that they filter rules by only passing on the core of relevant information. Most of the head teachers referred to the enormous amount of abstract texts in which rules are explained when talking about tempering or filtering rules. As the following two respondents stated:

> "I try to filter the rules. So, actually yes, you try to reduce it to what is actually interesting for your people." (Respondent A)

> "A lot of teachers have difficulties understanding those long complex texts. So that's why I simplify the rule or I give them an example. Well, I extract the core information and discuss it." (Respondent B)

Eight respondents sometimes block rules completely. As one respondent explained:

> "If you can estimate that a rule is not that important, you don't apply it. And if a rule just doesn't feel right, you don't apply it either. But, if we think a rule has meaning and utility, we implement it." (Respondent C)

Five respondents try to temper the influence of the rules by exploring the boundaries of the latter:

> "Rules and regulations usually have been formulated in woolly language, enabling all sorts of interpretations and possible follow-up. It should be kept this way." (Respondent D)

> "Dutch legislation usually consists of rules and exceptions. Well, those exceptions can be used in a flexible way. Entirely at your own discretion." (Respondent E)

The most important explanations given for buffering rules are to unburden personnel and to keep the situation workable:

> "As head teacher, you are familiar with the rules. You have some background information. A lot of the teachers in my team are not interested in those complicated stories. So, I think, those teachers are already busy teaching and fulfilling education-related tasks and that is complicated enough." (Respondent F)

"So, you really have to think about it. Because I have to burden the 50 members of my staff with those rules. And, you don't want rules to increase the workload, which they usually do." (Respondent C)

In addition, the respondents who sometimes block or temper rules indicated that when deciding how to react, their judgement of the usefulness of the rule is important. Four respondents explained that they sometimes block or temper rules because they deem these specific rules to be inconsistent with the situation at their school and the nature of its populations of pupils. An example is the head teacher who, in contrast to the rule, decided not to offer English lessons to the pupils in his classes, aged seven to nine, because the latter were already having too much trouble with Dutch, mathematics and basic skills. Two of the head teachers indicated that they only block or temper rules when they know that the frequency and consequences of control will be limited. The explications that the head teachers gave for passing on rules relate to the knowledge and responsibility of their personnel. As one respondent explained: "I must admit that some of my staff have more knowledge about some things than I do" (Respondent G). The two respondents who stated to formulate additional rules hoped to make the rules more applicable by doing so. Furthermore, they argued that this manner of acting gives them more control over the work of their personnel.

Organisational characteristics

As mentioned, it was expected that 'discretionary authority' and 'control' as organisational characteristics are explanatory factors for the ways in which head teachers react to rules. During the interviews, evidence was found that both characteristics do, indeed, matter. With regard to discretionary authority, all head teachers stated that they experience freedom to act. Five of the 16 head teachers indicated that they actively use ('take') the available space for action: "As yet, I still go my own way, doing my thing. I know where we are heading for as a school, so I do not bother too much" (Respondent D). Four of the five head teachers who 'take' space to act indicated that they sometimes try to temper the influence of rules. A majority of the respondents observed that the action space granted to them is successively being diminished. At the same time, it was acknowledged that control by school district managers seldom has consequences:

"I have never experienced that, no. Never have there been consequences that I was called to account and that you were told 'Hey, you didn't stick to the rules' or 'This was not what we have agreed upon'. This fact sometimes amazes me." (Respondent A)

The factor 'control' in this study refers to the frequency and consequences of control by the school board. There does not appear to be a connection between head teachers' reactions to rules and their experiences concerning control by the school board, discussed during the interviews. However, as discussed earlier, two respondents mentioned that they only block or temper rules when they know that the frequency and consequences of control are limited. These head teachers were referring to control in general, not only to control by the school board. Therefore, it can be stated that control is taken into consideration by some head teachers when deciding how to react to a rule.

Action characteristics

In this study, action characteristics have been defined as 'formal and informal contacts'. The frequency of formal and informal contacts between head teachers and their personnel, their peers and their manager was discussed during the interviews. The frequency of formal contacts with the school district manager was more or less equal across all the respondents. Only in one district were informal contacts also reported. Two of the 16 head teachers appeared to be most active outside their school. The majority, however, said that they spend at least 80% of their working time inside their school building. Most respondents, however, found it difficult to assess the time they spend having contact with the teachers at their school because such contacts occur continuously. Only two head teachers stated that they more frequently have formal than informal contacts with 'their' teachers. Despite the fact that there were, albeit small, differences between the contacts that head teachers maintain, it was not possible to link these action characteristics to head teachers' reactions to rules. It is possible that this is a result of the limited number of respondents.

Work perceptions

The work perceptions of the head teachers were studied in order to determine whether there is a connection between their perceptions and the way in which they process rules. To find out if role conception is a relevant explanatory factor, all head teachers were asked to describe their main task. The head teachers mentioned five themes in the following order: their teaching staff; the organisation; providing good education; the environment of their school; and the school board. Thus, most respondents put 'people and organisation' upfront. None of the seven head teachers who stated that their main task is related to their personnel pass on rules downward or formulate additional rules. They only describe buffering methods as a manner of reacting to rules. The two respondents who declared that they formulate extra rules were the only ones who mentioned the environment of the school and the school board. Based on this information, a distinction can be made between head teachers who mention their personnel first when describing the heart of their work and those who mention something else.

In addition to role conception, the experienced workload of head teachers was studied. All respondents remarked that they have a busy agenda. Two head teachers experienced the workload negatively. After studying the findings, it turned out that the experienced workload does not influence head teachers' reactions to rules. In addition, none of the head teachers described a situation in which their workload influenced the way in which they processed rules.

Person-bound characteristics

As noted earlier, it was also expected that 'gender' and 'knowledge and expertise' would play a role in explaining the ways in which head teachers react to rules. As only four female head teachers participated in this study, it is not possible to make a clear distinction between the responses of males and females.

As to 'knowledge and expertise', the head teachers were questioned about their education and training, number of years of experience in their present job, and years of experience in the field of education in general. All respondents were trained to be a teacher and 13 of them had received additional training to become a head teacher. Three respondents obtained a master's degree or were obtaining one during this study. In addition, the head teachers all attended courses and workshops provided by the school board. Of the 16 respondents, 13 had been working in the field of education for 30 to 40 years. Only two of the respondents had less than 20 years of experience working in this field. In order to get a complete picture, all head teachers were asked to give a self-assessment of their knowledge of rules and regulations and their skills to deal with these. None of the respondents indicated that they had problems with this. Most of them explained that this was due to their long experience in the field of education. After studying the findings, it turned out that the education and training and the experience of the head teachers did not influence head teachers' reactions to rules. As the self-assessments of the head teachers were quite similar, it was not possible to relate this assessment to the manner of reacting to rules.

Discussion and conclusion

How do head teachers of primary schools process rules, and what factors influence variation in this rule processing? That was the central research question in this chapter. It was found that head teachers process rules in varying ways, but mostly by buffering those rules. There is variation among head teachers, but – perhaps more striking – also per person, dependent on the character of rules involved. A few head teachers formulate additional rules now and then (*strengthening*), some pass rules (*passing*), but all try to capture rules, either by tempering rules when they receive them, by only passing on the core of relevant information or by blocking them (*buffering*).

Most head teachers indicated that they aim to bother the teachers as little as possible with new rules; buffering is the dominant mode. The majority of the head teachers state that their ad hoc assessment of the usefulness of the rules involved is at the basis of their preference to block or temper those rules. As reasons for acting like this, the head teachers mentioned their wish to unburden their personnel while keeping the situation that the latter have to work in workable. At the same time, almost half of the interviewed head teachers answered that they pass rules, sometimes literally, on to the teachers that they are supervising. They think that the latter also have a responsibility of their own, or simply want them to be informed. Two head teachers indicated that they sometimes add additional rules. They expressed two reasons for their action: first, they want to make new rules applicable; and, second, in this way, they want to exercise control over the actions of their subordinates. Unless one embraces a subjective definition, it seems possible to observe an origin of 'red tape' here, one could add.

Hence, buffering as a way of rule processing is a prevalent fact. On the side of the explanatory variables, the findings indicate that the causes of variation do, indeed, differ, but exactly how and to what extent could not be established definitively in this small study. The head teachers all work in schools with similar organisational characteristics, but their approaches to rules varied in terms of discretionary authority and control. Control is taken into consideration by some head teachers when deciding how to react to a rule. Two indicated that they practise the blocking or tempering of rules as ways of rule processing only when knowing that the frequency and consequences of control will be limited. These head teachers were referring to control in general, not only to control by the school board. Once the granted discretion is used, this mostly happens through buffering rules instead of just passing them downward.

Action characteristics, measured as formal and informal contacts (networking), do not seem to have much influence in this case. In the perspective of O'Toole and Meier's (1999) assumption that networking matters, the rather inward orientation of the head teachers studied here seems worthwhile to note. It is not the case that experienced workload seems to influence rule processing much, although all respondents perceived it as high. Role conception, however, seems to make a difference. Head teachers who put their staff 'central' seem to choose to buffer rules rather than to pass them on or formulate additional rules, in contrast to their peers with a different view of their role. As person-bound characteristics, knowledge and expertise do not seem to differentiate much. While it is obvious that we are talking about a small n here, the assumption that women would be less inclined to buffer rules than men (Portillo and DeHart-Davis, 2009) was not confirmed.

Given the small n, as just mentioned, it is clear that only limited statements can be made about the causal determinants of different ways of rule processing. At the same time, there is clear evidence of rule buffering. The findings of this empirical study can put two alternative views in perspective. In opposition to the top-down view of policy implementation, one can state that policy goals as formulated in official policy statutes do not predict policy outputs because what happens in 'Oakland' with those goals does have a dynamic of its own. At the same time, Lipsky's approach disregards the role of some key actors, namely, first-line managers, in that process.

Instead, the way in which first-line supervision is practised appears to have an impact on the actions within the black box of street-level bureaucracies. As the 'puppet who pulls the strings' (Schartau, 1993), the first-line supervisor co-decides whether and how rules and regulations reach subordinate public officials. The exact ways in which this happens, under which conditions, the underlying causal factors and the consequences all need specification. The *first-line supervision matters* hypothesis can only be articulated here; it needs to be tested in further empirical research.

As granted freedom for judgement, discretion is not only being *formulated* on varying layers in the vertical dimension of public administration, but also being *used* on a variety of layers as well – not only at the street level itself. Among all these spots in the hierarchy, the relevance of the ones closest to the state–citizen interaction at that level cannot be overlooked. First-line supervisors are discretionary actors in their own right.

FOURTEEN

Service workers on the electronic leash? Street-level bureaucrats in emerging information and communication technology work contexts

Tino Schuppan

Work organisation in e-government

E-government enables on the basis of information and communication technology (ICT), new organisational forms that can increasingly be observed in practice, such as in one-stop government. This particular form of e-government consists of a central entry point to all public services that can be implemented through physical access channels (eg a walk-in office) or through the telephone channel, such as the single Public Service Number (PSN). No matter what channels are used, providing an entire array of diverse services from a single point makes new cross-organisational cooperation at operational level necessary. The structure and dynamics of work organisation have changed. In particular, due to the use of ICT as the main communication channel, the day-to-day work of call centre agents in public organisations has changed: they confront a wider variety of citizens' requests and have to decide about the delivery of a larger amount of information and information sources. Which skills and discretion levels the agents apply to their tasks might be very diverse, affecting their characterisation as street-level bureaucrats. In this chapter, we argue that ICT does not decreases the decision capacities and discretion of call centre agents, but, to some extent, requires an extension of decision autonomy during the ICT-mediated interaction with citizens. Thus, e-government work, particularly in one-stop government contexts, can be characterised as street-level bureaucracy. I base my arguments on an empirical exploration of the extent of change at the working and management level in ICT-based one-stop government.

Lipsky's (2010) theory of street-level bureaucrats forms the theoretical basis for this chapter, in combination with some system-theoretical considerations on so-called boundary spanners. This theoretical perspective will be used to explore and discuss the implications for the change of work organisation and its control. Based upon these theoretical considerations, it is possible to derive the hypothesis that ICT, on the one hand, reduces the scope of action of and contributes to tighter control in a one-stop government organisation, which may result in the deskilling of street-level staff. On the other hand, we can argue that the scope of action will increase since a wide range of services must be conducted by a single person. The central issue is whether one-stop government and the way in which ICT is adopted will broaden or reduce street-level bureaucrats' scope of action and the controlling capacity of management.

Conceptualising work organisation in one-stop government

Worldwide, the concept of one-stop government has been closely related to e-government as its implementation requires ICT. The main idea of one-stop government is to provide a single access point for all or for a broad range of public services for citizens (see Hagen and Kubicek, 2000). ICT plays a key role in implementing one-stop government because it enables new forms of cooperation between organisations, which are necessary when access to services is to be bundled together at a single point. Cooperation is the main challenge of one-stop government, regardless of whether one-stop government is implemented by telephone or through online government (Dunleavy et al, 2008; Lenk et al, 2010). Thereby, ICT is seen as a tool for changing work organisation and the related work processes across existing administrative boundaries and independent of physical location (Davenport, 1995). One-stop government is one means of joining up government, with which the existing fragmentation of public administration can be overcome (Ling, 2002; Pollitt, 2003; Dunleavy et al, 2008, p 187; Davies, 2009; Askim et al, 2011; Keast, 2011, p 22).

However, although the general concept of one-stop government promises better service delivery at a macro-level of work organisation, one-stop government also challenges the micro-level of one-stop government day-to-day work. Work organisation refers to the concrete working steps to be taken by a person working in a single workplace and using ICT support. An analysis of work organisation thus encompasses the activities that are carried out to accomplish a task, the way in which and extent to which ICT is used in accomplishing this task, and the individual skills required. All of these elements of work organisation are closely interdependent. This means that they must be considered together. The delivery of the broad range of services necessary to implement one-stop government from a single workplace requires these three elements of work organisation. For a long time, work organisation in public administration was based upon the principles of the Weberian model, which, at the working level, could be seen as the counterpart to Taylor's model of mass production in the industrial sector. In Taylor's model, the ideal is for a single person to carry out, to the greatest extent possible, small and very similar working steps towards a small set of objects (eg documents) with a high rate of repetition, thus achieving higher specialisation. Examples of typical working steps in public administration include checking the facts in an application or document, calculating a certain quantity or amount, collecting information, making decisions, and so on. As a result, to date, rigid principles of work sharing, a high degree of formalisation, long processing times and complicated approval and co-signing procedures are still essential characteristics of work organisation in many public organisations. These characteristics have even often survived mandatory managerial reforms, which have mainly affected the management level (see Lenk, 2007). In other words, New Public Management did not take account of the working level of organisations; the consideration of single working steps would require a business process perspective (see eg Schedler and Utz, 2009).

As a consequence, the modern management techniques that are implemented often end up being used to control outdated working structures. This means that in the work practice, public servants enact obsolete bureaucratic rules while confronting new situations requiring new skills. To what extent these new situations also affect public servants' discretion is an open question.

Concretely regarding work organisation in one-stop government, there is a need to conceptually clarify which new models emerge due to ICT usage. Only some references can be found in the business literature. Essentially, two extreme forms of work organisation are discussed, one known as so-called high-road organisation and the other as low-road organisation (Milkman, 2002; Brödner and Latniak, 2002). In a high-road organisation, functional work sharing is reduced because ICT is used for more information processing at a single workplace (see Dejonckheere et al, 2001, p 3). Hence, a single workplace can integrate and process more tasks. For the employees, this can strengthen their identification with their work, something that tends to get lost if functional work sharing is too rigid. For this reason, high-road organisations are also characterised as *post-Tayloristic*. This, in turn, leads to a higher scope of action which requires that the workers themselves are higher skilled, so that they can fulfil these higher levels of responsibility. Not only is more knowledge needed to carry out the task at hand, but also more skills, such as the ability to stay organised or to work independently. In a low-road organisation, on the other hand, work sharing and standardisation are increased, contributing to higher specialisation. Such organisations reduce the scope of action and are characterised as *neo-Tayloristic* as they contribute to the industrialisation, and higher formalisation, of the service sector. This is possible because ICT not only enables automation, but also makes it possible to divide tasks into many small elements or functions, which, in turn, can be easily spatially distributed and coordinated by ICT (Murray and Willmott, 1997, p 165). Whether the work organisation of one-stop government tends to be a high-road organisation with higher-skilled workers or a low-road organisation with lower-skilled workers should be empirically analysed. A crucial question related to this is whether public servants working in one government context in both models act as street-level bureaucrats, using their discretion in direct and constant contact twith citizens. In the next section, I discuss this question in relation to the use of ICT in day-to-day work in order to theoretically base the empirical study.

Street-level bureaucrats without and with information and communication technology

According to street-level bureaucracy theory, management through the use of instructions and regulations is only possible to a limited degree. Street-level bureaucrats are often confronted with problems and solutions that cannot be predefined and prescribed in advance through legal regulations or guidelines. The law does not provide a definitive basis for decision making at the level of work practices. Street-level bureaucrats need a certain scope of discretion and room for interpretation when they take decisions while interacting with individual citizens. Lipsky uses the term 'discretion' in the sense that civil servants have room for interpretation when making a decision on the basis of a law. The term 'discretion' is slightly different than the term mainly used in this chapter, which is 'scope of action'. This refers more to work organisation itself and to the question about the extent of predefinition and standardisation of the working steps of street-level bureaucrats and the requirements that emerge through their use of

ICT. In other words, scope of action is related not only to decision-making, but also to problem understanding and defining in uncertain situations and to connecting the interdependent and diverse worlds of the administration and the citizens. Regarding this, Lipsky (2010, p 161) argues that 'Street-level bureaucrats have discretion because the nature of service provision calls for human judgment that cannot be programmed and for which machines cannot substitute'. Depending on the discretionary scope of the street-level bureaucrat, he or she must organise their work to a high degree themselves. Street-level bureaucrats are therefore more closely related to the high-road organisation than to the low-road organisation. This means that the work organisation of street-level bureaucrats is rather informal and characterised by greater numbers of ambiguous situations. Therefore, Lipsky (1980, p 147) mentions the greater need for higher skill levels and for individuals to be able to organise their work. Street-level bureaucracy is characterised by high levels of subjectivity in work organisation. This aspect is also taken into account by systems theory, which considers people working at organisational boundaries between different interdependent subsystems, such as street-level bureaucrats or agents in call centres, as acting as boundary spanners who translate the differing subsystems' inherent logics between each other. They have to translate external organisational requirements, such as those of citizens, into the internal world of the organisation and vice versa. They translate unfiltered and raw information into the language of the respective system (Luhmann, 1995, p 224). Therefore, in particular, boundary spanners have to collect, process, interpret and make sense of a lot of information (Adams, 1980), for which they must have well-developed individual skills. Furthermore, boundary spanners conduct activities such as filtering inputs and outputs, searching and collecting information, and representing the organisation to its external environment (Adams, 1980). The literature on call centres has emphasised that organisations need to mobilise the extra skills and knowledge reserves of employees and to match these with the organisational demands of quality and efficiency. In this way, organisations confront the dilemmas emerging from achieving rationalisation and quality service at the same time (Bain and Taylor, 2002; Batt and Moynihan, 2002; Taylor and Bain, 2003; Holman, 2004; Thompson et al, 2004; Batt and Nohara, 2009; Batt et al, 2009; Huws, 2009; Pierre and Tremblay, 2011, 2012).

The scope of action at the execution level also affects the leadership of street-level bureaucrats. Managers have scarce information about the common task practices of street-level bureaucrats: 'Under the best conditions, only a small part of their behaviour can be overseen and so the alienation resulting from close supervision may, in many cases, actually lead to decreased rather than increased compliance' (Prottas, 1978, p 301). Broad scopes of action mean less or other forms of control by managers. The use of tight guidelines or incentives does not completely solve the control gap problem. Instead, soft control mechanisms such as trust or informal arrangements are more effective. Recent leadership literature, increasingly focusing on the network nature of organisation, also emphasises these aspects. An important consequence of the control gap between managers and employees and the high degree of subjectivity at the working level is the great amount of uncertainty that managers must confront.

The extent to which ICT affects street-level bureaucracy was later brought into the discussion by other scholars. Two works refer explicitly to the theory of street-level bureaucracy: Snellen (1998) and Bovens and Zouridis (2002). The key question at hand is whether ICT changes the street-level bureaucrats' scope of action, or, in other words, and following the concept of street-level bureaucrats referred to in Chapter One, to what extent and how their discretion, their function as policy co-makers and their certain craftsmanship in fulfilling their tasks are affected by their use of ICT. Snellen (1998, p 500) emphasises that, in general, ICT reduces the scope for manipulation and interpretation. Automation plays a special role for Snellen because routine cases can be automatically assessed and decided (Snellen, 1998, p 501). If a reason must be provided for a decision, predefined text passages can be used. In such a system, managers only decide upon those cases that are more difficult and require higher competencies. Moreover, electronic monitoring systems offer executives better control possibilities to easily correct emerging mistakes. The result, according to Snellen, is a reduction in managers' uncertainty and higher formalisation at the work level.

Bovens and Zouridis (2002) develop a similar argument when they distinguish between so-called screen-level and system-level bureaucrats. Characteristic for screen-level bureaucrats is that the contact with citizens takes place via computer screens: 'Public servants can no longer freely take to the streets, they are always connected to the organisation by the computer' (Bovens and Zouridis, 2002, p 177). Screen-level bureaucrats are largely similar to Snellen's bureaucrats as their working processes are standardised and automated, such as the input of customer data in an electronic form. Nevertheless, Bovens and Zouridis (2002, p 177) argue that even when using ICT and although knowledge management systems and electronic guidelines strongly limit freedom of action, interaction with the citizen is only standardised to a limited extent: 'Many decisions are no longer made at the street-level by the worker handling the case; rather, they have been programmed into the computer in the design of the software'. Moreover, managers have the possibility to control the contents of electronic documents and can evaluate them automatically according to defined criteria, also reducing control uncertainties.

For Bovens and Zouridis, the next step of ICT usage is represented by system-level bureaucracy, in which comprehensive decision-making processes are supported and controlled by ICT. In a system-level bureaucracy, there are three groups of employees: (1) the system developer and system manager, who are responsible for data processing; (2) managers, who control service provision; and (3) information managers or helpdesk employees, who work at the interface with the citizen – 'The hundreds of individual case managers have all vanished. Their pivotal role in the organisation has been taken by systems and process designers' (Bovens and Zouridis, 2002, p 180). Moreover, boundaries between organisations become fluid because customer data are exchanged and processes are outsourced to other organisations to a great extent. The system developers and ICT experts become the new street-level bureaucrats because they define political implementation through the design of the software. This means that scopes of action now become available to these system-level bureaucrats, who implement legal requirements in form of algorithms, decision trees and graphic representations of decision rules. It is questionable, however, whether this applies to one-stop government because of its network character. The specific question is whether ICT-enabled network organisations, such as one-stop government, also change the scope of action through an increasing pre-structuration of work, resulting in a shift towards system developers and executives. From the literature review, it turns out that managers receive better control ability in an ICT-pervaded organisation, which was not the case in the previous non-ICT environment. Furthermore, ICT is able to reduce the uncertainty for the manager regarding the working level because managers are better able to control the content of documents and can analyse the whole working organisation with predefined criteria. Picot and Neuburger (2008), referring to enterprises, argue that employees at the working level are hanging on an electronic leash that allows managers a tight control of behaviour. Especially when conducting standardised work, a control is possible that goes beyond the classical hierarchical structures (Picot and Neuburger, 2008, p 232).

Summing up, the theory of street-level bureaucrats provides some useful information to better understand the working level. In particular, it addresses the scope of action and the limits of standardisation related to citizen interaction without the use of ICT. Nevertheless, to explore the ICT impact on work organisation in one-stop government, and particularly for the day-to-day practices of public servants, further aspects have to be considered. A major critique that can be levelled against the work of Snellen, Bovens and Zouridis is that they concentrate solely on ICT, neglecting other variables in the context of ICT usage, such as the nature of the task itself (eg standardised or non-standardised work), the organisational environment (eg stable or dynamic) and the organisational form of work (eg networked or hierarchical). These variables can offer a clue as to how to concretely analyse those aspects that enhance the explanatory power of Lipsky's theory emphasised in Chapter One: examining the nature of the task and the organisational form, we could better understand to what extent ICT plays a role in the scope of action of street-level bureaucrats. Moreover, the organisational environment can vary, for example, because the tasks are related to a particular time-limited project. Thus, tasks can be outsourced and the scope of action of the street-level bureaucrats can change. Both outsourced tasks and the scope of action of the street level bureaucrats are overshadowed by the particular effects of ICT use in the organisations, such as the shifting or even reduction of discretion due to automation of certain tasks and work processes (see, eg, Pollitt, 2011). This perspective supports Buffat's (2013) findings on the specific issue of street-level bureaucrats and ICT. Buffat, Snellen as well as Bovens and Zouridis are authors who favour the so-called 'curtailment thesis' regarding front-line discretion, while other authors, such as Jorna and Wagenaar (2007), favour the 'enabling thesis', in which ICT is only conceived as an additional contextual factors (among others). Furthermore, not only are different forms of ICT application insufficiently considered, but the scope of different ICTs and their various usages in a certain organisational context are also neglected. These research gaps should be taken into account in the analysis of ICT-enabled organisation, such as one-stop government, because the organisational impact often depends upon the concrete socio-technical design of a working system. This chapter looks at service workers in call centres, considering the particular socio-technical design of their work environments. It aims at contributing to further develop Lipsky's concept of street-level bureaucrats in the context of ICT-based public service delivery. The central question of the chapter is whether front-line workers have less latitude of choice or, in other words, less scope of action due to their new 'electronic leashes'. As empirical illustration,

I analyse the case of the PSN in Germany. The applied methodology and empirical findings are presented in the following sections.

Empirical findings: the case of the Public Service Number 115 in Germany

Methodology

To answer my research question, I selected a case study of public servants working in call centres, implemented as one-stop government and, more concretely, as a specific type of networked e-government, as empirical illustration. A qualitative approach focusing on interactions between the different actors involved at the work organisation level is needed to extend Lipsky's insights. This examines how the use of ICT affects the particular scope of action of the public servants, and, more concretely, analyses whether the nature of their tasks, how they used certain kinds of ICT tools to accomplish their tasks and what skills and training they needed might characterise them as street-level bureaucrats. More concretely, I focus on the following characteristics of the one-stop government's work organisation: Cooperation, Skills, Standardisation, Team Work and Leadership.

I combined several qualitative methods, including document analysis, 10 interviews using semi-standardised questionnaires and work observations at the call centres. The qualitative materials were collected from call centres in two large German cities (> 1 million inhabitants), Hamburg and Berlin. The cities have been chosen for a most similar case design. Both are large German cities with similar starting conditions and both are considered forerunners in e-government, including the use of call centres as one-stop government. The PSN is suitable for evaluating the working level of one-stop government because a tangible change in the work organisation can already be observed in connection with ICT use. The fieldwork took place from January 2011 to the end of September 2011. Each interview took about 90 minutes and was transcribed, summarised into a case description and then analysed.

Case description

The PSN 115 began operating in Berlin and Hamburg in 2009, in addition to each city's already-existing citizen telephone number. Thus, in both cities, two telephone access numbers and their corresponding infrastructures coexisted, with different levels of accessibility and service spectrums. In both cities, the 115 number offers a broader service spectrum than the city's own telephone number, but with shorter opening hours. In this aspect, PSN's call centre differs from a traditional switchboard. A switchboard provides no services, but merely forwards the incoming calls, whereas a PSN seeks to provide information and services directly over the phone.

In both cities, the call centres are organised as independent units. In Berlin, only one 115 team exists, with seven employees. This team is part of the larger service centre that operates the city's own phone line, Berlin phone, with more than 100 employees. In Hamburg, there are five teams, each led by a team leader.

Work performed

Citizens can call 115 to request information on more than 100 public services. Frequently, the information is for orientation purposes, for example, to prepare citizens for their visit to the administration, such as opening hours, documents to be presented or eligibility criteria for a service. In order to give an appropriate answer and to deal with the broad range of tasks, call centre agents use the ICT-based knowledge management system as a knowledge source. If a call centre agent cannot answer a question, he or she forwards the call to another level. This means that if a citizen's inquiry cannot be answered at the first service level by the call centre agent, they have to collaborate with other organisations or government levels. This results in different service levels in the organisational structure (a tripartite service architecture).

The conducted task at the work level has changed for the call centre agents as they must have knowledge on a broad range of services. Although they use an ICT-based knowledge management system for this purpose, this system addresses the comprehensive information requirements of the citizens only to some extent. The way of presenting the information in the knowledge management system was insufficiently prepared, so that it is very difficult to adequately provide high-quality information to the caller during the phone call in case of difficult requests. The socio-technical design is insufficient here. At the same time, the inadequately prepared information increases the requirements for the employees because they have to 'translate' the technical language of the knowledge management system into citizens' language. Some employees had difficulties coping with the technical aspects in this context.

Regarding citizens' inquiries that could not be answered by the call centre agents, they developed quite different practices in Berlin and Hamburg. Employees in Berlin responded by developing evasive mechanisms, such as calling citizens back later in order to have time to search for the required information. This, however, also impairs the service quality due to the delayed response time. The call centre agents in Berlin, however, seem to be more strongly motivated to answer the questions by themselves. In Hamburg, the call centre agents immediately forwarded citizens' inquiries to the next level if they were not able to answer them. Thus, despite the fact that the positions of the call centre agents in Berlin and Hamburg are very similar, in practice, the two groups tend to carry out their work in quite different ways. One possible explanation for that might be that the city administration in Hamburg employed their call centre agents from private sector call centres, which seem to be more formalised and more standardised as they used to sell only a limited number of products. Hamburg hired private sector call centres with the purpose of having professionals handle interactions with customers or citizens but they had no professional background in public administration, as the call centre agents in Berlin have.

For routine inquiries, the existing working system with the ICT tools was quite appropriate. Approximately 80% of calls received are standard requests for which a simple search of the knowledge database is sufficient. Here, a trend was evident that employees were working beneath their capabilities. In both call centres, cooperation with other public departments turns out to be difficult because these other departments are rather unwilling to share information with the call centre agents. To make up for this lack of cooperation, call centre employees in Berlin closely share information within their team to improve their level of knowledge. Sometimes, such an exchange even takes place during a call. In comparison, in Hamburg, cooperation is less evident. In this case, cooperation with specialists from other departments is essentially limited to forwarding the phone calls.

It became obvious that the work in the evaluated call centres requires new skills independently of the concrete knowledge requirements: in particular, the ability to multitask, an increased information processing capacity and stronger self-reflection regarding one's work were mentioned. It was found that even though the knowledge databases slightly mitigated the technical requirements, the requirements for non-routine cases have grown significantly. Employees permanently have to take in new information from several sources, process and forward them. They have to be able not only to communicate across organisational boundaries, but also to adopt a holistic approach to request and think beyond the boundaries of their own organisation.

Furthermore, despite using ICT, call centre employees are facing new requirements because they have to constantly respond to different work situations due to a high number of changing conversation partners. In particular, employees have to be able to switch quickly between different topics under time pressure and to adjust to the quick sequences of new conversation partners. They also have to switch between routine situations and unexpected cases. The environmental dynamics have increased significantly for the administrative staff. Employees also demonstrated a trend towards overstraining in this respect, in particular, the older employees.

In Berlin as well as in Hamburg, the staff had worked in existing call centres and joined the 115 teams, so that the employees already had previous knowledge. Indeed, it appeared that in Hamburg, the available staff were less highly skilled that those in Berlin. In Hamburg, special training was provided lasting up to eight weeks, while in Berlin, the training lasted only a few days.

Information and communication technology usage

The work in the call centre is heavily dependent upon a variety of ICT applications: the control of the telephone system, in particular, the distribution of the caller to the individual agents, is mainly carried out by software. The ICT system automatically measures performance indicators such as the waiting time of the caller, the phone call's duration and the workload of individual employees. However, it is the knowledge management system that makes up the core of the call centre. Some of the information contained in the knowledge management system is entered into the system centrally and some is entered by the call centre employees themselves. Nevertheless, observations show that the knowledge management system alone is often not enough to be able to answer incoming inquiries right away. Problems arise because certain information is not available in the system, or because the information available is not in a language that is understandable for citizens. Texts tend to be formulated in rather abstract terms that must be translated into citizens' language.

Furthermore, ICT is used to cooperate with other departments and agencies. Such cooperation is implemented using a so-called electronic ticket, in effect, a standardised e-mail that forwards the inquiry to the responsible department or agency. In practice, however, call centre agents rarely employ this system because it is complicated to use.

Control and team leadership

Although the ICT system provides the team leadership with more indicators of the team's performance, in practice, this only results in a partial increase in the ability to manage and control the working level. In particular, uncertainties exist about how individual employees carry out the tasks in the service centre and how they interact with citizens. For legal reasons, the indicators generated by the ICT system only apply to the team as a whole and do not allow insights into the performance of an individual employee. Without any doubt, a tighter control would be possible from a consequent ICT perspective, but it was not implemented in the German context.

Furthermore, although a cooperative style of leadership is expected from the team leaders, in fact, modern leadership instruments and control instruments were not available to them. For example, target agreements were not concluded with employees in either of the two call centres, even though such agreements could serve as a basis for performance discussions with the employees. Instruments to ensure service quality are either barely available or not permitted at all, as is the case with mystery calls. Team leaders may also not listen in on phone calls, a customary practice in private sector call centres. Standardised dialogue scripts with pre-formulated sentences that can be used in

Table 14.1: Summary: differences between the work organisation in Hamburg and Berlin

Characteristics of work organisation	Berlin	Hamburg
Cooperation	More collaboration and more informal collaboration to gain knowledge	More formal interaction, for example, the forwarding of inquiries
Skills	Less problems to cope with the dynamic environment, for example, fast-changing forms of communication	Problems with knowledge acquiring and information processing, less multitask-oriented
Standardisation	Lower	Rigid guidelines through training and written guidelines
Teamwork	More teamwork, informal communication	Vertical, formal communication, less horizontal communication
Leadership	Cooperative leadership style	More hierarchy leadership style with formal written guidelines

handling calls exist to a limited degree, such as in Hamburg, but are not used. Team leaders can only tell if fewer phone calls were accepted than agreed upon, something that can have many causes, for example, an ICT system failure. This means that the only option left to team leaders is to make a personal appeal to the call centre staff to accept more phone calls.

Furthermore, despite the similar work organisations, different leadership styles were observed in the two call centres. While in Hamburg, management can be characterised as being rather vertically oriented, a greater degree of freedom is given to the team in the Berlin call centre. Compared to Hamburg, more exchange among members of the team takes place in Berlin.

In sum, the work organisation in Berlin seems to be more flexible, collaborative and more dynamic than in Hamburg. Despite both call centres operating with very similar technical infrastructure, the scope of acting and using ICT is quite different. Thus, leadership style or the status of the staff as hired or permanent, rather than the ICT per se, affects the scope of work of the street-level bureaucrats in our case study.

Discussion of the empirical results

Characteristics of work organisation

These empirical findings show that standardisation is not a factor affecting the scope of work of the street-level bureaucrats in call centres. Only a limited degree of standardisation of work organisation exists. The broad range of services and topics covered in the explored call centres is associated with a high proportion of routine task requirements, which can be standardised to a certain degree. Although call centre tasks focused on delivering information are less related to decision-making than classical street-level bureaucrats' work, information provision is a core aspect of public service, even constituting the service itself in many cases (Hood, 1983). The government has to inform society, for example, about dangers such as the health risks of certain food. Based on information gathering and provision, the government can have steering effects on society. The analysis of our case studies reveals how difficult it is to handle information processing and how hard it is to standardise its delivery. As the results of the Hamburg example show, it is rarely possible to use predefined dialogue guidelines and text blocks for these tasks. The support instruments exist, but they are still not used. The callers' requests are too unpredictable and the interaction with the citizen itself cannot be standardised. This means that this type of task cannot be carried out by ICT. At the same time, the knowledge management system can easily be used to provide the content necessary to answer the calls, so that a certain deskilling trend can be deduced.

Difficult inquiries from citizens are clearly less standardised because they cannot be easily answered with the help of the knowledge management system. Skills requirements in these cases clearly go beyond the ability to use an ICT application. This means that subjectivity becomes a particularly crucial aspect of work organisation because of the interaction abilities needed to be able to respond to difficult inquiries. This is supported by ICT to only a very limited extent. Furthermore, the electronic ticket system is hardly used at all and is not sufficient to support the diverse cooperation requirements with the different back office organisations. In this regard, at best, ICT only plays a very limited role in predefining the actions of the call centre staff. Instead, the call centre staff have developed dynamic and varied mechanisms at the working level to cope with the somewhat inadequate socio-technical design and the insufficient support for inter-organisational cooperation. In particular, the scope of action has increased as the call centre agents must be able to organise themselves and their own work well.

Subsequently, system-level bureaucrats only gain an increased scope of action to a very restricted degree, if at all. In this respect, it appears that through the interaction with the citizen and the cooperation with the other departments alone, the subjectivity requirements for the work increases and the scope of action expands. A separate issue is the fact that the content of an answer can, indeed, be based on a knowledge management system. Only for standardised work could a limitation of scope of action be observed. However, this is not caused by ICT, but due to the nature of the conducted task.

Employees on an electronic leash?

The new working structures also influence team management because even though the level of ICT usage has increased, additional control over the employees is not possible. The subjective parts of the work organisation can hardly be directly controlled by ICT; indeed, they are only minimally based on ICT, or not at all. Especially in the case of managers, interaction with citizens and the extensive cooperation requirements cannot not be handled by ICT. Furthermore, in the specific German context, it is not allowed to use ICT to track the behaviour of a single person at the working level because it is rejected by the staff council. Thus, management-relevant information cannot be easily generated. Even though some indicators are collected, they cannot be tied to a single employee, meaning that the managers' level of uncertainty is not reduced. All in all, it appears that call centres can scarcely be managed hierarchically and directly. Rather, it becomes clear that the intensely interactive and cooperative character of one-stop government is beyond hierarchical control. The highly interactive and network character of one-stop government, as well as the method of handling difficult inquiries, reduce the possibilities of hierarchical control – even if the necessary data were collected through the ICT system. In particular, the communication between citizens and call centre employees and the behaviour of an employee during a conversation lie largely outside the instructions and control of the executives. In short, the new interfaces or organisational boundaries that were created by one-stop government produced new uncertainty for management, which could not be compensated for by ICT.

Conclusion: standardisation or subjectivity

In sum, the analysis of the case studies reveals that one-stop government in the form of a telephone access channel does not simply lead to standardisation, with a shift of control to system-level bureaucrats. Rather than leading to a reduction in the scope of action, the network character of this organisation makes it difficult to control through ICT. The subjectivity and decision-making requirements increase in the organisation, especially due to increasing difficult inquiries in the interaction between street-level bureaucrats and citizens. At the same time, in the case of simple inquiries, standardisation contributes to certain deskilling, resulting in a lack of challenge for the call centre agents. Thus, subjectivity and standardisation take place simultaneously and must be equally challenged by employees and executives. Even if the use of ICT, as well as the controlling systems, restrict the day-to-day work of public servants in one-stop government call centres to some extent, the work itself is so diverse and uncertain, and the interaction with citizens is so situation-dependent, that the public servants are continuously required to improvise in their decisions about the adequacy of the information they deliver. They act as policy co-makers at the level of interaction between citizens and public administrations. Thus, we conclude that call centre agents in one-stop government work as street-level bureaucrats, taking decisions about information delivery to citizens, their relevance and their effects for citizens' lives.

These insights can be transcribed in the following programme for the implementation of ICT usage in the day-to-day work of street-level bureaucrats:

1. A management sensitive to interactions across organisational boundaries is required. For example, it may not be possible to completely answer all inquiries in the call centres, but they must be understood in order to forward them to the party that can answer them. Call centre employees must be very able to handle highly divergent demands. This cannot be substituted by ICT. More research is needed at this point to explain how the scope of action of managers differently changes due to ICT usage in specifically emerging work constellations within public sector organisation contexts.
2. Furthermore, ICT has contributed to creating a new ambiguity in work organisation that has arisen because of the ICT-enabled network organisation, the high frequency of interaction and the broad spectrum of topics covered in one-stop government. The analysis of the PSN cases has shown that emerging work organisations do not simply result in either skilling or deskilling (Penn and Scattergard, 1985; Attewell, 1987), but that both phenomena can be observed at the same time. Although the intensive use of ICT may lead to deskilling effects for some jobs and positions, these deskilling effects are counteracted by networking and new interactions across organisational boundaries tied to that networking. Further research should explore both phenomena in depth, as well as the particular factors contributing to those changes. Moreover, specific continuous learning programmes should be designed in both cases in order to prevent work failures.
3. As far as system-level bureaucrats are concerned, no real shift of the kind Bovens and Zouridis described could be observed in one-stop government. Their conclusion about system-level bureaucrats seems rather normative and mechanistic from the presented experiences of one-stop government. It completely ignores the way that the specific organisational and cultural context affects the way in which ICT is adopted.

The comparative analysis of the German 115 call centres has shown some shortcomings in the design of their information systems; in particular, the knowledge management system did not meet the demands posed by the citizens' inquiries and the needs of its users, the call centre agents. Nevertheless, the call centre staff, as in Berlin, showed astonishing creativity in developing new procedures to compensate for these design faults, as, for example, when obtaining the information needed to answer an inquiry. Thus, more analysis about the design of the information systems in public service organisations and particularly of those systems designed for street-level bureaucrats is needed in order to overcome a lack of efficiency from both sides. Long-term participatory system design, taking into account work settings and their transformation, could be conceptualised as a result.

In conclusion, ICT expands the scope of action of street-level bureaucrats – or, in other words, extends their discretion, their function as policymakers and their particular craftsmanship in fulfilling their tasks – due to the uncertainties emerging in the new interaction mode with citizens. Thus, the expectation that the use of ICT will lead to the development of a system-level bureaucracy is too simple and does not do justice to the diversity of informatisation and the organisational design possibilities that go along with them. Rather, the empirical example makes clear that the new working structures tend to overwhelm street-level bureaucrats while, at the same time, leaving them feeling unchallenged in their work. Regarding one-stop government as a specific model of ICT-enabled organisation, ICT has only a very limited power to standardise the work level and to increase the controlling capacity of management. Lipsky's street-level bureaucrats, as triple boundary spanners, are thus confronted with new challenges between the logic of the organisation, that of diverse citizens and the one inserted in the ICT design itself. Further research is needed to examine deeper the particular agency dynamics (related to work structure, content and processes) of the electronic leash of street-level bureaucrats in other public service contexts.

Part Six
The promise of professionalism

FIFTEEN

Fulfilling the promise of professionalism in street-level practice

Paul van der Aa and Rik van Berkel

Introduction

As was argued in Chapter One, street-level bureaucrats work in roles with bureaucratic and professional characteristics. In an era of complex social problems, professionalism may be seen by street-level bureaucrats, policymakers and public managers as a foundation for delivering public policy that looks more promising than bureaucratic control, which may therefore result in reconsidering the mix of professional and bureaucratic work characteristics. Professionalism as an occupational value (Evetts, 2009) favours street-level decisions based on the acknowledged occupational standards, craftsmanship and ethics of workers (Abbott, 1988; Freidson, 2001). Enactment of professionalism requires 'discretion-as-granted' for workers to be able to make their own judgements, as well as sufficient trust in their capacities to do so (Clarke and Newman, 1997; Hasenfeld, 1999; Freidson, 2001). Professionalism holds the promise of dealing effectively with wicked social problems and offering tailor-made public services. As was discussed in Chapter One, professionalism may offer a suitable reference for the horizontal, intercollegial accountability of street-level bureaucrats' behaviour, in addition to or as a replacement for traditional vertical modes of accountability.

Surprisingly, this potential promise of professionalism for public policy production has received modest attention among street-level bureaucracy researchers, on the one hand, and researchers of professionals, on the other (Evans, 2010). Lipsky (2010), of course, did observe that most street-level bureaucrats consider themselves to be professionals. However, he did not elaborate on how professionalism actually affects street-level decision-making. The sociology of professions has produced a large body of literature on contemporary professionalism in various fields (Evetts, 2003; Noordegraaf, 2011). However, in so far as these studies look at public professionals, they mainly focus on their professional roles in changing contexts, and less on their bureaucratic roles and impact on public policy production.

This relative lack of attention can be considered to be somewhat problematic as, for various reasons, the fulfilment of the promise of professionalism by street-level bureaucrats is far from self-evident. First of all, many street-level bureaucrats can be considered to be *organisational* professionals (Evetts, 2009), working in public agencies responsible for delivering public policies. Therefore, workers have to deal with standards for doing their work that originate in various sources: public policy, their organisation and their occupation. Whether the promise of professionalism can be fulfilled is likely to depend on the nature of these standards and the way in which they support or maybe oppose each other.

Second, many of these standards have been changing profoundly over the last decades in ways that potentially affect the promise of professionalism. Expectations regarding public services have been changing as a consequence of changing public policies and new forms of governance. New standards are being set by public policies and managers and trust in established occupational standards is not self-evident. The role of occupational standards may change in various ways. Their role may be reduced, resulting in de-professionalisation, which may thwart the promise of professionalism. However, other dynamics are possible as well. Occupational standards may change and lead to the redefinition of the nature of professionalism. Finally, entirely new professions, requiring new standards, may arise to deliver new public services that are considered to require professional expertise.

Third, given this context of various, changing standards, the promise of professionalism ultimately depends on the way in which street-level bureaucrats themselves enact professionalism. Standards are often ambiguous, require interpretation and prioritisation, and leave room for professional inference. Therefore, how workers themselves deal with changing standards and expectations in daily practice is bound to influence whether the promise of professionalism is ultimately fulfilled.

This chapter therefore aims to contribute to the street-level bureaucracy debate by examining theoretically and empirically how we can improve our understanding of street-level bureaucrats' agency by analysing their enactment of professionalism in policy production given the changing context in which they work. Moreover, we aim to critically reflect on the promise of professionalism as a potential source of horizontal accountability for street-level policy production.

Our theoretical focus is on the enactment of professionalism in the delivery of social policies and the challenge for street-level bureaucrats of working with various, contested standards. The actual manifestation of this challenge, however, will be related to the specific organisational, policy and occupational context in which workers operate. Empirically, we therefore specifically ground our argument in research on the enactment of professionalism by workers delivering the emerging profession of 'job activation' in The Netherlands. As will be argued, such emerging professions provide an especially relevant case to study the contemporary enactment of public professionalism.

The next section will elaborate on the changing standards that street-level bureaucrats have to deal with, as well as on the various strategies that they may pursue to enact professionalism. The section after that discusses our empirical data on the enactment of professionalism in job activation by Dutch case workers. Finally, we will reflect on the relevance of looking at professionalism in street-level bureaucracy research, as well as on the actual promise of professionalism as a potential source of horizontal accountability for street-level agency.

Street-level practice and the fulfilment of the promise of professionalism

Clarke and Newman (1997) describe how in post-war 'bureau-professional settlements' in many social policy and occupational fields, there was a certain understanding and agreement about the required balance between policy, organisational and occupational standards for delivering social policy in an accountable way. However, the growing influence of neoliberalism on social policies since the 1980s and, especially in Western-European countries, the rise of 'new welfare' in the 1990s (Taylor-Gooby, 2008; Bonoli and Natali, 2012), as well as changing views on the governance and management of policy implementation, have changed the playing field of street-level bureaucrats involved in policy production (Bach and Kessler, 2012). These changes have affected expectations regarding the policy, organisational and occupational standards that guide the work of street-level bureaucrats. Established occupations and professions have to act on these changes and new occupations develop. Workers have to enact professionalism in changing contexts.

This section will elaborate on what these changes imply for the enactment of professionalism in street-level bureaucracies. We will first look at relevant changes in social policies, governance and management and the resulting changing standards with which street-level bureaucrats have to cope in their daily work. Second, we will assess how, given these changes, the actual enactment of professionalism by workers may be understood.

A general assessment of social policy changes is tricky given differences between welfare states and policy fields. However, scholars on welfare state development (Gilbert, 2002; Taylor-Gooby, 2008; Bonoli and Natali, 2012) agree on a number of general changes occurring in social policy fields across countries:

- the alignment of social policy and social protection with economic policies;
- a greater emphasis on the conditionality of welfare state arrangements; and
- especially since the economic crisis of 2008, the reduction of spending on social policies and services and a greater emphasis on the value of financial efficiency.

Such policy changes influence the standards that social policies set for service delivery, put existing occupational standards to the test or give rise to new occupational standards. For example, workers are expected to have a greater focus on the labour market attachment of their clients, to focus more on the financial efficiency of their services or to implement 'disciplinary' instruments, such as financial sanctioning. These new policy standards do not necessarily fit well with existing occupational standards, as the literature on social workers made responsible for implementing these policies has shown (Van Berkel and Van der Aa, 2012).

Various authors have explored these potential tensions for the social work occupation, which, in many cases, has been a preferred supplier for various kinds of social policies (Clarke and Newman, 1997; Kirkpatrick et al, 2005). Abramowitz (2005) and Marston and McDonald (2012), for example, observe a growing discrepancy between the self-identity of social workers as critical agents in structural social change and policy development, and the actual role that they have come to play in the 'technical' delivery of (neoliberal) social policies. Jordan (2001) discusses how social policy increasingly accentuates the promotion of employment, a domain in which traditional social work has not been very active and, we could add, competent. Soss et al (2011b), Kjørstad (2005) and Hasenfeld (1999) discuss the tension between disciplinary social policies and social work ethics. Thus, these authors suggest clear tensions between social work occupational standards and the changed standards set by social policy.

Changes in the governance and management of social policy implementation potentially affect the organisational standards for service provision as well. Van Berkel et al (2011) state that widely observed changes in this respect are the redistribution of responsibilities for policymaking and implementation, the introduction of quasi-markets for service delivery, the stimulation of inter-agency cooperation, and the introduction of new managerial methods within agencies. These changes potentially influence the organisational standards that workers have to deal with, especially with respect to changing norms regarding the legitimate output and outcome of services, changing demands on accountability and shifting divisions of labour, and changing relations between professionals in both public and private agencies.

An example derived from this debate concerns the use of performance management. On the one hand, output targets, as well as the external definition of these targets by policymakers or managers, may conflict with occupational standards, may be at odds with professional ethics and may be experienced as an attack on professional discretion (Morgen, 2001; Thorén, 2008). On the other hand, performance management may go hand in hand with deregulation and less bureaucratic control, thus actually increasing room for occupational standards (Sandfort, 2000; Riccucci and Lurie, 2001).

Some authors, such as Diefenbach (2009), interpret these new management techniques as predominantly an attack on 'pure professionalism' (Noordegraaf, 2011) at the cost of occupational standards and professional autonomy. In this interpretation, they threaten the promise of professionalism. Other authors, however, take a more nuanced view (Exworthy and Halford, 1999; Kirkpatrick et al, 2005; Newman, 2005; Evetts, 2009; Noordegraaf, 2011). They point to the fact that the exact impact of these changes appears to be contextualised, depending on the nature of the changes themselves, as well as on the existing working and occupational contexts in which they are introduced. Moreover, occupational standards are not necessarily static, but may adapt to new expectations.

As was argued in the introduction, how workers experience and practice changing standards influences how professionalism is enacted. They have an imperative to act (Hill and Hupe, 2007). Therefore, it is important to understand how front-line workers themselves deal with ambiguity and conflict concerning the standards for their work and what this implies for the fulfilment of the promise of professionalism.

Recent studies predominantly focus on the question of how workers belonging to established professions may deal with 'pressures' resulting from the changing standards that were described earlier. Hupe and

Van der Krogt (2013) suggest that they can act both individually and collectively to deal with these pressures. In this chapter, we focus on individual strategies at the shop floor, although collective strategies such as political activism by occupational groups can, of course, also be expected to be influential.

Wallace and Pease (2011) offer useful concepts for understanding the diversified ways in which workers may deal individually with possibly conflicting standards. In their literature review of social work practice against the background of changing standards, they identify three ideal-typical forms of individual agency that we think are relevant for analysing the promise and enactment of professionalism in street-level bureaucracies: shielding, adapting and resisting.

The first type they call *shielding* from or avoiding the tensions between different sets of standards. In this strategy, workers try to focus on the aspects of service that (still) require professional inference based on their original occupational standards, such as therapeutic work or coaching, while ignoring the more businesslike imperatives that, for example, managerial standards may set.

Second, they suggest that workers may be adaptable and amenable to applying or developing new standards. Wallace and Peace interpret *adaptation* rather negatively because it could mean that workers forsake their occupational norms and thus undermine their own profession. A more positive interpretation considers adaptation as a sign of 're-professionalisation' (Jørgensen et al, 2010) at the shop floor, where workers rework and maybe reconcile various standards to arrive at new occupational standards. A central question, of course, would be whether these new standards can achieve legitimacy.

Finally, workers may *resist* the new standards. Resistance may be understood as opposition towards changing standards, refusing to apply them. This could lead to what Lipsky (2010) called rule-breaking. Thomas and Davies (2005) offer a more subtle interpretation of resistance, based on the inherent ambiguity of most standards. In their interpretation, the difference between shielding, adaption and resistance becomes more fluid. They understand resistance as 'a constant process of adaptation, subversion and re-inscription of dominant discourses' (Thomas and Davies, 2005, p 687), aimed at reconciling ambiguous standards with their personal working identity and ambitions. In their view, this may lead to personalised and diverse ways of interpreting and practising standards. For example, one worker may feel comfortable with performance management and aim to bend occupational standards to resolve possible conflicts, while another worker may bend performance standards to uphold certain occupational standards.

To understand the promise of professionalism, these various strategies are relevant as the fulfilment of this promise is likely to depend on whether these strategies result in practices that are considered accountable. However, a possible shortcoming of this 'pressure' approach is that it runs the risk of considering occupational standards and established professions as given. This is not satisfactory because, as was stated, occupational standards may develop and the rise of entirely new professions may occur. Therefore, these strategies should not only be interpreted as *reactions* to 'external' pressures on established professions, resulting from policy and management, but rather as possible strategies to *reconfigure and develop professionalism* by working with and possibly developing different sets of available standards (Noordegraaf, 2011). Which standards are available depends on the policy, organisational and occupational context in which workers practise. How workers pursue these strategies in enacting these standards influences the development of their profession and the resulting promise of professionalism.

Dutch job activation and the promise of professionalism

Our argument can be substantiated with empirical data on the enactment of professionalism by Dutch, municipal caseworkers responsible for the delivery of 'job activation' to recipients of social assistance (*Wet Werk en Bijstand*: the last-resort, means-tested public benefit). Job activation is meant to support unemployed people to find work and plays a core role in the policy objective to get more people on benefits into paid work.

In the national Dutch policy discourse, job activation is conceived of as a predominantly professional function: it is considered to require discretion-as-granted to provide 'people-changing' service technology (especially with respect to motivation to return to work), tailor-made services and craftsmanship. Since 2010, the Ministry for Social Affairs and Employment has stimulated various initiatives towards the professionalisation of activation work (Divosa, 2011).

National policies hardly regulate the contents of this work. Since the implementation of social assistance is decentralised to the municipal level, local activation policies influence how the profession can actually be practised. Although an overview of all municipalities is unavailable, several studies suggest that many municipalities follow the national discourse and deliberately grant substantial discretion to their workers to be able to use their professional judgement to decide upon the best strategy to achieve activation goals (Van Berkel et al, 2010; Polstra, 2011; Zandvliet et al, 2011).

For two reasons, Dutch job activation provides an interesting case for studying how street-level bureaucrats enact professionalism. First, Dutch activation policy constitutes a field in which many of the changes that were described earlier are visible: a greater emphasis on stimulating employment, as well as on the conditionality of benefits; and the introduction of new governance and management arrangements, such as the outsourcing of services to external providers, network cooperation and output-steering within public agencies. As such, the enactment of professionalism takes place against the backdrop of changing expectations of professional public service delivery.

Second, Dutch activation work is an example of a *newly emerging* profession that has been created by new social policy. New professions have not received much attention in earlier studies on changing public professionalism, which mostly focus on established professions. However, analysing the practices of workers in emerging professions is especially relevant for understanding the enactment of professionalism. Since emerging professions lack generally accepted occupational standards, the street-level practice of workers in new professions can be expected to be especially relevant for fulfilling the promise of professionalism (or not), by working with (new) policy and managerial standards, as well as by developing new occupational standards in daily practice.

This also holds true for Dutch activation workers. Although they are granted discretion to act as professionals, their new profession lacks well-established and generally acknowledged occupational standards (Van Berkel et al, 2010). There is no professional consensus on the best ways to 'get people back to work'. Being a new profession, the level of institutionalisation is low. An occupational association was established in 2012, but it is not in the position to claim jurisdiction. Also, contrary to the Scandinavian countries for example (Thorén, 2008; Jørgensen et al, 2010), but comparable to the UK (Sainsbury, 2008), social assistance workers in The Netherlands do not share a common occupational background in social work, but have diverse educational and occupational backgrounds, ranging from administrative and legal to social and personnel studies. As a result, Dutch job activation is an example in which workers themselves are very much individually confronted with the challenge of fulfilling the promise of professionalism.

Research design

Empirical data stem from a PhD study (Van der Aa, 2012) on professional and bureaucratic roles in the delivery of job activation in social assistance agencies in three Dutch cities. These cities do not constitute a representative sample of all Dutch municipalities. Nevertheless, findings reported in other publications (Polstra, 2011; Zandvliet et al, 2011) indicate that the results found in this study are also visible in other municipalities. Data were collected in 2010 via semi-structured individual and focus group interviews with 70 frontline workers and 25 observations of their interactions with clients. Furthermore, policy documents were studied and 25 managers and policy advisors were interviewed.

Standards for doing job activation

As was argued, understanding the promise of professionalism requires insight into the nature of the standards with which workers are expected to work, as well as the discretion with which they are granted.

The municipalities in our study set the objective of services, which was to stimulate the acceptance of any paid job as soon as possible or, for certain groups, to engage in voluntary work. How this objective was to be achieved was not very strictly regulated, which allowed for 'professional inference'. In addition, various other standards applied.

All workers had targets with respect to the number of people that had to find work. Moreover, workers had to realise activation plans with nearly all of their clients. For workers who activated unemployed people with (expected) good chances to find work, these targets were the main standards. They could more or less decide for themselves how to achieve them. They could offer personal guidance or invite people to participate in 'job clubs'. Also, limited possibilities existed to offer wage subsidies to employers or to reimburse costs for short training.

Workers who activated clients with fewer prospects to find work had to make use of contracted services by external providers. Policy set general standards for the type of services that clients could use, but it was up to the workers to determine which contracted service was best suited for individual clients. A range of services was available. Workers were free to invite clients for follow-up meetings for additional coaching and advice. They were supposed to monitor progress and discuss changes with providers and clients when progress was lacking.

Municipalities also set policies for the financial sanctioning of non-compliance by clients. These policies determined the levels of financial sanctioning, as well as the procedures to be followed. Determining whether clients were non-compliant and whether to apply sanctions or not was largely left up to the workers. Furthermore, workers had to deal with other administrative standards concerning registration and accounting.

Finally, despite the national discourse on the professionalisation of job activation, none of the municipalities demanded specific occupational standards for this work. Neither was there systematic organisational support for professionalisation. Some teams organised collegial consultation as a means of practice-based learning, but there was no general agency policy to support this.

Thus, workers had to deal with certain organisational and policy standards, but were granted ample discretion in making decisions regarding service delivery. These were framed as professional decisions, but were hardly guided by generally acknowledged occupational standards.

Fulfilling the promise of professionalism in activation practice

The data on activation practice reveals that the workers used various strategies to apply the available standards, as well as to deal with the absence of occupational standards in daily activation work. By doing so, they individually constructed their new profession in practice. We will illustrate this by elaborating upon three characteristic aspects of daily activation work: determining activation goals and services; sanctioning in case of non-compliance; and dealing with performance targets.

Determination of the activation plan

The start of activation consisted of 'diagnosing' the activation problem and deciding about the content of services. Wright (2003) and Thorén (2008) describe this 'diagnosis' as a predominantly rule-driven selection of activation programmes based on strict policy regulations. In our case, we found a more differentiated practice in which professional inference was visible.

Adaptation to the absence of clear standards was a prominent strategy, which took the form of deciding based on personal and sometimes shared – at team-level – standards about how to activate unemployed people. A standard shared by many workers was the idea that activation services had to be tailor-made and individualised: "every client is different. One may need control and discipline, the other needs support or contacts with employers. You cannot say one size fits all" (Worker203[1]).

Standards about *how* to individualise varied and depended on personal preferences and experience. Differences that were found related to the desirability of 'harsh' approaches versus empowering methods, the way in which motivation and ability to work was assessed, and the active role that unemployed people themselves were allowed in deciding about the pathway towards work: "I think we deal differently with people who don't want to work. You can have multiple conversations to understand why someone is resisting. Or you can place him in a Workfirst job [placement in a subsidised street-cleaning job]" (Worker503). Workers were aware of these differences, but considered these as differences in 'personal style' and not as differences in occupational standards, which might be problematic from a perspective of professional legitimacy based on shared and acknowledged standards.

Some of the workers were no proponent of individualisation at all. In a way, they *shielded* themselves from the need to make professional inferences. They took a bureaucratic stance by offering standardised contracted services as much as possible or by focusing on the obligatory nature of activation: "as a matter of speaking, when a client says he likes coconut or kiwi, I say: 'I know that you like that. But I can only offer you pear, apple or banana'" (Worker902). Apparently, shielding may refer not only to professionals protecting their occupational standards, but also to workers who are supposed to work as professional but do not know how to do that and 'fall back' on a bureaucratic stance.

Resistance could also be observed in some cases. This was mainly the case with respect to setting the goal of activation services. The policy standard was unequivocal about this: unemployed people were supposed to accept any job regardless of former experience or education and regardless of job quality and security. This standard was, however, resisted by several workers, who would allow clients to look for 'better-quality jobs': "you want to reach sustainable results, you don't want to see them back. I would not want a street-cleaning job or other simple job either" (Worker403). Thus, resistance did not consist of rejecting the policy goal of getting people back to work, but of bending the policy standard by setting additional, personal standards for the job quality to aim for.

Sanctioning

Workers were supposed to apply sanctions whenever clients did not comply with their individual activation plan or did not show up at meetings. Concerning this aspect of activation, little discretion was granted, although it depended on the individual activation plan as to what kind of behaviour was actually sanctionable.

Especially in the US literature, examples are given of workers who use sanctioning to discipline clients in order to reach organisational goals (Soss et al, 2011b). In our case, however, many workers *resisted* standards concerning sanctioning, meaning that they did not sanction clients automatically when they did not comply. Here, discretion was taken, but based on professional arguments. Workers described that they tried to approach clients in a supportive way first: they would first try to understand non-compliance and to motivate clients to change their behaviour. When this did not succeed, they would start issuing warnings about possible sanctions. After that, they could actually apply sanctions, but, in practice, this did not happen very often. Their justification was 'professional' in the sense that they would only apply sanctions when they felt that sanctions would have a positive impact on finding a job:

> "of course you may sanction people, and again, and again. But, in the end, you cannot match unmotivated people with employers because they [employers] will say: 'I don't want these welfare clients anymore'. So, in the end, motivating people is what works best." (Worker204)

Others, however, felt less need to resist and adapted to the policy standards because they felt that sanctions were a sound way to get people back to work:

> "personally, I think we are not harsh enough. You have to be clear-cut. If you don't work hard enough, you get a sanction. If it happens again, I cut your allowance completely.... But I know what it is like, I am the same. If I don't feel like doing things and I have room to do so, I won't do it." (Worker404)

Still other workers adapted by sticking to the rules and taking a bureaucratic stance: "there are procedures, 'we have to do our work', I always explain to the client. Certain behaviour has a consequence, which is a sanction. And the client can always appeal, which gives him a juridical back-up" (Worker604).

Working with performance targets

Contrary to findings in some other studies (Morgen, 2001; Thorén, 2008), output-steering regarding job placements did not influence decision-making in a substantial way: the influence of this standard was rather limited in our case. Workers found their targets to be easily achievable: "I don't really focus on my targets and I still realise sufficient placements in work, so I don't really care" (Worker303).

Moreover, they noticed that nothing serious happened when they did not meet their targets. Also, they did not feel that these targets conflicted with how they wanted to focus their work anyway, that is, to support people to find a job. So, we could say that these workers adapted to these standards because they did not demand much of them.

However, some workers mentioned that these targets focused them on the policy standard to place clients as fast as possible in whatever job. They stimulated quick job placements, including when this involved short-time, insecure jobs, for example, with temp agencies. So, the resistance against these policy standards we described earlier was somewhat softened by adapting to these performance targets:

> "because of the targets, I have focused my work a bit differently. Much more focused on leaving benefits for whatever kind of work, short-term or long-term. In the past, I was more inclined to achieve sustainable placements. That goal is the past now." (Worker102).

Contrary to job placement targets, the targets on activation plans, which were strictly monitored by management, did have a major impact on activation practice by the workers. They were supposed to realise an activation plan with 80–90% of their clients. Workers adapted to these targets by paying little attention to the monitoring of activation plans and external providers in favour of realising sufficient activation plans. The target could also lead to 'empty plans' without any delivery of services:

> "when I have a target of 100 more activation plans, I focus on clients that don't have a plan yet. They have to have a plan. If a client is 63 years old, you can say: 'he won't do anything anymore'. Then you can make a plan that says: 'until he is 65, he won't do anything anymore'. Then the plan is registered." (Worker603)

Both findings indicate that workers can and do adapt to performance standards. As such, performance standards may focus the use of occupational and policy standards.

Conclusion

This chapter aimed to better understand street-level bureaucrats' agency by specifically looking at their enactment of professionalism in their daily work given a context of changing policy, organisational and occupational standards. In this final section, we will draw conclusions based on three questions:

- What can we learn from this focus on professionalism for our understanding of street-level bureaucrats' behaviour?
- What does our exploration learn with respect to the actual fulfilment of the promise of professionalism?
- How could research on the enactment of professionalism by street-level bureaucrats be further advanced?

Many street-level bureaucrats delivering social policies not only consider themselves to be professional, but are often expected to act as professionals given the complex social problems that they are confronted with. However, what professionalism actually means for contemporary street-level bureaucrats is far from obvious. Concerning the lessons for street-level bureaucracy research, we have therefore argued that a better understanding of street-level bureaucrats' agency requires more explicit attention to the way in which workers enact professionalism. We have suggested that this can be achieved by studying how workers deal with standards originating in social policy, their organisation and their occupation in terms of shielding, adapting or resisting. We feel that this offers a refined perspective on contemporary public service practice, expanding on studies that predominantly focus on the enactment of policy regulations and organisational imperatives. Since the standards, as well as the strategies, of workers can vary, the enactment of professionalism in street-level bureaucracies is highly contextualised:

- it will vary across policy fields and depend upon often localised policy and managerial choices;
- it depends on the status and maturity of the profession(s) involved; and
- it depends on the way in which workers deal with standards.

Of course, whether the resulting practices actually fulfil the promise of professionalism and lead to horizontally accountable professional practices is ultimately a normative question, which may be answered differently by different stakeholders.

Concerning this question, our exploration of the enactment of professionalism in a new profession raises the issue of how to assess the differentiated individual strategies we found. A major concern may be that they may lead to very individualised forms of professionalism that are at odds with the traditional ideal type of professionalism based on shared standards. However, as a stage in the process of (re-)professionalisation, these strategies and workers' tacit knowledge may contribute to (re)defining their professions and to newly acknowledged occupational standards. To achieve shared and legitimate occupational standards would require an underlying strategy aimed at validating and systematising varied local knowledge to arrive (again) at shared occupational standards. When such as strategy is not pursued, the fulfilment of the promise may, indeed, be considered problematic.

With respect to the specific strategies, individual adaptation was a prominent strategy in our empirical study. Adaptation could be deemed undesirable coping by street-level bureaucrats because it affects the transparency and predictability of services and may lead to the bending of standards. A more positive interpretation, however, is that adaptation can potentially be a source for re-professionalisation or professionalisation, based on the tacit knowledge that workers develop when confronted with complex problems and multiple standards. The strategy of shielding may be considered to be more problematic for fulfilling the promise of professionalism in changing contexts. Sticking to 'old' habits may feel comfortable for the workers involved, but it does not really solve the problem of how to deal with contested professionalism and multiple standards. Individual resistance was not very prominent in our case. The difference with adaptation was more gradual than substantial. Resistance may be necessary to protect discretion-as-given for the accountable application of accepted professional methods. However, resistance in the context of weak occupational norms may actually undermine horizontal accountability and may be interpreted by managers or policymakers as undesirable coping strategies.

Finally, to further research on the enactment of professionalism in street-level bureaucracies, we would support the more comparative approach advocated in Chapter One. This explorative chapter has only looked at one type of public street-level work in an early stage of professionalisation. The argument could be developed further by comparing the street-level enactment of professionalism in different policy, organisational and occupational contexts. Comparative research could also provide better insight into the influence on street-level behaviour of various degrees of professionalisation.

Note

[1] Numbers have been randomly assigned to citations to illustrate the various workers who are being cited.

SIXTEEN

Professionals and discretion in street-level bureaucracy

Tony Evans

Introduction

Lipsky's (2010, cover blurb) *Street-level bureaucracy* is a '… a cautionary tale of how decisions made by overburdened workers in underfunded government agencies translate into ad-hoc policy changes impacting on people's lives and life opportunities'. It has received plaudits for its enduring contribution to the study of public policy. In this chapter, I want to acknowledge the contribution of *Street-level bureaucracy* to understanding the limits of managerial control on front-line practice. My main focus, however, is on a critical examination of *Street-level bureaucracy*, arguing that it constrains the investigation of discretion and limits the exploration of the location, construction and deployment of discretion within welfare services. *Street-level bureaucracy* does not take sufficient account of the role of different occupational status, particularly professional status, in the construction of discretion or in how discretion may be used in practice. In emphasising both the similarity of all front-line workers and their fundamental difference from their supervisors and managers, Lipksy ignores the ways in which, for professional staff particularly, this distinction is blurred and highly permeable. *Street-level bureaucracy* also brackets off the discretion of managers – the new organisational professionals *par excellence* – and characterises their use of discretion as simply motivated to implement the policy that they have been given as best they can. In short, my argument is that *Street-level bureaucracy* pays insufficient attention to the role of professional status in understanding the discretion granted and used by some front-line staff and by managers within public welfare organisations and the way in which this can influence the extent and use of discretion at different points in implementation. While the chapter does not report on a particular empirical research project, it draws upon my earlier work on discretion in social work practice to explore the adequacy of Lipsky's treatment of issues about professionalism and its management.

In the first section of this chapterm I will outline what I see as the strength of the street-level bureaucracy approach in terms of its critique of the idea of managerial control of front-line discretion, and I will consider the additional resources for discretion available to professional front-line staff. I will then consider the way in which *Street-level bureaucracy* characterises the uses of discretion as 'client-processing' and engages with ideas of professionalism in characterising uses of discretion on the front line. In the final section, I will look at managers as the new elite professionals within welfare organisations and the issues this raises for *Street-level bureaucracy* about the analysis of managerial discretion.

Indelible discretion

Street-level bureaucrats work directly with citizens. They provide public services and 'have considerable discretion in determining the nature, amount, and quality of benefits and sanctions provided by their agencies' (Lipsky, 2010, p 13). The extensive discretion of front-line staff, Lipsky argues, arises, in part, from the stand-off between managers and front-line workers. Managers are powerful; they can control and direct front-line staff, but they also face practical limitations in the nature and exercise of this power. Managers are 'constrained by law, labor agreements, political opposition and worker solidarity from dictating decisions' (Lipsky, 1991, pp 216–17). They also need workers to perform because 'Workers can punish supervisors who do not behave properly toward them, either by refusing to perform work of certain kinds, by doing only minimal work, or by doing work rigidly so as to discredit supervisors' (Lipsky, 2010, pp 24–5).

The intensely political nature of public welfare services also contributes to discretion: services are replete with promises and political rhetoric; and policies tend to be wide-ranging and vague, and sometimes impractical. Policies also exist in an environment of other policies, with which they may fit or conflict. Resources also tend to undershoot what politicians and policies promise. In fact, social service organisations rely on the use of discretion by staff to ensure that services do not grind to a halt or collapse in confusion and contradiction.

However, the extent of discretion involves more than just the balance of power between the worker and manager and the mismatch between policy rhetoric and resources. It is also embedded in the nature of the work of public welfare services. The human dimension of service cannot easily be proceduralised and controlled because the 'elaboration of rules, guidelines, or instructions cannot circumscribe the alternative' (Lipsky, 2010, p 15). Front-line discretion is necessary to respond to the unexpected and to ensure that services are responsive to individual need.

Management control

One of the challenges of applying Lipsky's work to contemporary services is, critics argue, that welfare services are now so closely managed, and front-line workers so subject to control, direction and surveillance from managers, that discretion has all but disappeared (Howe, 1991; Cheetham, 1993). These critics are right to point to a shift in power away from practitioner discretion towards practice as increasingly defined and supervised by managers. The terms of the stand-off between managers and front-line practitioners have changed. Managers have become more powerful and are more able to restrict the freedom previously enjoyed by front-line staff. Employment rights, for instance, have been eroded (Mangan, 2009) and managerialism – the idea that managers should have freedom to manage in line with principles drawn from business practice – has been promoted by governments (Harris, 2008).

From any perspective, the rise of managerial power has constrained the freedom of front-line staff. However, constrained freedom does not mean the elimination of freedom, and the constraints themselves can create new choices and freedoms – discretion is as much about spaces created in the wake of the unintended consequences of others' policy choices as it is about simply being left to one's own devices. Policy initiatives often raise questions about what policies mean, how they should be applied in particular settings, how they fit with other policies and procedures, and so on. Harrison et al (1992), for instance, talks about the puzzlement often experienced by those who are faced with policies to implement, and the degree and extent of constraint is not necessarily uniform: the extent and impact of management control varies between services and between and within occupational groups (Evans, 2010).

My interest in discretion has focused on questions about the continuation of professional (social worker) discretion in contemporary local government social services, particularly in the context of a widespread assumption that front-line discretion has been curtailed. Key questions here include: the extent of discretion granted (or withdrawn); how organisationally sanctioned discretion intersects with professional claims to discretion; and the ways in which discretion is used in practice. An influential view is that discretion has now all but disappeared and front-line workers are compliant with systems of management control. A recent study of the introduction of information and communication technology (ICT) systems in children's services, for instance, characterises these systems as the perfection of the managerial control of practice, which have so limited professional decision-making, in all but marginal areas, that 'procedures and rules (inscribed in ICTs) … increasingly constrain what can be done, and indeed determine behaviour in the sense that power is ceded to the rules' (Wastell et al, 2010, p 318). However, even if managers are relatively more powerful, strategies to reduce front-line discretion continue to be frustrated by the human and political dimensions of the work of street-level bureaucracies. In another national study of the introduction of major ICT systems in social care services, the new systems were found to be ineffective and burdensome, and required extensive discretion on the part of professional staff to make sense of categories and to make the system work at all (eg Shaw et al, 2009).

Furthermore, even if managers are more active in seeking to control front-line discretion, it is not clear that they can or want to eliminate discretion. Systems of control can be expensive and severely hampered by resource constraints (Evans, 2010). Politicians and executives are often reluctant to take responsibility for difficult decisions, preferring to support ideas such as clinical responsibility and professional discretion as ways of defending senior decision-makers from blame if things go wrong (Hood et al, 2001).

Historically, professional staff have been employed within welfare services to play a key role in resolving the tensions between citizens, policies and resources (Marshall and Rees, 1985). The expansion of traditional professions and the development of new professions, alongside the expansion of the post-war welfare state, were noted by Lipsky as key factors in the development of street-level bureaucracies.

Professional street-level bureaucrats

Given the significant role of professionals in the post-war welfare services, Lipksy's treatment of professionalism in *Street-level bureaucracy* is intriguing. He refers to street-level workers as professionals but his use of the term ranges from the broad sense of service/white-collar workers to a narrower conception of a recognised occupational group with status and authority (Evans, 2010) (ie professional status based on its knowledge claims, organisation and norms of practice and some ability to guide and direct its own work [Freidson, 1994; Noon and Blyton, 2002]).

Lipsky occasionally draws on this second, narrow sense of 'professional', talking about a subset of street-level bureaucrats who are 'expected to exercise discretionary judgement in their field ... [and who] are regularly deferred to in their specialised areas of work and are relatively free from supervision by superiors' (Lipsky, 2010, p 14). However, generally, he tends to use 'professional' in the broader sense to make the point that there is now little use in distinguishing (narrow conception) professional street-level bureaucrats from their non-professional street-level bureaucrats because 'even public employees who do not have claims to professional status exercise considerable discretion ... even though their discretion is formally circumscribed by rules and relatively closely supervised' (Lipsky, 2010, p 14).

Lipsky acknowledges that there may be differences between street-level bureaucrats arising from professional status, but he does not pursue this point. Rather, he emphasises the common characteristics of street-level bureaucrats despite the diverse nature of the public services workforce to which this term refers – receptionists, benefits clerks, judges, doctors, police officers, social workers, teachers and so on (Lipsky, 2010). This would perhaps make sense if one were to assume the de-professionalisation of staff in street-level bureaucracies. However, while professional workers, across a range of different settings, have seen changes that have constrained their work, they have also seen changes that have increased their power and status (Leicht and Fennell, 2001). In England, for instance, the professional status of social workers has been embedded in law for over a decade (Social Care Act 2000). Social workers are now registered, and only social workers registered by the professional body can operate as social workers. Furthermore, the number of social workers employed within social services in England has also increased by 24% in the decade 2000–10 (NHS, 2010).

In relation to street-level discretion, Lipsky's concern for the 'central tendencies' (Lipsky, 2010, p xix) risks missing particular factors in particular settings that may give greater or fewer resources to exercise discretion – particularly the ability to appeal to an idea of professionalism and associated ideas of professional discretion.

My own research (Evans, 2010, 2011, 2013, 2014), for instance, has looked at the continuing role of 'professionalism' as a factor influencing front-line discretion. The research study looked at social workers' experience of discretion within adult services in an English local authority – a classic case of a 'street-level bureaucracy' that provides an opportunity to critically explore and examine the theory. The study employed qualitative methods of data gathering: primarily interviews but also observational and documentary research. As a case study, the research study was designed to explore and critique theory and to identify areas for further exploration and discussion (Walton, 1992). I found that the professional status of social workers was an important factor in the levels of discretion expected and afforded in their practice. Policies limiting decision-making on the face of it, actually assumed a major role for professional judgement. For instance, the eligibility criteria that govern service users' entitlement to social care services are couched in terms of 'needs' and 'risks' – which may also be 'high', 'significant', 'major' and so on. These terms are not defined, but assume that professional staff will bring into play their own expertise to fill the gaps. Furthermore, professionalism is a significant factor in understanding the relationship between front-line professionals and their managers. Friedson (1994) also notes that front-line professionals tend to be first-line managed by a fellow professional. In my research, practitioners and front-line managers shared a professional background (social work) and shared a similar worldview that included respecting the role of professional judgement as a basis for discretion in front-line work.

Street-level discretion and client-processing

The idea that professional status can augment the already wide-ranging resources for discretion available to front-line workers should not, on the face of it, be a problem for the street-level bureaucracy approach. However, I now want to consider the way in which professionalism as an idea introduces problems into the analysis of front-line discretion in *Street-level bureaucracy*. The assumption is that front-line discretion is the problem. Front-line staff tend to frustrate policy and use discretion to make their work easier or more bearable at the expense of the organisation's interest and service users' interests. This is perhaps a surprising claim, certainly in the UK, given the continued high level of trust and satisfaction with public sector professionals noted in national surveys (Ipsos-MORI, 2009).

Lipsky uses the term 'client-processing' to refer to the routines and practices that street-level bureaucrats individually and collectively adopt in the use of their discretion to manage the stress of their situation. Front-line staff: create waiting lists or allow people to queue-jump; prefer some service users over others; understand rules too narrowly or too broadly; see service users as more or less culpable for the problems they face, focusing either too much on individual fault or on social disadvantage and structural inequalities; and focus on certain aspects of their job at the expense of other aspects. These very different practices are, for Lipsky, fundamentally the same in that they are all about managing stress and pressure and 'contribute to control over the work environment. This is consistent with perceiving routines as coping behaviours in which the confronting problem is the management of work stresses'(Lipsky, 2010, pp 85–6).

For Lipsky the problem of front-line discretion is part of the stressful working environment of street-level bureaucracies. Street-level bureaucrats (except for professionals – see later) are not bad people; they are changed by experience. Initially, people are attracted to work in public welfare services because they want to help others. However, the pressures and contradictions of working in street-level bureaucracies frustrate idealists, who then leave. Those who remain accept that they have to compromise their ideals to survive. They develop strategies and practices – 'client-processing' – to reduce the stress and strain of their work in such a way that allows them to reduce the discord between their ideals (the myth of altruism) and the nature of their day-to-day practice. Is such a catch-all explanation for such a wide range of different behaviours in different settings plausible? Do the uses of discretion by front-line workers come down to stress?

Official statistics indicate that 'workplace stress' is higher among occupations in public services, such as health and social work, education, and public administration, than in the work population as a whole; however, it still only affects a small proportion of these occupational groups (around 2–3%) (Health and Safety Executive, 2013). These figures may indicate the tip of an iceberg – only those who find the stress too much to bear reporting their experience – but, even accepting this, it seems unlikely that 'stress' is the primary and predominant phenomenon in street-level bureaucracies that Lipsky assumes in his explanation of such front-line routines as 'client-processing' as a set of stress-management strategies.

It is not clear what 'stress' means in the account of 'client-processing' in *Street-level bureaucracy*. The sense one gets is that stress is used as synonymous with pressured and demanding work. However, this common-sense idea of stress, while widespread, is vague. Ferrie (2004, p 6) argues that this common-sense idea of workplace stress is not helpful and suggests that it is better understood as 'an imbalance between the psychological demands of work on the one hand and the degree of control over work on the other.... It is the combination of high demand and low control.' Work stress entails more than demanding and pressured work; it also relates to other factors, such as the opportunity to use skills and expertise, a sense of control over the task, occupational status, and so on (Ferrie, 2004). Stress is unlikely to be a uniform experience in street-level bureaucracies – professional street-level bureaucrats, for instance, with a relatively greater ability to control their work, sense of status and so on, are less likely to experience the sort of stress that Lipsky assumes gives rise to client-processing than other street-level bureaucrats.

Interestingly, though, in the case of professionals, Lipsky's account of motivation and routines short-circuits 'stress' and simply asserts the venal character of professionals:

> studies of professional practice suggest that doctors, lawyers, and other professions tend to seek out higher-status clients at the expense of low-status clients, to neglect necessary services in favor of exotic or financially rewarding specialties, to allow the market for specialists to operate so as to create extreme inequalities in the distribution of available practitioners, to provide only meagerly for the professional needs of low-income people, and to respond to poor people in controlling and manipulative ways when they do serve them. (Lipsky, 2010, p 202)

Lipsky's notion of 'client-processing' categorises a wide range of discretionary behaviours as reflections of a single phenomenon: they reflect a common drive to deal with the difficult circumstances of front-line practice, to reduce stress. However, while stress may explain some discretionary behaviour, it is difficult to see how it can provide a sufficient explanation. If stress fails to hold these disparate approaches to discretion among front-line staff together, then what is the purpose of the term? It seems to me that rather than describing something out there, it is a term that reflects the concerns and values of the person using it. Client-processing defines a problem for Lipsky. The problem is not so much that front-line staff develop routines and so on, but that these routines and so on do not – from his viewpoint – advance agency objectives or responsiveness to service users (Lipksy, 2010, p 86). However, on what basis is this judgement of front-line practice made? Scratch the surface of Lipsky's account of client-processing and it is an assumption that front-line workers will choose to make their work life easier, more pleasant and less stressful in preference to being concerned with others' interests. In the case of professional staff, he believes that they will seek to control and manipulate in the pursuit of individual and collective interests. However, are such simple, damning and global accounts of motivation plausible? Stress management or venality cloaked in altruism are unlikely to be the only or even the most plausible explanations for the different ways in which discretion is used by different actors, in different settings and for different purposes. The approaches to discretion may reflect commitments, interest and concerns (Evans, 2010), professional understanding and analysis, or professional ideas of appropriate responses and interventions (Evans and Hardy, 2010). The problem with the idea of client-processing is that it sets aside these questions with a sweeping statement about what makes all street-level bureaucrats tick. However, any explanation of behaviour also needs to consider motive 'because it is not really possible to observe and describe behaviour at all (apart from the very simplest actions) without grasping the motives that it expresses' (Midgley, 2001, p 93).

What seems to lie behind Lipsky's evaluation of front-line discretion is a view that policy is handed down through the organisation in a pristine condition until it gets to the front line, where 'street ministers' (Lipsky, 2010, p 12) mess it up. However, how can policy be handed down in a pristine state when one of the key arguments in *Street-level bureaucracy* is that policy is imprecise, contradictory and vague? Lipsky seems to get over this problem by equating policy with what hierarchical superiors say it is. In this sense, while Lipsky's account of the operation of discretion looks 'bottom-up' in recognising the limitations of 'top-down' managerial control and direction, his approach to the evaluation of front-line discretion is 'top-down' in that the measure of legitimate discretion is to be found in compliance with policy in terms of the instructions of one's organisational superior – one's manager.

This brings us onto the fundamental problem with the approach to front-line discretion and the notion of client-processing: it is a covert ethical assessment of front-line practice from a top-down perspective. Putting aside the psychological-looking analysis of work stress, what actually remains is an ethical evaluation that lumps together the diverse ways in which front-line discretion is used under the rubric of client-processing. Furthermore, this evaluation is based on the point of view that discretion and its use should be evaluated in terms of obedience to managers.

Managing – a fractured chain of command

The contrast that Lipsky draws in *Street-level bureaucracy* between the motivation of managers and the motivation of front-line workers is stark. While front-line staff pursue their own needs and interests, managers share a commitment to the implementation of organisational objectives

(Lipsky, 1980, p 216). They focus on the 'aggregate achievement of the work unit and orientations directed toward minimizing autonomy' (Lipsky, 2010 [1980], p 25). Their prime concern is with implementing the policy that they are directed to put into effect, and with doing this as effectively as possible (Lipsky, 2010, p 18). They sometimes also have to compromise in the face of front-line recalcitrance, and strike practical bargains, but still with the goal of achieving the policy in the circumstances.

Managers in *Street-level bureaucracy* are the hierarchical superiors of street-level bureaucrats, including 'someone in an immediate supervisory position vis-à-vis street-level bureaucrats' (Lipsky, 2010, p 242). They are supervisors, their supervisor's supervisor and so on in the organisational chain of command. Interestingly, Lipsky suggests – in a footnote – that there may be broken links in the chain of management command: 'The focus on the divergence of objectives between the organisation and lowest-level workers could with some modifications be applied to the relation between lowest-level supervisor and the roles to which this position is subordinate' (Lipsky, 2010, p 242). However, he does not pursue or develop this observation. I want to look at this issue more closely.

Local managers

The distinction between front-line managers and workers is likely to be blurred where services involve professional staff. Many front-line managers also occupy hybrid roles that cross the manager–professional divide (Causer and Exworthy, 1999). Professional front-line staff tend to be first-line managed by supervisors from their own profession (Friedson, 1994). In the personal social services in the UK, for instance, information on the professional background of front-line managers is thin on the ground, but research examining recruitment suggests that Friedson's observation continues to be the case. Henderson and Seden (2003, p 87) examined 'job descriptions' and 'person specifications' for front-line managers in social services and found that there was 'little evidence of employers prioritising management expertise rather than professionally defined skills, abilities and experience'.

In my research (Evans, 2010, 2011, 2013, 2014), I found that the blurring of local management and practitioner roles in professional social work teams was widespread. All the local managers were professional social workers who had moved into management. Overwhelmingly, these managers strongly characterised themselves as professionals first, who managed fellow professionals. They also identified with front-line workers' concerns about the (in their view, distorted) priorities of the organisation, focusing on finances rather than care. Furthermore, front-line managers managed not only front-line staff, but also their own front-line caseload – they were both managers and street-level bureaucrats. These practitioners and their social work managers also tended to identify with each other and with a professional social work culture, in contrast to senior managers, who were seen as a having different concerns, priorities and interests.

That front-line managers and front-line workers share commitments and distinguish themselves from senior mangers reflects a recurrent finding in organisational research in social services (Harris, 1998). This fracture in the management hierarchy poses the question: where are the 'managers' described in *Street-level bureaucracy*? Lower-level managers managing staff in professional services do not match the picture of mangers as a quite different group from the street-level bureaucrats. In fact, these managers look more like the professionals they manage than the senior managers to whom they report.

Senior management

We have to look further up the management hierarchy to find Lipsky's 'managers'. These are the senior managers, whose primary concerns are formulating organisational goals and implementing policy, and who identify with other managers and are entrusted with implementing policy. They look like the managers that Lipsky describes. Their raison d'être is to make policy work – striving to narrow the gap between street-level performance and 'desired policy results' (Lipsky, 2010, p 223).

Managers, as an occupational group, have advanced a professional project over the last few decades. Managers have created a body of expertise (knowledge claims) and a narrative of service (norms) that has been deployed to assert the idea of managers' right to manage (discretion) (Leicht and Fennel, 2001). Since the 1980s, the idea of professional managers has been embraced and promoted in the public sector by neoliberal-oriented governments (Pollitt, 1993).

Looked at from this perspective, the distinction between 'managers' and 'professionals' is a false contrast. Far from being the scourge of professional privilege, managers are its beneficiaries; management is an occupation group that has successfully promoted its professional project and, as part of the process, has sought to displace other (established) professional groups from their pre-eminence in organisations (Leicht and Fennel, 2001).

Seeing managers in this way raises questions about the rather anodyne way in which management is presented in *Street-level bureaucracy*, particularly the paucity of close examination of the discretion that is granted to managers and the ways in which managers use this discretion.

Lipsky tends to present discretion as a problem of front-line freedom with which managers have to cope in their work of implementing organisational goals and making policy work. Managers try (unsuccessfully) to control discretion. However, discretion permeates public welfare; it operates, according to Davis's (1969, p 4) classic definition, wherever a public official is free to make a decision or exercise choice. On this definition, any employee within a public body at any level of the organisation can exercise discretion. The conditions that contribute to wide-ranging front-line discretion – mismatched policy aspirations and resources, vague and conflicting policy, and so on – presumably also apply to managers and require them to make choices and exercise discretion. Managers' discretion is also embedded in their professional status as managers – 'the right to manage'.

Furthermore, managers' discretion is significant. Their decisions translate and change policy in its journey through the organisation and, in the process, create the environment of discretion faced by front-line staff. While street-level bureaucrats play a role in changing and implementing policy on the ground, the response of street-level bureaucrats to their situation – such as rationing contact time – may be a management strategy, as opposed to a worker response (Anon, 1981). Interestingly, in the new edition of *Street-level bureaucracy*, Lipsky (2010) acknowledges that the context within which street-level bureaucrats act is, to some extent, already structured by organisational responses and options.

The extent and impact of managerial discretion is important in understanding who the key actors are in making sense of policy and making policy work – and, in the process, changing it. However, why is the discretion of managers not more in the picture in *Street-level bureaucracy*? One reason for the blinkered nature of the analysis may be that management decision-making is not seen as discretion because, according to Lipsky, managers are committed to policy implementation; policy is safe in their hands and it is only at risk when it finally arrives at the front line. Managers can be trusted with policy while front-line staff cannot. However, is this view plausible? Given Lipsky's view that professionals are primarily concerned with advancing their own interests, why does Lipsky assume that management professionals are different?

One way to make sense of the apparent contradiction is to see senior managers' self-interest and the interests of the organisation as coincident. Senior managers are the authors of organisational goals. The apex of the organisation is where management self-interest harmonises with organisational interests. However, this confuses senior managers' interests with those of the organisation that employs them, and confuses organisational goals with policy.

It is not self-evident that the interests of senior managers dovetail with the interests of the organisation employing them. Over the past decade, for instance, senior managers have been accused of executing serial 'pay heists' against the organisations that employ them. They have prioritised higher and higher pay for themselves at the expense of shareholders' interests by taking advantage of 'the separation of ownership from control, and the potential for mischief it creates' (Colvin, 2001). Of course, this observation relates to the private sector but, given the promotion of a more business-like public sector, particularly by neo-liberal-minded governments, public sector managers are as likely to reflect the unsavoury characteristics of management – that greed is good, for instance – as they are characteristics of virtuous management.

Policy in the public sector is seldom made and implemented within the same organisation. Even in the traditional Westminster model of top-down policy implementation through levels of public sector organisations from national to local, different organisations are often involved, for example, national government to local authorities. In the contemporary setting of policy governance, policy implementation involves disparate organisations, such as agencies and trusts, as well as national and local government, and is also outsourced to private and third sector organisations (Rhodes, 2007). We cannot assume that organisational interests and goals coincide with the concerns and commitments of policymakers (Carson et al, 2014). A recent example in the health service in the UK illustrates this point. Over the past few years, there has been a series of enquiries into the service provided by Mid Staffordshire Hospital within the National Health Service in which senior executives were found to have prioritised the aspirations of the hospital board and senior managers to become a more autonomous and independent hospital trust within the health service by focusing on financial control and cutting costs, while, at the same time, the standards of the health care they were entrusted to deliver were plummeting. The final enquiry was critical of the practice of a range of the front-line professionals working in the hospital, but there was particular criticism of senior managers for distorting national policy goals in their (self-serving) pursuit of trust status for their hospital regardless of the human costs for patients, families and front-line staff (Francis, 2013).

Greener (2004) warns against imposing the false binary of managers as either simply heroes or villains. The point here is not to characterise managers (as Lipsky characterises other professionals) as villainous, but to move beyond the equally problematic assumption of heroic management embedded in the analysis of discretion in *Street-level bureaucracy*. Managers have extensive discretion, and to understand front-line discretion, we need at least to understand the impact of managerial discretion on front-line options and choices and to identify the extent to which the services received by citizens are influenced not just by 'street-level ministers', but also by 'organisational ministers'. We also need to grasp what motivates the choices of senior management in particular contexts – the range and mix of motives underpinning senior managers' approach to discretion.

Conclusion

In this chapter, I have sought to outline what initially drew me to *Street-level bureaucracy* in terms of the analysis of the central and continuing role of discretionary decision-making within public services. However, the focus of my argument has been on the fact that Lipksy's analysis of the extent, location and ways of understanding discretion in street-level bureaucracies pays insufficient attention to the role of professionalism in understanding the construction and deployment of discretion, and that the discretion of managers is under-examined.

I have argued that the idea of professionalism is helpful in understanding the extent of some street-level bureaucrats' discretion. In looking at the uses of discretion at the street level, Lipsky emphasises survival and self-protection in a difficult work environment. (The idea of professional altruism is given short shrift as a smokescreen for self-interest.) He argues that discretion is used at the street level for 'client-processing' – to manage work stress and to reconcile the myth of altruism with the desire to make work easier or more pleasurable. Looking at discretionary choices in terms of individual and collective strategies to manage work stress may contribute something to our understanding of the uses of discretion but it is far from a sufficient explanation of the motives underpinning the use of discretion.

In contrast to front-line workers, managers in *Street-level bureaucracy* are not the subject of close scrutiny. This is despite the fact that the conditions that give rise to extensive discretion at the street level also apply to their work. Managers have extensive discretion, and because of their position, they influence and change the policy they transmit to the street level. Their choices also influence the context of discretion within which front-line workers operate.

The basis for the assumption in *Street-level bureaucracy* that managers' motives are primarily concerned with putting policy into effect is unclear – particularly when we recognise managers as a professional occupation and consider Lipsky's characterisation of professionals as self-serving.

However, my argument is not that we should see managers as purely venal and front-line staff as altruistic. Rather, we need to move beyond sweeping and crude characterisations of motivation and discretion, and examine actors' own evaluations and accounts of the use of discretion in order to understand what is happening in different situations. Part of this process is the need to move away from the disproportionate focus on front-line discretion and to consider the extensive discretion of professional managers in order to understand how managers' discretion creates the context and constraints or expands the choices of front-line workers in implementing policy.

SEVENTEEN

The moment of the street-level bureaucrats in a public employment service

Christopher Osiander and Joss Steinke

Introduction

Over the last decade, Germany fundamentally changed its labour market policies, following the developments in many other European countries that focused on the task of 'activation', new management ideas and new forms of governance (Eichhorst and Konle-Seidl, 2008; Eichhorst et al, 2008; Weishaupt, 2010). From 2002, the former red–green government under Chancellor Gerhard Schröder had put the so-called 'Hartz reforms' into effect, which were much praised for their success (Fehr and Sunde, 2009; Koch et al, 2009). Nevertheless, the reforms were also the subject of controversial public debate and were often seen as a means to curb the supposedly expanding welfare state. One of the central aims was to cut down the costs of unemployment by reducing the maximum duration of unemployment insurance benefits and integrating the unemployment and social assistance schemes into one benefit for the long-term unemployed and other needy job seekers (Fleckenstein, 2008). The reforms also referred to Giddens's (1986) idea of a new balance of 'rights and obligations' between the state and citizen, enhancing mutual responsibilities and contractual relationships.

The Federal Employment Agency (FEA; *Bundesagentur für Arbeit*) found itself under immense political pressure to increase efficacy and efficiency because of exaggerated and partly faked statistical data concerning job placements. The third law of the Hartz legislation (Hartz III) aimed at restructuring the FEA to enable it to provide modern services on the labour market (including a 'one-stop-shop system'; see Konle-Seidl, 2009). The FEA ought to be a service provider instead of a bureaucratic organisation, treating citizens as 'clients' on equal terms by, on the one hand, promoting support and enabling its clients and, on the other hand, demanding cooperation and increased efforts from job seekers ('carrots and sticks' or '*Fördern und Fordern*'). This was also a challenging task for the FEA's caseworkers, who have been expected to act like counsellors instead of bureaucrats ever since. In general, caseworkers play an increasingly important role in practically implementing activation policies that require the individual treatment of clients (Borghi and Van Berkel, 2007).

Another major aspect of the reforms was the restructuring of unemployment benefits and legal responsibilities for counselling through the fourth Hartz law (Hartz IV[1]), officially known as Social Code II. Job seekers that have been employed for at least 12 months during the last two years are entitled to unemployment insurance payments (Unemployment Benefit I [UB II] or *Arbeitslosengeld I*) for a maximum duration of 12 months if they are younger than 50 years. Long-term unemployed and other needy people with a minimum of work capability can receive tax-financed means-tested benefits (Unemployment Benefit II [UB II] or *Arbeitslosengeld II*), a merger of the former unemployment and social assistance (*Arbeitslosenhilfe* and *Sozialhilfe*). This led to a complex system of legal responsibilities: local employment agencies (*Agenturen für Arbeit*) are responsible for the job seekers entitled to UB I according to Social Code III (*Sozialgesetzbuch Drittes Buch*); needy recipients (UB II) are counselled by job centres, which are set up as cooperative organisations between municipalities and job centres, or some municipalities that are fully responsible, according to Social Code II (*Sozialgesetzbuch Zweites Buch*).[2]

The political context was controversial: some wanted the demanding elements of the reforms to be even more pronounced; others criticised that the punitive elements of the new regime outweigh the supportive aspects. One of the central questions became whether more discretion at the local level would be favourable, as many instruments of active labour market policies (ALMP) became a discretionary decision of local agencies and caseworkers instead of explicit entitlements for clients. Although a multitude of empirical studies has been published in the field of German labour market research over recent years, both caseworkers' role in implementing and shaping labour market policies and their influence on labour market outcomes has been a blind spot for a long time. From 2006 on, some research has been conducted in order to try to shed some light on the street level of service provision.

In this chapter, we analyse, in particular, how caseworkers in the FEA – who are an important example of Lipsky's (1969, 2010) street-level bureaucrats – deal with the new challenges as a result of the reforms. As Brodkin (2007) noted, welfare state reforms must affect service provision at the street level if they are to create meaningful change.

We look at three important aspects of their work: first, caseworkers' attitudes towards regulations of ALMP and the effects of job counselling and its implications; second, the introduction of contractual elements between job seekers and job centres in the course of the reforms; and, third, the conflict between the challenge to respond to individual needs, on the one hand, and organisational standards and regulations, on the other.

The remainder of this chapter is organised as follows. In the next part, we discuss similarities between the street-level bureaucracy approach and co-production theory. The central aim of our contribution is to show that different dimensions of job counselling matter, that is, they influence labour market outcomes, and that granting discretion is no panacea for labour market counselling. Then, we present data from different empirical studies in the context of the German labour market, the results of which we will discuss in detail. These analyses provide some insights into the significance of caseworkers in Germany's public employment service (PES).

Theoretical considerations

On the street level of service delivery, there might be a difference between discretion granted – for example, by organisations or policymakers – and discretion used, that is, actual behaviour (Hupe, 2013). In our case, the question is to what extent caseworkers in employment agencies or job centres use the degrees of freedom that institutional rules grant them. Since Lipsky's (1969, 2010) work, it has become clear that discretion is a central characteristic of certain jobs in virtually all public administrations, which makes them distinct from many other (manual) jobs. Caseworkers in employment agencies or job centres are a good example of these front-line workers who directly interact with job seekers in the course of their daily work. We use Lipsky's approach and add theoretical insights from the co-production literature to show that the major services of the PES – counselling and job search assistance – are a result of conjoint work between both the caseworker and client.

Caseworkers in the public employment service as street-level bureaucrats

Counselling and job search assistance for the unemployed are the central tasks of the PES. The success and failure of matching processes on the labour market are influenced by two important factors: the actors themselves and the institutional setting, that is, the staff that work at employment agencies or job centres and the structures at the macro- or meso-level, for example, the organisational setting and the macroeconomic environment. Despite their substantial contribution to these services, caseworkers have been largely neglected in German labour market research for a long time. Studies from different countries show that different dimensions of the relation between caseworkers and job seekers influence labour market outcomes, that is, employment prospects or the probability of receiving unemployment benefits (Frölich et al, 2007; Lechner and Smith, 2007; Behncke et al, 2010a, 2010b; Hofmann et al, 2010, 2012; Hainmüller et al, 2011; Lagerström, 2011; Pedersen et al, 2012; Boockmann et al, 2013).

For Switzerland, Behncke et al (2010b) show, for example, that caseworkers who do not emphasise a cooperative relationship devoid of conflicts with their clients increase the average employment probabilities of the unemployed compared to their more lenient colleagues. The same authors report statistically significant positive employment effects if the caseworker and job seeker belong to the same social group, the latter defined by gender, age, education and nationality (Behncke et al, 2010a). For Sweden, Lagerström (2011) estimates the effects of caseworkers on future employment rates, earnings and wages. The author finds that the probability of being employed within a year after registration clearly depends on the caseworker. For Germany, Hainmüller et al (2011) find in a field experiment that better (ie lower) caseworker-to-client ratios in employment agencies result in a decrease of job seekers' unemployment duration and, therefore, the rate of local unemployment.

From a theoretical point of view, caseworkers' discretion results from a huge number of potential sources, which have been widely discussed in the literature. Moreover, connections and theoretical affinities between street-level bureaucracy and other theoretical approaches have been examined (eg Ostrom, 1996; Winter, 2003; Hupe and Hill, 2007). It has been pointed out that street-level bureaucrats often deal with different political or administrative expectations (May and Winter, 2009), different organisational structures, vague or, at worst, conflicting goals (Lipsky, 2010), or rules and regulations that require repeated interpretation. The work context, in the narrow sense, also matters: huge caseloads (Blackmore, 2001), demand that exceeds supply (Lipsky, 2010; Hudson, 1993), heterogeneous clients (May and Winter, 2009), information asymmetries (Winter, 2003), financial restraints, and so on.

Job seekers are sometimes – like other clients of social services – irrational or poorly informed, which makes the street-level bureaucrats' work too complex for complete standardisation. The result is not only a powerful position of the front-line worker, but also a dilemma between the need to standardise, on the one hand, and the necessity for differentiated responses to individual problems, on the other (Lipsky, 2010).[3] In street-level bureaucracies, clients are categorised based on specific 'observable' characteristics like sex, age, schooling, working experience, health status and so on, and are treated in terms of these different categories (Prottas, 1978; see also Lipsky, 2010). This inevitably raises the issue of procedural justice: every client should be treated with respect to his individual situation, but categorisations are established to reduce complexity and to treat equal things equally. The question arises as to how caseworkers in practice find practical solutions for such situations.

Job counselling as 'co-production' and 'interactive service'

The co-production approach is a theoretically fruitful way to clarify some central aspects arising in street-level bureaucracies. Co-production implies that the results of counselling are always determined by both the caseworkers and clients. The concept was introduced into the scientific discussion in the early 1980s in the course of studying urban services (Sharp, 1980; Whitaker, 1980; Parks et al, 1981; Rich, 1981; Brudney and England, 1983; Levine, 1984; Percy, 1984; for Germany, see also Dunkel, 2011) and gained increasing attention over the following decades. Ostrom (1996) clearly shows that street-level bureaucracy and co-production theory are compatible approaches.

As is often the case in the social sciences, there is no single definition of the term. When we speak of 'co-production' here, we mean that clients are involved in 'producing' the outcomes of public services and therefore heavily influence the quantity and quality of the results. To quote Whitaker (1980, p 240):

> in 'delivering' services the agent helps the person being served to make the desired sorts of changes.... Only the individual served can accomplish the change. He or she is a vital 'coproducer' of any personal transformation that occurs.... Rather than an agent presenting a 'finished product' to the citizen, agent and citizen together produce the desired transformation.

This 'conjoint responsibility' (Sharp, 1980) contributes to higher quality and helps to meet the individual needs of the clients best. Coproducers participate in creating an output that they consume at least partially themselves and from which they receive personal utility or benefit (Alford, 2002). Therefore, it requires clients who are willing to donate time and effort in creating this utility (Alford, 2002). Vice versa, the execution of many services is not possible without the voluntary involvement of clients. They have to be willing to work by mutual agreements, cooperation and the reciprocal adjustment of problems (Whitaker, 1980). It also means that some direct or opportunity costs are shifted to the co-producing individual (Percy, 1984). However, this does not automatically imply a partnership of equals: caseworkers have greater resources from the organisation they work for, have more or special knowledge about the field, and/or have the legal authority to impose sanctions on clients (Lipsky, 2010; Whitaker, 1980).

Besides being co-produced, counselling and job placement are also 'interactive services'. Böhle (2011) stresses some aspects that distinguish interactive services from other types of work. Caseworkers' jobs consist mainly of social interaction with clients, though it requires the balancing of interests between different actors. Besides that, the work affects the emotions and feelings of the caseworkers and clients involved in the process, preventing complete standardisation. Last, but not least, clients are not only participants in delivering the services, but also judges and evaluators.

It has become clear that discretion is both a ubiquitous phenomenon and an ambiguous concept. Discretion per se might not lead to better results because clients' cooperation is required for successful job counselling. Therefore, we assume that the recent attempts to (formally) widen the discretionary power of street-level bureaucrats in Germany's FEA do not automatically lead to more discretion actually used. In the following section, we give an overview of the data we use to address this question.

Data and methods

We combine empirical data from three different studies. First of all, we use data from a research project that investigated professional service delivery and activation policies in Germany's labour market with a qualitative approach (for details, see Schütz et al, 2011b). Data collection was performed in 16 local employment agencies and job centres, which were chosen on the basis of different characteristics (region, labour market state, urban versus rural setting, organisational characteristics). In each job centre, the research team conducted non-participatory observations of intake and follow-up meetings between caseworkers and approximately eight unemployed job seekers. The fieldwork began in October 2008 and ended in December 2009. Meetings between caseworkers and clients were audio-recorded and transcribed, and a content analysis was conducted. Additional unobtrusive measures like document analyses and information from administrative data of the FEA were added to complete the picture.

Second, we use the results of case studies in 14 local employment agencies and job centres in Germany (Steinke et al, 2012). The case studies were conducted during a research project at the Institute for Employment Research (IAB) about the recent reforms of ALMP in Germany in 2009. The central task was to evaluate the consequences of giving more discretionary power to caseworkers instead of using legally binding rules. Data collection was performed by combining different methods of explorative research. The study is based on the principle of 'scientific source texts' (Apel et al, 1995; Apel, 2009). This approach within the context of ethnographic field research produces a single text for each unit of analysis (ie local employment agency or job centre), which includes all relevant results regardless of which method of data collection (eg expert interview, document analysis) is focused on. This text is used as a de facto primary source for all further analyses and interpretations. Following the grounded theory approach (Glaser and Strauss, 1967), data collection is finished when researchers themselves conclude that sufficient information has been collected. Expert interviews were conducted with caseworkers, supervisors, members of the board and special counsellors in the regional directorates (*Regionaldirektionen*) of the FEA. Local employment agencies and job centres for the interviews were also chosen on the basis of different characteristics like regional setting and labour market state. The field phase was from May 2010 until December 2010.

Third, we use data from a standardised mixed-method survey (combining online and paper-and-pencil data collection) among caseworkers from 26 German employment agencies and job centres (for details, see Boockmann et al, 2013). These were also chosen on the basis of different characteristics; participation in the survey was voluntary. The field phase of the project was between March and June 2009. The questionnaire included information about the socio-demographic characteristics of the participants, but also their preferences and strategies and some context variables regarding the institutional and organisational context. We created a unique data set combining survey data and rich administrative data about the job seekers. The gross sample consisted of 1,563 caseworkers, from which 537 (34%) responded. So far, this survey is – to the best of our knowledge – the only one for

Germany that provides insights into the 'inner workings' of the PES using quantitative survey and data analysis methods.[4]

Empirical results

In this section, we present selected results from the empirical studies mentioned earlier. We concentrate on three, in our view, central aspects of discretion: first, we focus on caseworkers' attitudes towards ALMP and the effects of job counselling on individual labour market outcomes; second, we show results for the role of integration agreements as legally binding contracts between the caseworker and client; and, third, we look at the dilemma between standardisation and clients' individual needs.

Attitudes towards active labour market policies, job counselling and labour market outcomes

Despite having been reduced over recent years, measures of ALMP are still important in quantitative terms in Germany and have a long tradition. Figure 17.1 illustrates this point.

The lion's share accounts for measures of activation and integration, for example, compensations for travelling costs or placement vouchers,

Figure 17.1: Monthly entries in measures of active labour market policies, differentiated according to types of measures

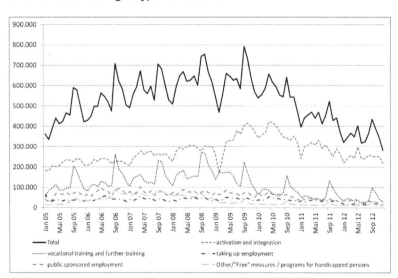

Source: Own calculations (minor subtypes grouped together), based on the Data Warehouse of the FEA.

whereas public-sponsored vocational and further trainings in German ALMP have been substantially reduced since 2009. These measures of ALMP are also relevant because, in most cases, job seekers are not legally entitled to participate in a given programme, but it is a discretionary decision that caseworkers have to make when interacting with clients.

Quite surprisingly, results from the quantitative study show that caseworkers highly appreciate internal recommendations of the FEA clarifying the allocation rules for the programmes of ALMP: 44% (Social Code III) and 48% (Social Code II) of the employees state that internal recommendations have 'high' or 'very high relevance' for their decisions as to whom to offer a programme. A possible explanation for this phenomenon is that many caseworkers may prefer legal certainty by official instructions because the interpretation of existing laws is often associated with uncertainty and requires specific knowledge. This also indicates that (increasing) discretion requires high-skilled caseworkers. First, there is a high density of regulations, combined with substantive discretion, especially under Social Code II. Moreover, the system of means-tested benefits was subject to a large number of legal changes even after its introduction in 2005. Both aspects highlight that skilled and experienced staff are necessary to provide high-quality services for the clientele. Therefore, giving more discretion to caseworkers might lead to uncertainty, especially among less-experienced staff. Similar observations are made by Jewell (2007), who finds that German caseworkers providing social assistance are constrained by the high demands of their work, for example, stemming from high regulatory complexity, frequently changing regulations and complex and voluminous areas like disability care.

Moreover, 58% (Social Code III) and 55% (Social Code II) state that the quantitative targets of the job office (eg the number of participants per period and programme) are important or very important. It is interesting to note that caseworkers' actions in this context seem to be structured by factors beyond their own control. Most programmes are centrally purchased and so their number is fixed at least in the short run. Consequently, and not surprisingly, over 70% of the caseworkers also say that the availability of measures is an 'important' or 'very important' aspect of their work.

Boockmann et al (2014) show with the same data that some of the caseworkers' individual attitudes and strategies influence the re-employment chances of 'their' clients. Table 17.1 provides an overview of the different effects on labour market outcomes.

For example, caseworkers who agree that clients are responsible for their own unemployment outperform those who do not: their job seekers have better chances to get back into employment in the short run. Job seekers who state that they often see their clients also achieve better results: their job seekers have better chances to leave unemployment than those of caseworkers who do not agree that they see their clients often. Caseworkers who stress the importance of regulations for their daily work perform better regarding exits into employment. They were also asked to evaluate if rules and regulations are an important prerequisite of their work or if they need a lot of discretion for their success. Interestingly, there is no difference in the labour market outcomes of job seekers regardless of whether a caseworker prefers strict rules or discretion. On the whole, this indicates that some – but not all – strategies and attitudes of caseworkers influence the labour market prospects of their clients.

Table 17.1: Effects of caseworkers' characteristics and attitudes on labour market outcomes

Caseworker's characteristics	Effect on:	
	probability of being re-employed	probability of leaving unemployment
High contact density	~	+ (in the short run)
Importance of regulations for own actions	+ (in the short run)	~
Clients responsible for own unemployment	~	+ (in the short run)
Focus on quick reintegration (versus sustained integration)	~	~
Sometimes using sanctions	~	~
Meet clients' wishes	~	~
Work perceived as self-determined	~	~

Notes: ~ = no significant effect on outcome; + = significantly positive effect on outcome; – = significantly negative effect on outcome.

Source: Own illustration, based on results published in Boockmann et al (2014).

Integration agreements

Integration agreements (*Eingliederungsvereinbarungen*) are formal contracts under public law that clarify the rights and obligations of both the client and employment agency or job centre. They take into account the specific strengths and weaknesses of every job seeker and are tailor-made (BA, 2011). Moreover, they are the basis for sanctions in cases of misdemeanour. However, empirical findings from different studies show that integration agreements are at least partially problematic because – as Baethge-Kinsky et al (2007) state – reciprocity is sometimes fictional in these contractual relationships. The authors find that the interaction between job centres under Social Code II and the client is asymmetrical and hierarchical in nature for two reasons. First, job seekers have no real practical alternative but signing the agreement because the job centre is otherwise authorised to specify rights and obligations even without the client's consent. The only possibility for the job seeker to avoid any sanction for certain is not to register at the job centre at all.[5] Second, the agreement's function as a basis for financial sanctions might thwart its intention because it counteracts the co-productive delivery of services (Schütz et al, 2011a). In fact, sanctions may indicate that cooperative behaviour is not desired because their very existence implies that clients are assumed to be not trustworthy, selfish and opportunistic (see also Alford, 2002).

In line with Baethge-Kinsky et al (2007), Schütz et al (2011a) also find in a more recent study that while the clients' obligations are often defined precisely, the duties of employment agencies or job centres, in contrast, are formulated rather vaguely or even 'state the obvious', for example, the fact that they will send vacancies (if there are any) and provide job counselling. The authors argue that especially among needy recipients – many of them having health or mental problems – the agreement is often not the result of negotiations on equal terms, but formulated by the caseworkers on the basis of legal regulations and expert knowledge. With regard to the client's obligations, most agreements specify precisely how many applications a job seeker has to write in a given time to fulfil the standards.

It is also highly questionable that the legally binding character of the agreements is downplayed or trivialised by caseworkers, who sometimes call the agreements misleadingly 'minutes' or 'summaries'. Moreover, integration agreements often include standardised expressions. This also counteracts specific formulations for clients' individual needs and problems. From the caseworkers' point of view, it seems to be rational behaviour because expressions that are both individually designed and not countervailable are much too time-consuming and demanding to create. This might indicate that the intended function of integration agreements is partially counteracted by caseworkers' discretionary power and organisational routines.

Considering this, it would be interesting to know how caseworkers themselves evaluate integration agreements. Figure 17.2 presents empirical results from the standardised survey among caseworkers concerning the item 'Generally, integration agreements are a useful tool of trade'. The ratings range from 'I totally agree' (1) to 'I totally disagree' (5).

Figure 17.2: 'Generally, integration agreements are a useful tool of trade'

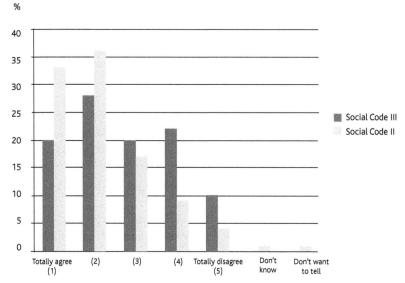

Source: Own calculations; based on a survey among caseworkers (Osiander and Steinke, 2011).

As can be seen, a majority of the caseworkers tends to be in favour of integration agreements in general. Almost 70% of the caseworkers under Social Code II support the use of the agreements (categories '1' and '2' added) compared to 58% of the caseworkers under Social Code III. Here, 32% of the caseworkers are sceptical about the utility of integration agreements (categories '4' and '5') compared to only 13% of the caseworkers under Social Code II.

The results also indicate that the reciprocity of rights and obligations does not seem to be fully implemented in practice. Rather, the clients' obligations in integration agreements are emphasised to a greater extent than their rights. Figure 17.3 shows the empirical results from the survey data.

In total, about 22% of the caseworkers say that integration agreements should specify rights as well as obligations in a fairly balanced way, though the caseworkers under Social Code II were twice as likely (28% versus 13%) as their colleagues under Social Code III to say that. This is also true for the specification of rights: 17% under Social Code II figure that the agreements mainly specify clients' rights; 8% under Social

Figure 17.3: 'What do integration agreements first and foremost specify?'

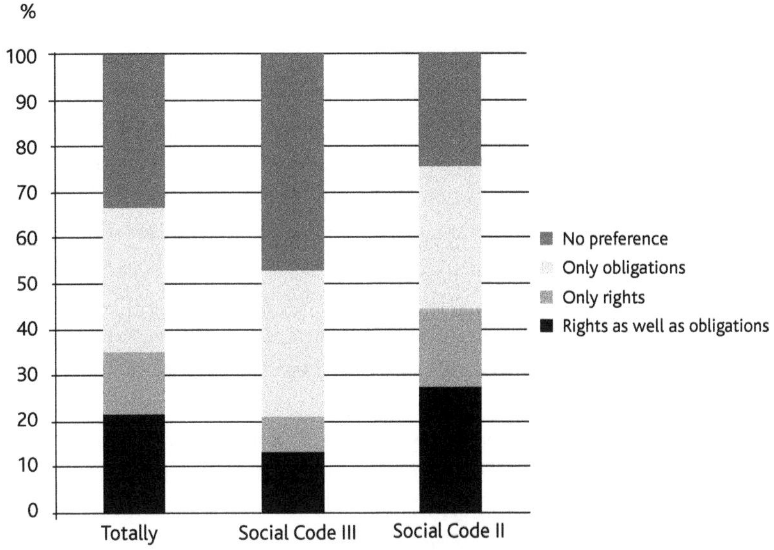

Source: Own calculations, based on a survey among caseworkers (Osiander and Steinke 2011).

Code III. About 30% in both cases find that integration agreements just specify clients' obligations. It is quite remarkable that under Social Code III, almost 50% of the caseworkers have no preference about integration agreements and see neither obligations nor rights as the essential part of the contracts.

To sum up the results for integration agreements, one can say that rights and obligations in integration agreements are not yet fairly balanced (Osiander and Steinke, 2011; Schütz et al 2011a). In principle, caseworkers accept integration agreements as a useful tool of trade for their day-to-day practice, but the emphasis is often on clients' obligations rather than on their rights. In addition, it seems problematic that the function of the contracts as a basis for potential financial sanctions is sometimes downplayed.

Discretion versus standardisation

In this section, we look at the dilemma between standardisation and discretion, which is fundamental in the PES. Rules and regulations frame the amount of discretion, but there is a dilemma between two dimensions of administrative action: rules are designed for making decisions justifiable and treating equal things equally. To the degree of discretion, equal cases may be treated differently, affecting procedural justice. So, how do caseworkers cope with increased discretion in Germany's PES?

In their qualitative study, Steinke et al (2012) find that supervisors in local employment agencies and job centres do not consider increased discretion as a high-priority problem. In general, equal treatment of clients is stressed as an important goal, but it is remarkable to note that more discretion on a legal basis does not automatically lead to an exercise of this latitude. Often, caseworkers themselves are interested in clear regulations. For example, recent reforms enabled caseworkers to use an 'integration budget' at their own discretion. The implementation of this integration budget varied substantially between local offices. The implementation process resulted in two different alternatives:

1. a fixed sum for the whole year that a caseworker was allowed to spend on *all* job seekers that he or she was responsible for, on his or her own responsibility; or
2. a fixed sum *per job seeker per year* that a caseworker was allowed to spend until it was gone

Interestingly, this did not lead to creative new ways to use the budget, but was counteracted by internal instructions that re-established the status quo ante, a process that was initiated upon the caseworkers' insistence (Steinke et al, 2012). This also clearly indicates that formal discretion and actually used discretion do not always coincide. More room for manoeuvre requires expert knowledge about existing regulations, which threatens to overwhelm caseworkers in their daily work. This is especially true for 'free' budgets, which can be used to create new innovative measures that have not yet been covered by other programmes.

Our standardised survey shows that in 73% of the employment agencies and job centres, there are specific instructions for caseworkers that clarify how to correctly interpret sometimes vague legal formulations.[6] Moreover, the orders specify which budget can be used per client, so that at least equal treatment in monetary terms is ensured. The budget per client is determined by expenditures in recent years or the categorisation of clients, or both, so that persons in each category get roughly the same budget. The supervisors consider this to be a proper (or, at least, formal) application of discretionary power. From the caseworkers' point of view, the instructions that guide them in the course of their work are effective. As part of the standardised survey, they were asked how specific instructions influence their discretionary power. Figure 17.4 shows the results.

Figure 17.4: 'How do specific instructions influence your discretionary power?'

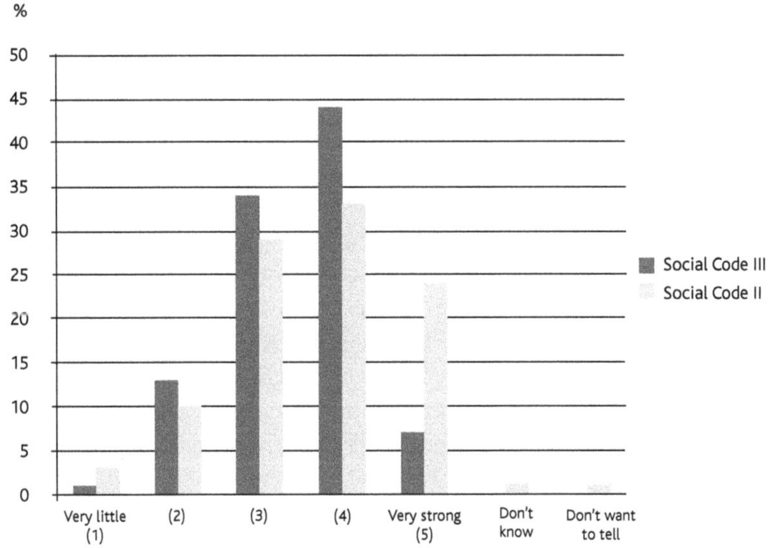

Source: Own calculations, based on a survey among caseworkers (Osiander and Steinke, 2011).

It becomes clear that, especially in the job centres under Social Code II, the specific instructions are important guidelines from the caseworkers' point of view: 57% of the caseworkers say that instructions influence discretion in a 'very strong' or 'strong' way; 13% believe that these instructions have no influence on their work; and, in employment agencies, 51% confirm the '(very) strong' influence of specific instructions. Needy recipients of UB II often do not take up regular employment due to barriers like poor health, substance abuse problems, low qualifications, long-term unemployment and so on. These clients need special treatment, so standardised instructions may not be interpreted as the appropriate way to deal with these cases. However, the caseworkers clearly identify the problem that regional and individual differences prevent 'perfect' equal treatment. Caseworkers stress that individual treatment and consideration of personal needs is a form of imbalance that has to be justified on a case-by-case basis. Some caseworkers interpret the dilemma between discretion and equality as a creative aspect of their work and a trend towards more discretion as a refreshing new element. However, they also identify problems. For them, it is particularly difficult to help clients with measures for personal matters, which include things like the refunding of hairdressing. In such cases, it is difficult, if not impossible, to evaluate in advance if the financial support is useful and appropriate (Steinke et al, 2012).

Conclusion

The aim of this article was to provide some insights into caseworkers' discretionary power in Germany's PES. Theoretically, we refer to Lipsky's (2010) street-level bureaucracy approach and co-production theory to show that success of counselling and job search assistance are heavily influenced by caseworkers and job seekers. We proposed that different dimensions of job counselling matter, that is, they influence the labour market outcomes of job seekers, and that granting more discretion to caseworkers is no cure-all solution.

Empirical results indicate that caseworkers' tasks in German employment offices and job centres are highly structured when it comes to measures of ALMP. Internal instructions, quantitative targets and the availability of programmes play an important role for them. Moreover, some caseworkers' attitudes and strategies shape the labour market outcomes of 'their' job seekers.

A problematic aspect arises when we consider the contractual elements of counselling. Originally intended as contracts on equal terms between the caseworker and job seeker, integration agreements are often hierarchical and asymmetrical in nature. Caseworkers themselves see the agreements as a useful tool of trade for their daily work, but their legally binding character is sometimes downplayed and trivialised. Moreover, the job seekers' duties are often specified precisely, whereas the obligations of the employment agency or job centre remain vague and/or simply state the obvious.

The third important aspect is the dilemma between standardisation and individual treatment. More discretion for caseworkers does not automatically mean that it is actually used. On the contrary, some elements of the recent reforms were counteracted by internal instructions that re-established the status quo ante. More room for manoeuvre sometimes seems to overwhelm caseworkers in their daily work. This also highlights the aspect that a huge amount of discretion has to go hand in hand with attempts to qualify the staff and strengthen street-level skills.

From a methodological point of view, the combination of qualitative and quantitative approaches to labour market and social policy research has improved our understanding of implementation challenges and deficits. Discretion itself, as Brodkin (2007, p 12) vividly describes it, is still 'both the hallmark and the horror of social welfare provision'.

Notes

[1.] The term 'Hartz IV' has even become part of everyday language, both as an abbreviated form of the reform package that gained most media and public attention and – wrongly – as a synonym for the means-tested benefits for needy recipients ('Unemployment Benefit II').

[2.] This was the result of a political compromise that followed a long debate about the appropriate government level for providing labour market policies within the federal system. In 2007, Germany's Federal Constitutional Court declared this combination of federal and municipal responsibilities unconstitutional. In 2010, the German Parliament amended the constitution to enable the continuation of the cooperation between the federal state and municipalities concerning labour market policies.

[3.] In the German literature, Oevermann (2000) describes similar situations. The author argues that caseworkers ought to respect procedural justice and strictly apply general rules and norms on a case-by-case basis. On the other hand, many individuals experience unemployment as a personal crisis that requires individual treatment and counselling to serve personal needs in an appropriate manner. Therefore, standardisation and individual treatment are equally important but conflicting goals.

[4.] The role model for this research project was the study by Frölich et al (2007), who conducted a similar survey among Swiss caseworkers. The research design and data collection had to be adjusted to the characteristics of Germany's PES.

[5.] From a more theoretical point of view, this is what Hirschman (1970) calls the 'exit' strategy. For job seekers, turning away from the PES is obviously a most difficult and risky choice because unemployment benefit receipt is determined by former formal registration.

[6.] This is the case for 71% of the employment agencies under Social Code III and 75% of the job centres under Social Code II.

Part Seven
Conclusion

EIGHTEEN

Conclusion: the present and future study of street-level bureaucracy

Peter Hupe, Michael Hill and Aurélien Buffat

Introduction

The object of this volume has been to explore the nature of the accumulated knowledge of street-level bureaucracy. In this concluding chapter, we review the contents of the book and make a case for further research. Some authors speak of 'street-level bureaucracy *theory*' (Maynard-Moody and Portillo, 2010). Indeed, since the publication of Michael Lipsky's (1980) book, the literature on street-level bureaucracy has developed in such a way that it offers a basis for the formulation of propositions that may be used to further understand and explain real-world phenomena, in a comparative perspective. Whether these propositions are called hypotheses depends upon one's stance on social science epistemology. The ever-present split between interpretivist and positivist orientations implies that the picture is mixed – as this volume shows. Knowledge and insights have been gained, in varying directions. 'Theory' (without an indefinite article) is used as an umbrella term for various sorts of contributions to street-level bureaucracy as a scholarly theme, where it would be inappropriate to speak of *a* theory.

With a variety in conceptualisations, research designs and epistemological stances, the state of knowledge on street-level bureaucracy can be characterised as one of *multiple diversity*. Against this background, we have tried to bring researchers together with respect to their shared interest in studying the subject matter central in this scholarly field. Some of the preceding chapters report on empirical analyses, while other are centred on concepts. The latter may assist us with the explanation or at least description of phenomena but do not necessarily lend themselves readily to hypothesis formation. In our view, this fact reflects the state of knowledge. The analyses of the phenomena in question are also influenced by normative concerns, summed up loosely as questions about 'who should be in charge' of policy outputs.

Therefore, in the next section, we go back to the book chapters and 'interrogate' them with respect to the aspects mentioned at the end of our introductory chapter, that is: the central question asked; theory and method; and the programmatic elements.

What do we learn: key issues and findings

Delivering services and benefits: street-level bureaucracy and the welfare state

After the introductory chapters, two parts of the book reflect a distinction between sorts of street-level bureaucracies as involved, respectively, in delivering services and benefits and in law enforcement. Part Two is about the first category, as typically connected with the welfare state. It starts with Chapter Three on the discretionary element in British social assistance. Carol Walker distinguishes between administrative discretion and the 'creative' discretion practised by first-line staff. Her historical description shows the importance of shifts in the locus from which discretion is granted within a largely centrally controlled delivery system. While, by definition, discretion remains *used* in the social interaction taking place at the street level, the limits of this discretionary usage has become much more firmly set by the government.

In Chapter Four, Stephen Harrison analyses the process of bureaucratisation and 'commodification' in British health services. The introduction of evidence-based medicine and the transformation of the National Health Service (NHS) into a quasi-market indicate policy changes with a direct impact on primary and secondary care. Since the claim of medical indeterminacy has come under challenge from within the profession, medical interventions appear to be possible objects of bureaucratisation.

In a Swiss context, Aurélien Buffat, in Chapter Five, looks at how taxing officers in a public employment fund exercise discretion. He finds that discretion may vary according to the task. While assessing clients' eligibility is a highly prescribed task, it enables less leeway – to the same functionary – than the task of sanctioning clients. These findings lead to a plea that discretion should be addressed as a task-dependent phenomenon. To explain variation in first-line discretion, the 'material economy of cases' matters, as well as the policy design, regulatory framework and control mechanisms at hand.

The chapters by Carol Walker and Aurélien Buffat both relate to what is, in broad terms, income maintenance. They offer an interesting contrast. Where Walker's is a study of the ways in which UK governments have sought to confine street-level discretion, Buffat is looking at actual practice in a system in which variable discretion is a fundamental aspect of the street-level task. Buffat is looking at what happens; Walker is showing how discretion in day-to-day practice has been confined and controlled.

In the case of Walker's contribution, success in confining discretion is implicit in the formulation of rules that make many forms of it impossible, notably, the elimination of powers to make additions to grants. However, at the margin, questions may still be asked about what happens in practice. There has been much controversy (at least in the newspapers) about social assistance administration centres regarding two phenomena that are forms of rule breaking: errors made by officials and claimant success in 'gaming' the system. Lying behind some of the issues, there is also a shift of the kind described by Bovens and Zouridis (2002): discretion has been moved from the street level to either the 'screen level' (where middle-rank officials are responsible for procedural rules) or, more particularly in this case, to the system level.

Stephen Harrison's chapter has a different concern, namely, medical discretion. His chapter, like Carol Walker's, draws upon a rich literature. What is particularly interesting about what he has to say is that he offers a challenge to the conventional view that medical discretion is at the very high end in terms of Dworkin's notion of 'an area left open' (see Chapter One). Moreover, where it has perhaps become conventional to see a conflict between managerial concerns and professional concerns, he traces an interesting convergence. Variation in practice from case to case is just as much a professional concern as a managerial one, and modern medicine offers a wide variety of ways in which efforts are being made to bring this variation under control.

Agents of the state: street-level bureaucracy and law enforcement

The three chapters of Part Three of the book, called 'Agents of the state', all focus on the behaviour of public officials with regulatory tasks. In Chapter Six, these officials are working in two federal police units and two labour inspection teams. In Chapter Seven, the work of inspectors of occupational health and safety, environmental safety, and fire precaution is examined, while Chapter Eight looks at inspectors concerned with agro-environmental regulations.

In Chapter Eight, Søren C. Winter and Peter J. May report on an empirical study rooted in a systematic research exercise designed to elicit evidence on the impact of the work of street-level bureaucrats on the farmers whose activities they regulate. Kim Loyens (Chapter Six) and Vibeke Lehmann Nielsen (Chapter Seven) focus on issues about the determinants of street-level bureaucrat behaviour. Kim Loyens uses ethnographic research methods to explore this, looking at the behaviour of two different groups of officials – police officers and labour inspectors – both dealing with illegal employment. In several chapters in this book, the point of departure is that there may be various types of ways in which street-level bureaucrats respond to their dilemmas. Hence, the authors treat the behaviour of street-level bureaucrats as more than simply determined by the task they have to do. Loyens's approach to this is to aim to delineate various coping styles.

Vibeke Lehmann Nielsen's contribution is an analysis of the ways in which street-level behaviour may be analysed, drawing on the empirical work of authors like Søren Winter and Peter May. Winter and May's work is specifically concerned with how street-level bureaucracy is received, Kim Loyens' is concerned with aspects of how it is shaped and Vibeke Lehmann Nielsen's is concerned with ways of looking at both together. All three chapters look at discretionary behaviour in law enforcement. While Kim Loyens develops a classification of coping styles, Vibeke Lehmann Nielsen distinguishes activities in terms of the level of the individual inspector, the level of interaction with the regulatee and the agency level. With this specification, she stresses three dimensions of variety. Jobs of street-level bureaucrats may differ in terms of: the core function of the street-level job; the political, organisational and managerial institutional setting involved; and the characteristics of the group of clients concerned (including the features of the interaction between the client and street-level bureaucrat). In Chapter Eight, Søren Winter and Peter May focus on this latter aspect. Client perceptions, in particular, trust in inspectors, assessment of their competence and views on the compliance of others, contribute to the calculation of the odds of being found to be non-compliant. This leads Winter and May to speak of 'regulatory deterrence'.

We have drawn a distinction between street-level tasks concerned with the delivery of benefits and services in Part Two and those dealing with law enforcement in Part Three. This being so, it is clear that the two key themes in the latter – about how activities are received and about how street-level bureaucrats cope with complexity – are applicable to the former as well.

Embedded in society: street-level bureaucrats as public actors

Central to Part Four of the book are the ways in which street-level bureaucrats reflect the context of society that they want to serve. As public actors, street-level bureaucrats may have a 'belief in a just world'. In the same conditions, public officials with a strong belief about people getting what they deserve will treat citizens differently than their peers without such a conviction. The personal values of street-level bureaucrats will influence their interaction with clients – that is the message that Vicky M. Wilkins and Jeffrey B. Wenger convey in Chapter Nine.

In Chapter Ten, Michael Musheno and Steven Maynard-Moody explore the use of discretion as influenced by a pervasive social context. Challenging the implementation–control–discretion narrative of the 'state-agent', their message is to avoid the word 'discretion' as such. With their focus on 'playing the rules', they, instead, introduce a novel vocabulary. Focusing on the centrality of judgements, they speak about 'agency', 'interactional hitches' and the 'choreography' of localised storytelling.

From a British context, Kathryn Ellis reports in Chapter Eleven on policy changes, particularly personalisation, in adult social work and their impact on the practice of that work. Highlighting the interplay of formal and informal frameworks of practices, Ellis characterises her case as being typical of a 'negotiated order' of these two dimensions at the street level.

All three contributions in Part Four explore social embeddedness through discussion, not so much reporting current empirical work as exploring ideas emergent from earlier research. They may be seen as developing themes important for future work. This is particularly the case with Vicky Wilkins and Jeffrey Wenger's chapter. Their starting point is an important theme in previous research on street-level bureaucracy, particularly in the US, where the social characteristics of officials (specifically their gender and/or ethnicity) have been seen as having an impact upon their decisions. They take this a stage further to discuss the extent to which psychological characteristics, especially pre-existing attitudes, may affect behaviour. This theme is echoed to some extent in Kathryn Ellis's chapter, where social workers are characterised in terms of their alternative models of their roles.

Behind these specific ways of characterising street-levels bureaucrats lie the wider concerns of exploring their roles in society, developed for some years in the work of Michael Musheno and Steven Maynard-Moody in terms of the 'client narrative' versus 'state-agent narrative'.

They move away from the rather specific focus on discretionary action that has been emphasised in much of this book, towards a wider concern with culture and agency. In methodological terms, that takes work on street-level bureaucracy very much in an ethnographic direction (for an exploration of the use of this approach, see Dubois, 2009). This perspective is shared by Kathryn Ellis's concerns to relate social work orientations to new demands. It stands in contrast to Vicky Wilkins and Jeffrey Wenger's interest in developing a way to operationalise a new approach to explaining a behavioural orientation in empirical terms.

The management of street-level bureaucrats

Issues about how street-level bureaucracies are managed and controlled are probably as old as the term coined by Lipsky. Therefore, in Part Five, attention is given to various modern modes and practices of managerial control.

The three chapters address different aspects of this theme, also adopting various theoretical lenses. In Chapter Twelve, Duco Bannink, Frédérique Six and Eelco van Wijk formulate a prescriptive and programmatic research question aiming at the identification of appropriate modes of control in contexts in which tasks are both highly complex and highly ambiguous. As they state, they adopt a 'logic of suitability of control mechanisms'. The two other chapters pose more descriptive-explanatory questions: 'What are the impacts of new technologies on street-level work and leeway in the case of call centre employees?' (Tino Schuppan, in Chapter Fourteen) and 'How do head teachers as first-line supervisors process rules coming from the top?' (Peter Hupe and Eva van Kooten, in Chapter Thirteen).

In terms of findings, all chapters lead to interesting results that both converge with the existing literature and suggest new directions for research. Five elements are worth considering.

First, all chapters indicate difficulties in effecting top-down control. In the organisations studied by Duco Bannink and his colleagues, no proper control mechanisms seem to exist for addressing the double challenge of high complexity and high ambiguity. Managerial control also seems very limited, as when the very people in charge of supervising school teachers themselves tend to buffer rules coming from the top in order to protect their personnel (Peter Hupe and Eva van Kooten) or even when street-level bureaucrats have an 'electronic leash' (Tino Schuppan)! On the latter, new technologies and information and communication technology (ICT) seem particularly ineffective for documenting the 'subjective parts of the work organisation' and do not improve managerial control. New technologies do not eliminate street-level discretion, but lead to new uncertainties and, hence, new dilemmas for individuals. This result gives further legitimacy to the argument that technological change is only one among (many) other factors influencing first-line discretion (for further discussion of the link between street-level bureaucracy and e-government, see Buffat, 2013).

This is probably linked to the second convergent observation, namely, that management and control tools are never just technical aspects. They are often linked to uncertainties, tensions or conflicts within street-level organisations. Duco Bannink and his colleagues observe that the combination of a mix of (bureaucratic, professional and managerial) controls leads to tensions, in particular, conflicts between task-related mechanisms and externally imposed mechanisms. In the case of Dutch school teachers and head teachers, first-line supervisors actually resist some rules coming from their hierarchy, while in German call centres, new control technologies contribute to create new uncertainties and, hence, new dilemmas for workers.

A third convergent result is about the shielded professionalism discovered in one third of the organisations analysed by Duco Bannink et al, the same result being observed by Peter Hupe and Eva van Kooten for Dutch head teachers who buffer rules. This means that first-line managers protect the autonomy of street-level bureaucrats against external control mechanisms. Tony Evans (in Chapter Sixteen) highlights similar discretionary behaviour by social work managers. Thus, the book provides three different cases in which: a) active or passive modes of resistance exist against control attempts coming from the top of the state; and b) these efforts to protect policy discretion are mainly located at the level of middle-range managers or first-line supervisors. This is an interesting result, showing that first-line managers are discretionary actors as well.

A fourth aspect concerns the increasing hybridity of modern practices of control at the street level. This is particularly highlighted in the chapter by Duco Bannink et al, in which all studied street-level organisations apply a mix or combination of several control mechanisms stemming from a bureaucratic, managerial and professional source. In contemporary organisations, street-level bureaucrats are held accountable to requirements stemming from various sources (Hupe and Hill, 2007). Not only are they expected to act in conformity with formal rules (compliance), but they are also supposed to comply with performance indicators (performance) and to act as professionals (professionalism). New modes of control through New

Public Management or professional norms do not eliminate ancient bureaucratic modes of control. Rather, they add to each other in a process of sedimentation of control mechanisms, creating tensions, new dilemmas and potential conflicts at the operational level. As public organisations in general, street-level organisations may, indeed, increasingly transform into hybrid types (Emery and Giauque, 2014). Then, it becomes interesting to look at how, precisely, street-level workers and their managers deal with the new series of dilemmas and tensions stemming from the increased hybridity of their organisations.

A fifth convergent result is that control mechanisms are closely connected to the type of task involved. This is true in the cases investigated by Duco Bannink and his colleagues, in which most of the control mechanisms found seem to primarily respond to the nature of the task at hand. Some tasks are monitored through bureaucratic means, whereas others are controlled via managerial or professional norms. The same applies for Schuppan, who argues that 'examining the nature of the task and the organisational form, we could better understand to what extent ICT plays a role in the scope of action of street-level bureaucrats' (p 250). In particular, a difference is to be made between standardised or non-standardised work, the former being much more easily monitored through electronic means than the latter, which tends to remain blurry for the 'electronic leash'.

The promise of professionalism

This leads us on to issues about 'The promise of professionalism', explored in Part Six of the book. Chapter Seventeen, however, presents a study suggesting that much granted discretion is not always used. In Chapter Seventeen, Christopher Osiander and Joss Steinke observe that 'More room for manoeuvre sometimes seems to overwhelm caseworkers' (p 310). In the case of German public employment services, a dilemma occurs between standardisation and individual treatment. In this context – counselling and job search assistance – more discretion is no panacea.

In a similar area – job activation – Paul van der Aa and Rik van Berkel, in Chapter Fifteen, stress that fulfilling the promise of professionalism is not self-evident and depends on local contexts. They conclude that, despite a discourse supporting professionalism, policy and new public management remain the most important reference for legitimate discretionary decision-making since diverse, individual, occupational standards are likely to remain disputed.

However, in Chapter Sixteen, Tony Evans explores an area of work – social work in the UK – where managers often originate from a professional background. He indicates, moreover, that even without such a background, managers have discretion and, one way or another, use it. Thus, their behaviour 'creates the context and constraints or expands the choices of front-line workers in implementing policy' (p 293). This discretionary dimension in respect of the behaviour of these managers appears quite similar to the one depicted by Peter Hupe and Eva van Kooten, in Chapter Thirteen, regarding the Dutch context of school first-line management.

These contrasts pose questions about what is meant by professionalisation. As indicated in Chapter One, the concept of the street-level bureaucrat cuts across a popular distinction between bureaucrats and professionalism. The latter is highlighted by Freidson's observation of a contrast between the negative word 'bureaucracy' and the positive word 'profession'. Essentially, Lipsky bypasses the distinction and so we have a range of activities, including medicine, teaching and social work, as well as very sophisticated regulatory tasks, as examples of street-level work.

We also suggest in Chapter One that the professional–bureaucrat distinction seems to very much rest upon the issue of the extent of discretion. In Part Six, two chapters have been concerned with job activation, with one highlighting the 'promise' of professionalism while the other focuses on caseworkers' 'fear' of freedom. The third chapter is about an occupational group where professionalism aspirations are very apparent (see also Chapter Eleven). Elsewhere in the book, we have seen Stephen Harrison suggesting that there has been a tendency for the extent of medical discretion to be exaggerated. The question is: are we just observing points on the discretion continuum between low and high, or is there something qualitatively different about a 'profession'?

That leads on to two questions. One of these is perhaps outside the street-level bureaucracy research agenda as such: to what extent is the distinction made (or denied) as part of a battle over rights to control occupations? The other is: to what extent does the ideal of professionalism embody an approach to the exercise of discretion – the 'promise of professionalism' – in which high levels of trust in respect of street-level work contribute to the realisation of desired goals? To take that further, of course, we need to dig a little deeper into the notion of desired goals. These cannot be specified in value-free terms. Job activation provides a good illustration of this since a contrast can be drawn between a view of this activity as about maximising individual work aspirations and as about minimising claims upon state benefits for unemployed people.

Comparative findings

While many of the observations about the parts of the book look across the book as whole, we need to make some overarching observations on the 15 chapters. Most chapters report on empirical studies. A few chapters are primarily descriptive: one presents a typology, one concerns a theory and another provides a research agenda. Apart from this diversity, the convergence of substantive findings is striking. Similar conclusions are reached, for instance, regarding the following aspects:

- The layer of the (national) system matters, while the factors and mechanisms active there need to be specified. In particular, the macro-policy context has an impact (Harrison; Ellis). Also, institutional settings, like the system of intergovernmental relations and shifts within in it, are influential (Walker). Convergent global developments, like office technologies, have divergent effects (Schuppan).
- Not only at the street level, but on various layers formally above 'the street', can discretionary actors be observed, notably, first-line managers (Evans; Hupe and Van Kooten; Bannink et al).
- The micro-level obviously matters, but it can also be specified. Persons matter; hence the need for attention to the traits of street-level bureaucrats (Wilkins and Wenger), and of their clients (Lehmann Nielsen). Not in the least, then, the interaction between the two is important (Lehmann Nielsen; Winter and May).
- When studying discretion, it seems important to specify the tasks involved (Musheno and Maynard-Moody; Buffat; Schuppan; Bannink et al), while the related questions about the role of trust in such contexts also need attention.

Key research questions for the future

Based on what has been learnt here, what would constitute promising research in the future? What does the next generation of studies on street-level bureaucracy need to look like? In Chapter Two, Evelyn Z. Brodkin calls for two key issues to be addressed in the future: to 'deepen our socio-political understanding' of street-level organisations; and to 'build a broader comparative research agenda' (p 39). Based on the latter, we will now list a range of research questions that the community of street-level bureaucracy researchers could work on in the coming years. Then, in the next section, we will elaborate some lines on how to make street-level bureaucracy studies both generalisable and comparative in the future.

Type of task

Future research should elaborate further, that is, in more systematic and comparative ways, how tasks and the types of tasks may constitute important explanatory factors of usages of discretion at the street level. As various chapters have shown, task variety has different implications on modes of control put into practice, requirements of accountability or types of regulation.

Issues about amounts of discretion

While the debates about how much discretion should be exercised by street-level bureaucrats have a normative core, they need to be informed by more examination of the feasibility of greater or lesser degrees of control for effective operation. The strengthening or weakening of levels of control, and the related issues about trust, have substantive consequences about which judgements can be made. Comparisons may yield answers to questions like these.

Effects of the hybridisation and digitalisation of street-level bureaucracies

As shown in this book, many modern street-level bureaucracies are experiencing important changes such as the increased role played by new technologies (ICT) or logics of action and modes of control coming from different universes of reference (eg public or private status). How ICT impacts street-level work is important and should be further investigated.

Role, function and discretion of first-line managers

One striking insight that the book has produced is that discretion can be observed not only at the street level, but also at other layers, such as the ones where first-line managers are active. First-line managers are street-level bureaucrats in their own right. This implies the peculiarity that they have a certain leeway in defining the organisational conditions of policy work achieved by street-level workers. The view that street-level bureaucrats simply sit at the bottom of a hierarchy that 'manages' them needs to be replaced by a recognition that there is often a 'nested', Russian doll-like, system of layers of discretion. Future theorising should specify the factors accounting for the more or less important room for manoeuvre at these layers. What are the favourable conditions for a buffering-oriented usage of discretion to resist the strict implementation of rules? All in all, following Tony Evans's suggestion, it is now time for the community of street-level bureaucracy researchers to investigate with more sustained effort the role, function and discretionary behaviours of middle-range managers, like school directors, group leaders in welfare departments and others.

Where do we go from here? Making the study of street-level bureaucracy both generalisable and comparative

Generalisation implies contextualised comparison

In this section, we will do three things. First, in this introduction to the section, we explore what is involved in developing further generalisations about street-level bureaucracy and suggest that this development has to involve comparative work of some kind. The second element in this discussion involves an examination of some of the potential dimensions of variety to be compared. Then, the third element addresses more specifically what is involved in making the study of street-level bureaucracy comparative.

The chapters in this book demonstrate the variety of aspects of the phenomena indicated as street-level bureaucracy. What calls for further consideration is the nature of the observed variety and the ways in which to study it. Lipsky's perspective on this draws our attention to similarities across different policy contexts. He states: 'I identify the common elements of occupations as apparently disparate as, say, police officer and social worker' (Lipsky, 2010, p xix). In the next sentence, he goes on to write of a need to 'identify which features of people-processing are common, and which are unique, to the different occupational milieux in which they arise' (Lipsky, 2010, p xix).

Hence, Lipsky (2010, p xix) speaks of an 'essentially comparative approach'. The research implications are that there are similarities of behaviour that may be detected across street-level bureaucracies broadly defined. The assumption is that across occupations, street-level bureaucrats act in the same vein because their working conditions are similar. In fact, this is the rationale behind the common denominator as such: fulfilling tasks as public officials at the street level, they deal similarly with given work circumstances. Faced with dilemmas as individuals, their actions – processing clients and rationing services from the perspective of controlling clients and their work situation – add up to general 'patterns of practice'. However, in contrast, Winter (2002) stresses that individual differences, in terms of ideology, policy preferences and other dimensions, do have an effect on behaviour and the interaction with clients. Hence, such differences contribute to the explanation of empirical variation in policy outputs.

The chapters of this book provide evidence for both arguments. As a general phenomenon, street-level bureaucracy is inherent to the modern state, and, to a certain extent, to the state as such. While even Weber's ideal-type of bureaucracy itself does not preclude 'the human factor', it seems justified to assume the relevance of both common and divergent factors. This book shows not only that street-level bureaucracy has many manifestations, but also that a range of dimensions of variety is involved. Apart from person-bound differences (gender and sociocultural background, but also, for instance, beliefs), there is a variety of sorts of street-level organisations, organisational structure and culture, organisational management, and organisational settings. At the system layer, intergovernmental relations have an influence on the practice of street-level bureaucracy, next to policy design and political attention – to mention a few variables.

However, when understanding street-level bureaucracy is at stake, what needs explanation has to be specified. It can be noted that, in Chapter Ten, Michael Musheno and Steven Maynard-Moody prefer to explore this in terms of the concept of 'agency'. Doing so, they stress the 'horizontal' perspective of the 'citizen-agent'. Perhaps more traditionally, we accept the case for specifying the research object of street-level bureaucracy research in terms of variation in the ways in which discretion is granted (cf a 'state perspective') and is being used (cf a 'citizen perspective'). We justify our preference in terms of the links between the academic concerns to explore and explain discretionary variation and the ever-present 'quest for control' (Van Gunsteren, 1976). This means that we approach as empirical questions the ways in which individual street-level actors act as embedded in a micro-web of *both* vertical and horizontal relations. In any case, specifying the research object is required when street-level phenomena are being studied in their own right (cf the work of Brodkin, 1990, 2010), as well as when used in relation to explaining variation in 'government-in-action' (Hill and Hupe, 2014), particularly policy outputs (cf Winter, 2002). In many studies of street-level bureaucracy, discretion-as-used will be what needs explanation, while discretion-as-granted will be an important explanatory variable – a distinction pointed out in Chapter One. Different than in a top-down view of implementation, however, granted discretion cannot be seen as empirically completely determining street-level behaviour. Where, then, do we seek additional variables to explain that behaviour?

Concerning potential explanatory variables, the theoretical question is how to avoid two extremes. One is to put a specific cluster of variables forward with the – implicit – claim to provide an overall account, like Lipsky's categorical explanation. At the other end, an inclination is observable to approach the empirics of street-level bureaucracy mainly in terms of highly individual characteristics, providing an 'everybody is unique' picture. In both instances, it becomes difficult to specify what is general and what is particular, and to distinguish between what seem to be patterns and what is idiosyncratic. This difficulty is enhanced when the conceptualisations used vary as well. What is merely variation in discourse and what stands for 'real' variation in empirical reality then becomes hard to discern.

In their overview of the field, Meyers and Nielsen (2012) suggest that there is an overestimation of the relevance of factors related to the individual public servants working at the street level. They observe:

> A handful of studies have used multivariate techniques to examine the link between the behaviors of front-line workers and policy achievement by capitalizing on cross-site variation. Findings about the explanatory power of worker behavior from these have been mixed and suggest that results are sensitive to both model specification and to the measurement of the dependent variable. (Meyers and Nielsen, 2012, p 312)

As Meyers and Nielsen (2012, p 313) go on to state, efforts to measure the impact of street-level discretion on policy outcomes via multivariate models 'have found relatively weak effects'; 'This contradictory portrait of street-level bureaucrats reflects both the lack of sufficient theory and methods for studying street-level workers and the failure to fully contextualize the evaluation of their performance'.

While Lipsky mentions a distinction between common and unique features, he seems to stress shared features of behaviour across occupational borders. Taking a cue from this distinction, and from Meyers and Nielsen's comment, we make the following case for generalisation here. Generalisation presupposes contextualised comparison. In other words, the 'test' for any generalisation about street-level bureaucracy must lie in exploring variation in similar and varying contexts. Then, a specification is needed of the relevant dimensions of variety. The next subsection does this.

Specifying dimensions of variety

The literature that extends representative bureaucracy theory into explorations of the impact of race, gender and so on upon street-level decision-making provides the most obvious way into the examination of dimensions of variety. We start by looking at this, noting the way in which it is developed in Chapter Nine by Wilkins and Wenger. Other dimensions of variety concern differences in tasks and contexts, focusing more on what is being done where, rather than who is doing it, so we move onto these.

The impact of the personal characteristics of street-level bureaucrats

To a certain extent, street-level work will be influenced by characteristics of workers that are independent of the tasks they perform. It is particularly here that some interesting work has already been done. This explores the predispositions of street-level staff in terms of the extent to which they have characteristics that influence the way in which they exercise their discretion, and how this carries advantages (or disadvantages) for their clientele. In this work, questions are asked about the impact of the ethnicity, gender or social class of implementers upon their decisions. Much of this work on *representative bureaucracy* is based on the distinction between 'active' and 'passive' representation, addressing the question: 'Do ascribed characteristics of an individual ... relate to or predict policy preferences, as well as actions to achieve certain policy *outcomes*?' (Riccucci and Meyers, 2004, p 586, emphasis in original).

The question raised here regarding generalisation about street-level work is whether there are propositions about decision-making dispositions that hold across all (or most) activities. Clearly, there is a problem about the extent to which many of them are likely to be task-specific. They are particularly pertinent to activities where there are issues about racial or sexual discrimination affecting policy. However, Lipsky's original work also raises questions about stereotyping as an aspect of efforts by street-level bureaucrats to simplify their tasks, especially when under pressure. Steven Maynard-Moody and Michael Musheno (2003; see also Chapter Ten) raise important questions about the ways in which street-level bureaucrat behaviour reflects social values. In Chapter Nine, Vicky Wilkins and Jeffrey Wenger explore this theme and take it a stage further by arguing that there may be differences in overriding attitudinal dispositions that influence street-level work.

How may these ideas lead to a generalisation that can be subject to testing in a comparative perspective? Psychological studies on roles suggest areas for further research on relationships between underlying dispositions and attitudes and socialisation into work. These issues are important, but it requires a big leap from this to propositions that might generally predict street-level behaviour. An alternative is to focus on differences between tasks.

The impact of specific tasks

Under the heading of *Bureaucracy*, Wilson (1989) focuses on 'what government agencies do and why they do it'. Like Lipsky, he stresses what 'operators' have in common, but he places them in a specified context of organisational subtypes. Wilson makes a distinction based upon the extent to which outcomes may be identified (and evaluated) in respect of the outputs of different workers and uses this to label varying kinds of organisations. It is clear that the soldier literally at the front-line in wartime and the teacher in the classroom do quite different work. Hence, Wilson makes a case for a comparative look at the work of the soldier and that of the teacher, however different. Until then, actual comparisons between street-level bureaucrats doing different tasks had received little attention. Wilson's typology refines the street-level bureaucracy perspective, particularly because of its focus on activities.

Another approach to task variety involves distinctions between the provision of benefits, the provision of services and regulation. This is one that can be seen when contributions to this book are compared. Such distinctions need to be handled with care because street-level tasks may involve combinations of the three. In particular, officials providing benefits and services regulate behaviour. Moreover, instrument choice theory shows how these may be alternative routes to the same political goals (Howlett, 1991).

Of course, it can be rash to assume that a task carried out in one nation is exactly the same as its equivalent carried out in another. Social assistance, a topic that has been studied comparatively, provides an example where two particular phenomena – the extent of related benefit cover by way of social insurance and the extent of involvement of social workers – may have very different manifestations at the street level (see Hvinden, 1994; Eardley et al, 1996).

Although directing attention primarily to similarities, among all dimensions of variety, Lipsky points to occupation-bound differences between tasks. Wilson took, one could say, 'tasks and their environment' seriously. The scope of 'task environment' has thus been theoretically widened, but so far little has been done to extend the street-level bureaucracy theme comparatively by looking at broadly similar tasks performed in different institutional and cultural settings. The effects of variety in institutional arrangements within nations cannot be overlooked, particularly where there is a federation or other sources of high local autonomy. In any case, it is clear that 'public task fulfilment in context' is a comparative theme in the cross-national sense *par excellence*.

This takes the arguments for future work in a different direction, not looking for substantive differences between tasks, but rather examining how similar tasks may be performed in different contexts. Tasks may be considered as perhaps the most 'elementary particle' that street-level bureaucracy can be broken down to. The latter exercise, however, directly enlarges the task environment, implying the need to incorporate a multitude of potentially relevant variables.

Similar tasks in different contexts

A pioneering study of cross-national variation is Jewell's (2007) study of welfare administration in the US, Germany and Sweden. Jewell observes 'three worlds of social welfare', making a connection here with Esping-Andersen's (1990) more macro-level comparative work. Jewell links 'macro-' and 'micro-'analysis by connecting 'national culture, institutional history, and agency organization to ground-level practice' (Jewell, 2007, p 34). Micro-level differences may, in a 'nested' way, be related to system differences, resulting in varying regulatory environments. Addressing 'welfare caseworker behaviour' and 'activation caseworker behaviour' as dependent variables, Jewell places them in a context where it seems to be the choices of institutional settings that are important. Street-level bureaucrats in the US, Germany and Sweden may be different kinds of people (one must not be indifferent to psychological theory that explores interactions between roles and personality). What is crucial is that they carry out similar and, therefore, comparable tasks in different institutional frameworks.

Following the idea behind Jewell's study, there are other examples where street-level bureaucrats have specific tasks that are remarkably similar across nations. The authors of this chapter include two people who have, albeit at different points in time, worked on similar issues about discretion in respect of unemployed people (Buffat, in Chapter Five, and Hill [1969; Hill et al, 1973]). Paul van der Aa and Rik van Berkel's discussion of job activation in The Netherlands in Chapter Fifteen raises issues about the 'professionalisation' of this work that are similar to those raised by Buffat. This theme is actually echoed in other comparative work, but without a street-level bureaucracy focus (Lodemel and Trickey, 2001). Personalisation in social care services, examined with regard to developments in England by Kathryn Ellis in Chapter Eleven, has been given some attention in comparative work (see Ungerson, 1995). There are other areas of work – early education, child protection and the checking of food standards are but a few examples – where street-level bureaucracy tasks are remarkably similar across nations.

Therefore, the words of caution about generalisation across occupations that we set out earlier lead us to commending as conversely important the replication of research work already done on the same policy delivery issue in the same institutional context. There is obviously much to be done in this respect. Essentially, it can refine the original analysis, leading to larger overall understanding of the phenomenon in one policy field. More challenging is work that can follow Jewell's lead to explore more widely how institutional and cultural differences affect street-level behaviour in the implementation of broadly similar policies. This starts to raise the question that is considered further later. If we are looking not only at how discretion is used, but also at how discretion is granted, how can a feasible comparative approach to street-level bureaucracy be developed?

Making the study of street-level bureaucracy comparative

There are differences in the way in which discretion is granted. Do these undermine efforts to do comparative work on street-level bureaucracy, or can these differences be studied effectively? It seems important to us to try to study them. In particular, it seems relevant to look at empirical studies and how discretion is framed there. A survey of this topic revealed a confusingly large number of variables that have been used, for example:

- policy design, bureaucratic incentives, political forces, task requirements and economic capacity (Keiser and Meier, 1996);
- partisan control, funding decisions, values of state administrators and levels of demand (Keiser and Soss, 1998);

- organisation size, task complexity, number of rules and stakeholder consensus (Langbein, 2000);
- administrative factors and political predispositions (Keiser, 2001); and
- municipal politics and policy (May and Winter, 2009).

It would be hard to design comparative approaches to our topic that satisfactorily encompass the whole range of factors. What underlies the discussion here is the need to move away from both a categorical and an individualist focus on the 'street', and to acknowledge how power relations, politics and related institutional factors impact upon it. In our view, it is important to look at street-level bureaucracies as political institutions where the ultimate decisions about 'who gets what, when, how' (Lasswell, 1936) are made as embedded in a multidimensional web of vectors (cf Weatherly, 1980). These vectors regard forces at face value as stronger in their effects than in the clarity of their direction. Moreover, they tend to be analysed in ways that are rather distant from the methodological 'nitty gritty' of the practice of street-level research. Evelyn Brodkin (2010, p 61) speaks of the 'politics of practice'. Earlier (Brodkin, 1990), she developed this view while looking at implementation in terms of 'policy politics'. It seems relevant to elaborate such a view when seeking to make comparative statements. This implies addressing the inherent difficulty of separating out what determines how discretionary powers are structured and how discretion is then exercised. There is an interaction here, which substantively poses a theoretical and methodological puzzle. The puzzle concerns one of disentanglement and reconstruction, aimed at understanding and explaining empirical variation.

Where, then, does this discussion take us as far as the future street-level bureaucracy research agenda is concerned? We are reminded of complaints about implementation research as trying to work with 'too many variables' (Goggin, 1986) and the subsequent pleas for more structure within analysis (Matland, 1995; Meier, 1999). This reinforces the argument that comparisons concerned with explaining variation in how discretion is exercised need to look within the same or closely related contexts. Conversely, this implies that comparison between its exercise across the borders of such contexts – by looking at different organisations, occupations, policy areas and/or countries – is inherently problematical.

We move on, therefore, into a discussion of the that shape comparative studies may take. Our starting point is other literature on comparative policy analysis. We briefly suggest that classic approaches to this should not be forgotten and then go on to some quite specific issues about how comparative work on street-level bureaucracy may be framed. We highlight two approaches, one of them being a 'model cases' approach, which has the advantage of minimising research costs. The other is the idea of comparing 'public service gaps'.

Connections to other approaches to comparative policy analysis

Does the literature on comparative policy analysis help with this problem? The difficulty is that in this literature, comparisons between national systems are usually made at a high level of abstraction and in general terms. Most studies focus particularly on types of economies, political systems or constitutional frameworks. These analyses tell us little about, for example, differences between how aspects of the operation of the welfare state, like the treatment of disadvantaged groups, are experienced and shaped in different countries. This issue has more than just intellectual importance. Policy learning across countries is widespread. There are many assumptions made about countries that are believed to administer specific policies 'better'. Any appreciation of what specific policy systems are actually doing needs to be founded upon detailed street-level comparisons. We make this statement boldly while recognising the massive practical and methodological problems about making comparisons. At the same time, this does not mean the rejection of any comparative research agenda. With the study referred to earlier, Jewell has shown that it is possible to make comparative statements about what happens at the street level in different 'worlds of welfare' and to make micro–macro links. We have more to say on this in the next paragraph.

Here, it is worthwhile emphasising what comparative analysis involves. It is, as Lijphart (1971, p 683) argues, 'a method of discovering empirical relationships amongst variables', which is particularly applicable when more rigorous methods (notably, experimentation) are not feasible. Then, as Durkheim (1982, p 141) argued:

> We have only one way of demonstrating that one phenomenon is the cause of another. That is to compare the cases where they are both simultaneously present or absent, so as to discover whether the variations they display in these different combinations of circumstances provide evidence that one depends on the other.

Those generic propositions imply a wide range of alternative comparisons.

Kinds of comparisons

There is a variety of possibilities for comparison in respect of both the behaviour of street-level bureaucrats when fulfilling public tasks and the structuring of their freedom of action by vectors from their task environment. In principle, both public task fulfilment and its structuring determinants can serve as either dependent or independent variables. At the same time, adopting the issue of generalisation as related to the fundamental distinction between discretion as exercised and as structured has consequences for an agenda for comparative research. In other words, it seems useful and possible to document public task fulfilment and public task environment in a comparative way independently of each other. When, however, explanation is the objective, relevant combinations of dependent and independent variables may be sought in terms of empirical variation in *public task fulfilment*. *'Public task environment'*, then, may serve as an umbrella label for a range of potential explanatory variables among which a theoretically grounded selection is to be made.

Logically, the object of comparison can take several forms. One could think of comparing persons with each other, or organisations, or aggregate systems. Also, tasks, occupations, jurisdictions, policy programmes, policy areas, nations and so on can be compared. In fact, the list is endless. With an eye on what we have stated earlier, a pragmatic suggestion would be to address primarily the option of looking at the carrying out of a specific task in terms of: a) comparing different employees of the same street-level organisation at one point or over time; b) making a comparison within the same system but within varied organisations; and c) looking at the same task as carried out in different countries.

These options for making street-level bureaucracy research comparative are mentioned here in a cumulative order of complexity. Comparisons within single nation-states where there are federal differences or even differences arising from high levels of local government autonomy. Studies involving national comparisons may potentially generate even more useful insights, of course, but the practical implications cannot be underestimated. Comparative studies are likely to depend upon collaboration between scholars. The more these studies require clearances for research in various jurisdictions, the more costly they will be. Unless substantial financial resources are available, studies of actual behaviour will be difficult in this respect. Therefore, it is helpful if there are already-existing sources of information on street-level bureaucrat activities that can be used as implicit measures of behaviour. Here, our earlier observation about the selection of activities to compare is relevant. An appropriate degree of comparability is given where the basic work task is likely to be similar in the countries compared. It then seems desirable to be able to hypothesise potential differences (as Jewell does using regime theory) and to explore how these affect task performance. There could be a particular concern to explore exercised modes of control.

Comparing 'model cases'

In the absence of comparative studies that are explicitly about street-level bureaucrat behaviour, it is possible to develop some ideas from comparative studies that focus on outputs or outcomes. Here, in the absence of resources for the very elaborate replication of methods to acquire direct evidence, a useful starting point is the 'model individual' or 'model families' approach to comparative studies (see Bradshaw, 1993; Eardley et al, 1996; Johnson, 1999; Pacolet et al, 1999; Meyer et al, 2007). None of the studies cited here concerned themselves with the variation that might arise from the presence of discretionary powers, let alone their exercise. They are cited here as examples of using expert assessors who could, in those or similar situations, be asked to explore discretionary variation in particular dimensions. Such an approach may be described as a 'model cases' one.

Public service gaps

Another approach to comparison arises in connection with system changes over time. In an article, Hupe and Buffat (2014) propose the construct of a 'public service gap'. A distinction is made between a 'demand' and a 'supply' side, referring to the difference between what is being asked of and the resources offered to public officials doing their work in contact with citizens. A public service gap occurs when what is required of street-level bureaucrats (action prescriptions) exceeds what is provided to them (action resources) for the fulfilment of their tasks.

On the demand side, a range of action prescriptions are involved (Hupe and Van der Krogt, 2013, p 61; see also Hupe and Hill, 2007):

- formal rules, stemming from public administration;
- professional norms, such as occupational guidelines; and
- expectations from society ('public opinion').

Opposite of constraints, on the 'supply side', there are 'enablements'. The latter concerns an umbrella term used to indicate the range of acts that enable street-level bureaucrats to fulfil their tasks. Enablements consist of various kinds of action resources, such as training, education, professional experience, time, information, staff and, last but not least, the budget itself.

From all that has been written about street-level bureaucracy, it has been evidenced that such a gap, framed in whatever vocabulary, is ubiquitous. However, it can also be assumed that this gap will be larger in some situations than in others, that is to say, the task environments will be more or less imbalanced in terms of existing action prescriptions and available action resources. This takes us back to Durkheim's proposition about the comparative method, challenging us to compare situations in which it may be postulated that the gap between what is asked and what is available will differ. This is particularly likely to occur when situations at two different points in time can be compared.

In conclusion, the assumptions about comparison are that some of the practical and methodological problems that have so far inhibited the development of comparative work on street-level bureaucracy can be solved. This is particularly likely to be the case where the contrasts between jurisdictions are small. Much will depend upon the pre-existing availability of data, and, in general, the achievement of comparisons between systems seems more likely to be achievable than comparisons between actual behaviour. An articulate focus on the variation in the fulfilment of identifiable, similar, tasks, therefore, could be appropriate as inviting to be explained. Some of the research strategies indicated earlier, particularly the identification of public service gaps, could be helpful to such an explanation.

Conclusion

This book ends with the present chapter asking: where do we go from here? Taking our cue from Lipsky's observation that the perspective he introduced is, in essence, 'comparative', we see many questions to be explored about the varied forms that the phenomenon takes. Hence, we have attempted in this final chapter to make some connections, while aiming at the accumulation of knowledge and insights relevant to understanding street-level bureaucracy.

The multidimensional character of the empirical object is reflected in the variety of ways in which this object gets research attention – as shown. Even when street-level bureaucracy is treated as a delineated scholarly theme of its own, a rather fundamental concept like discretion appears to stand for varying circumscriptions and measurements (see

Hupe, 2013). This being so, it seems possible to draw some lines, identifying what may be seen as more or less feasible ways to go forward.

Making a case for generalisation implies addressing the question of how to practise contextualised comparative research. After all, any generalising statement about street-level bureaucracy must be based on an exploration of empirical variation in both similar and varying contexts. Therefore, relevant dimensions of variety have been specified. On the basis of the work reported in the chapters of this book, we have highlighted several such dimensions:

- task variety (in the context of scepticism regarding the scope for comparisons between very different tasks);
- levels of granted discretion and trust;
- effects of office and communication technology; and
- variation in the roles of first-line managers.

Going forward along lines like these would mean an extension of comparative policy analysis beyond the very high-level comparisons implied by regime theory and related work. We also see it as important for policy transfer between nations, where policy ideas are borrowed with little attention to the way in which they operate on the ground.

This book has been comparative in 'spirit' rather than practice. We have not assembled research findings from a shared research project; we have not even sought contributions around one specific manifestation of street-level bureaucracy in action. Rather, this book involves a sharing of ideas and aspirations, an exploration of common themes from various nations provided by authors who share a concern to advance the study of street-level bureaucracy. In this final chapter, we have delineated those themes and then gone on to make some observations about how truly comparative research work might be developed on street-level bureaucracy.

References

6, P. (2003) 'Institutional viability: a neo-Durkheimian theory', *Innovation*, vol 16, no 4, pp 395–415.

Abbott, A. (1988) *The system of professions. An essay on the division of expert labor*, Chicago, IL: The University of Chicago Press.

Abel-Smith, B. and Townsend, P. (1965) *The poor and the poorest*, London: Bell.

Abramovitz, M. (2005) 'The largely untold story of welfare reform and the human services', *Social Work*, vol 50, no 2, pp 174–86.

Ackroyd, S. (1996) 'Organization contra organizations: professions and organizational change in the United Kingdom', *Organization Studies*, vol 17, no 4, pp 599–621.

Ackroyd, S. and Muzio, D. (2007) 'Reconstructed professional firm: explaining change in English legal practices', *Organization Studies*, vol 28, no 5, pp 729–47.

Adams, J.S. (1980) 'Interorganizational processes and organization boundary activities', in B.M. Staw and L.L. Cummings (eds) *Research in organizational behavior* (vol 2), Greenwich, CT: Elsevier, pp 321–55.

ADASS (Association of Directors of Adult Social Services) (2009) *Personalisation and the law: implementing Putting People First in the current legal framework*, London: ADASS.

ADASS, DH (Department of Health), SFC (Skills for Care), BASW (British Association of Social Workers) and SCA (Social Care Association) (2010) *The future of social work in adult social services*, London: ADASS/DH/SFC/BASW/SCA.

Adler, M. (2013) 'Conditionality, sanctions, and the weakness of redress mechanisms in the British "New Deal"', in E.Z. Brodkin and G. Marston (eds) *Work and the welfare state*, Washington, DC: Georgetown University Press.

Adler, P. and Borys, B. (1996) 'Two types of bureaucracy: coercive versus enabling', *Administrative Science Quarterly*, vol 41, no 1, pp 61–89.

Albrow, M. (1970) *Bureaucracy*, London: Pall Mall.

Alford, J. (2002) 'Why do public-sector clients coproduce? Toward a contingency theory', *Administration and Society*, vol 34, no 1, pp 32–56.

Anon (1981) 'Review article: street-level bureaucracy', *Michigan Law Review*, vol 79, pp 811–14.

Apel, H. (2009) 'Das methodische Konzept der Fallstudien des ISG', ISG Working Paper 6/2009.

Apel, H., Engler, S., Friebertshäuser, B., Fuhs, B. and Zinnecker, J. (1995) 'Kulturanalyse und Ethnographie. Vergleichende Feldforschung im studentischen Raum', in E. König and P. Zedler (eds) *Bilanz qualitativer Forschung. Band II*, Weinheim: DSV, pp 343–75.

Argyris, C. (1957) *Personality and organization*, New York, NY: Harper and Row.

Argyris, C. (1964) *Integrating the individual and the organization*, New York, NY: John Wiley and Sons.

Arksey, H. and Baxter, K. (2012) 'Exploring the temporal aspects of direct payments', *British Journal of Social Work*, vol 42, no 1, pp 147–64.

Arksey, H. and Kemp, P. (2008) *Dimensions of choice: a narrative review of cash-for-care schemes*, Working Paper No DHP 2250, York: Social Policy Research Unit, University of York.

Arnold, R.D. (1990) *The logic of congressional action*, New Haven, CT: Yale University Press.

Askim, J., Fimreite, A.L., Moseley, A. and Pedersen, L. (2011) 'One-stop shops for social welfare: the adaptation of an organisational form in three countries', *Public Administration*, vol 89, no 4, pp 1451–68.

Atkinson, A.B. (1970) *Poverty in Britain and the reform of social security*, Cambridge: Cambridge University Press.

Attewell, P. (1987) 'The deskilling controversy', *Work and Occupations*, vol 14, no 3, pp 323–46.

BA (Bundesagentur für Arbeit [Federal Employment Agency]) (2011) 'Fachliche Hinweise zu § 15 SGB II', internal document.

Bach, S. and Kessler, I. (2012) *The modernisation of the public services and employee relations: targeted change*, Hampshire: Palgrave Macmillan.

Baethge-Kinsky, V., Bartelheimer, P., Henke, J., Wolf, A., Land, R., Willisch, A. and Kupka, P. (2007) 'Neue soziale Dienstleistungen nach SGB II', IAB-Forschungsbericht 15/2007.

Bain, P. and Taylor, P. (2002) 'Ringing the changes? Union recognition and organisation in call centres in the UK finance sector', *Industrial Relations Journal*, vol 33, no 3, pp 246–61.

Baker, M.R. and Kirk, S. (eds) (1996) *Research and development for the NHS: evidence, evaluation and effectiveness*, Oxford: Radcliffe Medical Press.

Baldwin, R., Scott, C. and Hood, C. (1998) 'Introduction', in R. Baldwin, C. Scott and C. Hood (eds) *A reader on regulation*, Oxford: Oxford University Press, pp 1–55.

Bannink, D., Lettinga, B. and Heyse, L. (2006) 'NPM, bureaucratisering en de invloed van op de professie', *Beleid and Maatschappij*, vol 33, no 3, pp 159–74.

Bardach, E. (1977) *The implementation game: what happens after a bill becomes a law*, Cambridge, MA: MIT Press.

Bardach, E. and Kagan, R.A. (1982) *Going by the book: the problem of regulatory unreasonableness*, Philadelphia, PA: Temple University Press.

Bardsley, M., Coles, J. and Jenkins, L. (1987) *DRGs and health care: the management of case mix*, London: King's Fund.

Barnard, C.I. (1968) *The functions of the executive*, Cambridge, MA: Harvard University Press.

Batt, R. and Moynihan, L. (2002) 'The viability of alternative call centre production models', *Human Resource Management Journal*, vol 12, no 4, pp 14–34.

Batt, R. and Nohara, H. (2009) 'How institutions and business strategies affect wages: a cross national study of call centers', *Industrial and Labor Relations Review*, vol 62, no 4, pp 533-52.

Batt, R., Holman, D. and Holtgrewe, U. (2009) 'The globalization of service work: comparative institutional perspectives on call centers', *Introduction to a Special Issue of Industrial and Labor Relations Review*, vol 62, no 4, pp 453-88.

Beazley, S. and Brady, A.M. (2006) 'Integrated pathways in orthopaedics: a literature review', *Journal of Orthopaedic Nursing*, vol 10, pp 171–8.

Becker, G. (1968) 'Crime and punishment: an economic approach', *Journal of Political Economy*, vol 76, no 2, pp 169–217.

Beckman, S. (1990) 'Professionalization: borderline authority and autonomy of work', in M. Burrage and R. Torstendahl (eds) *Professions in theory and history*, London: Sage Publications, 115-38.

Beddoe, L. (2010) 'Surveillance or reflection: professional supervision in "the risk society"', *British Journal of Social Work*, vol 40, no 4, pp 1279–96.

Bègue, L. and Bastounis, M. (2003) 'Two spheres of belief in justice: extensive support for the bidimensional model of belief in a just world', *Journal of Personality*, vol 71, no 3, pp 435–63.

Bègue, L. and Muller, D. (2006) 'Belief in a just world as moderator of hostile attributional bias', *British Journal of Social Psychology*, vol 45, no 1, pp 117–26.

Behncke, S., Frölich, M. and Lechner, M. (2010a) 'A caseworker like me – does the similarity between unemployed and caseworker increase job placements?', *The Economic Journal*, vol 120, pp 1430–59.

Behncke, S., Frölich, M. and Lechner, M. (2010b) 'Unemployed and their caseworkers – should they be friends or foes?', *The Journal of the Royal Statistical Society – Series A*, vol 173, no 1, pp 67–92.

Beltram, G. (1984) *Testing the safety net*, London: NCVO/Bedford Square Press.

Berdowski, Z. and Vennekens, A. (2008) *Demarcatie proces- en productvoorschriften in primair en voortgezet onderwijs*, Zoetermeer: Instituut voor Onderzoek van Overheidsuitgaven (IOO).

Beresford, P. (2009) 'Social care, personalisation and service users: addressing the ambiguities', *Research, Policy and Planning*, vol 27, no 2, pp 73–84.

Beresford, P. and Hasler, F. (2009) *Transforming social care: changing the future together*, London: Brunel University Press.

Berg, M. (1997) 'Problems and promises of the protocol', *Social Science and Medicine*, vol 44, no 8, pp 1081–8.

Berrien, F.K. (1968) *General and social systems*, New Brunswick, NJ: Rutgers University.

Berthoud, R. (1984) *The reform of social security*, London: PSI.

Beveridge, W. (1942) *Social insurance and allied services*, Cmd 6404, London: HMSO.

Black, J. (2002) 'Regulatory conversations', *Journal of Law and Society*, vol 29, no 1, pp 163–96.

Black, J. and Baldwin, R. (2010) 'Really responsive-based regulation', *Law and Policy*, vol 32, no 3, pp 183–213.

Blackmore, M. (2001) 'Mind the gap: exploring the implementation deficit in the administration of the stricter benefits regime', *Social Policy and Administration*, vol 35, no 2, pp 145–62.

Blauner, R. (1964) *Alienation and freedom*, Chicago, IL: University of Chicago Press.

Böhle, F. (2011) 'Interaktionsarbeit als wichtige Arbeitstätigkeit im Dienstleistungssektor', WSI-Mitteilungen 9/2011, pp 456–61.

Bonoli, G. and Natali, D. (2012) *The politics of the welfare state*, Oxford: Oxford University Press.

Boockmann, B., Osiander, C., Stops, M. and Verbeek, H. (2013) 'Effekte von Vermittlerhandeln und Vermittlerstrategien im SGB II und SGB III (Pilotstudie)', Abschlussbericht an das IAB durch das Institut für Angewandte Wirtschaftsforschung e. V. (IAW), Tübingen, IAB-Forschungsbericht, 07/2013.

Boockmann, B., Osiander, C. and Stops, M. (2014) 'Vermittlerstrategien und Arbeitsmarkterfolg. Evidenz aus kombinierten Prozess- und Befragungsdaten', *Journal for Labour Market Research*, online first.

Borghi, V. and Van Berkel, R. (2007) 'Individualised service provision in an era of activation and new governance', *International Journal of Sociology and Social Policy*, vol 27, nos 9/10, pp 413–24.

Bouckaert, G. and Halligan, J. (2008) *Managing performance, international comparisons*, London: Routledge.

Bourdieu, P. (2005) *The social structures of the economy*, Cambridge: Polity Press.

Bovens, M. and Zouridis, S. (2002) 'From street-level to system-level bureaucracies: how information and communication technology is transforming administrative discretion and constitutional control', *Public Administration Review*, vol 62, no 2, pp 174–84.

Bradach, J. and Eccles, R. (1989) 'Price, authority and trust: from ideal types to plural forms', *Annual Review of Sociology*, vol 15, pp 97–118.

Bradley, G. (2005) 'Movers and stayers in care management in adult services', *British Journal of Social Work*, vol 35, no 4, pp 511–30.

Bradshaw, J. (1993) *Support for children: a comparison of arrangements in 15 counties*, London: HMSO.

Braithwaite, J., Walker, J. and Grabosky, P. (1987) 'An enforcement taxonomy of regulatory agencies', *Law and Policy*, vol 9, no 3(July), pp 325–51.

Braman, A.C. and Lambert, A.J. (2001) 'Punishing individuals for their infirmities: effects of personal responsibility, just-world beliefs, and in-group/out-group status', *Journal of Applied Social Psychology*, vol 31, no 5, pp 1096–1109.

Brewer, G.A. (2005) 'In the eye of the storm: frontline supervisors and federal agency performance', *Journal of Public Administration Research and Theory*, vol 15, no 4, pp 505–27.

Briggs, E. and Deacon, A. (1973) 'The creation of the Unemployment Assistance Board', *Policy and Politics*, vol 2, no 1, pp 43–62.

Brodkin, E.Z. (1990) 'Implementation as policy politics', in D. Palumbo and D. Calista (eds) *Implementation and the policy process: opening up the black box*, Westport, CT: Greenwood Press, pp 107–31.

Brodkin, E.Z. (1997) 'Inside the welfare contract: discretion and accountability in state welfare administration', *Social Service Review*, vol 71, no 1, pp 1–33.

Brodkin, E. Z. (2007) 'Bureaucracy redux: management reformism and the welfare state', *Journal of Public Administration Research and Theory*, vol 17, no 1, pp 1–17.

Brodkin, E.Z. (2008) 'Accountability in street-level organizations', *International Journal of Public Administration*, vol 31, no 3, pp 317–36.

Brodkin, E.Z. (2010) 'Human service organizations and the politics of practice', in Y. Hasenfeld (ed) *Human services as complex organizations* (2nd edn), London: Sage, pp 61–78.

Brodkin, E.Z. (2011) 'Policy work: street-level organizations under new managerialism', *Journal of Public Administration Research and Theory*, vol 21, no 2, pp i253–i277.

Brodkin, E.Z. (2012) 'Reflections on street-level bureaucracy: past, present, and future', *Public Administration Review*, vol 72, pp 940–9.

Brodkin, E.Z. (2013) 'Street-level organizations and the welfare state', in E.Z. Brodkin and G. Marston (eds) *Work and the welfare state*, Washington, DC: Georgetown University Press.

Brodkin, E.Z. and Majmundar, M. (2010) 'Administrative exclusion: organizations and the hidden costs of welfare claiming', *Journal of Public Administration Research and Theory*, vol 20, no 4, pp 827–48.

Brödner, P. and Latniak, E. (2002) 'Der lange Weg zur "High Road" – Neue Untersuchungsergebnisse zu organisatorischen Veränderungen in Unternehmen', Institut Arbeit und Technik, Jahrbuch 2001/2002, pp 113–34.

Brudney, J.L. and England, R.E. (1983) 'Toward a definition of the coproduction concept', *Public Administration Review*, vol 43, no 1, pp 59–65.

Buffat, A. (2011) 'Pouvoir Discrétionnaire et Redevabilité de la Bureaucratie de Guichet. Les Taxateurs d'une Caisse de Chômage comme Acteurs de Mise en Œuvre', unpublished PhD thesis, University of Lausanne, CH.

Buffat, A. (2013) 'Street-level bureaucracy and e-government', *Public Management Review*, doi: 10.1080/14719037.2013.771699.

Bundt, J. (2000) 'Strategic stewards: managing accountability, building trust', *Journal of Public Administration Theory and Research*, vol 10, no 4, pp 757–77.

Burawoy, M. (1979) *Manufacturing consent. Changes in the labour process under monopoly capitalism*, Chicago, IL: University of Chicago Press.

Burawoy, M. (1999) *1999. Ethnography unbound: power and resistance in the modern metropolis*, Berkeley, CA: University of California Press.

Burby, R.J. and Paterson, R.G. (1993) 'Improving compliance with state environmental regulations', *Journal of Policy Analysis and Management*, vol 12, no 4, pp 753–72.

Calhoun, L.G. and Cann, A. (1994) 'Differences in assumptions about a just world: ethnicity and point of view', *The Journal of Social Psychology*, vol 134, no 6, pp 765–70.

Carlyle, T. (1870) 'The new Downing Street', *Latter day pamphlets: collected works*, vol 19, London: Chapman and Hall.

Carr, S. and Robbins, D. (2009) *SCIE Research Briefing 20: the implementation of individual budget schemes in adult social care*, London: Social Care Institute for Excellence.

Carson, E., Chung, D. and Evans, T (2014) 'Complexities of discretion in social services in the third sector', *European Journal of Social Work*. Available at: http://dx.doi.org/10.1080/13691457.2014.888049 (accessed January 2014).

Causer, G. and Exworthy, M. (1999) 'Professionals as managers across the public sector', in M. Exworthy and S. Halford (eds) *Professions and the new managerialism in the public sector*, Buckingham: Open University Press.

Checkland, K. (2004) 'National service frameworks and UK general practitioners: street-level bureaucrats at work', *Sociology of Health and Illness*, vol 26, no 7, pp 951–75.

Checkland, K., McDonald, R. and Harrison, S. (2007) 'Ticking boxes and changing the social world: data collection and the new UK general practice contract', *Social Policy and Administration*, vol 41, no 7, pp 693–710.

Checkland, K., Harrison, S., McDonald, R., Grant, S., Campbell, S. and Guthrie, B. (2008) 'Biomedicine, holism and general medical practice: responses to the 2004 General practitioner contract', *Sociology of Health and Illness*, vol 30, no 5, pp 788–803.

Cheetham, J. (1993) 'Social work and community care in the 1990s: pitfalls and potential', in R. Page and J. Baldock (eds) *Social policy review 5*, Canterbury: University of Kent, Social Policy Association.

Cheraghi-Sohi, S., McDonald, R., Harrison, S. and Sanders, C. (2012) 'Experience of contractual change in UK general practice: a qualitative study of salaried GPs', *British Journal of General Practice*, April, e282–e287: doi: 10.3399/bjgp12X636128.

Cheung, C. and Ngai, S.S. (2009) 'Surviving hegemony through resistance and identity articulation among outreaching social workers', *Child and Adolescent Social Work Journal*, vol 26, no 1, pp 15–37.

Cho, Ch., Kelleher, C.A., Wright, D.S. and Yackee, S.W. (2005) 'Translating national policy objectives into local achievements across planes of governance and among multiple actors: second-order devolution and welfare reform implementation', *Journal of Public Administration Research and Theory*, vol 15, no 1, pp 31–54.

Clark, C. (1998) 'Self-determination and paternalism in community care: practice and prospects', *British Journal of Social Work*, vol 28, no 3, pp 387–402.

Clarke, A., Cochrane, A. and McLaughlin, E. (eds) (1994) *Managing social policy*, London: Sage.

Clarke, J.S. (1943) 'The assistance board', in W. Robson (ed) *Social security*, London: Allen and Unwin.

Clarke, J. and Newman, J. (1997) *The managerial state: power, politics and ideology in the remaking of social welfare*, London: Sage.

Cochrane, A.L. (1972) *Effectiveness and efficiency: random reflections on health services*, London: Nuffield Provincial Hospitals Trust.

Cohen, S. (2001) *States of denial. Knowing about atrocities and suffering*, Cambridge: Polity Press.

Cole, A. (2005) 'UK GP activity exceeds expectations', *British Medical Journal*, vol 331, p 536.

Cole, D., with Utting, J. (1962) *The economic circumstances of old people*, Welwyn: Codicote Press.

Colvin, C. (2001) 'The great CEO pay heist. Executive compensation has become highway robbery – we all know that. But how did it happen? And why can't we stop it?', *Fortune Magazine*, 25 June. Available at: http://money.cnn.com/magazines/fortune/fortune_archive/2001/06/25/305448/

Connors, J. and Heaven, P.C. (1990) 'Belief in a just world and attitudes toward AIDS sufferers', *The Journal of Social Psychology*, vol 130, no 4, pp 559–60.

Considine, M. (2000) 'Selling the unemployed: the performance of bureaucracies, firms and non-profits in the new Australian "Market" for unemployment assistance', *Social Policy and Administration*, vol 34, no 3, pp 274–95.

Cooper, D., Hinings, B., Greenwood, R. and Brown, J. (1996) 'Sedimentation and transformation in organizational change: the case of Canadian law firms', *Organization Studies*, vol 17, no 4, pp 623–47.

Crisp, B., Anderson, M., Orme, J. and Green Lister, P. (2006) 'What can we learn about social work assessment from the textbooks?', *Journal of Social Work*, vol 6, no 3, pp 337–59.

Curtis, L., Moriarty, J. and Netten, A. (2010) 'The expected working life of a social worker', *British Journal of Social Work*, vol 40, no 5, pp 1628–43.

Dalbert, C., Montada, L. and Schmitt, M. (1987) 'Glaube an eine gerechte Welt als Motiv: Validierungskorrelate zweier Skalen', *Psychologische Beitrage*, vol 29, pp 596–615.

Davenport, T.H. (1995) 'Business process reengineering: where it's been, where it's going', in V. Grover and W.J. Kettinger (eds) *Business process change: concepts, methods and techniques*, Harrisburg, PA: Idea Group Publishing, pp 1–13.

Davies, J.S. (2009) 'The limits of joined-up government: towards a political analysis', *Public Administration*, vol 87, no 1, pp 80–96.

Davis, K.C. (1969) *Discretionary justice: a preliminary inquiry*, Baton Rouge, LA: Louisiana State University Press.

Davison, R.C. (1938) *British unemployment policy: the modern phase since 1930*, London: Longman Green.

De Bruijn, H. (2007) *Managing performance in the public sector*, London: Routledge.

Deci, E. and Ryan, R. (2000) 'The "what" and "why" of goal pursuits: human needs and the self-determination of behavior', *Psychological Inquiry*, vol 11, no 4, pp 227–68.

Dejonckheere, J., Flecker, J. and Van Hootegem, G. (2001) 'Der Beitrag der IKT zum Wandel der Arbeitsorganisation – Ursache, Trendsetter oder Hindernis?', in J. Flecker and H.G. Zilian (eds) *e_work: Neue Jobchancen – real oder virtuell?*, Denkwerkstätte Wien, Tagungsband, Wien: Arbeitsmarktservice Wien/FORBA, pp 1–17.

Denzin, N.K. (1978) *The research act: a theoretical introduction to sociological methods*, New York, NY: McGraw-Hill.

Derthick, M. (1972) *New towns in town*, Washington, DC: The Urban Institute.

DH (Department of Health) (2005) *Independence, well-being and choice: our vision for the future of social care for adults in England*, London: DH.

DH (2010a) *Putting people first: personal budgets for older people – making it happen*, London: DH.

DH (2010b) *Changing lives together: using person-centred outcomes to measure results in social care*, London: DH.

DHSS (Department of Health and Social Security) and SBC (Supplementary Benefits Commission) (1977) *Low incomes: evidence to the Royal Commission on the Distribution of Incomes and Wealth*, London: HMSO.

Dias, J.J. and Maynard-Moody, S. (2007) 'For-profit welfare: contracts, conflicts, and the performance paradox', *Journal of Public Administration Research and Theory*, vol 17, no 2, pp 189–211.

Dickens, J. (2011) 'Social work in England at a watershed – as always: from the Seebohm Report to the Social Work Task Force', *British Journal of Social Work*, vol 41, no 1, pp 22–39.

Diefenbach, T. (2009) 'New Public Management in public sector organisations: the dark sides of managerialistic "enlightenment"', *Public Administration*, vol 87, no 4, pp 892–909.

Divosa (2011) *Programma vakmanschap in de re-integratiesector*, Utrecht: Divosa.

Dodson, L. (2009) *The moral underground: how ordinary Americans subvert the unfair economy*, New York, NY: New Press.

Donnison, D. (1977) 'Against discretion', *New Society*, 15 September.

Donnison, D. (1982) *The politics of poverty*, Oxford: Martin Robertson.

Dubois, V. (2009) 'Towards a critical policy ethnography. Lessons from fieldwork on welfare control in France', *Critical Policy Studies*, vol 3, no 2, pp 219–37.

Dubois, V. (2010) *The bureaucrat and the poor: encounters in French welfare offices*, New York, NY: Ashgate Publishing.

Duffy, S. (1996) *Unlocking the imagination*, London: Choice Press.

Duffy, S. (2005) *Keys to citizenship: a guide to getting good support for people with learning disabilities*, Birkenhead: Paradigm.

Duffy, S. (2010) 'The citizenship theory of social justice: exploring the meaning of personalisation for social workers', *Journal of Social Work Practice*, vol 24, no 3, pp 253–67.

Dunkel, W. (2011) 'Arbeit in sozialen Dienstleistungsorganisationen: die Interaktion mit dem Klienten', in A. Evers, R.G. Heinze and T. Olk (eds) *Handbuch Soziale Dienste*, Wiesbaden: VS Verlag, pp 187–205.

Dunleavy, P., Margetts, H., Bastow, S. and Tinkler, J. (2008) 'Australian e-government in comparative perspective', *Australian Journal of Political Science*, vol 43, no 1, pp 13–26.

Durkheim, E. (1982) *The rules of sociological method and selected texts on sociology and its method* (ed S. Lukes), London: Macmillan.

Durose, M.R., Smith, E.L. and Langan, P.A. (2007) *Contacts between police and the public*, Washington, DC: Bureau of Justice Statistics.

Dworkin, R.M. (1977) *Taking rights seriously*, Cambridge, MA: Harvard University Press.

Eardley, T., Bradshaw, J., Ditch, J., Gough, I. and Whiteford, P. (1996) *Social assistance in OECD countries: synthesis report*, London: HMSO.

Ecorys-NEI (Netherlands Economisch Institute) (2004) *Regeldruk voor OCW-instellingen. Een onderzoek in de sectoren PO, BVE, OWB, WO en podiumkunsten*, Rotterdam: Donker van Heel, P.A., Zutphen, van F. and Zoon, C.P.A.

Edelman, L. (1992) 'Legal ambiguity and symbolic structures: organizational mediation of civil rights law', *American Journal of Sociology*, vol 97, pp 1531–76.

Edelman, M. (1964) *The symbolic uses of politics*, Urbana, IL: University of Illinois Press.

Ehrlich, I. (1972) 'The deterrent effect of criminal law enforcement', *Journal of Legal Studies*, vol 1, no 2, pp 259–76.

Eichhorst, W. and Konle-Seidl, R. (2008) 'Contingent convergence: a comparative analysis of activation policies', IZA Discussion Paper No 3905.

Eichhorst, W., Grienberger-Zingerle, M. and Konle-Seidl, R. (2008) 'Activation policies in Germany: from status protection to basic income support', in W. Eichhorst, O. Kaufmann and R. Konle-Seidl (eds) *Bringing the jobless into work?*, Berlin: Springer.

Elias, N. (2009) *Essays on the sociology of knowledge and the sciences*, Dublin: UCD Press.

Ellis, K. (1993) *Squaring the circle: user and carer participation in needs assessment*, York: Joseph Rowntree Foundation/Community Care.

Ellis, K. (2007) 'Direct payments and social work practice: the significance of "street-level bureaucracy" in determining eligibility', *British Journal of Social Work*, vol 37, no 3, pp 405–22.

Ellis, K. (2011) '"Street-level bureaucracy" revisited: the changing face of frontline discretion in adult social care in England', *Social Policy and Administration*, vol 45, no 3, pp 221–44.

Ellis, K. (2013a) 'Personalisation, ambiguity and conflict: Matland's model of policy implementation and the "transformation" of adult social care in England', *Policy and Politics*. Available at: doi. org/10.1332/030557312X655828

Ellis, K. (2013b) 'Professional discretion and adult social work: exploring its nature and scope on the front line of personalisation', *British Journal of Social Work*, doi: 10.1093/bjsw/bct076, pp 1–18.

Ellis, K., Davis, A. and Rummery, K. (1999) 'Needs assessment "street-level bureaucracy" and the new community care', *Journal of Social Policy and Administration*, vol 33, no 3, pp 262–80.

Elmore, R. (1979) 'Backward mapping: implementation research and policy decisions', *Political Science Quarterly*, vol 94, pp 601–16.

Emery, Y. and Giauque, D. (2014) 'Employment in the public and private sectors: toward a confusing hybridization process', *International Review of Administrative Sciences*', vol 71, no 4, pp 640–57.

Enthoven, A.C. (1985) *Reflections on the management of the National Health Service: an American looks at incentives to efficiency in health services management in the UK*, London: Nuffield Provincial Hospitals Trust.

Epp, C. and Maynard-Moody, S. (2010) 'Pulled over: mutual disrespect and punishing drivers during traffic stops', *Law and Society Association*, 27–30 May.

Epp, C., Maynard-Moody, S. and Haider-Markel, D. (2014) *Pulled over: how police stops define race and citizenship*, Chicago, IL: University of Chicago Press.

Esping-Andersen, G. (1990) *The three worlds of welfare capitalism*, Cambridge: Polity.

Etzioni, A. (1961) *A comparative analysis of complex organizations*, New York, NY: The Free Press.

Etzioni, A. (1969) *The semi professions and their organization*, New York, NY: Free Press.

Evans, T. (2010) *Professional discretion in welfare services*, Aldershot: Ashgate.

Evans, T. (2011) 'Professionals, managers and discretion: critiquing street-level bureaucracy', *British Journal of Social Work*, vol 41, no 2, pp 368–86.

Evans, T. (2013) 'Organisational rules and discretion in adult social work', *British Journal of Social Work*, vol 43, no 4, pp 739–58.

Evans, T. (2014) 'The moral economy of street-level service', in *Croatian and comparative public administration*, vol 14, no 2, pp 281-399.

Evans, T. and Hardy, M. (2010) *Evidence and knowledge for practice*, Cambridge: Polity.

Evans, T. and Harris, J. (2004) 'Street-level bureaucracy, social work and the (exaggerated) death of discretion', *British Journal of Social Work*, vol 34, no 6, pp 871–95.

Evetts, J. (2003) 'Professionalism. Occupational change in the modern world', *International Sociology*, vol 18, no 2, pp 395–415.

Evetts, J. (2009) 'New professionalism and New Public Management: changes, continuities and consequences', *Comparative Sociology*, vol 8, no 2, pp 247–66.

Expenditure Committee (General Sub-Committee) (1977) *The civil service* (vols I–III, 1976–77), July, London: HMSO.

Exworthy, M. and Halford, S. (eds) (1999) *Professionals and the new managerialism in the public sector*, Buckingham: Open University Press.

Ezzy, D. (2002) *Qualitative analysis: practice and innovation*, London: Routledge.

Federal Assembly (1982) 'Loi fédérale sur l'assurance-chômage obligatoire et l'indemnité en cas d'insolvabilité', 25 June, Berne.

Federal Council (1983) 'Ordonnance sur l'assurance-chômage obligatoire et l'indemnité en cas d'insolvabilité', 31 August, Berne.

Fehr, R. and Sunde, U. (2009) 'Did the Hartz reforms speed-up the matching process? A macro-evaluation using empirical matching functions', *German Economic Review*, vol 10, no 3, pp 284–316.

Feinstein, J.S. (1989) 'The safety regulation of US nuclear power plants: violations, inspections, and abnormal occurrences', *Journal of Political Economy*, vol 97, no 1, pp 115–54.

Ferguson, I. (2007) 'Increasing user choice or privatizing risk? The antinomies of personalisation', *British Journal of Social Work*, vol 37, no 3, pp 387–403.

Ferguson, I. (2012) 'Personalisation, social justice and social work: a reply to Simon Duffy', *Journal of Social Work Practice: Psychotherapeutic Approaches to Health, Welfare and the Community*, vol 26, no 1, pp 55–73.

Ferrie, J. (ed) (2004) *Work stress and health: the Whitehall II study*, London: Council of Civil Service Unions, Cabinet Office and University College London. Available at: http://www.ucl.ac.uk/whitehallII/pdf/Whitehallbooklet_1_.pdf

Fineman, S. (1998) 'Street level bureaucrats and the social construction of environmental control', *Organization Studies*, vol 19, no 6, pp 953–74.

Fink, H. and Wilkins, W. (1976) 'Belief in a just world, interpersonal trust, and attitudes', paper presented at the Eastern Psychological Association, 22 April.

Fleckenstein, T. (2008) 'Restructuring welfare for the unemployed: the Hartz legislation in Germany', *Journal for European Social Policy*, vol 18, no 2, pp 177–88.

Flynn, R. and Williams, G. (eds) (1997) *Contracting for health: quasi-markets and the National Health Service*, Oxford: Oxford University Press.

Flynn, R., Williams, G. and Pickard, S. (1996) *Markets and networks: contracting in community health services*, Buckingham: Open University Press.

Foldy, E.G. and Buckley, T.R. (2010) 'Re-creating street-level practice: the role of routines, work groups, and team', *Journal of Public Administration Research and Theory*, vol 20, no 1, pp 23–52.

Folkman, S. and Lazarus, R.S. (1980) 'An analysis of coping in a middle-aged community sample', *Journal of Health and Social Behavior*, vol 21, no 3, pp 219–39.

Foster, J. (2010) 'Thinking on the front line: how creativity can improve self-directed support', *Journal of Social Work Practice*, vol 24, no 3, pp 283–99.

Foster, M., Harris, J., Jackson, K., Morgan, H. and Glendinning, C. (2006) 'Personalised social care for adults with disabilities: a problematic concept for frontline practice', *Health and Social Care in the Community*, vol 14, no 2, pp 125–35.

Foster, M., Harris, J., Jackson, K. and Glendinning, C. (2008) 'Practitioners' documentation of assessment and care planning in social care: the opportunities for organisational learning', *British Journal of Social Work*, vol 38, no 3, pp 546–60.

Francis, R. (2013) *Independent inquiry into care provided by Mid Staffordshire NHS Foundation Trust, January 2005–March 2009, volume I*, London: The Stationery Office.

Freidson, E. (1970a) *Professional dominance*, New York, NY: Atherton.

Freidson, E. (1970b) *Profession of medicine: a study of the sociology of applied knowledge*, Chicago, IL: University of Chicago Press.

Freidson, E. (1994) *Professionalism reborn: theory, prophecy and policy*, Cambridge: Polity Press.

Freidson, E. (2001) *Professionalism, the third logic. On the practice of knowledge*, Chicago, IL: University of Chicago Press.

Frey, B. (1997) 'A constitution for knaves crowds out civic virtues', *Economic Journal*, vol 107, no 443, pp 1043–53.

Frölich, M., Lechner, M., Behncke, S., Hammer, S., Iten, R., Schmidt, N., Menegale, S. and Lehmann, A. (2007) 'Einfluss der RAV auf die Wiedereingliederung von Stellensuchenden', Abschlussbericht im Auftrag des seco: Seco Publikation 2007.

Furnham, A. and Gunter, B. (1984) 'Just world beliefs and attitudes towards the poor', *British Journal of Social Psychology*, vol 23, no 3, pp 265–9.

Furnham, A. and Procter, E. (1989) 'Belief in a just world: review and critique of the individual difference literature', *British Journal of Social Psychology*, vol 28, no 4, pp 365–84.

Furnham, A. and Procter, E. (1992) 'Sphere-specific just world beliefs and attitudes to AIDS', *Human Relations*, vol 45, no 3, pp 265–84.

Furnham, A., Swami, V., Voracek, M. and Stieger, S. (2009) 'Demographic correlates of just world and unjust beliefs in an Austrian sample', *Psychological Reports*, vol 105, no 3 pt 1, p 989.

Gardner, A. (2011) *Personalisation in social work*, Exeter: Learning Matters.

Geertz, C. (1973) *The interpretation of cultures*, New York, NY: Fontana.

Giddens, A. (1979) *Central problems in social theory: action, structure and contradiction in social analysis*, Berkeley and Los Angeles, CA: University of California Press.

Giddens, A. (1986) *The constitution of society: outline of the theory of structuration*, Berkeley and Los Angeles, CA: University of California Press.

Gilbert, B.B. (1970) *British social policy 1914–39*, Bedford: Batsford.

Gilbert, N. (2002) *Transformation of the welfare state. The silent surrender of public responsibility*, Oxford: Oxford University Press.

Gilliom, J. (2001) *Overseers of the poor: surveillance, resistance and the limits of privacy*, Chicago, IL: University of Chicago Press.

Glasby, J. and Littlechild, R. (2009) *Direct payments and personal budgets. Putting personalisation into practice* (2nd edn), Bristol: The Policy Press.

Glaser, B. and Strauss, A.C. (1967) *The discovery of grounded theory: strategies for qualitative research*, New York, NY: De Gruyter.

Glendinning, C. (2008) 'Increasing choice and control for older and disabled people: a critical review of new developments in England', *Social Policy and Administration*, vol 42, no 5, pp 451–69.

Glendinning, C., Arksey, H., Jones, K., Moran, N., Netten, A. and Rabiee, P. (2008) *The national evaluation of the Individual Budgets Pilot Programme: experiences and implications for care coordinators and managers*, York: Social Policy Research Unit, University of York.

Gofen, A. (2013) 'Mind the gap: dimensions and influence of street-level divergence', *Journal of Public Administration Research and Theory*, online first, 20 August 2013, doi: 10.1093/jopart/mut037.

Goggin, M.L. (1986) 'The "too few cases/too many variables" problem in implementation research', *Political Research Quarterly*, vol 39, pp 328–47.

Goldthorpe, J., Lockwood, D., Bechhofer, F. and Platt, J. (1968a) *The affluent worker. Industrial attitudes and behavior*, Cambridge: Cambridge University Press.

Goldthorpe, J., Lockwood, D., Bechhofer, F. and Platt, J. (1968b) *The affluent worker. Political attitudes and behavior*, Cambridge: Cambridge University Press.

Goldthorpe, J., Lockwood, D., Bechhofer, F. and Platt, J. (1969) *The affluent worker in the class structure*, Cambridge: Cambridge University Press.

Goodsell, C.T. (ed) (1981) *The public encounter*, Bloomington, IN: Indiana University Press.

Goodsell, C.T. (1983) *The case for bureaucracy*, New Jersey, NJ: Chatham House.

Gormley, W.T., Jr (1998) 'Regulatory enforcement styles', *Political Research Quarterly*, no 51, pp 363–83.

Gouldner, A. (1954) *Patterns of industrial bureaucracy*, Glencoe, IL: Free Press.

Gray, W.B. and Scholz, J.T. (1991) 'Analyzing the equity and efficiency of OSHA enforcement', *Law and Policy*, vol 13, no 3, pp 185–214.

Greener, I. (2004) 'Talking to health managers about change: heroes, villains and simplification', *Journal of Health Organization and Management*, vol 18, pp 321–35.

Greenwood, W. (1933) *Love on the dole*, London: Jonathan Cape.

Griggs, S., Norval, A.J. and Wagenaar, H. (2014) *Practice and freedom: decentred governance, conflict and democratic participation*, Cambridge: Cambridge University Press.

Gulland, J. (2011) 'Assessing capacity for work: Employment and Support Allowance in the U.K.', paper presented at the annual meeting of the European Social Policy Association (ESPAnet) Conference, Valencia, Spain.

Haas, E.B. (1964) *Beyond the nation-state. Functionalism and international organization*, Stanford, CA: Stanford University Press.

Haas, P.M. (1992) 'Epistemic communities and international policy co-ordination', *International Organisation*, vol 46, no 1, pp 1–35.

Hagen, M. and Kubicek, H. (eds) (2000) *One-stop-government in Europe: results from 11 national surveys*, Bremen: Universität Bremen.

Hainmüller, J., Hofmann, B., Krug, G. and Wolf, K. (2011) 'Do lower caseloads improve the effectiveness of active labor market policies? New evidence from German employment offices', LASER Discussion Papers 52.

Hall, A.S. (1974) *The point of entry: a study of client reception in the social services*, London: Allen and Unwin.

Hall, P., Land, H., Parker, R. and Webb, A. (1975) *Change, choice and conflict in social policy*, London: Heinemann.

Hallett, T. (2010) 'The myth incarnate: recoupling processes, turmoil, and inhabited institutions in an urban elementary school', *American Sociological Review*, vol 75, no 1, pp 52–74.

Hammersley, M. and Atkinson, P. (1995) *Ethnography. Principles in practice*, Routledge: London.

Handler, J.F. and Hollingsworth, E.J. (1971) *The 'deserving poor': a study of welfare administration*, Chicago, IL: Markham.

Harcourt, B.E. (2007) *Against prediction: punishing and policing in an actuarial age*, Chicago, IL: University of Chicago Press.

Harlow, E. (2003) 'New managerialism, social services departments and social work practice today', *Practice*, vol 15, no 2, pp 29–44.

Harris, D.A. (1997) '"Driving while black"' and all other traffic offenses: the Supreme Court and pretextual traffic stops', *Journal of Criminal Law & Criminology*, vol 87, no 2, pp 544–82.

Harris, D.A. (2002) *Profiles in injustice: why racial profiling cannot work*, New York, NY: The New Press.

Harris, J. (1998) 'Scientific management, bureau-professionalism and new managerialism. The labour process of state social work', *British Journal of Social Work*, vol 28, pp 839–62.

Harris, J. (2008) 'State social work: constructing the present from moments in the past', *British Journal of Social Work*, vol 38, pp 662–79.

Harrison, S. (1988) *Managing the National Health Service: shifting the frontier?*, London: Chapman and Hall.

Harrison, S. (2002) 'New Labour, modernisation and the medical labour process', *Journal of Social Policy*, vol 31, no 3, pp 465–85.

Harrison, S. (2004) 'Governing medicine: governance, science and practice', in A.G. Gray and S. Harrison (eds) *Governing medicine: theory and practice*, Buckingham: Open University Press, pp 180–7.

Harrison, S. (2009) 'Co-optation, commodification and the medical model: governing UK medicine since 1991', *Public Administration*, vol 87, no 2, pp 184–97.

Harrison, S. and Ahmad, W.I.U. (2000) 'Medical autonomy and the UK state 1975 to 2025', *Sociology*, vol 34, no 1, pp 129–46.

Harrison, S. and Checkland, K. (2009) 'Evidence-based practice in UK health policy', in J. Gabe and M.W. Calnan (eds) *The new sociology of the health service*, London: Routledge, pp 121–42.

Harrison, S. and Dowswell, G. (2002) 'Autonomy and bureaucratic accountability in primary care: what English general practitioners say', *Sociology of Health and Illness*, vol 24, no 2, pp 208–26.

Harrison, S. and Hunter, D.J. (1994) *Rationing health care*, London: Institute for Public Policy Research.

Harrison, S. and Lim, J. (2003) 'The frontier of control: doctors and managers in the NHS 1966 to 1997', *Clinical Governance International*, vol 8, no 2, pp 13–17.

Harrison, S. and McDonald, R. (2008) *The politics of health care in Britain*, London: Sage.

Harrison, S., Hunter, D., Marnoch, G. and Pollitt, C. (1992) *Just managing*, Basingstoke: Macmillan.

Harrits, G.S. and Møller, M.Ø. (2013) 'Prevention at the front line: how home nurses, pedagogues, and teachers transform public worry into decisions on special efforts', *Public Management Review*, vol 16, no 4, pp 447–80.

Hasenfeld, Y. (1983) *Human service organisations*, Englewood Cliffs, NJ: Prentice Hall.

Hasenfeld, Y. (1999) 'Social services and welfare-to-work: prospects for the social work profession', *Administration in Social Work*, vol 23, no 3, pp 185–99.

Hasenfeld, Y. (2010) 'The attributes of human service organizations', in Y. Hasenfeld (ed) *Human services as complex organizations* (2nd edn), London: Sage, pp 9–32.

Hasenfeld, Y. and Garrow, E.E. (2012) 'Non-profit human service organizations, social rights, and advocacy in a neo-liberal welfare state', *Social Service Review*, vol 86, no 2, pp 295–322.

Hatton, C., Waters, J., Duffy, S., Senker, J., Crosby, N., Poll, C., Tyson, A., O'Brien, J. and Towell, D. (2008) *A report on In Control's second phase: evaluation and learning 2005–2007*, London: In Control.

Hawkins, K. (1984) *Environment and enforcement, regulation and the social definition of pollution*, Oxford: Oxford University Press.

Haywood, S and Alaszewski, A. (1980) *Crisis in the health service: the politics of management*, London: Croom Helm.

Health and Safety Executive (2013) 'Stress and Psychological Disorders'. Available at: http://www.hse.gov.uk/statistics/index.htm

Hedge, D.M., Menzel, D.C. and Williams, G.H. (1988) 'Regulatory attitudes and behavior: the case of surface mining regulation', *Western Political Quarterly*, vol 41, pp 323–40.

Helland, E. (1998) 'The enforcement of pollution control laws: inspections, violations, and self-reporting', *Review of Economics and Statistics*, vol 80, no 1, pp 141–53.

Henderson, J. and Seden, J. (2003) 'What do we want from social care managers? Aspirations and realities', in J. Reynolds, J. Henderson, J. Seden, J. Charlesworth and A. Bullman (eds) *The managing care reader*, London: Routledge.

Henwood, M. and Hudson, B. (2007) *Here to stay? Self-directed support: aspiration and implementation. A review for the Department of Health*, Heathencote: Melanie Henwood Associates.

Herd, D., Mitchell, A. and Lightman, E. (2005) 'Rituals of degradation: administration as policy in the Ontario Works programme', *Social Policy and Administration*, vol 39, no 1, pp 65–79.

Héritier, A. and Eckert, S. (2008) 'New modes of governance in the shadow of hierarchy: self-regulation by industry in Europe', *Journal of Public Policy*, vol 28, pp 113–38.

Hernes, T. (2005) 'Four ideal-type organizational responses to New Public Management reforms and some consequences', *International Review of Administrative Sciences*, vol 71, no 1, pp 5–17.

Herzberg, F. (1990) 'One more time: how do you motivate employees?', in Harvard Business Review (ed) *Manage people, not personnel*, Boston, MA: Harvard Business Review.

Hill, C.J. (2006) 'Casework job design and client outcomes in welfare-to-work offices', *Journal of Public Administration Research and Theory*, vol 16, no 2, pp 263–88.

Hill, M. (1969) 'The exercise of discretion in the National Assistance Board', *Public Administration*, vol 47, no 1, pp 75–91.

Hill, M. (1976) *The state, administration and the individual*, Glasgow: Fontana.

Hill, M. (2013) *The public policy process* (6th edn), Harlow: Pearson.

Hill, M. and Hupe, P.L. (2003) 'The multi-layer problem in implementation studies', *Public Management Review*, vol 5, no 4, pp 471–90.

Hill, M. and Hupe, P.L. (2007) 'Street-level bureaucracy and public accountability', *Public Administration*, vol 85, no 2, pp 279–99.

Hill, M. and Hupe, P.L. (2014) *Implementing public policy* (3rd edn), London: Sage.

Hill, M., Harrison, R.M., Sargeant, A.V. and Talbot V. (1973) *Men out of work*, Cambridge: Cambridge University Press.

Hirschman, A.O. (1970) *Exit, voice and loyalty. Responses to decline in firms, organizations and states*, Cambridge, MA: Harvard University Press.

HM Government (1979) *Reform of the supplementary benefits scheme*, White Paper, Cmnd 7773, London: HMSO.

HM Government (1985) *Reform of social security* (vol 1), Cmnd 9517, London: HMSO.

HM Government (2007) *Putting people first: a shared vision and commitment to the transformation of adult social care*, London: HM Government.

Hofmann, B., Krug, G., Sowa, F., Theuer, S. and Wolf, K. (2010) 'Modellprojekt in den Arbeitsagenturen: Kürzere Arbeitslosigkeit durch mehr Vermittler', IAB-Kurzbericht 09/2010.

Hofmann, B., Krug, G., Sowa, F., Theuer, S. and Wolf, K. (2012) 'Wirkung und Wirkmechanismen zusätzlicher Arbeitsvermittler(innen) auf die Arbeitslosigkeitsdauer – Analysen auf Basis eines Modellprojektes', Zeitschrift für Evaluation 1/2012, pp 7–38.

Holman, D. (2004) 'Employee well-being in call centres', in S. Deery and N. Kinnie (eds) *Call centres and human resource management*, Basingstoke: Palgrave, pp 223–44.

Homans, G. (1950) *The humans group*, New York, NY: Harcourt, Brace.

Hood, C. (1983) *The tools of government*, London: Macmillan.

Hood, C. and Peters, G. (2004) 'The middle aging of New Public Management: into the age of paradox?', *Journal of Public Administration Research and Theory*, vol 14, no 3, pp 267–82.

Hood, C., Rothstein, H. and Baldwin, R. (2001) *The government of risk: understanding risk regulation regimes*, Oxford: Oxford University Press.

House of Commons (1943) *Hansard*, vol 395, London: HM Stationery Office.

Houston, S. (2010) 'Beyond homo economicus: recognition, self-realization and social work', *British Journal of Social Work*, vol 40, no 3, pp 841–57.

Howe, D. (1991) 'Knowledge, power and the shape of social work practice', in M. Davies (ed) *The sociology of social work*, London: Routledge.

Howlett, M. (1991) 'Policy instruments, policy styles and policy implementation: national approaches to theories of instrument choice', *Policy Studies Journal*, vol 19, no 2, pp 1–21.

Huby, M. and Dix, G. (1992) *Evaluating the Social Fund*, Department of Social Security Research Report, London: HMSO.

Hudson, B. (1993) 'Michael Lipsky and street level bureaucracy: a neglected perspective', in M. Hill (ed) *The policy process: a reader*, Hemel Hempstead: Harvester Wheatsheaf.

Hudson, B. (2009) 'Captives of bureaucracy', *Community Care*, 9 April.

Hunter, B. and Segrott, J. (2008) 'Re-mapping client journeys and professional identities: a review of the literature on clinical pathways', *International Journal of Nursing Studies*, vol 45, pp 608–25.

Hupe, P.L. (2010) 'The autonomy of professionals in public service', in T. Jansen, G. van den Brink and J. Kole (eds) *Professional pride: a powerful force*, Amsterdam: Boom, pp 118–37.

Hupe, P.L. (2012) 'Determinants of discretion: explanatory approaches in street-level bureaucracy research', working paper written during a Visiting Fellowship 2012–13 at All Souls College, Oxford.

Hupe, P.L. (2013) 'Dimensions of discretion: specifying the object of street-level bureaucracy research', *Der Moderne Staat. Zeitschrift für Public Policy, Recht und Management*, vol 6, no 2, pp 425–40.

Hupe, P.L. (2014) 'What happens on the ground: persistent issues in implementation research', *Public Policy and Administration*, vol 29, no 2, pp 164–82.

Hupe, P.L. and Buffat, A. (2014) 'A public service gap: capturing contexts in a comparative approach of street-level bureaucracy', *Public Management Review*, vol 16, no 4, pp 548–69.

Hupe, P.L. and Hill, M. (2006) 'The three action levels of governance: re-framing the policy process beyond the stages model', in B.G. Peters and J. Pierre (eds) *Handbook of public policy*, London: Sage, pp 13–30.

Hupe, P.L. and Hill, M. (2007) 'Street-level bureaucracy and public accountability', *Public Administration*, vol 85, no 2, pp 279–99.

Hupe, P.L. and Van der Krogt, T. (2013) 'Professionals dealing with pressures', in M. Noordegraaf and B. Steijn (eds) *Professionals under pressure. The reconfiguration of professional work in changing public services*, Amsterdam: Amsterdam University Press, pp 55–72.

Hutter, B.M. (1989) 'Variations in regulatory enforcement styles', *Law and Policy*, vol 11, no 2, pp 153–74.

Huws, U. (2009) 'Working at the interface: call centre labour in a global economy', *Work Organisation, Labour & Globalisation*, vol 3, no 1, pp 1–8.

Hvinden, B. (1994) *Divided against itself: a study of integration in welfare bureaucracy*, Oslo: Scandinavian Universities Press.

Ingram, H. (1977) 'Policy implementation through bargaining: the case of federal grants-in-aid', *Public Policy*, vol 25, pp 501–26.

Ipsos-MORI (2009) 'Opinion of professions – index to trend data'. Available at: http://www.ipsos-mori.com/researchpublications/researcharchive/96/Opinion-of-Professions-8212-Index-to-Trend-Data.aspx?view=wide

Isaacs, W. (1999) *Dialogue and the art of thinking together*, New York, NY: Currency-Doubleday.

Jacobsen, K.D., Jensen, T. and Aarseth, T. (1982) 'Fordelingspolitikkens forvaltning', *Sosiologi i dag*, no 3, pp 29–49.

Jamous, H. and Peloille, B. (1970) 'Changes in the French university-hospital system', in J.A. Jackson (ed) *Professions and professionalisation*, Cambridge: Cambridge University Press, pp 111–52.

Jeffries, D. (2003) 'Save our soul', *British Journal of General Practice*, vol 53, no 496, p 888.

Jervis, R. (1997) *System effects: complexity in political and social life*, Princeton, NJ: Princeton University Press.

Jewell, C.J. (2007) *Agents of the welfare state*, New York, NY, and Basingstoke: Palgrave Macmillan.

Jewell, C.J. and Glaser, B.E. (2006) 'Toward a general analytic framework: organizational setting, policy goals and street-level behaviour', *Administration and Society*, vol 38, no 3, pp 335–64.

Johnson, P. (1999) 'The measurement of social security convergence: the case of European public pension systems since 1950', *Journal of Social Policy*, vol 28, no 4, pp 595–618.

Jones, K. and Netten, A. (2010) 'The costs of change: a case study of the process implementing individual budgets across pilot local authorities in England', *Health and Social Care in the Community*, vol 18, no 1, pp 51–8.

Jordan, B. (2001) 'Tough love: social work, social exclusion and the third way', *British Journal of Social Work*, vol 31, no 4, pp 527–46.

Jordana, J. and Levi-Faur, D. (eds) (2004) *The politics of regulation: institutions and regulatory reforms for the age of governance*, Cheltenham: Edward Elgar.

Jørgensen, H. I. Nørup & K. Baadsgaard (2010), 'Employment policy restructuring and the "de-professionalization" question - Do recent Danish developments give an answer?' Aalborg: Paper for the RESQ conference, Copenhagen, June 2010.

Jorna, F. and Wagenaar, P. (2007) 'The iron cage strengthened? Discretion and digital discipline', *Public Administration*, vol 85, no 1, pp 189–214.

Kagan, R. (1984) 'Regulatory enforcement styles', paper prepared for the Annual Meeting of the Law and Society Association, Boston, MA, 7–10 June.

Kagan, R. (1994) 'Regulatory enforcement', in D.H. Rosenbloom and R.D. Schwartz (eds) *Handbook of regulation and administrative law*, New York, NY: Marcel Dekker, pp 383–422.

Kagan, R. and Scholz, J.T. (1984) 'The "criminology of the corporation" and regulatory enforcement strategies', in K. Hawkins and J. Thomas (eds) *Enforcing regulation*, Boston, MA: Kluwer-Nijhoff.

Kast, F.E. and Rosenzweig, J.E. (1972) 'General systems theory: applications for organization and management', *Academy of Management Journal*, vol 15, no 4, pp 447–65.

Kast, F.E. and Rosenzweig, J.E. (1973) *Contingency views of organization and management*, Chicago, IL: Science Research Associates.

Kaufman, H. (1960) *The forest ranger: a study in administrative behavior*, Baltimore, MD: The Johns Hopkins University Press.

Keast, R. (2011) 'Joined up governance in Australia: how the past can inform the future', *International Journal of Public Administration*, vol 34, no 4, pp 221–31.

Keast, R., Mandell, M. and Brown, K. (2006) 'Mixing state, market and network governance modes. The role of government in "crowded" policy domains', *International Journal of Organization Theory and Behavior*, vol 9, no 1, pp 27–50.

Keiser, L.R. (1999) 'State bureaucratic discretion and the administration of social welfare programs: the case of social security disability', *Journal of Public Administration Research and Theory*, vol 9, no 1, pp 87–106.

Keiser, L.R. (2001) 'Street-level bureaucrats, administrative power and the manipulation of federal social security disability programs', *State Politics and Policy Quarterly*, vol 1, no 2, pp 144–64.

Keiser, L.R. (2008) 'Politics, decision-making resources and program generosity', unpublished paper.

Keiser, L.R. and Meier, K.J. (1996) 'Policy design, bureaucratic incentives, and public management: the case of child support enforcement', *Journal of Public Administration Research and Theory*, vol 6, no 3, pp 337–64.

Keiser, L.R. and Soss, J. (1998) 'With good cause: bureaucratic discretion and the politics of child support enforcement', *American Journal of Political Science*, vol 42, no 4, pp 1133–56.

Keiser, L.R, Wilkins, V., Meier, K. and Holland, C. (2002) 'Lipstick and logarithms: gender, identity, and representative bureaucracy', *American Political Science Review*, vol 96, no 3, pp 553–65.

Kemshall, H. (2010) 'Risk rationalities in contemporary social work policy and practice', *British Journal of Social Work*, vol 40, no 4, pp 1247–62.

Kemshall, H., Parton, N., Walsh, M. and Waterson, J. (1997) 'Concepts of risk in relation to organizational structure and functioning within the personal social services and probation', *Social Policy and Administration*, vol 31, no 3, pp 213–32.

Kirkpatrick, I. (1999) 'The worst of both worlds? Public services without market of bureaucracy', *Public Money and Management*, vol 19, no 4, pp 7–14.

Kirkpatrick, I., Ackroyd, S. and Walker, R. (2005) *The new managerialism and public service professions. Change in health, social services and housing*, New York, NY: Palgrave MacMillan.

Kissling-Näf, I. and Wälti, S. (2007) 'The implementation of public policies', in U. Klöti, P. Knoepfel, H. Kriesi, W. Linder, Y. Papadopoulos and P. Sciarini (eds) *Handbook of Swiss politics* (2nd edn), Zürich: NZZ Verlag, pp 501–24.

Kjørstad, M. (2005) 'Between professional ethics and bureaucratic rationality: the challenging ethical position of social workers who are faced with implementing a workfare policy', *European Journal of Social Work*, vol 8, no 4, pp 381–98.

Klein, R.E., Day, P. and Redmayne, S. (1996) *Managing scarcity: priority setting and rationing in the National Health Service*, Buckingham: Open University Press.

Kleinke, C. and Meyer, C. (1990) 'Evaluation of rape victim by men and women with high and low belief in a just world', *Psychology of Women Quarterly*, vol 14, no 3, pp 343–53.

Klijn E.-H., Koppenjan, J. and Termeer, K. (1995) 'Managing networks in the public sector: a theoretical study of management strategies in policy networks', *Public Administration*, vol 73, pp 437–54.

Klijn, E. and Koppenjan, J. (1997) 'Beleidsnetwerken als theoretische benadering: Een tussenbalans', *Beleidswetenschap*, vol 2, no 2, pp 143–67.

Koch, S., Kupka, P. and Steinke, J. (2009) *Aktivierung, Erwerbstätigkeit und Teilhabe. Vier Jahre Grundsicherung für Arbeitsuchende*, IAB-Bibliothek, 315, Bielefeld: Bertelsmann.

Konle-Seidl, R. (2009) 'Neuregelung der Jobcenter für Hartz-IV-Empfänger', *Wirtschaftsdienst*, vol 89, no 12, pp 813–20.

Koppenjan, J.F.M. and Klijn, E.-H. (2004) *Managing uncertainties in networks*, London: Routledge.

Korteweg, A. (2003) 'Welfare reform and the subject of the working mother: "get a job, a better job, then a career"', *Theory and Society*, vol 32, no 4, pp 445–80.

Kupchik, A. (2010) *Homeroom security: school discipline in an age of fear*, New York, NY: NYU Press.

Kurunmaki, L. (2004) 'A hybrid profession: the acquisition of management accounting expertise by medical professionals', *Accounting, Organisations and Society*, vol 29, nos 3/4, pp 327–47.

Kwan, J. (2007) 'Care pathways for acute stroke care and stroke rehabilitation: from theory to evidence', *Journal of Clinical Neuroscience*, vol 14, pp 189–200.

Ladd, H. (2011) 'Education and poverty: confronting the evidence', Duke University, Sanford School of Public Policy, Working Paper Series, SAN11-01.

Lagerström, J. (2011) 'How important are caseworkers – and why? New evidence from Swedish employment offices', Working Paper Series 2011:10, IFAU – Institute for Labour Market Policy Evaluation.

Langbein, L.I. (2000) 'Ownership, empowerment and productivity: some empirical evidence on the causes and consequences of employee discretion', *Journal of Policy Analysis and Management*, vol 19, pp 427–49.

Larsen, F. (2013) 'Active labor market reform in Denmark: the role of governance in policy change', in E.Z. Brodkin and G. Marston (eds) *Work and the welfare state*, Washington, DC: Georgetown University Press.

Lasswell, H.D. (1936) *Politics: who gets what, when, how*, Cleveland, OH: Meridian Books.

Lechner, M. and Smith, J.A. (2007) 'What is the value added by caseworkers?', *Labour Economics*, vol 14, no 2, pp 135–51.

Leece, J. and Leece, D. (2011) 'Personalisation: perceptions of the role of social work in a world of brokers and budgets', *British Journal of Social Work*, vol 41, no 2, pp 204–23.

Leicht, K. and Fennel, M. (2001) *Professional work: a sociological approach*, Oxford: Blackwell.

Lempert, D. (2007) 'The belief in a just world and perceptions of fair treatment by police', ANES Pilot Study Report No nes012058.

Lenk, K. (2007) 'Reconstructing public administration theory from below', *Information Polity*, vol 12, no 4, pp 204–12.

Lenk, K., Schuppan, T. and Schaffroth, M. (2010) *Networked public administration. Organisational concept for a federal e-government Switzerland*, eCH-White Paper, Bern: Eidgenössisches Finanzdepartement.

Lens, V. (2013) 'Redress and accountability in work activation policies in the United States', in E.Z. Brodkin and G. Marston (eds) *Work and the welfare state*, Washington, DC: Georgetown University Press.

Lerner, M. (1974) 'The justice motive: equity and parity among children', *Journal of Personality and Social Psychology*, vol 29, no 4, p 539.

Lerner, M. (1980) *The belief in a just world: a fundamental delusion*, New York, NY: Plenum Press.

Lerner, M. (1991) 'The belief in a just world and the heroic motive: searching for constants in the psychology of religious ideology', *International Journal for the Psychology of Religion*, vol 1, no 1, pp 27–32.

Levi, M. (1988) *Of rule and revenue*, Berkeley, CA: University of California Press.

Levine, C.H. (1984) 'Citizenship and service delivery: the promise of coproduction', *Public Administration Review*, vol 44 (special issue), pp 178–89.

Lijphart, A. (1971) 'Comparative politics and the comparative method', *American Political Science Review*, vol 65, no 3, pp 682–93.

Lindhorst, T. and Padgett, J. (2005) 'Disjunctures for women and frontline workers: implementation of the family violence option', *Social Service Review*, vol 78, no 3, pp 405–29.

Ling, T. (2002) 'Delivering joined-up government in the UK: dimensions, issues and problems', *Public Administration*, vol 80, no 4, pp 615–42.

Lipkus, I.M., Dalbert, C. and Siegler, I.C. (1996) 'The importance of distinguishing the belief in a just world for self versus for others: implications for psychological well-being', *Personality and Social Psychology Bulletin*, vol 22, no 7, pp 666–77.

Lipsky, M. (1969) 'Toward a theory of street-level bureaucracy', discussion paper prepared for presentation at the Annual Meeting of the American Political Science Association, New York, 2–6 September, Institute for Research on Poverty Discussion Paper, University of Wisconsin.

Lipsky, M. (1971) 'Toward a theory of street-level bureaucracy', *Urban Affairs Quarterly*, vol 6, pp 391–409.

Lipsky, M. (1978) 'Standing the study of public policy implementation on its head', in W.D. Burnham and M. Wagner Weinberg (eds) *American politics and public policy*, Cambridge, MA: MIT Press, pp 391–402.

Lipsky, M. (1991) 'The paradox of managing discretionary workers in social welfare policy' in M. Adler (ed) *The sociology of social security*, Edinburgh: Edinburgh University Press.

Lipsky, M. (1980) *Street-level bureaucracy: dilemmas of the individual in public services*, New York, NY: Russell Sage Foundation.

Lipsky, M. (2010) *Street-level bureaucracy: dilemmas of the individual in public services* (30th anniversary expanded edn), New York, NY: Russell Sage Foundation.

Lister, R. (1976) *National welfare benefits handbook* (6th edn), London: CPAG.

Llewellyn, K.N. and Hoebel, E.A. (1941) *The Cheyenne way: conflict and case law in primitive jurisprudence*, Norman, OK: University of Oklahoma Press.

Lodemel, I. and Trickey, H. (eds) (2001) *An offer you can't refuse: workfare in international perspective*, Bristol: The Policy Press.

Long, C.P. and Sitkin, S.B. (2006) 'Trust in the balance: how managers integrate trust-building and task control', in R. Bachmann and A. Zaheer (eds) *Handbook of trust research*, Cheltenham: Edward Elgar, pp 87–106.

Loyens, K. (2012) 'Integrity secured. Understanding ethical decision making among street-level bureaucrats in the Belgian Labor Inspection and Federal Police', PhD dissertation, Leuven, KU Leuven.

Luhmann, N. (1995) *Funktionen und Folgen formaler Organisation* (5th edn), Berlin: Duncker und Humblot.

Lundman, R. and Kaufman, R. (2003) 'Driving while black: effects of race, ethnicity, and gender on citizen self-reports of traffic stops and police actions', *Criminology*, vol 41, no 1, pp 195–220.

Lundqvist, L. (1980) *The hare and the tortoise: clean air policies in the United States and Sweden*, Ann Arbor, MI: University of Michigan Press.

Lymbery, M. (1998) 'Care management and professional autonomy: the impact of community care legislation on social work with older people', *British Journal of Social Work*, vol 28, no 6, pp 863–78.

Lymbery, M. (2001) 'Social work at the crossroads', *British Journal of Social Work*, vol 31, no 3, pp 369–84.

Lymbery, M. (2010) 'A new vision for adult social care? Continuities and change in the care of older people', *Critical Social Policy*, vol 30, no 1, pp 5–26.

Lymbery, M. and Postle, K. (2010) 'Social work in the context of adult social care in England and the resultant implications for social work education', *British Journal of Social Work*, vol 40, no 8, pp 2502–22.

Lynes, T. (1977) 'Supplementary benefits: the legislative history', in *SBC Annual Report 1976*, Appendix A, London: DHSS/SBC.

Lyons, W. and Drew, J. (2006) *Punishing schools: fear and citizenship in American public education*, Ann Arbor, MI: University of Michigan Press.

Mangan, D. (2009) *Employment contracts for teachers as professional employees*, LSE Law, Society and Economy Working Papers 21/2009, London: London School of Economics and Political Science, Law Department.

Manning, P. (1997) *Police work*, Cambridge, MA: MIT Press.

Mannion, R. and Davies, H.T.O. (2008) 'Payment for performance in health care', *British Medical Journal*, vol 336, p 306.

Marshall, T. and Rees, A. (1985) *Social policy*, London: Hutchinson.

Marston, G. and McDonald, C. (2012) 'Getting beyond "heroic agency" in conceptualising social workers as policy actors in the twenty-first century', *British Journal of Social Work*, vol 42, no 6, pp 1022–38.

Matland, R. (1995) 'Synthesizing the implementation literature. The ambiguity-conflict model of policy implementation', *Journal of Public Administration Research and Theory*, vol 5, no 2, pp 145–74.

Maupin, J.R. (1993) 'Control, efficiency and the street-level bureaucrat', *Journal of Public Administration Research and Theory*, vol 3, no 3, pp 335–57.

May, P.J. (1993) 'Mandate design and implementation: enhancing implementation effort and regulatory styles', *Journal of Policy Analysis and Management*, vol 12, pp 634–63.

May, P.J. (1994) 'Analyzing mandate design: state mandates governing hazard-prone areas', *Publius*, vol 24, no 2, pp 1–16.

May, P.J. (2005) 'Compliance motivations: perspectives of farmers, homebuilders, and marine facilities', *Law and Policy*, vol 27, no 2, pp 317–47.

May, P.J and Burby, R.J. (1996) 'Regulatory styles and strategies: insights from the enforcement of building codes', paper prepared for the annual meeting of the Association for Public Policy and Management in Pittsburgh, 31 October–2 November, Washington and New Orleans, Department of Political Science, University of Washington and University of New Orleans.

May, P.J and Burby, R.J. (1998) 'Making sense out of regulatory enforcement', *Law and Policy*, vol 20, pp 157–82.

May, P.J. and Winter, S.C. (1999) 'Regulatory enforcement and compliance: examining Danish agro-environmental policy', *Journal of Policy Analysis and Management*, vol 18, no 4, pp 625–51.

May, P.J. and Winter, S.C. (2000) 'Reconsidering styles of regulatory enforcement: patterns in Danish agro-environmental inspection', *Law and Policy*, vol 22, no 2, pp 143–73.

May, P.J. and Winter, S.C. (2009) 'Politicians, managers, and street-level bureaucrats: influences on policy implementation', *Journal of Public Administration Research and Theory*, vol 19, no 3, pp 453–76.

May, P.J. and Winter, S.C. (2011) 'Regulatory enforcement styles and compliance', in C. Parker and V.L. Nielsen (eds) *Explaining regulatory compliance. Business responses to regulation*, Cheltenham: Edward Elgar Publishing, pp 222–44.

May, P.J. and Wood, R.S. (2003) 'At the regulatory frontlines: inspectors' enforcement styles and regulatory compliance', *Journal of Public Administration Research and Theory*, vol 13, no 2, pp 117–39.

Maynard, A.K. (1986) 'Performance Incentives', in G. Teeling-Smith (ed) *Health education and general practice*, London: Office of Health Economics.

Maynard-Moody, S. and Musheno, M. (2000) 'State agent or citizen agent: two narratives of discretion', *Journal of Public Administration Research and Theory*, vol 2, no 2, pp 329–58.

Maynard-Moody, S. and Musheno, M. (2003) *Cops, teachers, counselors: narratives of street-level judgment*, Ann Arbor, MI: University of Michigan Press.

Maynard-Moody, S. and Musheno, M. (2012) 'Social equities and inequities in practice: street-level workers as agents and pragmatists', *Public Administration Review*, vol 71, no S1, pp S16–S23.

Maynard-Moody, S. and Portillo, S. (2010) 'Street-level bureaucracy theory', in R.F. Durant and G.C. Edwards III (eds) *The Oxford handbook of American bureaucracy*, Oxford: Oxford University Press, pp 252–77.

Maynard-Moody, S., Musheno, M. and Palumbo, D. (1990) 'Street-wise social policy: resolving the dilemma of street-level influence and successful implementation', *The Western Political Quarterly*, vol 43, no 4, pp 833–48.

McDonald, A., Postle, K. and Dawson, C. (2008) 'Barriers to retaining and using professional knowledge in local authority social work practice with adults in the UK', *British Journal of Social Work*, vol 38, no 7, pp 1370–87.

McDonald, R. and Harrison, S. (2004) 'The micropolitics of clinical guidelines: an empirical study', *Policy and Politics*, vol 32, no 2, pp 223–38.

McDonald, R., Harrison, S., Checkland, K., Campbell, S.M. and Roland, M. (2007) 'Impact of financial incentives on clinical autonomy and internal motivation in primary care: an ethnographic study', *British Medical Journal*, vol 334, pp 1357–9.

McGregor, D.M. (1960) *The human side of enterprise*, New York, NY: McGraw-Hill.

Meier, K.J. (1975) 'Representative bureaucracy: an empirical analysis', *American Political Science Review*, vol 69, no 1, pp 526–42.

Meier, K.J. (1993) 'Representative bureaucracy: a theoretical and empirical exposition', in B.E. Perry (ed) *Research in public administration*, Greenwich, CT: JAI Press Inc., pp 1–35.

Meier, K.J. (1999) 'Are we sure Lasswell did it this way? Lester, Goggin and implementation research', *Policy Currents*, vol 9, no 1, pp 5–8.

Meier, K.J. and Nigro, L. (1976) 'Representative bureaucracy and policy preferences: a study in the attitudes of federal executives', *Public Administration Review*, vol 36, pp 458–69.

Meier, K.J. and O'Toole, J.J., Jr (2007) 'Modeling public management: empirical analysis of the management–performance nexus', *Public Management Review*, vol 9, no 4, pp 503–27.

Meier, K.J. and Stewart, J. (1992) 'Active representations in educational bureaucracies: policy impacts', *American Review of Public Administration*, vol 22, no 2, pp 157–71.

Meier, K.J., O'Toole, L.J., Jr and Hicklin, A. (2010) 'I've seen fire and I've seen rain: public management and performance after a natural disaster', *Administration and Society*, vol 41, no 8, pp 979–1003.

Merton, R.K. (1957) *Social theory and social structure*, Glencoe, IL: Free Press.

Meyer, J. and Rowan, B. (1977) 'Institutional organizations: formal structure as myth and ceremony', *American Journal of Sociology*, vol 83, pp 340–63.

Meyer, T., Bridgen, P. and Reidmüller, B. (eds) (2007) *Private pensions versus social inclusion: non-state provision for citizens at risk in Europe*, Cheltenham: Edward Elgar.

Meyers, M. and Nielsen, V.L. (2012) 'Street-level bureaucrats and the implementation of public policy', in B.G. Peters and J. Pierre (eds) *The Sage handbook of public administration* (2nd edn), London: Sage Publications, pp 305–18.

Meyers, M. and Vorsanger, S. (2003) 'Street-level bureaucrats and the implementation of public policy', in G. Peters and J. Pierre (eds) *Handbook of public administration*, London: Sage, pp 245–57.

Meyers, M., Glaser B. and MacDonald K. (1998) 'On the front lines of welfare delivery: are workers implementing policy reforms?', *Journal of Policy Analysis and Management*, vol 17, no 1, pp 1–22.

Meyers, M., Riccucci, N. and Lurie, I. (2001) 'Achieving goal congruence in complex environments. The case of welfare reform', *Journal of Public Administration Research and Theory*, vol 11, no 2, pp 165–201.

Midgley, M. (2001) *Science and poetry*, London: Routledge.

Milkman, R. (2002) 'High road or low road?', in J. Kelly (ed) *Industrial relations: critical perspectives on business and management*, London: Routledge.

Mills, P. and Margulies, N. (1980) 'Toward a core typology of service organizations', *Academy of Management Review*, vol 5, pp 255–65.

Mintzberg, H. (1979) *The structuring of organisations*, Englewood Cliffs, NJ: Prentice Hall.

Mintzberg, H. (1989) *Mintzberg on management*, New York, NY: The Free Press.

Monnat, S.M. (2011) 'The color of welfare sanctioning: exploring the individual and contextual roles of race on TANF case closures and benefit reductions', *The Sociological Quarterly*, vol 51, no 4, pp 678–707.

Montada, L. (1998) 'Belief in a just world: a hybrid of justice motive and self-interest', in L. Montada and M. Lerner (eds) *Responses to victimizations and belief in a just world: critical issues in social justice*, New York, NY: Plenum Press, pp 217–46.

Moore, S.T. (1987) 'The theory of street-level bureaucracy', *Administration and Society*, vol 19, no 74, p 94.

Morgen, S. (2001) 'The agency of welfare workers. Negotiating devolution, privatisation and the meaning of self sufficiency', *American Anthropologist*, vol 103, no 3, pp 747–61.

Morrill, C. and Musheno, M. (forthcoming) *Youth conflict: trust and control in an urban school*, Chicago, IL: University of Chicago Press.

Morrill, C., Yalda, C., Adelman, M., Musheno, M. and Bejarano, C. (2000) 'Telling tales in school: youth culture and conflict narratives', *Law and Society Review*, vol 34, no 3, pp 521–66.

Mosher, F. (1968) *Democracy and the public service*, New York, NY: Oxford University Press.

Moynihan, D.P. and Herd, P. (2010) 'Red tape and democracy: how rules affect citizenship rights', *American Review of Public Administration*, vol 40, no 6, pp 654–70.

Murray, C. (2006) 'State intervention and vulnerable children: implementation revisited', *Journal of Social Policy*, vol 35, no 2, pp 211–28.

Murray, F. and Willmott, H. (1997) 'Putting information technology in its place: towards flexible integration in the network age?', in B.P. Bloomfield, R. Coombs, D. Knights and D. Littler (eds) *Information technology and organisations*, Oxford and New York, NY: Oxford University Press, pp 162–87.

NAB (National Assistance Board) (1949) *Report of the National Assistance Board 1948*, Cmnd 7767, London: HMSO.

NAB (1966) *Report of the National Assistance Board 1965*, Cmnd 8900, London: HMSO.

Navarro, V. (1988) 'Professional dominance or proletarianisation? Neither', *Millbank Quarterly*, vol 66, supp 2, pp 57–75.

Needham, C. (2011) *Personalising public services. Understanding the personalisation narrative*, Bristol: The Policy Press.

Newman, J. (2005) 'Bending bureaucracy: leadership and multi-level governance', in P. du Gay (ed) *The values of bureaucracy*, Oxford: Oxford University Press, pp 191–210.

Newman, J., Glendinning, C. and Hughes, M. (2008) 'Beyond modernisation? Social care and the transformation of welfare governance', *Journal of Social Policy*, vol 37, no 4, pp 531–57.

NHS (National Health Service) Available at: https://catalogue. ic.nhs.uk/publications/social-care/staff/pers-soci-serv-staf-30-sep-eng-2010/pers-soci-serv-staf-30-sep-eng-2010-rep.pdf

NHS Executive (1996a) *Clinical guidelines: using clinical guidelines to improve patient care within the NHS*, London: Department of Health.

NHS Executive (1996b) *Promoting clinical effectiveness: a framework for action in and through the NHS*, London: Department of Health.

Nielsen, V.L. (2002) *Dialogens pris. Uformelle spilleregler, ressourceasymmetri og forskelsbehandling i offentligt tilsyn*, Århus: Forlaget Politica.

Nielsen, V.L. (2005) 'Power in public implementation – a complex but important part of power studies', *Scandinavian Political Studies*, vol 28, no 4, pp 349–75.

Nielsen, V.L. (2006a) 'Are street level bureaucrats compelled or enticed to cope', *Public Administration*, vol 84, no 4, pp 861–89.

Nielsen, V.L. (2006b) 'Are regulators responsive?', *Law and Policy*, vol 28, no 3, pp 395–416.

Nielsen, V.L. (2007) 'Differential treatment and communicative interactions: why the character of social interaction is important', *Law and Policy*, vol 29, no 2, pp 257–83.

Nielsen, V.L. and Parker, C. (2012) 'Mixed motives: economic, normative and social motivations in business compliance', *Law and Policy*, vol 34, no 4, pp 428–62.

Noon, M. and Blyton, P. (2002) *The realities of work*, Basingstoke: Palgrave.

Noordegraaf, M. (2007) 'From "pure" to "hybrid" professionalism, present-day professionalism in ambiguous public domains', *Administration and Society*, vol 39, no 6, pp 761–85.

Noordegraaf, M. (2011) 'Risky business. How professionals and professionals fields (must) deal with organizational issues', *Organization Studies*, vol 32, no 10, pp 1349–71.

Noordegraaf, M. and Abma, T. (2003) 'Management by measurement? Public management practices amidst ambiguity', *Public Administration*, vol 81, no 4, pp 853–71.

Noordegraaf, M., van der Steen, M. and van Twist, M. (2014) 'Fragmented or connective professionalism? Strategies for professionalizing the work of strategists and other (organizational) professionals', *Public Administration*, vol 92, pp 21–38.

Oberweis, T. and Musheno, M. (2001) *Knowing rights: state actors' stories of power, identity and morality*, Burlington, VT: Ashgate/Darmouth.

O'Connell, L. (1991) 'Investigators at work: how bureaucratic and legal constraints influence the enforcements of discrimination law', *Public Administration Review*, vol 51, no 2, pp 123–31.

O'Connor, W.E., Morrison, T.G., McLeod, L.D. and Anderson, D. (1996) 'A meta-analytic review of the relationship between gender and belief in a just world', *Journal of Social Behavior & Personality*, vol 11, no 1, pp 41–148.

Oevermann, U. (2000) 'Dienstleistung und Sozialbürokratie aus professionalisierungstheoretischer Sicht', in E.-M. von Harrach, T. Loer and O. Schmidtke (eds) *Verwaltung des Sozialen. Formen der subjektiven Bewältigung eines Strukturkonflikts*, Konstanz: UVK, pp 57–78.

O'Reilly, K. (2005) *Ethnographic methods*, London: Routledge.

Osiander, C. and Steinke, J. (2011) 'Street-level bureaucrats in der Arbeitsverwaltung. Dienstleistungsprozesse und reformierte Arbeitsvermittlung aus Sicht der Vermittler', *Zeitschrift für Sozialreform*, vol 57, no 2, pp 149–73.

Ostrom, E. (1996) 'Crossing the great divide: co-production, synergy, and development', *World Development*, vol 24, no 6, pp 1073–88.

Ostrom, E. (1999) 'Institutional rational choice: an assessment of the institutional analysis and development framework', in P.A. Sabatier (ed) *Theories of the policy process*, Boulder, CO: Westview Press.

O'Toole, L.J., Jr and Meier, K.J. (1999) 'Modelling the impact of public management: implications for the structural context', *Journal of Public Administration Research and Theory*, vol 9, no 4, pp 505–26.

O'Toole, L.J., Jr, Meier, K.J. and Nicolson-Crotty, S. (2005) 'Managing upward, downward, and outward: networks, hierarchical relationships and performance', *Public Management Review*, vol 7, no 1, pp 45–68.

Pacolet, J., Bouten, R., Lanoye, H. and Versieck, K. (1999) *Social protection for dependency in old age in the 15 EU Member States and Norway*, Luxembourg: European Commission.

Parks, R.B., Baker, P.C., Kiser, L., Oakerson, R., Ostrom, E., Ostrom, V., Percy, S.L., Vandivort, M.B., Whitaker, G.P. and Wilson, R. (1981) 'Consumers as coproducers of public services: some economic and institutional considerations', *Policy Studies Journal*, vol 9, no 7, pp 1001–11.

Parrott, L. and Madoc-Jones, I. (2008) 'Reclaiming information and communication technologies for empowering social work practice', *British Journal of Social Work*, vol 8, no 2, pp 181–97.

Pasquier, M. and Larpin, B. (2008) 'Analyse des problèmes politico-administratifs et de la gouvernance des caisses publiques de chômage', Chavannes-Lausanne, Cahiers de l'IDHEAP no 244a.

Pautz, M. (2010) 'Front-line regulators and their approach to environmental regulation in southwest Ohio', *Review of Policy Research*, vol 27, no 6, pp 761–80.

Pedersen, J.M., Rosholm, M. and Svarer, M. (2012) 'Experimental evidence on the effects of early meetings and activation', working paper.

Penn, R. and Scattergard, H. (1985) 'Deskilling or enskilling? An empirical investigation of recent theories of the labour process', *The British Journal of Sociology*, vol 36, no 4, pp 611–30.

Percy, S.L. (1984) 'Citizen participation in the coproduction of urban services', *Urban Affairs Review*, vol 19, no 4, pp 431–46.

Perrow, C. (1972) *Complex organizations: a critical essay*, Cleanview, IL: Scott Foresman.

Picot, A. and Neuburger, R. (2008) 'Arbeitsstrukturen in virtuellen Organisationen', in C. Funken and I. Schulz-Schaeffer (eds) *Digitalisierung der Arbeitswelt. Zur Neuordnung formaler und informeller Prozesse in Unternehmen* (1st edn), Wiesbaden: VS Verlag für Sozialwissenschaften.

Pierre, X. and Tremblay, D.G. (2011) 'Levels of involvement and retention of agents in call centres: improving well-being of employees for better socioeconomic performance', *Journal of Management Policy and Practice*, vol 12, no 5, pp 53–71.

Pierre, X., Tremblay, D.G. (2012) '*Attraction e rétention des centres d"appels: l"innovation socioterritoriale comme source d"avantages concurrentiels?*' *Revue Interventions économiques*, no 44.

Pitkin, H. (1967) *The concept of representation*, Berkeley, CA: University of California Press.

Pitts, D. and Lewis, G. (2009) 'Representation of lesbians and gay men in federal, state, and local bureaucracies', *Journal of Public Administration Research and Theory*, vol 21, no 1, pp 159–80.

Polanyi, M. (1967) *The tacit dimension*, London: Routledge and Kegan Paul.

Pollack, S. (2010) 'Labelling clients "risky": social work and the neo-liberal welfare state', *British Journal of Social Work*, vol 40, no 4, pp 1263–78.

Pollitt, C. (1990) *Managerialism and the public services: the Anglo-American experience*, Oxford: Blackwell.

Pollitt, C. (1993) *Managerialism and the public sector*, Oxford: Oxford University Press.

Pollitt, C. (2003) 'Joined up government: a survey', *Political Studies Review*, vol 1, no 1, pp 34–49.

Pollitt, C. (2011) 'Mainstreaming technological change in the study of public management', *Public Policy and Administration*, vol 26, no 4, pp 377–97.

Pollitt, C. and Bouckaert, G. (2004) *Public management reform, a comparative analysis* (2nd edn), Oxford: Oxford University Press.

Polstra, L. (2011) *Laveren tussen belangen*, Groningen: Kenniscentrum Arbeid Hanzehogeschool Groningen.

Pope, C. (2003) 'Resisting evidence: the study of evidence-based medicine as a contemporary social movement', *Health: An Interdisciplinary Journal for the Study of Health, Illness and Medicine*, vol 7, no 3, pp 267–82.

Portillo, S. and DeHart-Davis, L. (2009) 'Gender and organizational rule abidance', *Public Administration Review*, vol 69, no 2, pp 339–47.

Potter, S.J. and McKinlay, J.B. (2005) 'From a relationship to encounter: an examination of longitudinal and lateral dimensions in the doctor–patient relationship', *Social Science and Medicine*, vol 61, no 2, pp 465–79.

Power, M. (1997) *The audit society, rituals of verification*, Oxford: Oxford University Press.

Pressman, J.L. and Wildavsky, A. (1973) *Implementation*, Berkeley, CA: University of California Press.

Price, D. (1978) 'Policymaking in congressional committees: the impact of environmental factors', *American Political Science Review*, vol 72, pp 161–83.

Priestley, M., Riddell, S., Jolly, D., Pearson, C., Williams, V., Barnes, C. and Mercer, G. (2010) 'Cultures of welfare at the front line: implementing direct payments for disabled people in the UK', *Policy & Politics*, vol 38, no 2, pp 307–24.

Prime Minister's Strategy Group (2005) *Improving the life chances of disabled people*, London: Cabinet Office.

Prottas, J. (1978) 'The power of the street-level bureaucrat in public service bureaucracies', *Urban Affairs Quarterly*, vol 13, no 3, pp 285–312.

Prottas, J. (1979) *People processing. The street-level bureaucrat in public service bureaucracies*, Lexington: D.C. Heath and Company.

Provan, K.G. and Milward, H.B. (1991) 'Institutional-level norms and organizational involvement in a service-implementation network', *Journal of Public Administration Research and Theory*, vol 1, no 4, pp 391–417.

Provine, D.M. (2007) *Unequal under law: race in the war on drugs*, Chicago, IL: University of Chicago Press.

Rabiee, P., Moran, N. and Glendinning, C. (2009) 'Individual budgets: lessons from early users' experiences', *British Journal of Social Work*, vol 39, no 5, pp 918–35.

Rawlins, M.D. and Culyer, A.J. (2004) 'National Institute for Clinical Excellence and its value judgements', *British Medical Journal*, vol 329, pp 224–7.

Rees, S. (1978) *Social work face to face*, London: Edward Arnold.

Reichle, B., Schneider, A. and Montada, L. (1998) 'How do observers of victimization preserve their belief in a just world cognitively or actionally', in L. Montada and M. Lerner (eds) *Responses to victimizations and belief in a just world: critical issues in social justice*, New York, NY: Plenum Press, pp 55–64.

Reuss-Ianni, E. (1983) *Two cultures of policing: street cops and management cops*, New Brunswick, NJ: Transaction Books.

Reuss-Ianni, E. and Ianni, F.A.J. (1988) 'Street cops and management cops: the two cultures of policing', in M. Punch (ed) *Control in the police organization*, Cambridge, MA: MIT Press.

Rhodes, R. (1997) 'From marketisation to diplomacy: it's the mix that matters', *Australian Journal of Public Administration*, vol 56, no 2, pp 40–53.

Rhodes, R. (2007) 'Understanding governance: ten years on', *Organisational Studies*, vol 28, pp 1243–64.

Riccucci, N.M. (2005a) 'Street-level bureaucrats and intrastate variation in the implementation of Temporary Assistance for Needy Families policies', *Journal of Public Administration Research and Theory*, vol 15, no 1, pp 89–111.

Riccucci, N.M. (2005b) *How management matters: street-level bureaucrats and welfare reform*, Washington, DC: Georgetown University Press.

Riccucci, N.M. and Lurie, I. (2001) 'Employee performance evaluation in social welfare offices', *Review of Public Personnel Administration*, vol 21, no 1, pp 27–37.

Riccucci, N.M and Meyers, M.K. (2004) 'Linking passive and active representation: the case of frontline workers in welfare agencies', *Journal of Public Administration, Research and Theory*, vol 14, no 4, pp 585–97.

Riccucci, N.M., Meyers, M.K., Lurie, I. and Han, J.S. (2004) 'The implementation of welfare reform policy: the role of public managers in front-line practices', *Public Administration Review*, vol 64, no 4, pp 438–48.

Rich, R.C. (1981) 'Interaction of the voluntary and governmental sectors: toward an understanding of the coproduction of municipal services', *Administration and Society*, vol 13, no 1, pp 59–76.

Richards, L. and Morse, J.M. (2007) *Readme first for a user's guide to qualitative methods*, Thousand Oaks, CA: Sage.

Rihoux, B. and Ragin, C. (2009) *Configurational comparative methods. Qualitative comparative analysis (QCA) and related techniques*, London: Sage.

Robinson, R. and Le Grand, J. (eds) (1993) *Evaluating the NHS reforms*, London: King's Fund.

Robinson, R. and Steiner, A. (1998) *Managed health care: US evidence and lessons for the National Health Service*, Buckingham: Open University Press.

Roethlisberger, F.J. and Dickson, W.J. (1947) *Management and the worker*, Cambridge, Ma: Harvard University Press.

Roland, M. (2004) 'Linking physician pay to quality of care: a major experiment in the UK', *New England Journal of Medicine*, vol 351, pp 1488–54.

Rosenthal, P. and Pecci, R. (2006) 'The social construction of clients by service agents in reformed welfare administration', *Human Relations*, vol 59, no 12, paras 1633–58.

Roulstone, A. and Morgan, H. (2009) 'Neo-liberal individualism or self-directed support: are we all speaking the same language on modernising adult social care?', *Social Policy and Society*, vol 8, no 3, pp 333–45.

Rubin, Z. and Peplau, A. (1973) 'Belief in a just world and reactions to another's lot: a study of participants in the national draft lottery', *Journal of Social Issues*, vol 29, no 4, pp 73–93.

Ryan, R. and Deci, E. (2000) 'Self-determination theory and the facilitation of intrinsic motivation, social development, and well-being', *American Psychologist*, vol 55, no 1, pp 68–78.

Sackett, D.L., Tugwell, P. and Guyatt, G.H. (1991) *Clinical epidemiology: a basic science for clinical medicine* (2nd edn), Boston, MA: Little Brown.

Sackett, D.L., Rosenberg, W., Gray, J.A., Haynes, R.B. and Richarsdon, W.S. (1996) 'Evidence-based medicine: what it is and what it isn't', *British Medical Journal*, vol 312, pp 71–2.

Sætren, H. (2014) 'Implementing the third generation research paradigm in policy implementation research: an empirical assessment', *Public Policy and Administration*, vol 29, no 2, pp 84–105.

Sainsbury, R. (2008) 'Administrative justice, discretion and the "welfare to work" project', *Journal of Social Welfare and Family Law*, vol 30, no 4, pp 323–38.

Saltzstein, G. (1979) 'Representative bureaucracy and bureaucratic responsibility: problems and prospects', *Administration and Society*, vol 10, no 1, pp 465–75.

Sanders, T., Harrison, S. and Checkland, K. (2008) 'Evidence-based medicine and patient choice: the case of heart failure care', *Journal of Health Services Research and Policy*, vol 13, no 2, pp 103–8.

Sandfort, J.R. (2000) 'Moving beyond discretion and outcomes: examining public management from the front lines of the welfare system', *Journal of Public Administration Research and Theory*, vol 10, no 4, pp 729–56.

Satyamurti, C. (1981) *Occupational survival. The case of the local authority social worker*, Oxford: Blackwell.

SBC (Supplementary Benefits Commission) (1977) *SBC annual report 1976*, Cmnd 6910, London: HMSO.

Schartau, M.-B. (1993) 'The public sector middle manager: the puppet who pulls the strings?', PhD dissertation, University of Lund.

Schedler, K. and Utz, H. (2009) 'Process management in public sector organizations', in T. Bovaird and E. Löffler (eds) *Public management and governance*, Abingdon: Routledge, pp 181–98.

Scheuer, S. (2000) *Social and economic motivation at work. Theories of motivation reassessed*, Copenhagen: Copenhagen Business School Press.

Schneider, A.L. and Ingram, H. (1993) 'Social construction of target populations: implications for politics and policy', *American Political Science Review*, vol 87, no 2, pp 334–47.

Schneider, A.L. and Ingram, H. (1997) *Policy design for democracy*, Lawrence, KS: University Press of Kansas.

Scholz, J.T. (1991) 'Cooperative regulatory enforcement and the politics of administrative effectiveness', *American Political Science Review*, vol 85, pp 115–36.

Scholz, J.T. (1994) 'Managing regulatory enforcement', in D.H. Roosenbloom and R.D. Schwartz (eds) *Handbook of regulation and administrative law*, New York, NY: Marcel Decker, pp 423–63.

Scholz, J.T. and Lubell, M. (1998) 'Trust and taxpaying: testing the heuristic approach to collective action', *American Journal of Political Science*, vol 42, no 2, pp 398–417.

Scholz, J.T. and Pinney, N. (1995) 'Duty, fear, and tax compliance: the heuristic basis of citizenship behavior', *American Journal of Political Science*, vol 39, no 2, pp 490–512.

Scholz, J.T., Twombly, J. and Headrick, B. (1991) 'Street-level political controls over federal bureaucracy', *The American Political Science Review*, vol 85, no 3, pp 829–50.

SCHOOL (2010) 'Annual report 2010', Gluton.

Schulz, R.L. and Harrison, S. (1986) 'Physician autonomy in the Federal Republic of Germany, Great Britain and the United States', *International Journal of Health Planning and Management*, vol 1, no 5, pp 1213–28.

Schütz, H., Kupka, P., Koch, S. and Kaltenborn, B. (2011a) 'Eingliederungsvereinbarungen in der Praxis: Reformziele noch nicht erreicht', IAB-Kurzbericht 18/2011.

Schütz, H., Steinwede, J., Schröder, H., Kaltenborn, B., Wielage, N., Christe, G. and Kupka, P. (2011b) *Vermittlung und Beratung in der Praxis. Eine Analyse von Dienstleistungsprozessen am Arbeitsmarkt*, IAB-Bibliothek 330, Bielefeld: Bertelsmann.

Schwehr, B. (2010) 'Safeguarding and personalisation', *Journal of Adult Protection*, vol 12, no 2, pp 43–51.

SCIE (Social Care Institute for Excellence) (2010) *Enabling risk, ensuring safety: self-directed support and personal budgets*, Report 36, London: SCIE.

Scott, P.G. (1997) 'Assessing determinants of bureaucratic discretion: an experiment in street-level decision making', *Journal of Public Administration Research and Theory*, vol 7, no 1, pp 35–57.

Scott, P.G. and Pandey, S.K. (2000) 'The influence of red tape on democratic behaviour', *Journal of Policy Analysis and Management*, vol 19, no 4, pp 615–33.

Seeman, M. (1959) 'On the meaning of alienation', *American Sociological Review*, vol 24, no 6, pp 783–91.

Selden, S. (1997) *The promise of the representative bureaucracy: diversity and responsiveness in a government agency*, Armonk, NY: ME Sharpe.

Sewell, W. (1992) 'A theory of structure: duality, agency, and transformation', *American Journal of Sociology*, vol 98, no 1, pp 1–29.

Sharp, E.B. (1980) 'Toward a new understanding of urban services and citizen participation: the coproduction concept', *The American Review of Public Administration*, vol 14, no 2, pp 105–18.

Shaw, I., Morris, K. and Edwards, A. (2009) 'Technology, social services and organizational innovation or how great expectations in London and Cardiff are dashed in Lowestoft and Cymtyrch', *Journal of Social Work Practice*, vol 23, pp 383–400. Available at: http://dx.doi.org/10.1080/02650530903374937 (accessed 10 February 2010).

Shearing, C. and Ericson, R. (1991) 'Culture as figurative language', *The British Journal of Sociology*, vol 42, no 4, pp 481–506.

Shekelle, P. (2003) 'New contract for general practitioners', *British Medical Journal*, vol 326, no 7387, pp 457–8.

Simon, J. (2007) *Governing through crime: how the war on crime transformed American democracy and created a culture of fear*, New York, NY: Oxford University Press.

Sitkin, S., Cardinal, L. and Bijlsma Frankema, K. (eds) (2010) *Control is fundamental, organisational control*, Cambridge: Cambridge University Press.

Skinner, E.A. and Zimmer-Gembeck, M.J. (2007) 'The development of coping', *Annual Review of Psychology*, vol 58, pp 119–44.

Skinner, E.A., Edge, K., Altman, J. and Sherwood, H. (2003) 'Searching for the structure of coping: a review and critique of category systems for classifying ways of coping', *Psychological bulletin*, vol 129, no 2, pp 216–69.

Sklansky, D.A. (2008) *Democracy and the police*, Stanford, CA: Stanford University Press.

Smaling, A. (2003) 'Inductive, analogical, and communicative generalization', *International Journal of Qualitative Methods*, vol 2, no 1, pp 52–67.

Smith, B.C. (1988) *Bureaucracy and political power*, Brighton: Wheatsheaf.

Smith, B.D. and Donovan, S. (2003) 'Child welfare practice in organizational and institutional context', *Social Service Review*, vol 77, no 4, pp 541–63.

Smith, G. (1980) *Social need. Policy, practice and research*, London: Routledge and Kegan Paul.

Smith, K. and Green, D. (1984) 'Individual correlates of the belief in a just world', *Psychological Reports*, vol 54, no 2, pp 435–8.

Smith, S.R. (2012) 'Street-level bureaucracy and public policy', in B. Guy Peters and J. Pierre (eds) *The SAGE handbook of public administration* (2nd edn), London: Sage, pp 431–46.

Snellen, I. (1998) 'Street level bureaucracy in an information age', in I. Snellen and W. van de Donk (eds) *Public administration in an information age. A handbook*, Amsterdam: IOS Press, pp 497–505.

Soss, J., Fording, R.C. and Schram, S.F. (2009) 'Governing the poor: the rise of the neoliberal paternalistic state', Annual Meeting of the American Political Science Association, Toronto, Canada.

Soss, J., Fording, R.C. and Schram, S.F. (2011a) *Disciplining the poor: neoliberal paternalism and the persistent power of race*, Chicago, IL: University of Chicago Press.

Soss, J., Fording, R.C. and Schram, S.F. (2011b) 'The organization of discipline: from performance management to perversity and punishment', *Journal of Public Administration and Research Theory*, vol 21, suppl 2, pp 203–32.

Spandler, H. and Vick, N. (2005) 'Enabling access to direct payments: an exploration of care co-ordinators' decision-making practices', *Journal of Mental Health*, vol 14, no 2, pp 145–55.

Sparrow, M.K. (2000) *The regulatory craft*, Washington, DC: Bookings Institution Press.

SSAC (Social Security Advisory Committee) (1987) *Fifth report of the Social Security Advisory Committee 1986/7*, London: HMSO.

SSAC (1990) *Seventh report of the Social Security Advisory Committee 1989*, London: HMSO.

SSEA (State Secretariat for Economic Affairs) (2002) 'Circulaire relative à l'indemnité de chômage (IC)', January, Berne.

Stanford, S. (2011) 'Constructing moral responses to risk: a framework for hopeful social work practice', *British Journal of Social Work*, vol 41, no 8, pp 1514–31.

Steinke, J., Koch, S., Kupka, P., Osiander, C., Dony, E., Güttler, D., Hesse, C. and Knapp, B. (2012) 'Neuorientierung der Arbeitsmarktpolitik. Die Neuausrichtung der arbeitsmarktpolitischen Instrumente aus dem Jahr 2009 im Blickpunkt: Mehr Flexibilität und größere Handlungsspielräume für die Vermittler?', IAB-Forschungsbericht 02/2012.

Stevens, M., Glendinning, C., Jacobs, S., Moran, N., Challis, D., Manthorpe, J., Fernandez, J.-L., Jones, K., Knapp, M., Netten, A. and Wilberforce, M. (2011) 'Assessing the role of increasing choice in English social care services', *Journal of Social Policy*, vol 40, no 2, pp 257–74.

Stigler, G.J. (1970) 'The optimum enforcement of laws', *Journal of Political Economy*, vol 70, no 3, pp 526–36.

Stoker, R.P. and Wilson, L.A. (1998) 'Verifying compliance: social regulation and welfare reform', *Public Administration Review*, vol 58, no 5, pp 395–405.

Stowe, K.R. (1961) 'Staff training in the National Assistance Board: problems and policies', *Public Administration*, vol 39, no 4, pp 331–49.

Stowers, D. and Durm, M. (1998) 'Is belief in a just world rational?', *Psychological Reports*, vol 83, no 2, pp 423–6.

Sullivan, M.P. (2009) 'Social workers in community care practice: ideologies and interactions with older people', *British Journal of Social Work*, vol 39, no 7, pp 1306–25.

Swidler, A. (1986) 'Culture in action: symbols and strategies', *American Sociological Review*, vol 51, no 2, pp 273–86.

Syrett, K. (2003) 'A technocratic fix to the "legitimacy" problem? The Blair government and health care rationing in the United Kingdom', *Journal of Health Politics, Policy and Law*, vol 28, no 4, pp 715–46.

Taylor, F.W. (1911) *The principles of scientific management*, New York, NY: Harper.

Taylor, P. and Bain, P. (2003) '"Subterranean worksick blues": humour as subversion in two call centres', *Organization Studies*, vol 24, no 9, pp 1487–509.

Taylor-Gooby, P. (2008) 'The new welfare state settlement in Europe', *European Societies*, vol 10, no 1, pp 3–24.

Terpstra, J. and Havinga, T. (2001) 'Implementation between tradition and management: structuration and styles of implementation', *Law and Policy*, vol 23, no 1, pp 95–116.

Thelen, K. (2004) *How institutions evolve: the political economy of skills in Germany, Britain, the United States and Japan*, New York, NY: Cambridge University Press.

Thielemann, G. and Stewart, J. (1996) 'A demand-side perspective on the importance of representative bureaucracy: AIDS, ethnicity, gender, and sexual orientation', *Public Administration Review*, vol 56, no 2, pp 168–73.

Thomas, P. and Hewitt, J. (2011) 'Managerial organization and professional autonomy: a discourse-based conceptualization', *Organization Studies*, vol 32, no 10, pp 1373–93.

Thomas, R. and Davies, A. (2005) 'Theorizing the micro-politics of resistance: New Public Management and managerial identities in the UK public services', *Organization Studies*, vol 26, no 5, pp 683–706.

Thompson, G., Frances, J., Levaçic, R. and Mitchell, J. (eds) (1991) *Markets, hierarchies and networks. The coordination of social life*, London: Sage.

Thompson, P., Callaghan, G. and van den Broek, D. (2004) 'Keeping up appearances: recruitment, skills and norative control in call centres', in S. Deery and N. Kinnie (eds) *Call centres and human resource management*, Basingstoke: Palgrave, pp 129–52.

Thorén, K. (2008) *'Activation policy in action'. A street-level study of social assistance in the Swedish welfare state*, Vaxjo: Vaxjo University Press.

Thornton, D., Gunningham, N.A. and Kagan, R.A. (2005) 'General deterrence and corporate environmental behavior', *Law and Policy*, vol 27, no 2, pp 262–88.

Timmins, N. (2007) 'Farewell to dodging and weaving', *British Medical Journal*, vol 334, pp 877–8.

Titmuss, R. (1971) 'Welfare "rights", law and discretion', *Political Quarterly*, vol 42, no 2, pp 113–32.

Torstendahl, R. (1990) 'Essential properties, strategic aims and historical development: three approaches to theories of professionalism' in M. Burrage and R. Torstendahl (eds) *Professions in theory and history*, London: Sage Publications, pp 44–5.

Tummers, L.G. (2012) 'Policy alienation of public professionals: the construct and its measurement', *Public Administration Review*, vol 72, no 4, pp 516–25.

Tummers, L.G., Bekkers, V. and Steijn, B. (2009) 'Policy alienation of public professionals. Application in a New Public Management context', *Public Management Review*, vol 11, no 5, pp 685–706.

Tummers, L.G., Bekkers, V., Vink, E. and Musheno, M. (2013) 'Handling stress during policy implementation: developing a classification of "coping" by frontline workers based on a systematic review', IRSPM 2013, Prague.

Tummers, L.G., Vermeeren, B., Steijn, A.J. and Bekkers, V.J.J.M. (forthcoming) 'Public professionals and policy implementation: measuring and examining three role conflicts', *Public Management Review*.

Turner, V. (1977) 'Process, system, and symbol: a new anthropological synthesis', *Daedalus*, vol 106, no 3, pp 61–80.

Tyler, T.R. (1990) *Why people obey the law*, New Haven, CT, and London: Yale University Press.

Tyson, A., Brewis, R., Crosby, N., Hatton, C., Stansfield, J., Tomlinson, C., Waters, J. and Wood, A. (2010) *A report on In Control's third phase: evaluation and learning 2008–2009*, London: In Control.

UAB (Unemployment Assistance Board) (1936) *Report of the Unemployment Assistance Board 1935*, Cmnd 5177, London: HMSO.

UAB (1937) *Report of the Unemployment Assistance Board 1936*, Cmnd 5526, London: HMSO.

Umberson, D. (1993) 'Sociodemographic position, worldviews, and psychological distress', *Social Science Quarterly*, vol 74, pp 575–89.

Ungerson, C. (1995) 'Gender, cash and informal care: European perspectives and dilemmas', *Journal of Social Policy*, vol 24, no 1, pp 31–52.

Van Berkel, R. (2013) 'Triple activation: introducing welfare to work into Dutch social assistance', in E.Z. Brodkin and G. Marston (eds) *Work and the welfare state*, Washington, DC: Georgetown University Press.

Van Berkel, R. and Van der Aa, P. (2012) 'Activation work: policy programme administration or professional service provision?', *Journal of Social Policy*, vol 41, no 3, pp 493–510.

Van Berkel, R., Van der Aa, P. and Van Gestel, N. (2010) 'Professionals without a profession? Redesigning case management in Dutch local welfare agencies', *European Journal of Social Work*, vol 13, no 4, pp 447–63.

Van Berkel, R., De Graaf, W. and Sirovatka, T. (eds) (2011) *The governance of active welfare states in Europe*, Houndmills: Palgrave Macmillan.

Van der Aa, P. (2012) 'Activeringswerk in uitvoering. Bureaucratische en professionele dienstverlening in drie sociale diensten', PhD thesis, Utrecht University.

Van der Veen, R. (1995) '*De taal van het beleid. Precisering en verdere categorisering van beleid*', in L. Aarts et al (eds) *Het bedrijf van de verzorgingsstaat. Naar nieuwe verhoudingen tussen staat, markt en burger*, Amsterdam: Boom, pp 80–98.

Van Gool, S. (2008) 'Untouchable bureaucracy: unrepresentative bureaucracy in a North Indian State', dissertation.

Van Gunsteren, H.R. (1976) *The quest for control*, London: John Wiley and Sons.

Van Thiel, S. and Leeuw, F.L. (2002) 'The performance paradox in the public sector', *Public Performance and Management Review*, vol 25, no 3, pp 267–81.

Vinzant, J.C. and Crothers, L. (1998) *Street-level leadership: discretion and legitimacy in front-line public service*, Washington, DC: Georgetown University Press.

Walker, C. (1983) *Changing social policy: the case of the supplementary benefits review*, London: Bedford Square Press.

Walker, C. (1993) *Managing poverty: the limits of social assistance*, London: Routledge.

Wallace, J. and Pease, B. (2011) 'Neoliberalism and Australian social work: accommodation or resistance?' *Journal of Social Work*, vol 11, no 2, pp 132-42.

Walton, J. (1992) 'Making the theoretical case', in C. Ragin and S. Becker (eds) *What is a case? Exploring the foundations of social inquiry*, Cambridge: Cambridge University Press.

Warin, B. (2010) 'Safeguarding adults in Cornwall', *The Journal of Adult Protection*, vol 12, no 2, pp 39–42.

Wastell, D., White, S., Broadhurst, K., Peckover, S. and Pithouse, A. (2010) 'Children's services in the iron cage of performance management: street-level bureaucracy and the spectre of Švejkism', *International Journal of Social Welfare*, vol 19, pp 310–20.

Watkins-Hayes, C. (2011) 'Race, poverty, and policy implementation: inside the black box of racially representative bureaucracies', *Journal of Public Administration Research and Theory*, vol 21, suppl 2, pp i233–i251.

Weatherly, R. (1979) *Reforming special education: policy implementation from state level to street level*, Cambridge, MA: MIT Press.

Weatherly, R. (1980) 'Implementing social programs: the view from the front-line', paper presented at the Annual Meeting of the American Political Science Association, Washington, DC.

Weber, M. (1947) *The theory of social and economic organizations* (trans A.M. Henderson and T. Parsons), Glencoe, IL: Free Press.

Weibel, A. (2007) 'Formal control and trustworthiness: shall the twain never meet?', *Group and Organization Management*, vol 32, no 4, pp 500–17.

Weibel, A. (2010) 'Managerial objectives of formal control: high motivation control mechanisms', in S. Sitkin, L. Cardinal and K. Bijlsma-Frankema (eds) *Control is fundamental, organisational control*, Cambridge: Cambridge University Press.

Weibel, A. and Six, F.E. (2013) 'Trust and control: the role of intrinsic motivation', in R. Bachmann and A. Zaheer (eds) *Handbook of advances in trust research*, Cheltenham: Edward Elgar, pp 57–81.

Weishaupt, J.T. (2010) 'A silent revolution? New management ideas and the reinvention of European public employment services', *Socio-Economic Review*, vol 8, no 3, pp 461–86.

Weissert, C.S. (1994) 'Beyond the organization: the influence of community and personal values on street-level bureaucrats' responsiveness', *Journal of Public Administration Research and Theory*, vol 4, no 2, pp 225–54.

Wenger, J.B. and Wilkins, V.M. (2009) 'At the discretion of rogue agents: how automation improves women's outcomes in unemployment insurance', *Journal of Public Administration Research and Theory*, vol 19, no 2, pp 313–33.

Wennberg, J.E. (1984) 'Dealing with medical practice variations: a proposal for action', *Health Affairs*, vol 3, no 2, pp 6–32.

Whatley, M. (1993) 'Belief in a just world scale: unidimensional or ultidimensional?', *The Journal of Social Psychology*, vol 133, no 4, pp 547–51.

Whitaker, G.P. (1980) 'Coproduction: citizen participation in service delivery', *Public Administration Review*, vol 40, no 3, pp 240–6.

Wilensky, H.L. (1964) 'The professionalisation of everyone', *American Journal of Sociology*, vol 70, pp 137–58.

Wilson, J.Q. (1967) 'The bureaucracy problem', *The Public Interest*, winter, pp 3–9.

Wilson, J.Q. (1989) *Bureaucracy: what government agencies do and why they do it*, New York, NY: Basic Books.

Wilson, W. (1887) 'The study of administration', *Political Science Quarterly*, vol 2, pp 197–222.

Winter, S. (1994) 'Street-level bureaucrats and the implementation of political reforms: welfare, employment, and environmental policies in Denmark', unpublished paper, Aarhus, Department of Political Science, Aarhus University.

Winter, S. (1996) 'Causes and consequences of regulatory enforcement styles: Danish agro-environmental policy', paper prepared for presentation at the annual meeting of the Association for Public Policy and Management in Pittsburgh, 31 October–2 November, Aahus, Department of Political science, Aarhus University.

Winter, S. (2001) 'Effekter af forskellige tilsynsstrategier på landmændenes efterlevelse af Vandmiljøplanerne', Miljøforskning no 46 – Stok eller gulerod? Virkemidler i miljøpolitikken – del 2, Det strategiske Miljøforskningsprogram, pp 28–33.

Winter, S. (2002) 'Explaining street-level bureaucratic behavior in social and regulatory policies', paper prepared for the Annual Meeting of the American Political Science Association in Boston, 29 August–1 September, Danish National Institute of Social Research, Copenhagen.

Winter, S. (2003) 'Political control, street-level bureaucrats and information asymmetry in regulatory and social policies', draft paper presented at the Annual Meeting of the Association for Public Policy Analysis and Management held in Washington, DC, 6–8 November, Danish National Institute of Social Research, Copenhagen.

Winter, S. (2012) 'Introduction to part 5 "implementation"', in B.G. Peters and J. Pierre (eds) *SAGE handbook of public administration* (2nd edn), London: SAGE, pp 255–63.

Winter, S. and May, P. (2001) 'Motivation for compliance with environmental regulations', *Journal of Policy Analysis and Management*, vol 20, no 4, pp 675–98.

Winter, S. and May, P. (2002) 'Information, interests, and environmental regulation', *Journal of Comparative Policy Analysis*, vol 4, no 2, pp 115–42.

Winter, S., Nielsen, V.L. and May, P. (forthcoming) 'Coersion at the frontlines in regulatory and social policies: the role of power and social construction of target populations', paper prepared for the Bi-Annual Research Meeting of the Association for Public Management Research Association in Syracuse, 2–4 June 2011.

Wood, G.D. (1981) 'Rural class formation in Bangladesh 1940–1980', *Bulletin of Concerned Asian Scholars*, vol 1, pp 2–15.

Wright, S.E. (2003) 'Confronting unemployment in a street-level bureaucracy: jobcentre staff and client perspectives', PhD thesis, University of Stirling.

Ybema, S., Yanow, D., Wels, H. and Kamsteeg, F.H. (2009) *Organizational ethnography: studying the complexity of everyday life*, London: Sage Publications.

Yin, R. (1994) *Case study research. Design and methods* (2nd edn), London: Sage.

Yin, R. (2003) *Case study research. Design and methods* (3rd edn), Thousand Oaks, CA: Sage Publications.

Zacka, B. (2011) 'The two bodies of the bureaucrat', *Public Administration Review*, vol 72, pp 1–3.

Zandvliet, K., Gravesteijn, J., Tanis, O., Collewet, M. and de Jong, N. (2011) *Procesanalyse re-integratie. Reconstructie van re-integratiedienstverlening. Onderzoek uitgevoerd in opdracht van de Raad voor Werk en Inkomen*, Rotterdam: SEOR.

Zimmer-Gembeck, M.J. and Skinner, E.A. (2011) 'Review: the development of coping across childhood and adolescence: an integrative review and critique of research', *International Journal of Behavioral Development*, vol 35, no 1, pp 1–17.

Zinner, S. (2011) 'The stories public administrators tell', *Public Integrity*, vol 13, no 4, pp 385–96.

Index

in social care (UK) 192, 200, 201
regulation of public services, and
    discretion 303–304
regulatory inspections (Denmark)
    115–131
    characteristics of regulation 117–120
    deterrent-based enforcement, factors
        impacting 135–138, 147–151
    discretionary choices and interaction
        dynamics 126–131
    enforcement behaviour 120–126,
        134–137
    Lipsky on 115
    research on 121–125, 138–146, 152
Reichle, B. 162–163
representative bureaucracy, role of in
    SLB research 13, 156–159, 166–167,
    329
resistance, as response to conflicting
    standards 268, 273, 274
risk management 196, 198–200
Rubin, Z. 162, 163
rules
    awareness of, and regulatory
        compliance 138, 144–145, 148–149
    definition 229
    discretion and 17–18, 84–85, 93,
        307–309
    impact of 172–173
    as positive response to discretionary
        decisions 51
    processing of by middle managers
        227–231, 234–237, 239–241

S

sanctions on benefits 86–92, 271–272,
    273–274, 304
Scholz, J.T. 135, 147
schools
    punitive schooling and interactional
        hitches (US) 175–179, 184
    rule processing by headteachers
        (Netherlands) 227– 228, 233–241
Schütz, H. 305
scientific management (Taylorism) 5,
    127, 245, 246
Sewell, W. 173–174
Shearing, C. 172, 173
shielded professionalism 222–223
shielding, as response to conflicting
    standards 268, 273
Skinner, E.A. 100–101, 108
Smith, K. 162
Snellen, I. 248, 250

social assistance, evolution of (UK)
    45–60
    historic context 45–47
    National Assistance 48–52
    Supplementary Benefits 52–56
    Income Support 56, 57, 58, 59
    Social Fund 57–58, 59
    see also unemployment benefits;
        welfare-to-work programmes
social care see adult social care
Social Fund 57–58, 59
social injustice, rationalisation of 156,
    159–167
Social Penal Code (Belgium) 102–103
Social Security Acts (UK) 54–57, 59
social workers, discretion and 193–202,
    266
socio-political studies 36–38
Stanford, S. 199
state-agent narrative 169–170, 171–172
street-level bureaucracy
    current research and theory 27–33,
        39–42, 246–251
    definition and use of term 3–4, 16,
        25, 115, 211, 279
    functions of 206
    future research, recommendations for
        324–338
    individual, role of in research 12, 328,
        329–330
    Lipsky's approach (overview) 8–11
    policy outcomes, impact of on 32–33,
        36–39, 206
    as a scholarly theme 11–18
    'street-level bureaucrat' type in care
        management 190, 197–198
    strengthening, as method of rule
        processing 229–230
    stress in the workplace 117, 284–287,
        285–286
    structure and agency 173
    'Study of administration, The' (Wilson) 5
    supervision of SLBs see control of SLBs;
        management; managerialism
Supplementary Benefits (UK) 52–56
Switzerland, unemployment benefits
    in see unemployment benefits
    (Switzerland)
system-level bureaucracy 249, 257, 259
systems theory 101–102, 247

T

task environment and discretion 92,
    206–214, 221–222, 330–332